RHCSA®

Red Hat® Enterprise Linux® 9
Certification Study Guide
(Exam EX200)

T0266287

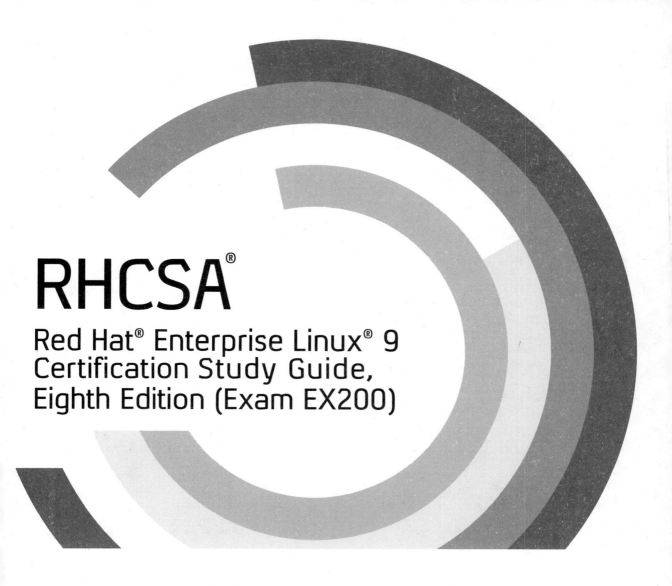

RHCSA®

Red Hat® Enterprise Linux® 9 Certification Study Guide, Eighth Edition (Exam EX200)

Michael Jang
Alessandro Orsaria

McGraw Hill is an independent entity from Red Hat®, Inc. and is not affiliated with Red Hat, Inc. in any manner. This study/training guide and/or material is not sponsored by, endorsed by, or affiliated with Red Hat, Inc. in any manner. This publication and accompanying media may be used in assisting students to prepare for a Red Hat RHCSA certification exam. Neither Red Hat nor McGraw Hill warrant that use of this publication and accompanying media will ensure passing any exam. Red Hat®, Red Hat Enterprise Linux®, RHCE®, RHCSA®, and the Red Hat logo and Red Hat "Shadowman" logo are trademarks or registered trademarks of Red Hat, Inc. in the United States and certain other countries. All other trademarks are trademarks of their respective owners.

Mc
Graw
Hill

New York   Chicago   San Francisco
Athens   London   Madrid   Mexico City
Milan   New Delhi   Singapore   Sydney   Toronto

McGraw Hill books are available at special quantity discounts to use as premiums and sales promotions, or for use in corporate training programs. To contact a representative, please visit the Contact Us pages at www.mhprofessional.com.

RHCSA® Red Hat® Enterprise Linux® 9 Certification Study Guide, Eighth Edition (Exam EX200)

Copyright © 2024 by McGraw Hill. All rights reserved. Printed in the United States of America. Except as permitted under the Copyright Act of 1976, no part of this publication may be reproduced or distributed in any form or by any means, or stored in a database or retrieval system, without the prior written permission of publisher, with the exception that the program listings may be entered, stored, and executed in a computer system, but they may not be reproduced for publication.

All trademarks or copyrights mentioned herein are the possession of their respective owners and McGraw Hill makes no claim of ownership by the mention of products that contain these marks.

1 2 3 4 5 6 7 8 9   LCR   29 28 27 26 25 24 23

ISBN   978-1-260-46207-4
MHID   1-260-46207-2

Sponsoring Editors
Tim Green

Project Editor
Rachel Fogelberg

Acquisitions Coordinator
Caitlin Cromley-Linn

Technical Editor
Sam Doran

Copy Editor
William McManus

Proofreaders
Paul Tyler and Lisa McCoy

Indexer
Arc Indexing, Inc.

Production Supervisors
Thomas Somers and Lynn M. Messina

Composition
KnowledgeWorks Global Ltd.

Illustration
KnowledgeWorks Global Ltd.

Art Director, Cover
Anthony Landi

Information has been obtained by McGraw Hill from sources believed to be reliable. However, because of the possibility of human or mechanical error by our sources, McGraw Hill, or others, McGraw Hill does not guarantee the accuracy, adequacy, or completeness of any information and is not responsible for any errors or omissions or the results obtained from the use of such information.

For the young widows and widowers:
may they find the courage to face their fears,
to navigate their way through the pain,
and to find hope for a brighter future.

ABOUT THE AUTHORS

Michael Jang (RHCE, LPIC-2, UCP, LCP, Linux+, MCP) is currently a Lead Technical Writer for Forescout. His experience with computers goes back to the days of jumbled punch cards. He has written other books on Linux certification, including *LPIC-1 in Depth, Mike Meyers' Linux+ Certification Passport,* and *Sair GNU/Linux Installation and Configuration Exam Cram.* His other Linux books include *Linux Annoyances for Geeks, Linux Patch Management,* and *Security Strategies in Linux Platforms and Applications.* He has also written or contributed to books on Microsoft operating systems, including *MCSE Guide to Microsoft Windows 98* and *Mastering Windows XP Professional, Second Edition.*

Alessandro Orsaria (RHCE, RHCA, CCIE x 2) is an IT professional with more than 20 years' experience in the industry. He has authored articles for technical Linux magazines and is currently employed by a proprietary trading firm. Alessandro is Red Hat RHCE and RHCA certified and has achieved two Cisco CCIE certifications in Routing & Switching and Datacenter. He holds an MBA from Imperial College of London and a degree in physics.

About the Technical Editor

Sam Doran is a Principal Software Engineer at Red Hat. He served in the U.S. Air Force as an aircraft mechanic and is a proud alumnus of the Virginia Tech Corps of Cadets. Prior to joining Red Hat, he worked for the U.S. government as well as private industry in jobs ranging from site reliability engineering to information security. He has used RHEL professionally since 2003 as well as a number of other Linux distributions.

CONTENTS AT A GLANCE

CONTENTS

ix

ACKNOWLEDGMENTS

I'd like to thank Ed Tittel, who gave me my first chance to write for publication, as well as Tim Green, for helping me write what BookAuthority has named the best Red Hat Linux book of all time! I'd also like to thank various mentors over the years: Penny Yao, Susan Tacker, Mark Craig, and Carole Jelen for supporting my work. I'd also like to thank Alessandro Orsaria for taking on the work required to update this book. We would not have the last two editions without him. I'd like to pay tribute to my dog, Katie, who was this man's best friend for 15 years. Most importantly, I'd like to thank my sweet wife, Donna; you are the love of my life.

—Mike Jang

My profound appreciation extends to Mike Jang and Tim Green, whose confidence in my abilities enabled me to contribute to the eighth edition of this book. I also wish to extend my gratitude to the editorial team of McGraw Hill, whose stellar efforts have been indispensable. To Emiliano and Julia, whose unwavering support was my beacon during the arduous process of creating this work, I offer my deepest thanks and love. A final thought goes to Maria, for her constant support in all that I have done.

—Alessandro Orsaria

PREFACE

Linux is booming, and Red Hat is leading this growth with the help of skilled Red Hat Certified Systems Administrators (RHCSA).

Linux, which is free, became popular because it offered companies a cheaper alternative to the more costly Unix systems. But Linux has more to offer than just cost savings. Thanks to the Linux community, this operating system works well with many kinds of hardware. Today, you can use Linux on everything from laptops and mobile devices to servers and mainframes. This makes Linux a versatile option for many different situations.

Linux is also known for its strong security. Because it is open source, any security problems can be quickly found and fixed by the community. Linux also has strong rules about permissions and access, which makes it tough for harmful software to break in. Regular updates also help keep Linux safe and secure.

Linux also provides good support for virtualization, which lets users create and manage virtual machines (VMs) efficiently. With tools like Kernel-based Virtual Machine (KVM) and Xen, Linux allows users to run more than one operating system at the same time on a single machine. This is really useful in server environments, where virtualization makes things like software deployment and resource management easier.

On top of this, Linux is the go-to platform for container technologies like Docker and Kubernetes. Containers create isolated environments for applications, making them easier to move and run on different systems. Linux's built-in features, such as namespaces and cgroups, are the backbone of containerization. These features make it easier to manage resources, isolate processes, and scale up. By bringing together Linux and containerization, software development and deployment have become faster and more efficient.

Having discussed the diverse capabilities and advantages of Linux, it's essential to recognize the challenges that come with mastering it. Red Hat exams, for instance, are tough, and not many first-time test-takers pass the RHCSA exam. But don't let that scare you. While passing isn't guaranteed, this book is designed to help you prepare for and hopefully pass the RHCSA exam. The skills described in this book can also help you in your job as a Linux administrator. However, this book isn't a replacement for the Red Hat prep courses, which we'll talk about soon.

To prepare for the RHCSA exam, you should have a laptop or computer with at least 8GB of RAM so that you can run a couple of virtual machines. It doesn't matter whether your computer runs Linux, Windows, or macOS; you simply need to be able to create two VMs. In this book, we use VMware Workstation Player as our hypervisor, but you can choose another option like KVM, especially if you're running Linux on your computer.

You could also use cloud instances for the labs and exercises in this book, although some cloud providers' version of Red Hat Enterprise Linux might be slightly different from the standard one. You might also be unable to do some tasks, like installing the operating system from an ISO image. For these reasons, we recommend installing VMware Workstation Player, as explained in Chapter 1, or another hypervisor of your choice.

Getting Red Hat Enterprise Linux

Red Hat exams, including the RHCSA, test your proficiency with Red Hat Enterprise Linux. You might believe that you need to buy a subscription to RHEL to meet the exam objectives, such as installing software packages and updates via Red Hat Subscription Management (RHSM). However, Red Hat currently provides a no-cost Developer Subscription for Individuals if you join the Red Hat Developer program. This subscription includes access to Red Hat Enterprise Linux and a variety of other technologies. Joining the program, which you can do for free at https://developers.redhat.com/register, is the only requirement. Chapter 1 provides detailed instructions on how to join and install Red Hat Enterprise Linux.

Alternatively, you can choose to install one of the many derivatives of Red Hat Enterprise Linux. These derivatives are built from the RHEL source code, which is mostly released under the Linux General Public License (GPL) or other open-source licenses. These licenses grant anyone the right to construct Red Hat Enterprise Linux from the released Red Hat source code. However, if you're comfortable with the terms and conditions of the Red Hat Developer program, there's no clear advantage to using a derivative distribution for RHCSA exam preparation.

Red Hat also provides several Enterprise Linux subscriptions. While not required for RHCSA exam prep, familiarity with these can be beneficial if you plan to (or already) work with Red Hat Enterprise Linux systems:

- RHEL Server provides varying levels of support for three different CPU architectures, with costs based on the number of CPU sockets and supported virtual guests.
- RHEL Workstation includes varying levels of support ideal for workstation use.
- RHEL Developer Suite offers download access to RHEL 9 and several additional software packages, intended solely for development.
- RHEL add-ons enhance functionality in areas such as high availability, resilient storage, and load balancing, among others.

This book was developed using RHEL 9.1 Server. While RHEL's source code is open source, access to the binary packages requires a subscription. This can be free of charge if you select the Red Hat Developer Subscription for Individuals.

Enterprise-level operating systems like RHEL 9 offer the benefit of stability. When an enterprise upgrades to RHEL 9, they can trust that configuration revisions will be a one-time affair, with security updates and bug fixes handled automatically. Red Hat strives to ensure enterprises won't need to overhaul their systems for minor releases, such as RHEL 9.1. A necessity to reconfigure for minor updates would escalate costs.

Minor releases also should not impact Red Hat exam objectives. While RHEL 9.2 introduces bug fixes, security updates, and new features, it doesn't alter the defaults of any configuration files detailed in this book.

We expect future minor releases, such as RHEL 9.3, RHEL 9.4, and beyond, to follow this pattern. Our close monitoring of RHEL releases over the past ten years suggests no significant exam objective changes based solely on a minor release. Still, you should routinely check the exam objectives listed on the Red Hat website to ensure they align with the content of this study guide.

In This Book

Chapter 1 of this book is designed to assist you in preparing a study system for the RHCSA exam and offers detailed insight into the exam experience.

Except for Chapter 1, every chapter begins by outlining the objectives pertinent to that chapter's material. Following this, the topics are dissected and explained. We have chosen to present the topics in an order that we believe will be most beneficial to the majority of candidates, which doesn't necessarily follow the sequence of the exam objectives. However, if you are already well-versed with Linux, feel free to skip over certain sections or entire chapters during your initial reading.

Toward the end of each chapter, we've included a Self Test, a series of questions, along with their answers. While Red Hat exams don't typically involve multiple-choice questions, these types of questions can still be a valuable tool in assessing your understanding and retention of the chapter material. Furthermore, the short-answer questions format emphasizes the practical experience necessary for the exam.

Following this Self Test is a "Lab Questions" section that directs you to the companion website to access the lab exercises for the chapter. The solutions to the lab exercises are included in the book, at the end of each chapter. Please see Appendix D, "About the Online Content."

Remember, Red Hat exams are hands-on. Therefore, practice is key. You should repeatedly exercise your skills until you reach a level of confidence where you can complete tasks without the assistance of this book. The Red Hat RHCSA exam is designed to test candidate qualifications as Linux systems administrators. If you pass the exam, it's not because you've memorized a canned set of answers—it's because you have a set of Linux administrative skills and know how to use them under pressure, whether it be during an exam or in a real-world situation.

While this book is organized to serve as an in-depth review for the RHCSA exam for both experienced Linux and Unix professionals, it is not intended as a substitute for Red Hat courses—or, more important, real-world experience. Nevertheless, each chapter covers a major aspect of the exam, with an emphasis on the "why" as well as the "how to" of working with and supporting RHEL as a systems administrator or engineer.

Conventions and Abbreviations

Although logging in to the root user account is a risky practice on production systems, it is the fastest way to administer RHEL during the exam. The command prompt assumes use of that account. When logged in to the root account, you'll see a command-line prompt similar to the following:

```
[root@server1 root]#
```

As the length of this prompt would lead to a number of broken and wrapped code lines throughout this book, we've normally abbreviated the root account prompt as

```
#
```

Be careful. The hash mark (#) is also used as a comment character in Linux scripts and programs. When logged in as a regular user, you will see a slightly different prompt; for user michael, it would typically look like the following:

```
[michael@server1 michael]$
```

Similarly, we've abbreviated this as

```
$
```

There are a number of command lines and blocks of code interspersed throughout the chapters. Commands embedded within regular text, such as **ls -l**, are shown in bold. User entries and some variables in regular text are also shown in bold.

Sometimes commands exceed the available length of a line. Take this example:

```
# virt-install -n outsider1.example.org -r 1024 --disk
path=/var/lib/libvirt/images/outsider1.example.org.img,size=16
-l ftp://192.168.122.1/pub/inst -x ks=ftp://192.168.122.1/pub/ks1.cfg
```

Unless this command is carefully formatted, line breaks might appear in unfortunate places, such as between the two dashes in front of the **--disk** switch. One way to address this is with the backslash (\), which "escapes" the meaning of the carriage return that follows. (The backslash can also "escape" the meaning of a space, making it easier to work with multiple-word filenames.) Therefore, while the following command appears as if it is on four different lines, the backslashes mean that Linux reads it as one single command:

```
# virt-install -n outsider1.example.org -r 1024 --disk \
> path=/var/lib/libvirt/images/outsider1.example.org.img,size=16 \
> -l ftp://192.168.122.1/pub/inst \
> -x ks=ftp://192.168.122.1/pub/ks1.cfg
```

In some code snippets, we could not use the backslash character to split the output on more than one line. In those cases, we used a continuation arrow, as shown next:

```
5 2 * * 6 root /usr/bin/tar --selinux -czf /tmp/etc-backup-\$(/bin/date ↵
+\%m\%d).tar.gz /etc > /dev/null
```

Sometimes, you'll need to actually type in a command or a response to a question at a command line. In that case, you'll see an instruction such as "Type **y**." Alternatively, some menus require a keypress; for instance, you may be asked to press P to access a password prompt. In that case, the letter *p* is not added to the screen when you press that key. In addition, the A, despite its appearances, is in lowercase. In contrast, A is the uppercase version of that letter.

One area where some publishers have trouble is with the double-dash. Some publishing programs change the double-dash to an em dash (—). But that can be a problem. The double-dash is common in many Linux commands. For example, the following command lists all packages currently installed on the local system:

```
# rpm --query --all
```

When we ran this command on our RHEL 9 systems, it listed over 1000 packages.

In contrast, the following command lists all files in all packages on the local system:

```
# rpm --query -all
```

When we ran this command on our RHEL 9 system, it listed over 150,000 files, a rather different result. So pay attention to the dashes, and rest assured that the team who produced this book took care to make sure that double-dashes are shown as is!

Exam Readiness Checklist

At the end of the Introduction, you will find an Exam Readiness Checklist. This table has been constructed to allow you to cross-reference the official RHCSA exam objectives with the objectives as they are presented and covered in this book. The checklist also allows you to gauge your level of expertise on each objective at the outset of your studies. This should allow you to check your progress and make sure you spend the time you need on more difficult or unfamiliar sections. The checklist lists all the objectives exactly as Red Hat presents them (www.redhat.com/en/services/training/ex200-red-hat-certified-system-administrator-rhcsa-exam?section=objectives) and cross-references the corresponding coverage in this book, including chapter and page references. Additionally, the table features a column of blank boxes next to each objective. Readers can check these boxes when they feel confident that they are prepared for that specific exam objective.

In Every Chapter

For this series, we've created a set of chapter components that calls your attention to important items, reinforces important points, and provides helpful exam-taking hints. Take a look at what you'll find in every chapter:

- Every chapter begins with the **Certification Objectives**—the skills you need to master in order to pass the section on the exam associated with the chapter topic. The Objective headings identify the objectives within the chapter, so you'll always know an objective when you see it.

- **Exam Watch** notes call attention to information about, and potential pitfalls in, the exam. These helpful hints are written by authors who have taken the exams and received their certification—who better to tell you what to worry about? They know what you're about to go through!

| This book's coverage of the RHCSA exam objectives can be found in the | RHCSA Exam Readiness Checklist at the end of this front matter. |

- **Practice Exercises** are interspersed throughout the chapters. These are step-by-step exercises that allow you to get the hands-on experience you need in order to pass the exams. They help you master skills that are likely to be an area of focus on the exam. Don't just read through the exercises; they are hands-on practice that you should be comfortable completing. Learning by doing is an effective way to increase your competency with a product. Remember, the Red Hat exams are entirely "hands on"; there are no multiple-choice questions on these exams.

- **On the Job** notes describe the issues that come up most often in real-world settings. They provide a valuable perspective on certification- and product-related topics. They point out common mistakes and address questions that have arisen from on-the-job discussions and experience.

- **Inside the Exam** sidebars highlight some of the most common and confusing problems that students encounter when taking a live exam. Designed to anticipate what the exam will emphasize, they will help ensure you know what you need to know to pass the exam. You can get a leg up on how to respond to those difficult-to-understand labs by focusing extra attention on these sidebars.

- **Scenario & Solution** sections lay out potential problems and solutions in a quick-to-read format.
- The **Certification Summary** is a succinct review of the chapter and a restatement of salient skills regarding the exam.

✓
- The **Two-Minute Drill** at the end of every chapter is a checklist of the main points of the chapter. It can be used for last-minute review.

Q&A
- The **Self Test** offers questions designed to help test the practical knowledge associated with the certification exams. The answers to these questions, as well as explanations of the answers, can be found at the end of each chapter. By taking the Self Test after completing each chapter, you'll reinforce what you've learned from that chapter. This book does not include multiple-choice questions because Red Hat does not include any such questions on its exams.
- The **Lab Questions** at the end of the Self Test section offer a unique and challenging question format that requires the reader to understand multiple chapter concepts to answer correctly. These questions are more complex and more comprehensive than the other questions because they test your ability to take all the knowledge you have gained from reading the chapter and apply it to complicated, real-world situations. Starting with Chapter 2, all lab questions are available only from the companion website that accompanies this book, consistent with the electronic format associated with the Red Hat exams. Remember, the Red Hat exams contain *only* lab-type questions. If you can answer these questions, you have proven that you know the subject!

Additional Resources

If you would like to pursue further reading beyond this book, perhaps the best way to do so is with Red Hat documentation. Much of what we've learned about RHEL 9 comes from the documents available at https://access.redhat.com/documentation/en/red_hat_enterprise_linux/9. For your purposes, the following may be the most important of these guides:

- **Performing a Standard RHEL 9 Installation** Although Red Hat exams are given on preconfigured systems, every Linux administrator should be able to install the operating system from scratch.
- **Configuring Basic System Settings** This system administrator guide includes essential skills that you should be able to master in your job.
- **Managing Software with the DNF Tool** This guide could serve as an additional resource that expands upon the software installation procedures detailed in Chapter 4.
- **Using SELinux** SELinux often poses a challenging topic for many candidates. This guide details various strategies that can aid in bolstering your SELinux policy's security.
- **Configuring and Managing Networking** Despite a majority of this guide's chapters being beyond the scope of the RHCSA exam, the initial chapters establish a strong foundation on network configuration.

Some Pointers

Once you've finished reading this book, set aside some time to do a thorough review. You might want to return to the book several times and make use of all the methods it offers for reviewing the material:

- *Reread all the Exam Watch notes.* Remember that these notes are written by authors who have taken the exam and passed. They know what you should expect—and what you should be on the lookout for.
- *Review all the Scenario & Solution sections* for quick problem solving.
- *Retake the Self Tests.* Focus on the labs, as there are no multiple-choice questions on the Red Hat exams. We've included questions just to test your mastery of the practical material in each chapter.
- *Complete the exercises.* Did you do the exercises when you read through each chapter? If not, do them! These exercises are designed to cover exam topics, and there's no better way to get to know this material than by practicing. Be sure you understand why you are performing each step in each exercise. If there is something you are not clear on, reread that section in the chapter.

The Red Hat Exam Challenge

This section covers the reasons for pursuing industry-recognized certification, explains the importance of the RHCSA certification, and prepares you for taking the actual examination. It gives you a few pointers on how to prepare, what to expect, and what to do on exam day.

This book covers every published exam objective at the time of writing. For the latest objectives, see www.redhat.com/en/services/certification/rhcsa. Red Hat has also published a syllabus for each of its prep courses for these exams, described shortly. While the published exam objectives are accurate, the prep course syllabi provide additional information. Each Red Hat prep course provides an excellent grounding in systems administration, network administration, security, and more. To that end, this book also includes coverage based on the public syllabi of Red Hat courses RH124 and RH134, described later.

Nevertheless, this book is not intended to be a substitute for any Red Hat course.

Leaping Ahead of the Competition!

Red Hat's RHCSA certification exam is a hands-on exam. As such, it is respected throughout the industry as a sign of genuine practical knowledge. If you pass, you will be head and shoulders above the candidate who has passed only a "standard" multiple-choice certification exam.

Red Hat has offered its hands-on exams since 1999. They've evolved over the years. As detailed in Chapter 1, the RHCSA is a three-hour exam. The requirements are detailed in the Exam Readiness Checklist later in this Introduction.

Why a Hands-On Exam?

Most certifications today are based on multiple-choice exams. These types of exams are relatively inexpensive to set up and easy to proctor. Unfortunately, many people without real-world skills are good at taking multiple-choice exams. In some cases, the answers to these multiple-choice exams are already available online. This results in problems on the job with "certified" engineers who have an image as "paper tigers" and do not have any real-world skills.

INSIDE THE EXAM

The RHCSA exam is a Red Hat exam. Knowledge of Unix or a Linux distribution such as Ubuntu is certainly helpful, as well as real-world experience with Linux and containers. However, it is important to know how to set up, configure, install, and perform tasks using Red Hat Enterprise Linux.

In response, Red Hat wanted to develop a certification program that matters. In our opinion, they have succeeded with the RHCSA, the RHCE, and their other advanced certifications.

Linux administrators sometimes have to install Linux on a computer or virtual machine. In fact, the RHCSA includes several objectives on this subject. Depending on the configuration, they may need to install Linux from a central source through a network. Installing Linux is not enough to make it useful. Administrators need to know how to configure Linux: add users, install and configure services, set up firewalls, and more.

Red Hat Certification Program

Red Hat offers several courses that can help you prepare for the RHCSA exam. Most of these courses are four or five days long. In some cases, the courses are offered electronically.

These aren't the only Red Hat courses available; there are a number of others related to the Red Hat Certified Engineer (RHCE), Red Hat Certified Architect (RHCA), Red Hat Certified OpenShift Administrator, and several Certificates of Expertise in specific areas such as server hardening and performance tuning. But focus on passing the RHCSA exam first; the RHCSA is a prerequisite for more advanced certifications such as the RHCE and RHCA.

Should You Take an RHCSA Course?

This book is *not* intended as a substitute for any particular Red Hat RHCSA prep course. However, the topics in this book are based in part on the topics listed in course outlines provided at www.redhat.com/en/services/training/all-courses-exams. By design, these topics may help Linux users qualify as real-world administrators and can also be used as such. Red Hat can change these topics and course outlines at any time, so monitor www.redhat.com for the latest updates. Table 1 describes those courses associated with the RHCSA exam.

The courses given by Red Hat are excellent. The Red Hat instructors who teach these courses are highly skilled. If you have the resources, it is the best way to prepare for the RHCSA exam. If you feel the need for classroom instruction, read this book and then take the appropriate course.

TABLE 1	Red Hat RHCSA-Related Courses

Course	Description
RH024	A free, on-demand video course that provides an introduction to Red Hat Enterprise Linux
RH124	System Administration I: Core system administration skills
RH134	System Administration II: Command line skills for Linux administrators (RH135 without the RHCSA exam)
RH135	System Administration II with the RHCSA exam
RH199	RHCSA rapid-track course for experienced administrators
RH200	RH199 + RHCSA exam
EX200	Just the RHCSA exam

If you're not sure you're ready for the course or book, read Chapter 1. It includes a rapid overview of the requirements associated with the RHCSA certification. If you find the material in Chapter 1 to be overwhelming, consider one of the books noted near the start of the chapter or one of the other lower-level Red Hat courses. In addition, Chapter 1 includes a lab that prompts you to examine the requirements of the Linux Professional Institute for its Level 1 certification (LPIC-1). Linux geeks like yourself who are ready to study for the Red Hat exams often take the LPIC-1 exams first.

Alternatively, you may already be familiar with the material in this book. You may have the breadth and depth of knowledge required to pass the RHCSA exam. In that case, use this book as a refresher to help you focus on the skills and techniques needed to pass the exam.

Signing Up for the RHCSA Course and/or Exam

Red Hat provides convenient web-based registration systems for the courses and tests. To sign up for any of the Red Hat courses or exams, navigate to www.redhat.com, click the link for Training & Services | All Courses and Exams, and select the desired course or exam. As shown back in Table 1, exams may be taken independently from a course. For example, the RHCSA exam is associated with exam codes EX200. Exams may also be taken as part of an online or instructor-led course. Alternatively, contact Red Hat Enrollment Central at training@redhat.com or (866) 626-2994.

Discounts may be available for a limited time for candidates who have been previously certified as an RHCSA. Current discounts are shown at https://www.redhat.com/en/services/training/specials/.

RHCSA Exam Readiness Checklist

Certification Objective	Study Guide Coverage	Ch #	Pg #	Exam Ready?
Category: Understand and Use Essential Tools				
Access a shell prompt and issue commands with correct syntax	Shells	2	46	
Use input-output redirection (>, >>, |, 2>, etc.)	Shells	2	46	
Use grep and regular expressions to analyze text	Managing Text Files	2	68	
Access remote systems using SSH	Administration with Secure Shell and Secure Copy	3	73	
Log in and switch users in multiuser targets	User and Shell Configuration	6	236	
Archive, compress, unpack, and uncompress files using tar, star, gzip, and bzip2	Archives and Compression	9	367	
Create and edit text files	Managing Text Files	2	68	
Create, delete, copy, and move files and directories	Standard Command-Line Tools	2	51	
Create hard and soft links	Standard Command-Line Tools	2	51	
List, set, and change standard ugo/rwx permissions	File Permissions	2	60	
Locate, read, and use system documentation including man, info, and files in /usr/share/doc	Accessing the Documentation	2	78	
Category: Create Simple Shell Scripts				
Conditionally execute code (use of: if, test, [], etc.)	Bash Scripts	9	377	
Use Looping constructs (for, etc.) to process file, command line input	Bash Scripts	9	377	
Process script inputs ($1, $2, etc.)	Bash Scripts	9	377	
Processing output of shell commands within a script	Bash Scripts	9	377	
Category: Operate Running Systems				
Boot, reboot, and shut down a system normally	Bootloaders and GRUB 2, Between GRUB 2 and Login	5	177, 189	
Boot systems into different targets manually	Between GRUB 2 and Login	5	189	
Interrupt the boot process in order to gain access to a system	Bootloaders and GRUB 2	5	177	
Identify CPU/memory-intensive processes and kill processes	Resource Management and System Tuning	9	355	

Certification Objective	Study Guide Coverage	Ch #	Pg #	Exam Ready?
Adjust process scheduling	Resource Management and System Tuning	9	355	
Manage tuning profiles	Resource Management and System Tuning	9	355	
Locate and interpret system log files and journals	Local Log Files	9	388	
Preserve system journals	Local Log Files	9	388	
Start, stop, and check the status of network services	Network Configuration and Troubleshooting	3	59	
Securely transfer files between systems	Administration with Secure Shell and Secure Copy	3	73	
Category: Configure Local Storage				
List, create, and delete partitions on MBR and GPT disks	Storage Management and Partitions	7	255	
Create and remove physical volumes	Logical Volume Manager (LVM)	7	282	
Assign physical volumes to volume groups	Logical Volume Manager (LVM)	7	282	
Create and delete logical volumes	Logical Volume Manager (LVM)	7	282	
Configure systems to mount file systems at boot by universally unique ID (UUID) or label	Filesystem Management	7	288	
Add new partitions and logical volumes, and swap to a system non-destructively	Basic Linux Filesystems and Directories, Filesystem Management	7	279, 288	
Category: Create and Configure File Systems				
Create, mount, unmount, and use vfat, ext4, and xfs filesystems	Filesystem Formats, Filesystem Management	7	274, 288	
Mount and unmount network file systems using NFS	Filesystem Management	7	288	
Configure autofs	The Automounter	7	296	
Extend existing logical volumes	Logical Volume Manager (LVM)	7	282	
Create and configure set-GID directories for collaboration	Special Groups	6	240	
Diagnose and correct file permission problems	File Permissions	2	60	

Certification Objective	Study Guide Coverage	Ch #	Pg #	Exam Ready?
Category: Deploy, Configure, and Maintain Systems				
Schedule tasks using at and cron	Running Tasks on a Schedule: cron and at	9	369	
Start and stop services and configure services to start automatically at boot	Control by Target	5	200	
Configure systems to boot into a specific target automatically	Between GRUB 2 and Login	5	189	
Configure time service clients	Time Synchronization	5	204	
Install and update software packages from Red Hat Network, a remote repository, or from the local file system	The RPM Package Manager, More RPM Commands, Dependencies and the dnf Command	4	87, 94, 99	
Modify the system bootloader	The Boot Process, Bootloaders and GRUB 2	5	175, 177	
Category: Manage Basic Networking				
Configure IPv4 and IPv6 addresses	A Networking Primer, Network Configuration and Troubleshooting, An Introduction to IPv6	3	51, 59, 69	
Configure hostname resolution	Network Configuration and Troubleshooting	3	59	
Configure network services to start automatically at boot	Network Configuration and Troubleshooting	3	59	
Restrict network access using firewall-cmd/firewall	Basic Firewall Control	8	313	
Category: Manage Users and Groups				
Create, delete, and modify local user accounts	User Account Management	6	216	
Change passwords and adjust password aging for local user accounts	User Account Management	6	216	
Create, delete, and modify local groups and group memberships	User Account Management	6	216	
Configure superuser access	Administrative Control	6	232	
Category: Manage Security				
Configure firewall settings using firewall-cmd/firewalld	Basic Firewall Control	8	313	
Manage default file permissions	File Permissions	2	60	

Certification Objective	Study Guide Coverage	Ch #	Pg #	Exam Ready?
Configure key-based authentication for SSH	Securing SSH with Key-Based Authentication	8	324	
Set enforcing and permissive modes for SELinux	A Security-Enhanced Linux Primer	8	329	
List and identify SELinux file and process context	A Security-Enhanced Linux Primer	8	329	
Restore default file contexts	A Security-Enhanced Linux Primer	8	329	
Manage SELinux port labels	A Security-Enhanced Linux Primer	8	329	
Use boolean settings to modify system SELinux settings	A Security-Enhanced Linux Primer	8	329	
Diagnose and address routine SELinux policy violations	A Security-Enhanced Linux Primer	8	329	
Category: Manage Containers				
Find and retrieve container images from a remote registry	Building and Using Container Images	10	416	
Inspect container images	Building and Using Container Images	10	416	
Perform container management using commands such as podman and skopeo	Managing Containers	10	422	
Build a container from a Containerfile	Building and Using Container Images	10	416	
Perform basic container management such as running, starting, stopping, and listing running containers	Fundamentals of Container Technology, Getting Started with Containers	10	407, 412	
Run a service inside a container	Getting Started with Containers	10	412	
Configure a container to start automatically as a systemd service	Managing Containers	10	422	
Attach persistent storage to a container	Managing Containers	10	422	

Chapter 1

Prepare for the Red Hat RHCSA Certification

T he Red Hat exams are an advanced challenge. This book covers the Red Hat Certified System Administrator (RHCSA) exam, a practical lab test that evaluates an individual's proficiency in Red Hat Enterprise Linux. Successfully passing it not only boosts one's professional appeal but also demonstrates their mastery of Linux. The RHCSA certification also is the foundation for those who want to earn the Red Hat Certified Engineer (RHCE) and serves as the initial step toward more advanced Red Hat certifications. Red Hat offers several courses to help prepare for these exams, as described in the front matter and in this chapter.

The focus of this chapter is installation, to create a lab environment as a test bed for the lab exercises in subsequent chapters. We assume that you have a PC available, either a desktop or a laptop, running Linux or a Windows operating system. On your PC, you will install two virtual machines (VMs) running Red Hat Enterprise Linux 9 (RHEL 9). Alternatively, you can use a "rebuild" distribution such as AlmaLinux, as it's built from the same source code as RHEL 9. We discuss the only relevant differences in Chapter 4.

Today, containers have become a key part of IT systems because of their unique ability to neatly pack up an application in its own box with everything it needs to run. This makes moving and running applications much easier and quicker. Plus, with containers, you can easily add or reduce resources based on the demand for your app, a feature known as *scalability*. Because containers play such a big role in modern IT operations, the RHCSA exam now includes a whole section about them. We'll go into all the details in Chapter 10 of this book.

If you are new to Linux or Unix, this book may not be enough for you. Red Hat suggests that RHCSA candidates have one to three years of experience with the bash shell, user administration, system monitoring, basic networking, software updates, and more. In this book it's not possible to provide sufficient detail, at least in a way that can be understood by newcomers to Linux and other Unix-based operating systems. Nevertheless, we tried to keep the topics easy to follow even for the reader who has very little experience with Linux. If after reading the first chapters of this book you find gaps in your knowledge, you can refer to one of the following guides:

- *Linux Administration: A Beginner's Guide, Eighth Edition*, by Wale Soyinka (McGraw Hill, 2020), provides a step-by-step guide to Linux.
- *LPIC-1 in Depth* by Michael Jang (Course Technology PTR, 2009) covers the certification many Linux professionals qualify for prior to working for the RHCSA. The book dates back to 2009, but the fundamentals of Linux are still the same.

Before installing RHEL 9, you need to ensure that your system has the right hardware. The installation of RHEL 9 is supported on systems with 64-bit CPUs. In addition, to set up a lab environment with virtual machines, you need a CPU that supports hardware virtualization. Details are discussed in this chapter. As such, while the RHCSA exam is, by and large, not a hardware exam, some basic hardware knowledge is a fundamental requirement for any Linux administrator. As for the operating system itself, you can purchase a subscription to RHEL, or you can use a "rebuild" distribution such as AlmaLinux, where the operating system software is compiled by the open-source community from source code publicly released by Red Hat.

If you're experienced with other Unix-type operating systems such as Solaris, AIX, and HP-UX, prepare to leave some defaults at the door. There are even significant differences between the Ubuntu and Red Hat distributions. When Red Hat developed its Linux distribution, the company made some choices that differed from other Unix implementations. When one of the authors of this *Study Guide* took one of Red Hat's System Administration courses, some students with these backgrounds had difficulties with the course and the RHCSA exam.

For the purposes of this book, we'll be running most commands as the Linux administrative user, root. Logging in as the root user is normally discouraged for security reasons. Also, if you make a mistake on the command line as the root user, you could potentially harm your system very seriously. However, since the RHCSA is a time-based exam, you may find that running commands as the root user is appropriate, because it is quicker and requires less typing than using a normal user account for administrative purposes. Just remember that out of the exam room, this is not recommended.

INSIDE THE EXAM

OS Installation and Virtualization

This chapter does not cover any RHCSA exam objectives. While the previous versions of the RHCSA exam included skills related to the installation of Red Hat Enterprise Linux and to the management of virtual guests, the current version of the RHCSA exam does not.

For RHEL 9, the installation process of RHEL is relatively simple. Automated installations (using Kickstart) and virtualization management are now covered in other certification exams: specifically, in the Red Hat Certified Specialist in Deployment and System Management exam (EX403) and in the Red Hat Certified Specialist in Virtualization exam (EX318).

Nevertheless, to set up the lab environment that we will use in the rest of the book, you will need to go through the installation of RHEL and the basic configuration of virtual machines.

These procedures will not be tested in the RHCSA exam, but are essential skills that you must be very familiar with.

Using Other Versions of Red Hat

For the purposes of this chapter, you can install RHEL 9 using a no-cost developer subscription provided by the Red Hat Developer Program. You can also use AlmaLinux. However, whereas RHEL 9 is based in part on the work done by many open-source contributors, it's also based on the Fedora Linux 34 release. Don't use Fedora to study for the Red Hat exams. If you use Fedora, some configuration settings and commands may differ from RHEL 9. Later versions of Fedora are likely to have features not found in RHEL 9.

CERTIFICATION OBJECTIVE 1.01

The RHCSA Exam

Red Hat first started giving certification exams in 1999. Since that time, its exams have evolved. The former Red Hat Certification Technician (RHCT) was a complete subset of the RHCE.

In addition, Red Hat has focused the exams more on hands-on configuration. Multiple-choice questions were removed from the exam in 2003. Later, in 2009, Red Hat simplified the exam by removing the requirement to install Linux on a "bare-metal" system.

Then, the RHCSA certification was introduced as a replacement for the RHCT certification to better align with industry demands and to reflect the evolving role of a Linux system administrator.

Today, the RHCSA exam tests your ability to configure live physical and virtual systems for networking, security, custom filesystems, package updates, user management, and more. In essence, the RHCSA exam covers those skills required to configure and administer a Linux system in the enterprise.

on the
job

For those keen on progressing their Red Hat credentials, the RHCE certification is the next logical step. The RHCE exam tests your ability to manage multiple systems using Ansible and evaluates your expertise in system automation and administration. Achieving this certification augments one's professional standing and underscores their expertise in Linux.

The Exam Experience

Red Hat's certification tests are hands-on exams. As a result of this, they are respected throughout the industry as a sign of genuine practical knowledge. When you pass a Red Hat exam, you will stand head and shoulders above the candidate who has passed only a "standard" multiple-choice certification exam.

When the RHCSA exam starts, you'll be faced with a live RHEL 9 system. You'll be given actual configuration problems associated with the items listed in the RHCSA EX200 exam objectives, shown at the following (click the Objectives tab):

https://www.redhat.com/en/services/training/ex200-red-hat-certified-system-administrator-rhcsa-exam

Naturally, this book is dedicated to helping you gain the skills described on those web pages.

exam
watch   **An overview of this book's coverage of the items listed in the RHCSA exam objectives can be found in the introduction for this book.**

The RHCSA exam lasts three hours. Any changes that you make must survive a reboot. When you've completed the given tasks, the person grading the exam will check if the system is configured to meet the requirements. For example, if you are told to "create, delete, and modify local user accounts," it doesn't matter whether you modify the associated configuration files with the **vi** editor or by using other command-line tools. As long as you don't cheat, it's the results that count.

While you won't have Internet access during the exam, you will have access to online documentation such as man and info pages, as well as documentation in the /usr/share/ doc/ directories, assuming appropriate packages are installed.

In addition, Red Hat provides the exams in electronic format. Although the basic instructions may be in a local language such as English, the RHCSA exam is available in several different languages. If you prefer to take the exam in a language other than English, you should contact Red Hat training to be sure the exam is available in that language at training@redhat.com or 1-866-626-2994.

Red Hat also has prep courses for the RHCSA exam. The outlines for those courses are available from https://www.redhat.com. Although this book is not intended as a substitute for such courses, it is consistent with their outlines. This book covers the objectives associated with the RHCSA exam.

ⓦatch	**Red Hat provides "pre-assessment" tests for its exam prep courses. These tests are available at https://rhtapps.redhat.com/assessment**

Evolving Requirements

Red Hat regularly updates the RHCSA exam to keep up with the changing landscape of Linux system administration and technology trends. This ensures that certified professionals remain current and relevant in their skills and knowledge.

Future changes to the RHCSA exam may be based on topics covered in the Red Hat RHCSA Rapid Track course, RH199/RH200. So if you are not planning to take the RHCSA exam within the next few months, watch the outline for that course. It may, in effect, be a preview of where Red Hat wants to take the RHCSA exam in the future.

CERTIFICATION OBJECTIVE 1.02

Basic Hardware Requirements

Now it is time to explore in detail the hardware that a computer requires to support Red Hat Enterprise Linux. Although some manufacturers include their own Linux hardware drivers, most Linux hardware support comes from third parties, starting with the work of volunteers. Fortunately, there is a vast community of Linux developers, many of whom produce drivers for Linux and distribute them freely on the Internet. If a certain piece of hardware is popular, you can be certain that Linux support for that piece of hardware will pop up somewhere on the Internet and will be incorporated into various Linux distributions, including Red Hat Enterprise Linux.

Hardware Compatibility

RHEL 9 can be installed only on 64-bit systems. Fortunately, all PCs and servers sold today are 64-bit systems. Even the lowly Intel i3 CPU can handle 64-bit operating systems. There are even 64-bit versions of the Intel Atom CPU, common on netbook systems and tablets. Similar comparisons can be made for CPUs from Advanced Micro Devices.

Be careful when purchasing a new computer to use with Linux. Although Linux hardware compatibility has come a long way the last few years, and you should have little problem installing it on most modern servers or PCs, you shouldn't assume Linux will install or run flawlessly on *any* computer, especially if the system in question is a state-of-the-art laptop computer. Laptops are sometimes designed with proprietary configurations that work with Linux only after some reverse engineering.

If you want hardware compatible with and supported by Red Hat, consult the hardware compatibility list at https://catalog.redhat .com/hardware.

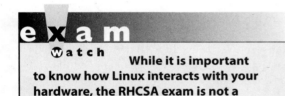

While it is important to know how Linux interacts with your hardware, the RHCSA exam is not a hardware exam.

Architectures

The architecture of a server or PC defines the components it uses as well as the way those components are connected. In other words, the architecture describes much more than just the CPU. It includes standards for other hardware such as memory, data paths such as computer buses, general system design, and more. All software is written for a specific computer architecture.

Although RHEL 9 has been built for a variety of architectures, you can focus on the Intel/AMD 64-bit or x86_64 architecture for the RHCSA exam. As of this writing, this exam is offered only on computers with such CPUs, so you need not worry about special architecture-specific issues such as specialty bootloaders or custom proprietary drivers. Nevertheless, customized Red Hat distributions are available for a variety of platforms.

You can install RHEL 9 on systems with a wide variety of CPUs. Red Hat supports four different basic 64-bit CPU architectures:

- Intel/AMD64 (x86_64)
- 64-bit ARM

- IBM Power Systems, Little Endian
- IBM System Z

To identify the architecture of a running RHEL system, run the following command:

```
# uname -p
```

To practice with the labs in this book, you need to configure virtual machines. Be sure to choose a system that supports hardware-assisted virtualization, along with Basic Input/Output System (BIOS) or Unified Extensible Firmware Interface (UEFI) menu options that allow you to activate hardware-assisted virtualization. All new PCs will meet these requirements today. However, if you are running an old system, look at the processor specifications on the vendor's website.

RAM Requirements

Although it's possible to run RHEL 9 on less, the RAM requirements are driven by the needs of the Red Hat installer. For basic Intel/AMD-based 64-bit architectures, Red Hat officially requires 1.5GiB of RAM.

Of course, actual memory requirements depend on the load from every program that may be run simultaneously on a system. That can also include the memory requirements of any virtual machine that you might run on a physical RHEL 9 system. There is no practical maximum RAM because, theoretically, you could run 64TB of RAM on RHEL 9. But that's just theory. The maximum RAM supported and tested on RHEL 9 for 64-bit Intel/AMD-based systems is 48TB, which is still twice than the 24TB supported on RHEL 8.

on the job

If you're setting up Linux as a server, RAM requirements increase with the number of applications that may need to run simultaneously. The same may be true if you're running several different VMs on a single system. However, administrators typically "overcommit" RAM on VMs configured with different functionality. VMs can also transparently share memory pages to further improve efficiency.

Storage Options

Before a computer can load Linux, the BIOS or UEFI firmware has to recognize the active primary partition on the disk drive. This partition should include the Linux boot files. The BIOS or UEFI can then set up and initialize that disk drive, and then load Linux boot files from that active primary partition. You should know the following about disk drives and Linux:

- The number of drives that can be installed on modern computers has increased. On commodity hardware it's relatively easy to get 16 or 24 Serial Advanced Technology Attachment (SATA) or Serial Attached SCSI (SAS) internal drives on a system. Moreover, the use of Non-Volatile Memory Express (NVMe) drives is steadily growing, particularly in applications requiring high performance.

- You need both a UEFI firmware and a GPT-partitioned disk to boot from a drive larger than 2TB. UEFI is a firmware interface that is meant to replace the traditional BIOS, and today is available on many PCs on the market. The GUID Partition Table (GPT) is a partitioning format that supports drives larger than 2TB, but you also require a UEFI firmware (rather than a traditional BIOS firmware) to boot from such device.
- You can install RHEL 9 on a storage area network (SAN) volume. RHEL 9 supports more than 10,000 storage device paths.

Networking

As Linux was originally designed as a clone of Unix, it retains the advantages of Unix as a network operating system. However, not every network component works with Linux. As an example, several manufacturers of wireless network devices have not built Linux drivers. In most such cases, Linux developers have been working endlessly to develop appropriate drivers and to get those drivers incorporated into the major distributions, including RHEL.

Virtual Machine Options

Virtualization makes it relatively easy to set up a large number of systems, so it can help you configure machines, each dedicated to a specific service. To that end, virtualization can be classified into different categories. Some solutions can belong to more than one category. As an example, VMware ESXi is a bare-metal, hypervisor-based virtualization solution that supports hardware-assisted virtualization and provides optional paravirtual drivers to be installed on the guest OS.

- **Application level vs. VM level**   Software tools such as Wine (originally an acronym for Wine Is Not an Emulator) support the installation of a single application. In this case, Wine allows an application built for Microsoft Windows to be running on Linux. On the other end, VM-level virtualization emulates a number of complete computer systems for the installation of separate guest OSs.
- **Hosted vs. bare-metal hypervisor**   Applications such as VMware Player and VirtualBox are hosted hypervisors ("type-2" hypervisors) because they run on a conventional OS such as Microsoft Windows 11. Conversely, bare-metal virtualization systems, such as VMware ESXi and Citrix Hypervisor ("type-1" hypervisors), include a minimal OS dedicated to VM operations.
- **Paravirtualization vs. full virtualization**   Full virtualization allows a guest OS to run unmodified on a hypervisor, whereas paravirtualization requires specialized drivers to be installed in the guest OS.

The KVM (Kernel-based Virtual Machine) solution that comes with RHEL 9 is known as a hypervisor—a VM monitor that supports the running of multiple operating systems concurrently on the same CPU.

on the job

KVM replaced Xen as the default hypervisor starting in RHEL 5 and has replaced Xen in many open-source distributions. Citrix Hypervisor (formerly XenServer) is owned by Citrix.

Another virtualization approach that is very popular today is Linux containers, such as those provided by Docker or Podman. This solution is not hypervisor-based but rather relies on the process and filesystem isolation techniques available in the Linux kernel (that is, cgroups and namespaces) to run multiple isolated Linux systems on the same physical host. Kubernetes (and OpenShift, which is based on it) provides an orchestration platform for the management and deployment of containers.

CERTIFICATION OBJECTIVE 1.03

Get Red Hat Enterprise Linux

The RHCSA exam is based on your knowledge of RHEL. To get an official copy of RHEL, you typically need a subscription. However, for development purposes Red Hat also offers a subscription at no cost as part of the Red Hat Developer Program. As an alternative, third-party rebuilds such as AlmaLinux are available. AlmaLinux uses the same source code as RHEL and, except for the trademarks and the connection to the Red Hat Customer Portal, is essentially functionally identical to RHEL.

Once you get a subscription, you'll be able to download RHEL 9 from the Red Hat Customer Portal at https://access.redhat.com/downloads. Downloads are available for the operating system in a format appropriate for a DVD. There's also a download available for a network boot ISO image. You'll even be able to download files with the source code for associated packages. These downloads are in ISO image format, with an **.iso** extension. Such files can be burned to appropriate media, using standard tools such as balenaEtcher, K3b, Brasero, and even corresponding tools on Microsoft systems. Alternatively, you can set up a VM where the virtual CD/DVD drive hardware points directly to the ISO file.

exam watch

Although it is important to know how to get RHEL, that skill is not a part of the objectives for the RHCSA exam.

Get a Subscription at No Cost

Red Hat currently offers a RHEL subscription at no cost, if you enroll in the Red Hat Developer Program at https://developers.redhat.com. If you want to learn RHEL and use it for development purposes, this is certainly the most affordable option. However, keep in mind that you may not be allowed to use this subscription on production systems. The Red Hat Developer subscription offers self-service support through resources such as knowledge base articles and discussion groups on the Red Hat Customer Portal.

Purchase a Subscription

Different subscriptions are available for workstations, servers, and development machines. You may want to purchase a subscription if you want to be able to contact Red Hat Support.

A variety of server subscriptions are available, the price of each depending on the number of CPU sockets and virtual guests and on the support level. A system associated with a standard RHEL subscription is limited to two CPU sockets and two virtual nodes. Each socket can have a multicore CPU. Significant discounts for academic users are available.

Red Hat also offers a Red Hat Enterprise Linux Workstation subscription, currently priced at $299 per year in the United States. This subscription provides full support from Red Hat and download access to RHEL and several types of add-on software.

Third-Party Rebuilds

To comply with the Linux General Public License (GPL), Red Hat releases the source code for just about every RHEL package. However, the GPL only requires Red Hat to make the source code available to its customers. Red Hat does not have to make the binary packages compiled from that source code publicly available.

 on the job   **The description in this book of the GPL, trademark law, and Red Hat legal agreement for subscription services is not a legal opinion and is not intended as legal advice.**

Under trademark law, Red Hat can prevent others from releasing software with its trademarks, such as the Red Hat logo. Nevertheless, the GPL gives anyone the right to compile that source code. If they make any modifications, all they need to do is release their changes under the same license. And some "third parties" have taken this opportunity to remove the trademarks from the released source code and have compiled that software into their own rebuilds, functionally equivalent to RHEL.

The RHEL source code is available at the Red Hat Customer Portal. However, the building of a distribution, even from source code, is a tricky process. But once complete, the rebuild has the same functionality as RHEL. However, rebuild distributions don't have a connection to and can't get updates from the Red Hat Customer Portal. Installing packages from Red Hat Subscription Management (RHSM) is part of the RHCSA exam objectives, so you will not be able to practice this skill if you use a rebuild distribution. Nevertheless, this is the only limitation.

e x a m
watch

In the current RHCSA exam objectives, RHSM is referred to by its previous name, the "Red Hat Network." While there's a possibility of Red Hat making updates to this in the future, for the RHCSA exam's scope, both RHSM and the "Red Hat Network" represent the same service, which offers access software packages and updates provided by Red Hat.

CentOS Linux, once the most prominent RHEL rebuild, was discontinued in 2021. It was replaced by CentOS Stream, a Linux distribution designed to function as a midstream bridge between Fedora Linux's upstream development and RHEL's downstream development. As such, it's not a rebuild of RHEL but rather an upstream development platform for it.

Among the third-party rebuilds, AlmaLinux continues to be a viable option. For more information, see https://almalinux.org.

Check the Download

For downloads from its website, Red Hat provides checksums based on the 256-bit Secure Hash Algorithm (SHA256). You can check these ISO files against the given checksum numbers with the **sha256sum** command. For example, the following command calculates the SHA256 checksum for the RHEL 9.1 DVD file:

```
# sha256sum rhel-baseos-9.1-x86_64-dvd.iso
```

At the time of writing, the most recent version of RHEL available was 9.1. Throughout this book, we've tailored the examples and exercises to align with RHEL 9.1 specifics. However, readers should find it straightforward to modify and apply these examples to newer releases of RHEL 9. It's essential to stay updated and adaptable, recognizing that the core principles typically remain consistent across minor version updates.

EXERCISE 1-1

Get Red Hat Enterprise Linux

In this exercise, you will enroll in the Red Hat Developer Program and download a RHEL 9 ISO image. You can skip this exercise if you already have a RHEL subscription, or if you wish to use AlmaLinux or another RHEL derivative distribution to practice for the Red Hat exams.

1. Point your browser to https://developers.redhat.com. Click Log In in the upper-right corner, then click Register in the same location.

2. Complete the registration form and click Create My Account to activate your account.

3. Go to https://developers.redhat.com/products/rhel/download and download the latest Server DVD ISO image for RHEL 9, x86_64 architecture.

4. Calculate the SHA256 checksum of the RHEL 9 Server DVD ISO file. If you are on a Linux machine, type this command (the filename may differ slightly for a release of RHEL other than 9.1):

   ```
   # sha256sum rhel-baseos-9.1-x86_64-dvd.iso
   ```

   On Windows, start PowerShell and run

   ```
   # Get-FileHash rhel-baseos-9.1-x86_64-dvd.iso
   ```

5. Go to https://access.redhat.com/downloads and click Red Hat Enterprise Linux. You can also get the DVD ISO image from this page, but the most important thing is that here you will find the SHA checksum of the DVD ISO file that you have previously downloaded. Compare the SHA256 checksum with the one that you calculated in Step 4 and check that the two values are the same. If not, you may have had an issue during the download of the file.

6. Go to https://access.redhat.com/management/products. You should see a Red Hat Developer Subscription for Individuals in your active subscriptions. Click it and have a look at the products included with your Developer Subscription. In the list, you should recognize Red Hat Enterprise Linux for x86_64. There will be lots of products listed, but we won't cover all of those in this book.

CERTIFICATION OBJECTIVE 1.04

An Environment for Practice Labs

Red Hat provides "pre-installed systems" for its exams, with questions presented "electronically." So you won't start from scratch, but you'll still need to set up practice systems.

In other words, when seated for an exam, you'll see an installed copy of RHEL 9 on the test system, with questions in some electronic format. No public information is available on the format of the questions.

The installation requirements described in this section are suited to the creation of an environment for practice labs. That environment may also work as a baseline for other RHEL systems. On many real networks, new virtual systems are created or cloned from that baseline. Those new systems are then dedicated for a single service.

For the purposes of our lab environment, we will use VMware Workstation Player virtualization software to set up some RHEL virtual machines for testing. We chose VMware Workstation Player because it is freely available, and you can install it on a desktop PC or laptop, whether you have a Windows or Linux system running on it. Of course, if you already have a physical system running Linux, you may choose to use KVM, the Red Hat virtualization hypervisor. Or you can install other virtualization products, such as VirtualBox. However, we cannot cover every possible scenario in this book, so we'll assume you will be using VMware Workstation Player.

The baseline for the RHEL 9 systems configured in this chapter is relatively simple. You will need about 20GiB of disk space. Part of that space will be organized as shown in Table 1-1. Some of the space will be configured as regular partitions. The remaining space on the disk drive will be left empty for potential configuration during the lab exercises as logical volumes.

on the **Ü** o b

The notation MiB indicates a mebibyte, which is equivalent to 1024KiB (1024 "kibibytes"), or 1024 × 1024 = 1,048,576 bytes. Similarly, a GiB is a gibibyte and is the same as 1024MiB, and so on. However, in the notation of the International System of Units, MB indicates a megabyte, which is equivalent to 1000KB (1000 kilobytes), or 1000 × 1000 = 1,000,000 bytes. You may have noticed that operating systems usually show a disk size in GiB (or TiB), while disk vendors advertise their disk sizes in GB (or TB). Can you guess why? Which is larger?

The 20GiB virtual hard disk is the recommended size to provide enough room for the labs that you will complete in later chapters. If space is limited on your system, you might go as low as 10GiB, which is the minimum disk size supported by RHEL 9, or even lower. Swap space in Linux is used as an extension of local RAM, especially when that resource runs short, and is not strictly necessary.

TABLE 1-1	Location	Size	
	/boot	1GiB	
Filesystem Mount Points	/	15GiB	
	/home	1GiB	
	Swap	1GiB	

The baseline minimum installation of RHEL 9 does not include a GUI. Although it is fairly easy to install the package groups associated with the GUI after installation is complete, that process requires the installation of several hundred megabytes' worth of packages. And that takes time. Since Red Hat provides a pre-installed system to reduce the time required for the exam, it is reasonable to suggest that the system provided by Red Hat includes the GUI. And the default GUI for Red Hat systems is the GNOME Desktop Environment.

on the Job

GNOME was initially an acronym within an acronym. It stood for the GNU Network Object Model Environment. GNU is itself a recursive acronym because it stands for GNU's Not Unix. Linux is filled with similar recursive acronyms, such as PHP: Hypertext Preprocessor (PHP).

The amount of RAM to allocate is more complex, especially on a VM. For the purposes of this book, we've configured VMs with 2GiB of RAM to comfortably enable GUI-based illustrations of the RHEL installation process. However, 1.5GiB of RAM is the minimum required, and you could run RHEL 9 with even less. Since different VMs rarely use all the RAM simultaneously, it's possible to "overcommit" RAM; for example, it may be possible to set up two VMs, with 2GiB of RAM each, on a physical host system with less than 4GiB of physical RAM. Some RAM on the VMs will remain unused, available to the physical host system.

System Roles

In this chapter, you will set up two RHEL 9 virtual machines. The installation of the first system will be explained in the next Certification Objective section, "RHEL 9 Installation," while you will install the second system in Lab 1 at the end of the chapter.

Table 1-2 lists the roles appropriate for each of the two systems that you will install.

Getting VMware Workstation Player

To get VMware Workstation Player, navigate to the official VMware website, specifically to https://www.vmware.com/products/workstation-player.html. Click the Download For Free link, and then click Go To Downloads. Following that, you'll be presented with two

TABLE 1-2	System	Roles
Roles for Test Systems	server1	Main server to practice with the labs in this book, configured as server1.example.com on the 172.16.0.0/24 network. This book assumes a fixed IP address of 172.16.0.100.
	tester1	Secure Shell server that supports remote access, configured as tester1.example.com on the 172.16.0.0/24 network. May be used to test network connectivity and firewall rules. This book assumes a fixed IP address of 172.16.0.50.

download options, one for Linux and one for Windows. Click the Download Now button for the one that fits your operating system.

Once the software is downloaded, locate the installation file in your Downloads folder or wherever your browser defaults to save files. The installation file generally ends with .exe for Windows or .bundle for Linux. To start the installation process, double-click the file.

For Windows, an installation wizard opens to guide you through the process. Click Next and follow the onscreen instructions, accepting the End-User License Agreement and choosing the location of installation (if not the default).

On Linux, open the terminal, navigate to the directory containing the .bundle file, and use the command **sudo sh ./VMware-Player-<version_number>.bundle** to start the installation process. Follow the prompts, accepting the license agreement and choosing the relevant options.

Upon successful installation, you can launch VMware Workstation Player. To do this, either navigate to the program through your system's start menu or type **VMware Workstation Player** into your system's search bar and press ENTER.

When you open VMware Workstation Player, a window appears that is similar to what is shown in Figure 1-1. This is your main control panel for managing and interacting with your virtual machines. From here, you can create new VMs, open existing ones, change settings, and much more.

FIGURE 1-1   VMware Workstation Player

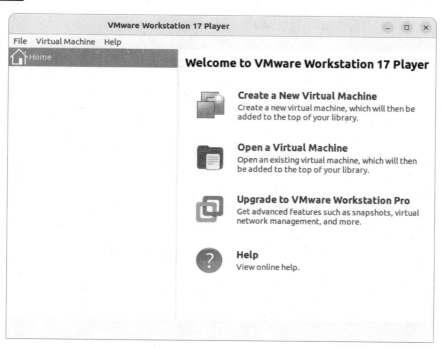

Virtual Networks on a Hypervisor

The free version of VMware Workstation Player offers three types of networks that you can configure for your virtual machines:

■ **Bridged**   This mode bridges your physical network adapter and your virtual machine's adapter, allowing the VM to appear as a separate device on the same network that your host machine is connected to. It means that the VM will get an IP address within the same subnet as your host machine.

■ **Network Address Translation (NAT)**   In NAT mode, your VM shares the IP address of your host machine. The VMware hypervisor software acts as a network router for the VM and manages a private network connection between the host machine and the VM. The VMs connected via NAT mode will be able to access the Internet but won't be directly accessible from the external network, as they'll be on a separate subnet.

■ **Host-only**   With a host-only network, your VM can only communicate with the host machine. It will not have any access to the external network, the Internet. This is useful when you want to isolate the VM from your network for security or testing purposes.

In our lab environment, we will be using the NAT mode for our Linux VMs. This configuration provides the VMs with Internet access while keeping them isolated from the outside, making it an ideal balance for our purposes.

VMware Workstation Player automatically allocates a subnet for NAT mode. To determine the subnet used by VMware for NAT, follow this procedure on a Windows system, as shown in Figure 1-2:

1. Open Control Panel and click Network And Internet (in Category view).
2. Click Network And Sharing Center.
3. On the left side of the Network And Sharing Center window, click Change Adapter Settings. This opens a screen with all of your network connections.
4. Locate the VMware Network Adapter VMnet8. This adapter is used for the NAT network in VMware Workstation Player.
5. Right-click the name of the adapter and select Properties.
6. In the Properties window, click Internet Protocol Version 4 (TCP/IPv4) and then click the Properties button.
7. The next window displays the IP address and subnet mask for the VMnet8 adapter.

If you have installed VMware Workstation Player on Linux, open a terminal and type the command **ip address show vmnet8**. This will display the IP address and subnet mask for the vmnet8 adapter.

FIGURE 1-2

The VMnet8
adapter properties

Internet Protocol Version 4 (TCP/IPv4) Properties ☒

General

You can get IP settings assigned automatically if your network supports
this capability. Otherwise, you need to ask your network administrator
for the appropriate IP settings.

○ Obtain an IP address automatically
⦿ Use the following IP address:

IP address: 172 . 16 . 0 . 1
Subnet mask: 255 . 255 . 255 . 0
Default gateway: . . .

○ Obtain DNS server address automatically
⦿ Use the following DNS server addresses:

Preferred DNS server: . . .
Alternate DNS server: . . .

☐ Validate settings upon exit

Advanced...

OK   Cancel

on the
Job

**VMware Workstation Player will take care to avoid IP address conflicts with
existing hardware on the local network, such as with routers and wireless
access points. For example, if your wireless access point uses the subnet
192.168.56.0/24, the VMware software will not use this range.**

If you need help with networking, refer to Chapter 3. For now, all you need to know is that
VMware Workstation Player has created a network subnet for NAT mode on your physical
host. This subnet is not visible to the external world, and the VMs that you create will be
attached to it so that they will run and communicate on this isolated network segment.

The NAT subnet can be changed according to your preferences or requirements, but
this is not necessary. Throughout this book, we'll be working under the assumption that the
subnet is set to 172.16.0.0/24. However, it is essential to remember that your own system's
configuration might differ from this.

For instance, suppose that the subnet created by VMware Workstation Player on your machine happens to be 192.168.219.0/24. In such a case, the corresponding IP address you would assign to server1 would then be 192.168.219.100 rather than 172.16.0.100. Here, you'll notice that the final octet is the same, whereas the first three octets reflect the NAT subnet address. So, the key takeaway is to ensure that the first three octets that you assign to your VM's IP address match those of your NAT subnet.

Configure a Virtual Machine on VMware Workstation Player

Return to the main window of VMware Workstation Player. With the following steps, you'll set up the VM that will host the server1.example.com system introduced in Table 1-2:

1. Click File | Create a New Virtual Machine to open the New Virtual Machine Wizard.

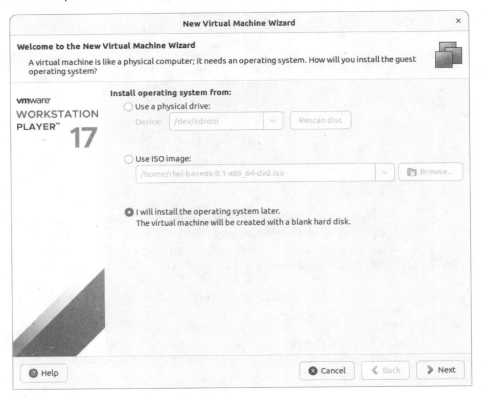

2. Select "I will install the operating system later" and click Next.
3. Set the guest operating system to Linux, version Red Hat Enterprise Linux 9 64-bit.
4. Type a name for the new VM; to match the discussion in the remainder of this book, you should name this VM **server1**. Click Next. In the next screen, set the disk size to 20GB.

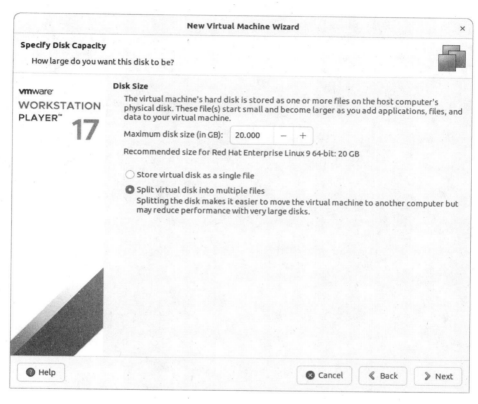

5. Click Next, then Finish. The virtual machine is created and is shown in VMware Workstation Player in a "Powered Off" state.

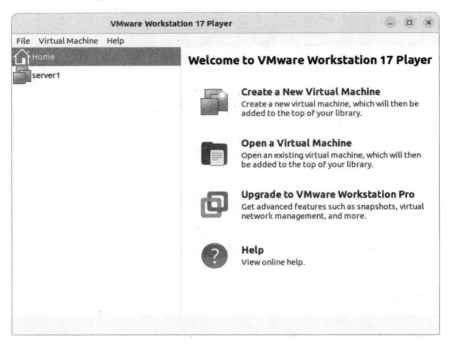

6. Now you need to point VMware Workstation Player to your installation media. Select the newly created VM and click Edit Virtual Machine Settings. In the new window that opens, select CD/DVD (SATA) and ensure that the option Connect At Power On is selected. Then, click the Browse button and browse until you find the path of the RHEL 9 ISO image that you have previously downloaded. This image will be mounted as if it were a DVD inserted in the drive of the machine. Then, click Save to return to VMware Workstation Player.

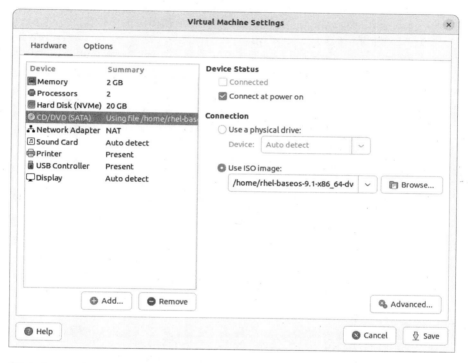

7. Click Start. The VM should power on and boot from the RHEL 9 DVD image that you have attached to it.

8. To power off the virtual machine, from the Virtual Machine menu select Power | Power Off Guest.

on the **job**

If you click your mouse pointer inside the virtual machine display window of VMware Workstation Player, this will cause the VM to capture the host mouse pointer and keyboard so that you can use the mouse and type inside the VM. Press CTRL-ALT to release it and restore control to the main operating system.

CERTIFICATION OBJECTIVE 1.05

RHEL 9 Installation

Even most new Linux users can install RHEL 9 from a CD/DVD. Although this section addresses some of the options associated with installation, it is focused on the creation of the first of the two systems listed in Table 1-2.

In addition, the installation process is an opportunity to learn more about RHEL 9, not only boot media, but the logical volumes that can be configured after installation is complete. However, because pre-installed physical systems are now the norm for Red Hat exams, detailed discussions of logical volumes have been consolidated in Chapter 7.

The steps described in this section assume that you have downloaded the RHEL 9 DVD image, as explained earlier in the chapter, and followed the steps in the previous section to create a VM in VMware Workstation Player.

Boot Media

When you are installing RHEL 9, the simplest option is to boot it from the RHEL 9 DVD. But that's not the only available installation option. In essence, five methods are available to start the RHEL 9 installation process:

- Boot from a RHEL 9 Binary DVD.
- Boot from a USB drive containing the RHEL 9 Binary DVD image.
- Boot from a minimal RHEL Boot CD.
- Boot from a USB key containing a minimal RHEL Boot CD image.
- Boot from a Kickstart server using a PXE network boot card.

The last three options generally assume that you're going to install RHEL over a network and that package repositories will be available on a web server, FTP server, or NFS share. The installation and boot media are available from the Red Hat Customer Portal for users with a subscription. They are also available from servers associated with "rebuild" distributions.

If you followed the steps in the previous section, you can boot the server1.example.com VM from the installation DVD. After a few seconds, a RHEL installation screen should appear, as illustrated in Figure 1-3, with at least the following three options:

- Install Red Hat Enterprise Linux 9.1
- Test this media & install Red Hat Enterprise Linux 9.1
- Troubleshooting

FIGURE 1-3

The installation
boot screen

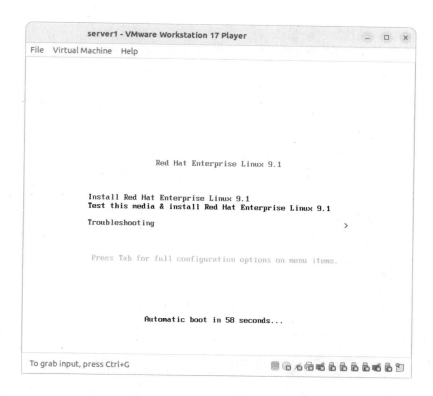

The first option should work for most users. If you want to check the integrity of the installation media before starting the installation process, select the second option.

Two modes are associated with the Red Hat installation program (also known as "Anaconda"): text mode and graphical mode. Although the graphical mode is the recommended method, you would be automatically redirected to text mode if the installation program does not properly detect your video card. Fortunately, this will not be the case on VMware Workstation Player, because the hosted hypervisor will emulate a video card that is supported by Linux.

You can also force installation in text mode if you wish. To do so, highlight the Install Red Hat Enterprise Linux 9.1 option and press the TAB key. When you do, the following options are revealed on that screen, on one line:

```
> vmlinuz initrd=initrd.img inst.stage2=hd:LABEL=RHEL-9.1.0-
BaseOS-x86_64 quiet
```

To force installation in text mode, add **inst.text** to the end of this line.

Basic Installation Steps

The basic RHEL installation is straightforward and should already be well understood by any Red Hat certification candidate.

The sequence of steps for the installation process varies depending on whether you're installing in text mode or graphical mode. The sequence also may vary if you're using a rebuild distribution of RHEL 9. So be flexible when reading the following instructions:

1. Boot your computer from the RHEL DVD. Three options are normally shown, as illustrated in Figure 1-3. Select the first option and press ENTER.

2. Select a language to use during the installation process, as shown in Figure 1-4. English is the default; over 50 options are available.

3. The next screen is the Installation Summary screen, shown in Figure 1-5. From this interface you can review and edit all installation settings. One item in the Installation Summary screen is marked with a "warning" symbol. This indicates that you must configure the corresponding section before being able to proceed with the installation.

4. From the Installation Summary screen, review the date and time zone of the local system, and make appropriate changes if necessary.

FIGURE 1-4

Select a language for installation.

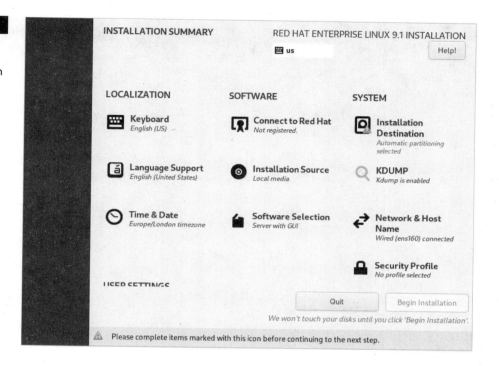

FIGURE 1-5

The Installation Summary screen

5. Similarly, you can review the keyboard configuration and the language settings if needed.

6. The next option in the Installation Summary screen relates to the installation source. Because you are installing from a DVD image, leave this setting as "Local media."

7. Review the Network & Host Name settings in the Installation Summary screen, as shown in Figure 1-6. The left panel lists the network interfaces detected by the installation program. Select the Ethernet interface, and move the switch at the top-right corner to the ON position.

8. Click the Configure button and select the IPv4 Settings tab to choose how you want IP addressing to be configured. You will see the window shown in Figure 1-7. In the Method field, set the configuration method to Manual to manually enter a static IP address. Then, click Add and enter the settings shown in Figure 1-7. Save your configuration.

9. In the Host Name field shown at the bottom left in Figure 1-6, set **server1.example .com** as the hostname for the system and click Apply. Once you have completed your configuration changes, click the Done button.

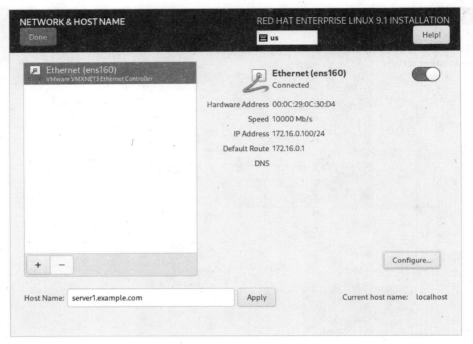

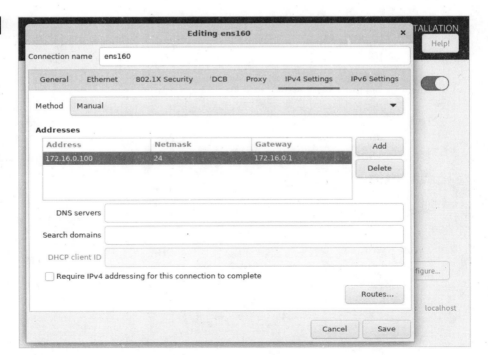

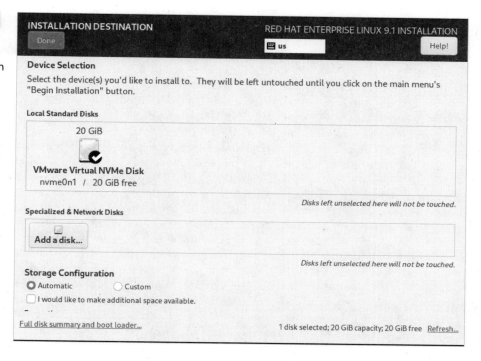

FIGURE 1-8

The Installation
Destination screen

10. Click the Installation Destination item from the Installation Summary screen, and you will see the screen shown in Figure 1-8. From this screen, you can determine how space on configured disk drives, local and remote, is used. Here, you can choose between automatically and manually configured partitioning. For automatic partitioning, you can select the check box "I would like to make additional space available" if you want to reconfigure space from other existing partitions. Optionally, you can select "Encrypt my data." For the purposes of this installation, select Custom and click Done to continue.

The Installation Perspective on Partitions

Disk partitions are a way to slice a disk drive into multiple regions. Once a partition is created, you can configure Linux to mount a partition on a directory, or "mount point." For example, a partition can be mounted on the top of the Linux filesystem, which is the root partition (or "/"), or it can be mounted under a different directory, such as /home.

To define a partition, you may need some background on naming conventions, the configuration of different filesystems, and uses of swap space and logical volumes. This is just an overview. Detailed information is available in Chapter 7.

Naming Conventions

Linux has a simple naming standard for disk partitions: three letters followed by a number. The first letter identifies the type of drive (s is for SATA or SAS, and v is for virtual disks on KVM-based VMs). The second letter is d for disk, and the third letter represents the relative position of that disk, starting with a. For example, the first SATA drive is sda, followed by sdb, sdc, and sdd. (NVMe drives, such as that detected in Figure 1-8, are named nvme$X$nY, where X indicates the index or number of the NVMe controller, and nY refers to the namespace or logical unit within the NVMe controller.)

The number that follows the three letters is based on the relative position of the partition. Two partitioning schemes are available on modern PCs: the traditional Master Boot Record (MBR) and the newer GUID Partition Table (GPT) scheme.

In the MBR scheme, partitions can be one of three types: primary, extended, or logical. Primary partitions can contain the boot files for an operating system. Disk drives can also be configured with one extended partition, which can then contain a number of logical partitions.

Disk drives are limited to four primary partitions. When four partitions are not enough, an extended partition can be substituted for the last primary partition. That extended partition can then be subdivided into logical partitions. So when planning a partition layout, make sure that the extended partition is big enough. Although it's possible to create more, you should not create more than 12 logical partitions on any individual SATA, SAS, or virtual disk drive.

The GPT partitioning scheme does not have such limitations and, on RHEL 9, by default can support up to 128 partitions. This number can be increased further if necessary, although such a scenario is quite rare and not commonly used.

Each partition is associated with a Linux device file. At least that is straightforward; for example, the device filename associated with the third partition on the first SATA drive is /dev/sda3. (For NVMe drives, the third partition on /dev/nvme0n1 would be indicated as /dev/nvme0n1p3.)

A volume is a generic name for a formatted segment of space that can be used to contain data. Volumes can be partitions or those logical volumes associated with Logical Volume Management (LVM). A filesystem exists inside a volume and provides the ability to store files. Filesystems handle the conversion of blocks on the volumes to files. For example, Red Hat uses the XFS filesystem as the default format for its volumes. The standard way to access data in Linux is to first mount that filesystem onto a directory. For instance, when the /dev/sda1 partition is formatted to the XFS filesystem, it can then be mounted on a directory such as /boot. It is common to say something like, "The /dev/sda1 filesystem is mounted on the /boot mount point." You will review these concepts in more depth in Chapter 7.

Separate Filesystem Volumes

Normally, you should create several volumes for RHEL 9. Even in the default configuration, RHEL is configured with at least three volumes—a top-level root directory (/), a /boot directory, and Linux swap space. Additional volumes may be suitable for directories such as /home, /opt, /tmp, and /var. They're also suitable for any custom directories such as for websites, dedicated groups of users, and more.

Although it's important to configure the /boot directory on a regular partition, other directories can readily be configured on logical volumes.

Dividing the space from available disk drives in this manner keeps system, application, and user files isolated from each other. This helps protect the disk space used by system services and various applications. Files cannot grow across volumes. For example, a user's home directory with lots of files can't crowd out space needed by a system service.

While there are many advantages to creating more volumes, it isn't always the best solution. When disk space is limited, the number of partitions should be kept to a minimum. For example, if you have a 12GiB disk drive and want to install 5GiB of packages, having dedicated /var and /home volumes could lead to a situation where disk space runs out far too quickly.

Linux Swap Space

Linux swap space is normally configured either on a dedicated partition or on a logical volume. Such space is used to extend the amount of effective RAM on a system as virtual memory for currently running programs. But normally you should not just buy extra RAM and eliminate swap space. Linux moves infrequently used programs and data to swap space even if you have gigabytes of free RAM.

The way Red Hat recommends to assign swap space is based on the amount of RAM on a system. For systems of up to 2GiB, the recommended swap space size is twice the amount of installed RAM. For systems between 2GiB and 8GiB, it's equal to the amount of RAM. Above 8GiB, it's half the amount of RAM. But those are not "hard and fast" rules. Workstations with several gigabytes of RAM frequently use very little swap space. However, certain application workloads may need a big swap partition, such as applications that use large tmpfs filesystems (tmpfs is a temporary filesystem stored in RAM that relies on swap space as a backing store if the server is under memory pressure). In any case, the default installation configures swap space, not in a dedicated partition, but as a logical volume.

Basic Information on Logical Volumes

The creation of a logical volume from a partition requires the following steps. Details on these concepts, as well as the actual commands required to execute these steps, are described in Chapter 7. Some of these steps are run automatically if you create a logical volume during the installation process.

- Label a partition as a Linux LVM volume.
- Initialize the labeled partition as a physical volume.
- Combine one or more physical volumes as a volume group.
- Subdivide a volume group into logical volumes.
- Format a logical volume to a Linux filesystem or swap space.
- Mount a formatted logical volume on a directory or as swap space.

Partition Creation Exercise

Now we return to the installation process. If you followed the steps described so far in this chapter, you should see the Manual Partitioning screen shown in Figure 1-9.

At this screen, the drop-down menu gives you the opportunity to configure filesystems on standard partitions, on LVM volumes, and on thin-provisioned LVM volumes. The /boot mount point will be always configured on a standard partition, regardless of the partition scheme settings you have selected in this screen.

1. Select Standard Partition from the partitioning scheme drop-down menu. LVM will be discussed in Chapter 7.
2. Configure standard mount points as described earlier in Table 1-1. Larger partitions are acceptable if you have the space. At the bottom left of the screen, the + button supports the creation of a new mount point, as shown in Figure 1-10.

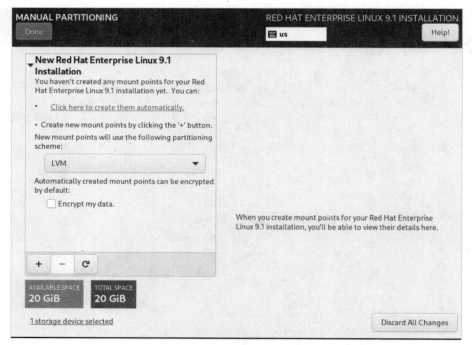

FIGURE 1-9

The Manual Partitioning screen

FIGURE 1-10

Adding a
mount point

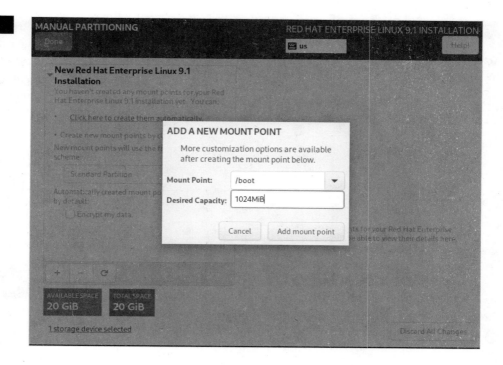

3. Back in the Manual Partitioning screen, you should now see the settings shown in Figure 1-11. This window supports a number of choices:

- **Mount Point**   This is the directory (such as /boot) whose files will be stored on the partition.

- **Desired Capacity**   Indicate the desired capacity of the partition; in this case, the partitions to be configured for this baseline system are defined in Table 1-1.

- **Device Type**   This is the device type, which you previously set to Standard Partition from the partitioning scheme menu.

- **File System**   Select the filesystem type; in this case, the default xfs filesystem is selected.

- **Label**   You can provide an optional label.

Now it's time for an exercise. First, we examine how to create and configure partitions during the installation process. We'll also look at how to allocate a filesystem to a partition or a logical volume.

FIGURE 1-11

Configuration for
the /boot partition

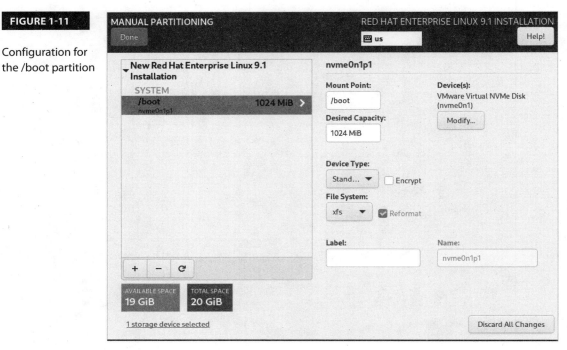

EXERCISE 1-2

Partitioning During Installation

This exercise is based on the assumption that you have followed the installation steps in
the previous section of this chapter. It is easy to recover from mistakes because you can
click the Reload Storage Configuration button to discard any configuration changes. This
exercise starts with the Manual Partitioning screen shown in Figure 1-9 and continues with
the screens shown in Figures 1-10 and 1-11.

1. If you have made any configuration changes to the partitioning layout, click the
   Reload Storage Configuration button (the rotating arrow button at the bottom left
   in Figure 1-9) to discard all of them.
2. Select the LVM partitioning scheme from the drop-down menu on the left of Figure 1-9.
3. At the bottom left of the screen, click the + button to add a new mount point.
4. Set up an appropriate mount point, such as /boot, set the capacity to 1GiB, and click
   the Add Mount Point button.

5. Note that despite your having selected the LVM partitioning scheme, the /boot mount point has been created on a standard partition. This is because the Anaconda installer forces the /boot volume to be on a standard partition.

6. Click the File System drop-down menu and review the available options. You will see several filesystem types, such as xfs, vfat, ext4, and so on.

7. Create an additional volume for the swap space. Under Mount Point, select "swap" and set the size to 1GiB.

8. Leave the swap space on a standard partition. Ensure that the swap partition is selected and change the Device Type setting from LVM to Standard Partition.

9. Create an additional mount point for the root filesystem, using the steps just described. Select / in the Mount Point input box and set the size to 15GiB. Note how the Available Space and Total Space figures shown at the bottom left of the window have changed.

10. Repeat the preceding step to create a mount point for the /home filesystem and set the size to 1GiB.

Now that the exercise is complete, the partition configuration should reflect at least the minimums shown in Table 1-1. One version is shown in Figure 1-12. If a mistake is made, highlight a partition and edit its configuration settings. Do not be concerned with small errors; modest variations in size are not relevant in practice—and the Red Hat exams reflect what happens in practice.

FIGURE 1-12

Sample partition configuration

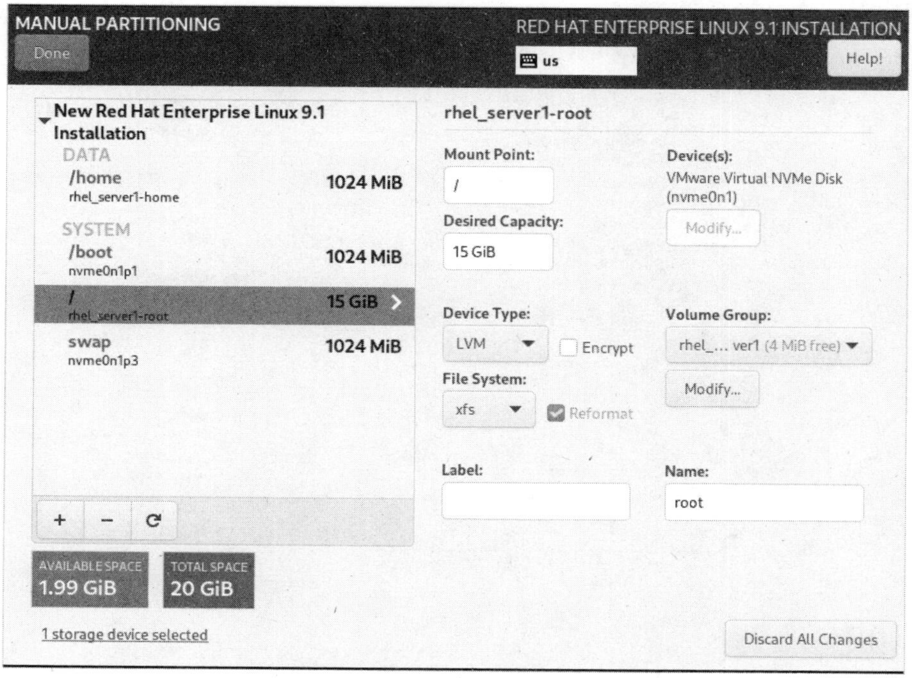

To complete this part of the process, click Done. You will see a Summary of Changes screen. This is your last chance to cancel before proceeding. Assuming you're satisfied, click Accept Changes to continue.

Wow, Look at All That Software!

Over 6600 software packages are available just from the RHEL 9 installation DVD. That figure does not include a number of packages available only through other subscription channels on the Red Hat Customer Portal. With so many packages, it's important to organize them into groups. Click Software Selection from the Installation Summary screen (shown earlier in Figure 1-5). You'll see the options shown in Figure 1-13, which allow you to configure the local system to a desired functionality. The selection depends on your objective. If you're installing on a production physical system to set up KVM-based virtualization, select Virtualization Host. If you're setting up virtual guests (or other dedicated physical servers), select Server with GUI. During a Red Hat exam, you'll be installing most additional software after basic operating system installation is complete. Other options are listed in Table 1-3.

FIGURE 1-13

Software
Selection screen

SOFTWARE SELECTION   RED HAT ENTERPRISE LINUX 9.1 INSTALLATION

Done   us   Help!

Base Environment

○ **Server with GUI**
An integrated, easy-to-manage server with a graphical interface.

○ **Server**
An integrated, easy-to-manage server.

○ **Minimal Install**
Basic functionality.

○ **Workstation**
Workstation is a user-friendly desktop system for laptops and PCs.

○ **Custom Operating System**
Basic building block for a custom RHEL system.

○ **Virtualization Host**
Minimal virtualization host.

Additional software for Selected Environment

☐ **Debugging Tools**
Tools for debugging misbehaving applications and diagnosing performance problems.

☐ **DNS Name Server**
This package group allows you to run a DNS name server (BIND) on the system.

☐ **File and Storage Server**
CIFS, SMB, NFS, iSCSI, iSER, and iSNS network storage server.

☐ **FTP Server**
These tools allow you to run an FTP server on the system.

☐ **Guest Agents**
Agents used when running under a hypervisor.

☐ **Infiniband Support**
Software designed for supporting clustering, grid connectivity, and low-latency, high bandwidth storage using RDMA-based InfiniBand, iWARP, RoCE, and OPA fabrics.

☐ **Mail Server**
These packages allow you to configure an IMAP or SMTP mail server.

☐ **Network File System Client**

TABLE 1-3	Installation Software Categories

Category	Description
Minimal Install	Includes a minimal list of packages for the operating system
Server	Installs basic packages for Red Hat as a server
Workstation	A desktop installation for laptops and PCs
Virtualization Host	Configures a system for running VMs using the KVM hypervisor
Server with GUI	Same as Server, plus a GUI
Custom Operating System	If your use case does not fit with any of the above

For a truly secure baseline in a production environment, consider the minimal installation. Fewer packages mean fewer vulnerabilities. You can then add just the packages needed for the desired functionality. Any software that isn't installed can't be exploited by a "black hat" hacker.

on the job **In the security world, the term "white hat" hackers refers to good people who break into systems for nonmalicious reasons, such as for a security penetration test. The term "black hat" hackers refers to people who want to break into other systems with evil intent.**

Baseline Packages

In this section, you'll get a basic overview of what's available during the RHEL 9 installation process. During the exams, you may refer to one of these package groups with the Red Hat Add/Remove Software tool. You can also find a list of available package groups with the **dnf group list** command. More information is available in Chapter 4.

Red Hat package groups are organized logically. It's important to choose only the package groups you need. Fewer installed packages means more room for personal files, as well as the log files needed to monitor systems.

For the purposes of this installation, select Server with GUI from the Software Selection screen shown in Figure 1-13. Click the Root Password option and enter a password for the root administrative user twice. Later during the installation, you can create a regular user for the system. Finally, click Done and then click Begin Installation. Anaconda then proceeds to the installation process.

During the Installation

After the installation of the software packages is initiated, you will see the screen shown in Figure 1-14.

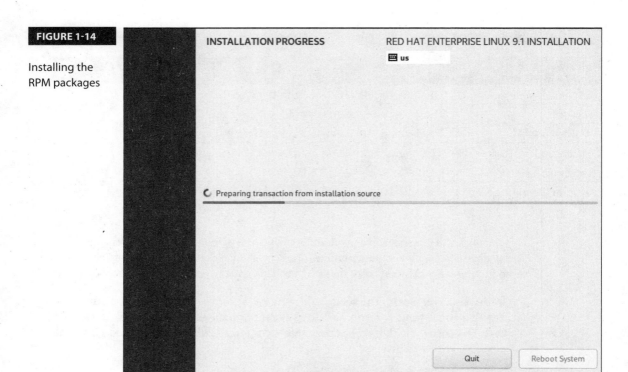

FIGURE 1-14

Installing the
RPM packages

When the installation is complete, you'll see a final message to that effect, with an option to reboot the system. Don't forget to remove the installation DVD image; otherwise, the system may boot again from the DVD media. To do so, select the Virtual Machine menu, click Removable Devices, and under CD/DVD click Disconnect.

Initial Setup

Upon completion of the installation process, when RHEL 9 boots to the graphical user interface for the first time, the Initial Setup screen will appear, as shown in Figure 1-15. Follow these steps:

1. At the Initial Setup screen, you can enable or disable location services and connect your online accounts, such as Google or Microsoft. Click Skip to go to the next screen.
2. Create a regular user account by providing a username and password of your choice.
3. Click Start Using Enterprise Linux.
4. On a RHEL 9 system, you're offered to take a tour of the system. If you are new to RHEL 9, click Take Tour.

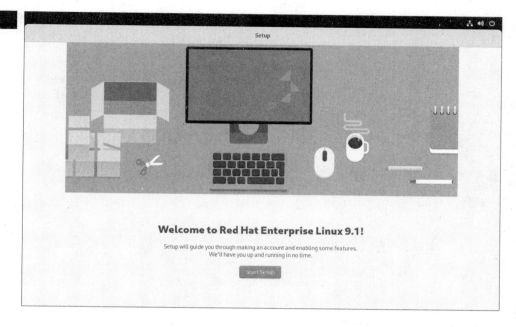

FIGURE 1-15

The Initial Setup screen

5. You're prompted to connect the system to the Red Hat Subscription Management. To register, you'll need a Red Hat account with an available subscription, which you should have obtained in Exercise 1-1. However, you will complete the registration of the system in Chapter 4.

CERTIFICATION SUMMARY

The RHCSA exam is not for beginners. It's a hands-on, practical test that assesses your abilities on a live RHEL system through problem-solving and system configuration tasks. The examination primarily focuses on evaluation of your core system administration skills, simulating real-world scenarios.

RHEL 9 supports different architectures. For the RHCSA exam, you need a system with an Intel/AMD 64-bit CPU (also known as x86_64 architecture).

This chapter helped you to obtain and install a basic RHEL system, with the packages and settings suitable for the remainder of this book. With a subscription to the Red Hat Customer Portal, you can download RHEL installation ISO files from the associated account. Since RHEL software is released under open-source licenses, third parties such as AlmaLinux OS Foundation have used that source code to build a new Linux distribution without Red Hat trademarks. You can also use AlmaLinux to study for the RHCSA exam.

This chapter also helped you to create and configure an installation of RHEL 9 to practice the skills you'll learn in subsequent chapters. You'll configure a second system in upcoming Lab 1. Although many users don't have spare physical computers to dedicate to their studies, VMs make it possible to set up these systems on a single physical computer.

Because the installation of RHEL 9 is relatively easy even for newer Linux users, not every detail was covered in this chapter. After installation comes the Initial Setup screen. However, this varies depending on whether you've installed a GUI.

TWO-MINUTE DRILL

Here are some of the key points from the certification objectives in Chapter 1.

The RHCSA Exam

❑ The RHCSA exam is a separate exam from the RHCE exam.

❑ Red Hat exams are all "hands-on"; there are no multiple-choice questions.

Basic Hardware Requirements

❑ Although RHEL 9 can be installed on several different platforms, you'll need hardware with 64-bit CPUs and hardware-assisted virtualization for the RHCSA exam.

❑ Red Hat supports RHEL 9 installations on systems with at least 1.5GiB of RAM. Less is possible, especially on systems without a GUI.

❑ RHEL 9 can be installed on a local drive or a variety of storage network devices.

Get Red Hat Enterprise Linux

❑ The RHCSA exam uses Red Hat Enterprise Linux.

❑ Production and development subscriptions of RHEL 9 are available.

❑ Since Red Hat releases the source code for RHEL 9, third parties are free to "rebuild" the distribution from the Red Hat source code (except for the trademarks).

❑ A rebuild of RHEL 9 is functionally identical to the original, except for access to Red Hat Customer Portal to download software packages.

❑ Reputable third-party rebuilds are available, such as AlmaLinux.

An Environment for Practice Labs

❑ Red Hat states that exams are presented on "pre-installed systems" with questions presented "electronically."

❑ The native RHEL 9 VM solution is KVM. In this book, we use VMware Workstation Player, because it is open source and freely available for Linux and Windows operating systems.

❑ It's useful to set up multiple VMs to simulate network communications.

RHEL 9 Installation

❑ You can start the installation process from a variety of boot media.

❑ RHEL 9 can be installed from DVD, from a local drive, from an NFS directory, from a web server, or from an FTP server.

❑ RHEL 9 should be configured on separate volumes for at least the top-level root directory (/), the /boot directory, and Linux swap space.

❑ RHEL 9 includes installation package groups in a number of categories.

❑ The first post-installation steps involve the Initial Setup screen.

SELF TEST

The following questions will help you measure your understanding of the material presented in this chapter. Because there are no multiple-choice questions on the Red Hat exams, there are no multiple-choice questions in this book. These questions exclusively test your understanding of the chapter. It is okay if you have another way of performing a task. Getting results, not memorizing trivia, is what counts on the Red Hat exams.

The RHCSA Exam

1. How many multiple-choice questions are there on the RHCSA exam?
2. How much time is allocated for installation during the RHCSA exam?

Basic Hardware Requirements

3. Assuming Intel-based PC hardware, what's the default virtualization technology for RHEL 9?

4. Which Intel/AMD CPU architectures can be used on RHEL 9?

Get Red Hat Enterprise Linux

5. Name one third-party distribution based on RHEL 9 source code.

An Environment for Practice Labs

6. Is VMware Workstation Player a type-1 or type-2 hypervisor?

RHEL 9 Installation

7. Name two different options for installation media that will boot the RHEL 9 installation program.

8. Name two types of volumes that can be configured and formatted during the RHEL 9 installation process to store data.

9. What are the different types of base environments available in the Software Selection screen that is accessed from the Installation Summary screen?

10. What application is started during the first boot of a new RHEL 9 system?

LAB QUESTIONS

The first lab is fairly elementary, aimed to complete the installation of the environment for practice labs that you have started in this chapter. The second lab suggests that you look at the requirements associated with the Linux Professional Institute for a different perspective on system administration.

Lab 1

In this lab, you will install the tester1.example.com system described earlier in Table 1-2. To do so, follow the steps you performed earlier to install server1.example.com in the "Configure a Virtual Machine on VMware Workstation Player" and "RHEL 9 Installation" sections.

Select a text-based installation and perform a minimal installation.

Lab 2

The Red Hat exams are an advanced challenge. In this lab, you'll examine the Red Hat exam prerequisites from a slightly different perspective. If you're uncertain about your readiness for the RHCSA exam, the Linux Professional Institute (LPI) has Level 1 exams that test basic skills in more detail. In addition, they cover a number of related commands that we believe are implied prerequisites for the Red Hat certifications.

To that end, examine the detailed objectives associated with LPIC-1 exams 101 and 102. Links to those objectives are available at https://www.lpi.org/our-certifications/lpic-1-overview. If you're comfortable with most of the files, terms, and utilities listed in the objectives for those exams, you're ready to start your studies for the Red Hat exams.

SELF TEST ANSWERS

The RHCSA Exam

1. There are no multiple-choice questions on any Red Hat exams. It has been more than a decade since the Red Hat exams had a multiple-choice component. The Red Hat exams are entirely "hands-on" experiences.

2. There is no correct answer to this question. Although the Red Hat exams are now presented on pre-installed systems, keep in mind that requirements may change at any time.

Basic Hardware Requirements

3. The default virtualization technology for RHEL 9 is KVM. Although there are many excellent virtualization products available, KVM is the default option supported by Red Hat on RHEL 9.

4. To install RHEL 9, you need a system with one or more 64-bit CPUs.

Get Red Hat Enterprise Linux

5. AlmaLinux is one of the distributions built on RHEL 9. CentOS Linux was discontinued in 2021.

An Environment for Practice Labs

6. VMware Workstation Player is a type-2 (or "hosted") hypervisor, because it runs on a conventional operating system such as Linux, macOS, or Windows.

RHEL 9 Installation

7. Options for installation boot media for RHEL 9 include a DVD, and a USB drive.

8. You can configure and format regular partitions and logical volumes during the installation process to store data.

9. The base environments are Server with GUI, Server, Minimal Install, Workstation, Custom Operating System, and Virtualization Host.

10. Initial Setup is started during the first boot.

LAB ANSWERS

Lab 1

This lab assumes you've downloaded the DVD ISO image for RHEL 9, as explained in the section "Get Red Hat Enterprise Linux" in this chapter. Follow the same steps you performed to create a virtual machine for the server1.example.com system in "Configure a Virtual Machine on VMware Workstation Player," but set the system name to tester1.example.com. Next, install RHEL 9 by following the instructions in the "RHEL 9 Installation" section. Refer to the partitioning scheme in Table 1-1 and be sure to configure the network settings provided in Table 1-2.

Once you have completed the installation, you will have a tester1.example.com virtual machine identical to server1.example.com, except for the hostname and IP address settings.

Lab 2

This lab may seem odd given that it references the requirements for a different Linux certification. However, many Linux administrators take the exams of the Linux Professional Institute seriously. LPI creates excellent certifications. Many Linux administrators study for the LPIC Level 1 certification. Passing the LPIC-1 101 and 102 exams provides an excellent foundation for the RHCSA exam.

If you feel the need to get more of a grounding in Linux, refer to either or both of the books described at the beginning of this chapter.

The Red Hat exams are an advanced challenge. Some of the requirements for the RHCSA exam may seem intimidating. It's okay if some of them seem beyond your capabilities at the moment, because that is the reason you are reading this book. However, if you're uncomfortable with basic command-line tools such as **ls**, **cd**, and **cp**, you might need more of a grounding in Linux first. Most candidates are successfully able to fill in the gaps in their knowledge with some self-study and practice.

Chapter 2

Fundamental Command-Line Skills

The Red Hat exams are an advanced challenge. This chapter covers RHCSA requirements related to essential Linux command-line tools. Many of these requirements specify basic command-line tools associated with entry-level certifications such as those offered by the Linux Professional Institute.

While command-line skills are no longer official prerequisites, they are required to achieve the exam objectives. As most candidates for the RHCSA exam should already be familiar with these command-line tools, this chapter covers the related topics with minimum detail. If after reading this chapter you feel the need for more guidance about these topics, the excellent beginning Linux books described in Chapter 1 can help.

Linux gurus should recognize that we've "oversimplified" a number of explanations to keep this chapter as short as possible. However, because most IT professionals are specialists, you may feel a bit uncertain about a few topics in this chapter. That is okay. In fact, it's natural that many experienced Linux administrators don't frequently use every command. Many candidates are successfully able to fill in the gaps in their knowledge with some self-study and practice.

INSIDE THE EXAM

Shells

The related RHCSA exam objective is pretty generic:

- Access a shell prompt and issue commands with correct syntax

The default shell for Linux is bash, the "Bourne-again shell." In fact, the original release of the RHCSA objectives specified the use of bash. Whatever shell you prefer, you need to know how to get to a shell prompt and run regular commands from that prompt. Some basic commands are described in some of the other objectives. It's fairly easy to open a shell prompt from a console and within the GUI.

Pipelines and Redirection

Data into and out of a shell is often thought of in Linux as a stream of information. One basic Linux skill is the ability to redirect such streams. As described in the RHCSA requirements, that's the ability to

- Use input/output redirection (>, >>, |, 2>, etc.)

The operators in parentheses can redirect the streams from command output, command error, data files, and more.

File and Directory Management

Now that you have access to a command line, file and directory management is next. With related commands, you can navigate around the Linux directory tree, as well as perform all the tasks suggested in the related objectives:

- Create, delete, copy, and move files and directories
- Create hard and soft links

File Permissions

Security in Linux starts with the permissions given to files. As "everything is a file" in Linux, assigning file permissions is an excellent start to implementing security. In any case, the related exam objectives, once understood, are fairly straightforward:

- List, set, and change standard ugo/rwx permissions
- Diagnose and correct file permissions problems
- Manage default file permissions

Standard permissions for Linux files are defined for users, groups, and others, which leads to the *ugo* concept. Those permissions are read, write, and execute, or *rwx*.

The Analysis of Text Output

Most Linux configuration files are text files. It is important to understand and analyze the flow of text as it is sent to the terminal or "piped" through different commands. Tools such as the **grep** command can help you focus on needed information. In this chapter, you will examine how to meet the following objective:

- Use grep and regular expressions to analyze text

The Use of Text Editors

To configure Linux, you need to know how to edit text files. And for those newer to Linux, that requires a different paradigm. Although word processors such as OpenOffice.org Writer and Microsoft Word can save files in text format, a mistake with a key configuration file can render a Linux system unbootable, and these editors can inject hidden data or otherwise cause problems when used for simple text editing. Therefore, you need to know how to handle the following objective with standard non-GUI utilities:

- Create and edit text files

The Variety of Local Documentation

Internet access is not available during the Red Hat exams, but that's okay. Google is not your only friend. Linux has some excellent documentation installed with most packages. Command manuals are also available. The following objective is straightforward; it describes the commands and directory associated with most Linux online documentation:

- Locate, read, and use system documentation including man, info, and files in /usr/share/doc

Shells

A *shell* is a user interface. A text-based shell is also used as a command-line interpreter. In Linux, the shell is the interpreter that allows you to interact with the operating system using various commands. With the right file permissions, you can set up commands in scripts to run as needed, even at a certain time. Linux shells can process commands in various sequences, depending on how you manage the input and output of each command. The way commands are interpreted is in part determined by variables and parameters associated with each shell.

As previously introduced, the default shell in Linux is bash, so the focus of commands in this book is based on how they're used in bash. However, a number of other shells are available that are popular with many users. As long as the appropriate RPMs are installed, users can start any of these shells. If desired, you can change the default shell for individual users in the /etc/passwd file.

Other Shells

Users can choose between four command-line shells in RHEL 9. Although bash is the default, longtime Linux and Unix users may prefer something else. This is a partial list of the most common shells:

- **bash** The default Bourne-again shell, based on the command-line interpreter originally developed by Stephen Bourne
- **ksh** The Korn shell, developed by David Korn at Bell Labs in the 1980s, to incorporate the best features of the Bourne-again and C shells
- **tcsh** An enhanced version of the Unix C shell
- **zsh** A sophisticated shell, similar to the Korn shell

These shells are located in the /bin directory. If a user prefers one of these options as their default shell, it's easy to change. The most direct method is to change the default shell in the /etc/passwd file. For example, the line that applies to one of the authors' regular accounts is

```
michael:x:1000:1000:Michael Jang:/home/michael:/bin/bash
```

As an example, to change the default shell to ksh, change /bin/bash to /bin/ksh. You also need to install the corresponding RPM package for the Korn shell. Package management will be covered in Chapter 4.

Virtual Consoles

If you have access to the console of a RHEL system, you can use six virtual consoles (or "virtual terminals") to open six independent login sessions. However, only one virtual console is activated by default. The other login prompts are launched dynamically when you switch to an unused terminal. Virtual consoles are defined by the logind.conf file in the /etc/systemd directory. If you look at that file, you'll see an option named NAutoVTs, which defines the maximum number of virtual consoles that can be activated. Virtual consoles are associated with device files /dev/tty1 through /dev/tty6. When a GUI is configured, it takes /dev/tty1.

Even though it should be trivial for most Linux users, a part of one RHCSA objective is to "access a shell prompt." You should now know how to set up access to different shell prompts.

Normally, to change between virtual consoles, press ALT and the function key associated with that terminal. For example, the ALT-F3 key combination moves to the third terminal. However, in the RHEL GUI, the ALT-F*n* key combinations are used to provide other functionalities, such as to start the Run Application tool via ALT-F3. Therefore, you'll need to press CTRL-ALT-F*n* to move to the *n*th virtual console from the GUI.

At a text console login, you'd see the following prompt, which depends a bit on the release of RHEL, the version number of the kernel, and the system hostname:

```
Red Hat Enterprise Linux 9.1 (Plow)
Kernel 5.14.0-162.6.1.el9_1.x86_64 on an x86_64
server1 login:
```

The graphical login, which requires the installation of the GNOME Display Manager (GDM), is more intuitive, as shown in Figure 2-1.

GUI Shell Interfaces

Once you are logged in to the GUI, access to the bash shell is easy. If you're in the default GNOME desktop environment, choose Activities | Terminal. Traditionally, administrators have worked from the console. But in many cases, working on the command line from the GUI can be helpful, especially because you can place windows side by side. A right-click on a GUI terminal screen supports opening of additional terminals in different windows or in tabs. It also supports copy and paste as needed.

The screenshots of the command line taken for this book are from the GUI-based command line using a "Light" theme, in part because dark text on a white screen is easier to read. To change the theme of your GNOME terminal, choose Edit | Preferences and click the General tab, as shown in Figure 2-2.

FIGURE 2-1

A first GUI login console

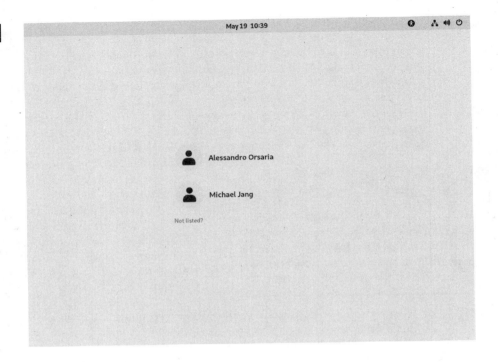

FIGURE 2-2

Option to change the GNOME terminal theme

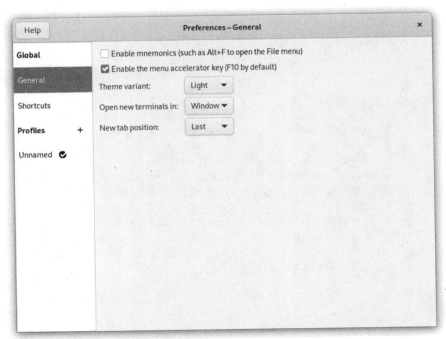

Differences Between Regular and Administrative Users

What you can do at the command line depends on the privileges associated with the login account. Two basic prompts are available. The following is an example of what you might see when logged in as a regular user:

```
[michael@server1 ~]$
```

Note how it includes the username, the hostname of the local system, the current directory, and a $ prompt. The $ prompt is the standard for regular users. As noted in the introduction to the book, examples of commands run from a regular user account just show the following:

```
$
```

In contrast, take a look at a prompt for the root administrative user on the same system. It should look familiar. Except for the name of the account, the only consistent difference is the prompt.

```
[root@server1 ~]#
```

In this book, examples of commands run from the root administrative account just show the following:

```
#
```

Besides ownership and permissions, other differences between regular and administrative accounts are discussed in Chapter 6.

Standard Streams and Command Redirection

Linux uses three basic data streams. Data goes in, data comes out, and errors are sent in a different direction. These streams are known as standard input (*stdin*), standard output (*stdout*), and standard error (*stderr*). Every process has the stdin, stdout, and stderr configured to a device. Normally, input comes from the keyboard, whereas standard output and standard error go out to the screen terminal. In the following example, when you run **cat /etc/fstab**, the contents of the /etc/fstab file are sent to the screen as standard output (as are any errors):

```
# cat /etc/fstab
```

You can redirect each of these streams to or from a file. For example, if you have a program named database and a datafile with a lot of data, the contents of that datafile can be sent to the database program with a left redirection arrow (<). As shown here, datafile is taken as standard input:

```
# database < datafile
```

Standard input can come from another command as well. For example, if you need to scroll through the boot messages, you can combine the **dmesg** and **less** commands with a pipe:

```
# dmesg | less
```

on the job

The sequence of commands separated by a pipe symbol is a *pipeline*.

The output from **dmesg** is redirected as standard input to **less**, which then allows you to scroll through that output as if it were a separate file.

Standard output is just as easy to redirect. For example, the following command uses the right redirection arrow (>) to send the standard output of the **ls** command, which lists the contents of the current directory, to the file named filelist.txt:

```
# ls > filelist.txt
```

exam watch

Command redirection symbols such as >, >>, 2>, and | are associated with the "input/output redirection" objective in the RHCSA exam objectives.

The file filelist.txt will be created if it does not exist. If it does exist, its contents will be overwritten. You can add standard output to the end of an existing file with a double redirection arrow with a command such as **ls >> filelist.txt**.

If you want to save the error messages of a program into a file, redirect the error stream from it with a command such as the following:

```
# program 2> err-list.txt
```

Sometimes you may want to discard all errors. This can be achieved by redirecting the error stream to the special device file /dev/null:

```
# program 2> /dev/null
```

Another useful redirection operator is the ampersand and right arrow (&>), which sends both the standard output and error to a file or device. An example is shown here:

```
# program &> output-and-error.txt
```

Another way to achieve the same result is shown next:

```
# program > output-and-error.txt 2>&1
```

Here, the first operator (>) sends the standard output to the file indicated, while the next operator (2>&1) sends the standard error stream to the same file as standard output.

Table 2-1 summarizes the redirection operators that we have described so far.

TABLE 2-1	Redirection Operators

Operator	Description
< *file*	Redirects standard input from *file*
> *file*	Redirects standard output to *file*
>> *file*	Appends standard output to *file*
2> *file*	Redirects standard error to *file*
&> *file* or > *file* 2>&1	Redirects standard output and standard error to *file*
command1 | command2	Redirects the standard output of *command1* as standard input to *command2*

CERTIFICATION OBJECTIVE 2.02

Standard Command-Line Tools

While newer Linux users may prefer to use the GUI, the most efficient way to administer Linux is from the command-line interface. Although excellent GUI tools are available, the look and feel of those tools varies widely by distribution. In contrast, if you know the standard command-line tools, you'll be able to find your way around every Linux distribution.

Remember, in any bash session you can go through the history of previous commands, using the UP- and DOWN-ARROW keys, and use CTRL-R to make a search. You can also take advantage of text completion, which allows you to use the TAB key almost as a wildcard to complete a command, a filename, or a variable (if the text begins with the $ character).

e x a m

ⓦatch

This section covers only the most basic of commands available in Linux. It describes only a few capabilities of each command. Nevertheless, it allows you to "issue commands with correct syntax," as described in the RHCSA objectives.

Almost all Linux commands include options (or "switches") and arguments. Command options allow you to change the behavior of a command and are usually prepended by one or two dashes (such as **ls -a** or **ls --all**). Arguments specify files, devices, or other targets that a command should act on. Only a few commands are covered in this chapter. If you're less familiar with some of them, use the documentation. Study the command options. Try them out! Only with practice, practice, and more practice can you really understand the power behind some of these commands.

Two basic groups of commands are used to manage Linux files. One group helps you get around Linux files and directories. The other group actually does something creative with the files. Those commands will be covered in the next sections, but first we'll review some basic filesystem concepts.

File and Directory Concepts

As noted previously, everything in Linux can be reduced to a file. Directories are special types of files that serve as containers for other files. To navigate and find important files, you need some basic commands and concepts to tell you where you are and how to move from directory to directory. One of the most important commands is **pwd**, which prints the current directory; a variable that always points to a user's home directory is the tilde (~); and the concept that describes where you are in the Linux directory tree is the path. Closely related are the directories searched when a command is typed in, which is based on the environment variable known as the PATH. Once these concepts are understood, you can navigate between directories with the **cd** (short for "change directory") command.

pwd

At the command-line interface, the current directory may be either the top-level root (/) directory or a subdirectory. The **pwd** command identifies the current directory. Try it out. It'll give you a directory name relative to the / directory. With this information in hand, you can move to a different directory if needed. Incidentally, **pwd** is short for "print working directory" (which has nothing to do with modern printers, but respects the days when output was printed on a teletype). For example, when the user michael runs that command in his home directory, he gets the following output:

```
/home/michael
```

The Tilde (~)

Upon a standard login, every Linux user is taken to a home directory. The tilde (~) can be used to represent the home directory of any currently active user. For example, when user john logs in, he's taken to his home directory, /home/john. In contrast, the home directory of the root administrative user is /root.

Thus, the effect of the **cd** ~ command depends on your home directory. For example, if you've logged in as user mj, the **cd** ~ command navigates to the /home/mj directory. If you've logged in as the root user, this command navigates to the /root directory. You can list the contents of your home directory from anywhere in the directory tree with the **ls** ~ command. The **cd** and **ls** commands are described shortly. When you log in as the root administrative user and run the **ls** command, you should see the following filename being listed:

```
anaconda-ks.cfg
```

Incidentally, this file describes what happened during the installation process, the packages that were installed, and the users and groups added to the local system. The **anaconda-ks.cfg** command is also important for automated Kickstart installations, but this is outside the scope of the RHCSA exam.

Directory Paths

You need to know two path concepts when working with Linux directories: absolute paths and relative paths. An absolute path describes the complete directory structure in terms of the top-level directory, root (/). A relative path is based on the current directory. Relative paths do not start with a slash. However, they may initiate with "./". The dot symbol signifies the current directory in this context.

The difference between an absolute path and a relative one is important. Commands referencing a wrong directory by using a relative path may lead to unintended consequences. For example, say you're in the top-level root directory /, and you have backed up the /home directory using its relative path to the root, home (notice the lack of a leading slash). If you happen to be in the /home directory when restoring that backup, the files for user michael, for example, would be restored to the /home/home/michael directory.

In contrast, if the /home directory was backed up using the absolute path /home (notice the leading slash), the current working directory doesn't matter when you are restoring these files. That backup will be restored to the correct directories.

PATH Environment Variable

PATH is a special environment variable that a shell, such as bash, will search for executable commands. PATH contains a list of directories that are searched for the command that the user just typed at the command prompt. Strictly speaking, it is best to use the full path to a command, such as **/bin/ls** instead of **ls**. In practice, this is tedious, which is why the PATH environment variable was created. The only place absolute paths are recommended is in shell scripts or when the PATH is unknown or inconsistent across various machines. There is normally no need to use absolute paths when entering commands in an interactive shell, unless the command happens to be in a directory that is not in your PATH.

To determine the PATH for the current user account, run the **echo $PATH** command. You should see a series of directories in the output. The differences between the PATH for a regular user and one for a root user are shown next::

```
$ echo $PATH
/home/michael/.local/bin:/home/michael/bin:/usr/local/bin::/usr/bin

# echo $PATH
/root/.local/bin:/root/bin:/usr/local/sbin:/usr/local/bin:/usr/sbin:/usr/bin
```

The directories in the PATH for regular users and the root administrative user are slightly different. But the differences matter because the directories are searched in order. For example, the **useradd** command is available from the /usr/sbin directory. As you can see from the default PATH for regular and root users, the command is not in the PATH of regular users, since /usr/sbin is not in the list.

The PATH is determined globally by current settings in the /etc/profile file or by scripts in the /etc/profile.d directory.

As well as the global settings, the PATH for individual users can be customized with an appropriate entry in that user's home directory, in the hidden files named ~/.bash_profile or ~/.profile.

cd

It's easy to change directories in Linux. Just use **cd** and cite the absolute path of the desired directory. If you use the relative path, just remember that the destination depends on the current working directory.

By default, the **cd** command with no arguments navigates to your home directory. The tilde is not required for that command. Another common shortcut is two consecutive dots (..) to represent the directory that is one level up in the hierarchy. Thus, **cd ..** moves to the parent directory of the current working directory.

File Lists and ls

Now that you've reviewed those commands that can navigate from one directory to another, it's time to see what files exist in a directory—and that's the province of the **ls** command.

The Linux **ls** command (short for "list"), with the right switches, can be quite powerful. The right kind of **ls** can tell you everything about a file, such as last modification time, last access time, and size. It can help you organize the listing of files in just about any desired order. Important variations on this command include **ls -a** to reveal hidden files (which are files whose names begin with a dot, "."), **ls -l** for long listings, **ls -t** for a list sorted by modification time, and **ls -i** for inode numbers (inodes are internal data structures in a filesystem that store information about a file). Other useful command options are **-r**, to reverse the listing order, and **-R**, to list the contents of all subdirectories recursively.

You can combine switches; we often use the **ls -ltR** command to display a recursive long listing with the most recently changed files last. The **-d** switch, when combined with others, can give you more information on the current directory, or on a directory that you have passed as an argument to the **ls** command.

One important feature that returns SELinux contexts is the **ls -Z** command. Take a look at the output in Figure 2-3. The system_u, object_r, var_t, and s0 output demonstrates the current SELinux contexts of the noted files. During the RHCSA exam (and RHCE as well),

FIGURE 2-3	Current SELinux contexts

```
[root@server1 ~]# ls -Zl /var
total 16
drwxr-xr-x.  2 root root system_u:object_r:acct_data_t:s0        19 Jan 25 15:17 account
drwxr-xr-x.  2 root root system_u:object_r:var_t:s0               6 Aug  9 2021 adm
drwxr-xr-x. 19 root root system_u:object_r:var_t:s0            4096 May 15 05:53 cache
drwxr-xr-x.  2 root root system_u:object_r:kdump_crash_t:s0       6 Jul 11 2022 crash
drwxr-xr-x.  3 root root system_u:object_r:system_db_t:s0        18 Jan 25 15:16 db
drwxr-xr-x.  2 root root system_u:object_r:var_t:s0               6 Aug  9 2021 empty
drwxr-xr-x.  3 root root system_u:object_r:public_content_t:s0   17 May 14 19:00 ftp
drwxr-xr-x.  2 root root system_u:object_r:games_data_t:s0        6 Aug  9 2021 games
drwxr-xr-x.  3 root root system_u:object_r:var_t:s0              18 Feb 22 11:19 kerberos
drwxr-xr-x. 58 root root system_u:object_r:var_lib_t:s0        4096 May  1 08:09 lib
drwxr-xr-x.  2 root root system_u:object_r:var_t:s0               6 Aug  9 2021 local
lrwxrwxrwx.  1 root root system_u:object_r:var_lock_t:s0         11 Jan 25 15:15 lock -> ../run/lock
drwxr-xr-x. 18 root root system_u:object_r:var_log_t:s0        4096 May 28 15:07 log
lrwxrwxrwx.  1 root root system_u:object_r:mail_spool_t:s0       10 Aug  9 2021 mail -> spool/mail
drwxr-xr-x.  2 root root system_u:object_r:var_t:s0               6 Aug  9 2021 nis
drwxr-xr-x.  2 root root system_u:object_r:var_t:s0               6 Aug  9 2021 opt
lrwxrwxrwx.  1 root root system_u:object_r:var_run_t:s0           6 Aug  9 2021 preserve
drwxr-xr-x. 11 root root system_u:object_r:var_spool_t:s0         6 Jan 25 15:15 run -> ../run
drwxrwxrwt. 15 root root system_u:object_r:tmp_t:s0             121 May 15 05:53 spool
drwxr-xr-x.  5 root root system_u:object_r:httpd_sys_content_t:s0 4096 May 29 17:36 tmp
drwxr-xr-x.  2 root root system_u:object_r:var_yp_t:s0           46 May  1 09:28 www
[root@server1 ~]#                                                  6 Aug  9 2021 yp
```

you'll be expected to configure a system with SELinux enabled. Starting with Chapter 8, this book covers how SELinux can be configured for every service that's installed.

File-Creation Commands

Two commands are used to create new files: **touch** and **cp**. Alternatively, you can let a text editor such as vi create a new file. Although the **ln**, **mv**, and **rm** commands don't create files, they do manage them in related ways.

touch

Perhaps the simplest way to create a new empty file is with the **touch** command. For example, the **touch abc** command creates an empty file named abc in the local directory. The **touch** command is also used to change the time of the last modification of a file. For example, try the following three commands:

```
# ls -l /etc/passwd
# touch /etc/passwd
# ls -l /etc/passwd
```

Note the timestamps listed with the output of each **ls -l** command, and compare them with the current date and time returned by **date**. After you run the **touch** command, the timestamp of /etc/passwd is updated to the current date and time.

cp

The **cp** (copy) command allows you to take the contents of one file and place a copy with the same or different name in the directory of your choice. For example, the **cp** *file1 file2* command takes the contents of *file1* and saves the contents in *file2* in the current directory. One of the dangers of **cp** is that it can easily overwrite files in different directories, without prompting you to make sure that's what you really wanted to do.

Another usage of the **cp** command is with multiple file sources to be copied into a single destination directory. In this case the syntax is **cp** *file1 file2 ... dir*.

The **cp** command, with the **-a** switch, supports recursive changes and preserves all file attributes, such as permissions, ownerships, and timestamps. For example, the following command copies all subdirectories of the noted directory, along with associated files, into /mnt/backup:

```
# cp -a /home/michael/. /mnt/backup/
```

mv

Although there is a "rename" command in Linux, you can use **mv** (short for "move"). The **mv** command puts a different label on a file. For example, the **mv** *file1 file2* command changes the name of *file1* to *file2*. Unless you're moving the file to a different filesystem, everything about the file, including the inode number, remains the same.

The **mv** command can also be used to move files and directories into the directory specified as the last argument. The following example creates two files named "a" and "b" in the current directory and then moves them into the /tmp directory:

```
# touch a b
# mv a b /tmp
```

ln

Linked files allow users to refer to the same file using different names. When linked files are devices, they may represent more common names, such as /dev/cdrom. File links can be hard or soft.

Hard links are directory entries (or "dentries") that point to the same inode. They must be created within the same filesystem. You could delete a hard-linked file in one directory, and it would still exist in the other directory (files are only deleted when the number of dentry records pointing to them hits 0, which is tracked via a counter per file). For example, the following command creates a hard link from the actual Samba configuration file to smb .conf in the /root directory:

```
# ln /etc/samba/smb.conf /root/smb.conf
```

On the other hand, a soft link serves as a redirect; when you open a file created with a soft link, the link redirects you to the original file. If you delete the original file, the file is lost. Although the soft link is still there, it has nowhere to go. The following command is an example of how you can create a soft-linked file:

```
# ln  -s /etc/samba/smb.conf /root/smb.conf
```

rm

The **rm** command is somewhat dangerous. At the Linux command line, there is no trash bin. So if you delete a file with the **rm** command, it's at best difficult to recover that file.

The **rm** command is powerful. For example, let's assume that you downloaded the source files for the Linux kernel in the /root/rpmbuild/BUILD/kernel-5.14.0-162.el9_1 directory. Several thousand files are included in that directory. If you don't need those files anymore, obviously it's not practical to delete them one by one. Therefore, the **rm** command includes some powerful switches. The following command removes all of those files in one go:

```
# rm -rf /root/rpmbuild/BUILD/kernel-5.14.0-162.6.1.el9_1
```

The **-r** switch works recursively, and the **-f** switch overrides any safety precautions, such as the **-i** switch (which prompts for confirmation) shown in the output to the **alias** command for the root administrative user. It's still quite a dangerous command. For example, a simple typing mistake such as putting a space between the first forward slash and the directory name, as shown here, would first delete every file starting with the top-level root directory (/) before looking for the root/rpmbuild/BUILD/kernel-5.14.0-162.6.1.el9 subdirectory:

```
# rm -rf / root/rpmbuild/BUILD/kernel-5.14.0-162.6.1.el9_1
```

This would delete every file on the system, and you would have to restore all its contents from backup.

Directory Creation and Deletion

The **mkdir** and **rmdir** commands are used to create and delete directories. The ways these commands are used depend on the already-discussed concepts of absolute and relative paths. For example, the following command creates the test subdirectory to the current directory. If you're currently in the /home/michael directory, the full path would be /home/michael/test.

```
# mkdir test
```

Alternatively, the following command creates the /test directory:

```
# mkdir /test
```

If desired, you can use the following command to create a series of directories:

```
# mkdir -p test1/test2/test3
```

That command is equivalent to the following commands:

```
# mkdir test1
# mkdir test1/test2
# mkdir test1/test2/test3
```

Conversely, the **rmdir** command deletes a directory only if it's empty. If you're cleaning up after the previous **mkdir** commands, the **-p** switch is useful there as well. The following command deletes the noted directory and subdirectories, as long as all of the directories are otherwise empty:

```
# rmdir -p test1/test2/test3
```

alias

The **alias** command can be used to simplify a few commands. For the root administrative user, the default aliases provide a bit of safety. To see the aliases for the current user, run the **alias** command. The following output shows some of the default Red Hat aliases for the root user:

```
alias cp='cp -i'
alias egrep='egrep --color=auto'
alias fgrep='fgrep --color=auto'
alias grep='grep --color=auto'
alias l.='ls -d .* --color=auto'
alias ll='ls -l --color=auto'
alias ls='ls --color=auto'
alias mv='mv -i'
alias rm='rm -i'
```

Some of these aliases help protect key files from mistakes. The **-i** switch prompts the user for confirmation before a file is deleted or overwritten with the **cp**, **mv**, or **rm** command. Just be aware, the **-f** switch supersedes the **-i** switch for the noted commands.

Wildcards

Sometimes you may not know the exact name of the file or the exact search term. That is when a wildcard is handy, especially with the commands described throughout the book. Three basic wildcards are shown in Table 2-2.

The use of wildcards is sometimes known in the Linux world as *globbing***.**

TABLE 2-2	Wildcards in the Shell

Wildcard	Description
*	Any number of characters (or no characters at all). For example, the **ls ab*** command would return the following filenames, assuming they exist in the current directory: ab, abc, abcd.
?	One single character. For example, the **ls ab?** command would return the following filenames, assuming they exist in the current directory: abc, abd, abe.
[]	A range of options. For example, the **ls ab[123]** command would return the following filenames, assuming they exist in the current directory: ab1, ab2, ab3. Alternatively, the **ls ab[X-Z]** command would return the following filenames, assuming they exist in the current directory: abX, abY, abZ.

File Searches

Most users who study Linux for a while become familiar with key files. For example, named.conf is the key configuration file for the standard DNS (Domain Name Service) servers, based on the Berkeley Internet Name Domain (BIND). But not many people remember that a sample named.conf file, with all kinds of useful configuration hints, can be found in the /usr/share/doc/bind/sample/etc directory.

To that end, there are two basic commands for file searches: **find** and **locate**.

find

The **find** command searches through directories and subdirectories for a desired file. For example, if you wanted to find the directory with the named.conf DNS sample configuration file, you could use the following command, which would start the search in the root directory:

```
# find / -name named.conf
```

But the speed of that search depends on the memory and disk speed available on the local system. Alternatively, if you know that this file is located in the /usr subdirectory tree, you could start in that directory with the following command:

```
# find /usr -name named.conf
```

That command should now find the desired file more quickly.

e x a m

ⓦ a t c h When you take Red Hat exams, you can run updatedb **early on to find needed files more quickly later on without delay.**

locate

If this is all too time-consuming, RHEL allows you to set up a database of installed files and directories. Searches with the **locate** command are almost instantaneous—and **locate** searches don't require the full filename. The drawback is that the **locate** command database is normally updated only once each day.

CERTIFICATION OBJECTIVE 2.03

File Permissions

The basic security of a Linux computer is based on file permissions. Default file permissions are defined by the **umask** command. Special permissions can be configured to give all users and/or groups additional privileges. These are known as the set user ID (SUID), set group ID (SGID), and sticky permission bits. Ownership is based on the default user and group IDs of the person who created a file. The management of permissions and ownership involves commands such as **chmod**, **chown**, and **chgrp**. Before exploring these commands, it's important to understand the permissions and ownership associated with a file.

File Permissions and Ownership

Linux file permissions and ownership are straightforward. As suggested by the related RHCSA objective, they're read, write, and execute, classified by the user, the group, and all other users. However, the effect of permissions on directories is more subtle. Table 2-3 shows the exact meaning of each permission bit.

TABLE 2-3   Permissions on Files and Directories

Permission	On a File	On a Directory
read (r)	Permission to read the file	Permission to list the contents of the directory
write (w)	Permission to write (change) the file	Permission to create and remove files in the directory
execute (x)	Permission to run the file as a program	Permission to access the files in the directory

Position	Description
1	Type of file; - = regular file, *d* = directory, *b* = device, *l* = symbolic link
234	Permissions granted to the owner of the file
567	Permissions granted to the group owner of the file
890	Permissions granted to all other users on the Linux system

TABLE 2-4

Description of File Permissions

Consider the following output from **ls -l /sbin/fdisk**:

```
-rwxr-xr-x. 1 root root 175376 Sep 21 10:45 /sbin/fdisk
```

The permissions are shown on the left side of the listing. Ten characters are shown. The first character determines whether it's a regular file or a special file. In this example, the first character is a dash (-), which indicates that this is a regular file. The remaining nine characters must be read in groups of three, and each group applies, respectively, to the file owner (user), the group owner, and everyone else on that Linux system. The letters are straightforward: *r* = read, *w* = write, *x* = execute. These permissions are described in Table 2-4.

Hence, in the previous example, the root user has rwx permissions to the /sbin/fdisk file, while the root group and everyone else have only rx permissions. It's common for the user and group owners of a file to have the same name. In this case, the root user is a member of the root group. But they don't have to have the same name. For example, directories designed for collaboration between users may be owned by a special group. As explained in Chapter 6, that involves groups with several regular users as members.

Keep in mind that permissions granted to the group take precedence over permissions granted to all other users. Similarly, permissions granted to the owner take precedence over all other permissions categories. Thus, in the following example, although everyone else has full permissions to the file, the members of the group "mike" have not been granted any permissions, and as such they won't be able to read, modify, or execute the file:

```
$ ls -l setup.sh
-rwx---rwx. 1 root mike 127 Dec 13 07:21 setup.sh
```

There's a relatively new element with permissions—and it's subtle. Notice the dot after the last x in the output to the **ls -l setup.sh** command? It specifies that the file has an SELinux security context. If you've configured ACL permissions on a file, that dot is replaced by a plus sign (+). But that symbol doesn't override SELinux control.

You need to consider another type of permission: the special permission bits. These include the SUID and SGID bits and another special permission known as the *sticky bit*. The effects of the special permission bits on files and directories are shown in Table 2-5.

TABLE 2-5	Special Permission Bits	
Special Permission	**On an Executable File**	**On a Directory**
SUID	When the file is executed, the effective user ID of the process is that of the file.	No effect.
SGID	When the file is executed, the effective group ID of the process is that of the file.	Give files created in the directory the same group ownership as that of the directory.
Sticky bit	No effect.	Files in the directory can be renamed or removed only by their owners.

An example of the SUID bit is associated with the **passwd** command in the /usr/bin directory. Executing the **ls -l** command on that file leads to the following output:

```
-rwsr-xr-x. 1 root root 32648 Aug 10 2021 /usr/bin/passwd
```

The **s** in the execute bit for the user owner of the file is the SUID bit. It means the file can be executed by other users with the authority of the file owner, the root administrative user. But that doesn't mean that any user can change other users' passwords. Access to the **passwd** command is further regulated by Pluggable Authentication Modules (PAM), although this is out of scope of the RHSCA exam. The SUID permission is required because the user's password is stored in /etc/shadow, and that file can be accessed only by the root user.

An example of the SGID bit can be found with the **locate** command, also in the /usr/bin directory. Executing the **ls -l** command on that file displays the following output:

```
-rwx--s--x. 1 root slocate 41032 Aug 10 2021 /usr/bin/locate
```

The **s** in the execute bit for the group owner of the file (group nobody) is the SGID bit. The **locate** command has the SGID bit set because it keeps track of all the files in the system in the database /var/lib/mlocate/mlocate.db, which is readable only by the root and slocate users.

Finally, an example of the sticky bit can be found in the permissions of the /tmp directory. It means that users can copy their files to that directory, but no one else can remove those files, apart from their respective owners (which is the "sticky"). The **ls -ld** command on that directory shows the following output:

```
drwxrwxrwt. 40 root root 4096 Dec 15 17:15 /tmp
```

The **t** in the execute bit for other users is the sticky bit. Note that without the sticky bit, everyone will be able to remove everyone else's files in /tmp because write permissions have been granted to all users on that directory.

The Loophole in Write Permissions

It's easy to remove write permissions from a file. For example, if you wanted to make the license.txt file read-only, the following command removes write permissions from that file:

```
$ chmod a-w license.txt
```

You may notice that, under certain conditions, if a change is made in the vi text editor, the user who owns that file can override a lack of write permissions with the bang character, which looks like an exclamation point (!). In other words, while in the vi editor, the user who owns the file can run the following command to override the lack of write permissions:

```
w!
```

Although this may seem surprising, in practice the **w!** command of the vi editor is not bypassing the Linux file permission system. The **w!** command overwrites a file—that is, it deletes the existing file and creates a new one with the same name. As you can see from Table 2-3, the permission bit that grants the privilege to create and delete files is the write permission on the parent directory, not the write permission on the file itself. Hence, if a user has write permission on a directory, she can overwrite the files in it, regardless of the write permission bits set on files.

Commands to Change Permissions and Ownership

Key commands that can help you manage the permissions and ownership of a file are **chmod**, **chown**, and **chgrp**. In the following subsections, you'll examine how to use those commands to change permissions along with the user and group that owns a specific file, or even a series of files.

One tip that can help you change the permissions on a series of files is to use the **-R** command option. It is the recursive switch for all three of these commands. In other words, if you specify the **-R** switch with any of the noted commands on a directory, it applies the changes recursively. The changes are applied to all files in that directory, including all subdirectories. *Recursion* means that the changes are also applied to files in each subdirectory, and so on.

The chmod Command

The **chmod** command uses the numeric value of permissions associated with the owner, group, and others. In Linux, permissions are assigned the following numeric values: $r = 4$, $w = 2$, and $x = 1$. In numerical format, permissions are represented by an octal number, where each digit is associated with a different group of permissions. For example, the permission number 640 means that the owner is assigned permission 6 (4 + 2, read and write), whereas the group has permission 4 (read) and everyone else has no permissions. The **chown** and **chgrp** commands adjust the user and group owners associated with the cited file.

The **chmod** command is flexible. You don't always have to use numbers. For example, the following command sets execute permissions for the user owner of the script.sh file:

```
# chmod u+x script.sh
```

Note how the **u** and the **x** follow the ugo/rwx format specified in the associated RHCSA objective. To interpret, this command adds (with the plus sign) for the user owner of the file (with the **u**) execute permissions (with the **x**).

These symbols can be combined. For example, the following command disables (with the minus sign) write permissions (with the **w**) for the group owner (with the **g**) and all other users (with the **o**) on the local file named document.txt:

```
# chmod go-w document.txt
```

Rather than adding or removing permissions with the + and – operators, you can set the exact mode of a permission group using the equal operator (=). As an example, the following command changes the group permissions of the file named document.txt to read and write and clears the execute permission if it was set:

```
# chmod g=rw document.txt
```

While you can use all three group permission types in the **chmod** command, it's not necessary. The following command makes the script.sh file executable by all users:

```
# chmod +x script.sh
```

For the SUID, SGID, and sticky bits, some special options are available. If you choose to use numeric bits, those special bits are assigned numeric values as well, where SUID = 4, SGID = 2, and sticky bit = 1. However, to define the special bits you need one more digit in the octal representation. For example, the following command configures the SUID bit (with the first 4 digits in permission mode). It includes rwx permissions for the user owner (with the 7), rw permissions for the group owner (with the 6), and r permissions for other users (with the last 4) on the file named testfile:

```
# chmod 4764 testfile
```

If you'd rather use the ugo/rwx format, the following command activates the SGID bit for the local testscript file:

```
# chmod g+s testscript
```

And the following command turns on the sticky bit for the /test directory:

```
# chmod o+t /test
```

For the **chmod** command, changes don't have to be made by the root administrative user. The user owner of a file is allowed to change the permissions associated with her files.

The chown Command

The **chown** command can be used to modify the user who owns a file. For example, take a look at the ownership for the first figure that we created for this chapter, based on the **ls -l** command:

```
-rw-r--r--. 1 michael examprep 855502 Oct 25 14:07 F02-01.tif
```

The user owner of this file is michael; the group owner of this file is examprep. The following **chown** command changes the user owner to user elizabeth, but must be executed as root:

```
# chown elizabeth F02-01.tif
```

You can do more with **chown**; for example, the following command changes both the user and group owner of the noted file to user donna and group supervisors, assuming that user and group already exist:

```
# chown donna.supervisors F02-01.tif
```

Only the root administrative user can change the user owner of a file, whereas group ownership can be modified by root and also by the user who owns the file.

The chgrp Command

You can change the group owner of a file with the **chgrp** command. For example, the following command changes the group owner of the noted F02-01.tif file to the group named project (assuming it exists):

```
# chgrp project F02-01.tif
```

Special File Attributes

In addition to regular rwx/ugo permissions, files also have attributes. Such attributes can help you control what anyone can do with different files. Whereas the **lsattr** command lists current file attributes, the **chattr** command can help you change those attributes. For example, the following command protects /etc/fstab from accidental deletion, even by the root administrative user:

```
# chattr +i /etc/fstab
```

With that attribute, if you try to delete the file as the root administrative user, you'll get the following response:

```
# rm /etc/fstab
rm: remove regular file '/etc/fstab'? y
rm: cannot remove '/etc/fstab': Operation not permitted
```

TABLE 2-6	File Attributes

Attribute	Description
append only (**a**)	Prevents deletion, but allows appending to a file—for example, if you've run **chattr +a tester, cat /etc/fstab >> tester** would add the contents of /etc/fstab to the end of the tester file. However, the command **cat /etc/fstab > tester** would fail.
no dump (**d**)	Disallows backups of the configured file with the **dump** command.
immutable (**i**)	Prevents deletion or any other kind of change to a file.

The **lsattr** command shows an active "immutable" attribute on /etc/fstab:

```
# lsattr /etc/fstab
----i---------------- /etc/fstab
```

Of course, the root administrative user can unset that attribute with the following command. Nevertheless, the initial refusal to delete the file should at least give pause to that administrator before changes are made.

```
# chattr -i /etc/fstab
```

Several key attributes are described in Table 2-6. Other attributes, such as **c** (compressed), **s** (secure deletion), and **u** (undeletable), don't work for files stored in the ext4 and XFS filesystems.

A Basic Introduction of User and Group Concepts

Linux, like Unix, is configured with users and groups. Everyone who uses Linux is set up with a username, even if it's just "guest." There's even a standard user named "nobody." Take a look at /etc/passwd. An excerpt from this file is shown in Figure 2-4.

As shown, all kinds of usernames are listed in the /etc/passwd file. Even a number of Linux services such as mail, news, ftp, and apache have their own usernames. In any case, the /etc/passwd file follows a specific format, described in more detail in Chapter 6. For purposes of this discussion, note that the only regular users shown in this file are alex and michael; their user IDs (UID) and group IDs (GID) are, respectively, 1000 and 1001; and their home directories match their usernames. The next user gets UID and GID 1002, and so on.

This matching of UIDs and GIDs is based on the Red Hat user private group scheme. Now run the **ls -l /home** command. The output should be similar to the following:

```
drwx------. 4 alex    alex    4096 Dec 15 16:12 alex
drwx------. 4 michael michael 4096 Dec 16 14:00 michael
```

FIGURE 2-4   The /etc/passwd file

```
dbus:x:81:81:System message bus:/:/sbin/nologin
polkitd:x:998:996:User for polkitd:/:/sbin/nologin
avahi:x:70:70:Avahi mDNS/DNS-SD Stack:/var/run/avahi-daemon:/sbin/nologin
tss:x:59:59:Account used for TPM access:/dev/null:/sbin/nologin
colord:x:997:993:User for colord:/var/lib/colord:/sbin/nologin
clevis:x:996:992:Clevis Decryption Framework unprivileged user:/var/cache/clevis:/usr/sbin/nologin
rtkit:x:172:172:RealtimeKit:/proc:/sbin/nologin
sssd:x:995:991:User for sssd:/:/sbin/nologin
geoclue:x:994:990:User for geoclue:/var/lib/geoclue:/sbin/nologin
libstoragemgmt:x:993:989:daemon account for libstoragemgmt:/var/run/lsm:/sbin/nologin
setroubleshoot:x:992:988:SELinux troubleshoot server:/var/lib/setroubleshoot:/sbin/nologin
pipewire:x:991:986:PipeWire System Daemon:/var/run/pipewire:/sbin/nologin
flatpak:x:990:985:User for flatpak system helper:/:/sbin/nologin
gdm:x:42:42::/var/lib/gdm:/sbin/nologin
cockpit-ws:x:989:984:User for cockpit web service:/nonexisting:/sbin/nologin
cockpit-wsinstance:x:988:983:User for cockpit-ws instances:/nonexisting:/sbin/nologin
gnome-initial-setup:x:987:982::/run/gnome-initial-setup/:/sbin/nologin
sshd:x:74:74:Privilege-separated SSH:/usr/share/empty.sshd:/sbin/nologin
chrony:x:986:981::/var/lib/chrony:/sbin/nologin
dnsmasq:x:985:980:Dnsmasq DHCP and DNS server:/var/lib/dnsmasq:/sbin/nologin
tcpdump:x:72:72::/:/sbin/nologin
systemd-oom:x:978:978:systemd Userspace OOM Killer:/:/usr/sbin/nologin
alex:x:1000:1000:Alessandro Orsaria:/home/alex:/bin/bash
michael:x:1001:1001:Michael Jang:/home/michael:/bin/bash
[root@server1 ~]#
```

Pay attention to the permissions. Based on the rwx/ugo concepts described earlier in this chapter, only the named user owner has access to the files in his or her home directory.

The umask

Every time you create a new file, the default permissions are based on the value of umask. When you type the **umask** command, the command returns a four-digit octal number such as 0002. If a bit of the umask is set, then the corresponding permission is disabled in newly created files and directories. To find the relevant permission bits, you need to subtract the umask value from the number 777 (or 666 for a file). As an example, a umask of 0245 would cause newly created directories to have 0532 octal permissions (0777 − 0245 = 0532), which is equivalent to the following permission string:

```
r-x-wx-w-.
```

In the past, the value of umask affected the value of all permissions on a file. For example, if the value of umask was 000, the default permissions for any file created by that user were once 777 − 000 = 777, which corresponds to read, write, and execute permissions for all users. They're now 666, since regular new files can no longer get executable permissions when they are created. Directories, on the other hand, require executable permissions so that any file contained therein can be accessed.

The Default umask

With that in mind, the default umask is driven by the /etc/profile and /etc/bashrc files, specifically the following stanza, which drives a value for umask depending on the value of the UID:

```
if [ $UID -gt 199 ] && [ "`id -gn`" = "`id -un`" ]; then
    umask 002
else
    umask 022
fi
```

In other words, the umask for user accounts with UIDs of 200 and above is 002. In contrast, the umask for UIDs below 200 is 022. In RHEL 9, service users such as adm, postfix, and apache have lower UIDs; this affects primarily the permissions of the log files created for such services. Of course, the root administrative user has the lowest UID of 0. By default, files created for such users have 644 permissions (666 – 022 = 644); directories created for such users have 755 permissions (777 – 022 = 755).

In contrast, regular users have a UID of 1000 and above. Files created by such users normally have 664 permissions. Directories created by such users normally have 775 permissions. Users can override the default settings by appending a **umask** command in their ~/.bashrc or ~/.bash_profile.

CERTIFICATION OBJECTIVE 2.04

Managing Text Files

Linux and Unix are typically managed through a series of text files. Linux administrators do not normally use graphical editors to manage these configuration files. Editors such as OpenOffice.org Writer or Microsoft Word normally either save files in a binary format or change the encoding of plain-text files. Unless text files are preserved in their original format, changes that are made can render a Linux system unbootable.

Linux commands have been set up to manage text files as streams of data. You've seen tools such as redirection arrows and pipes. However, that data can be overwhelming without tools that can sort through that data. Even before files are edited, it's important to know how to read these files at the command-line interface.

Commands to Read Text Streams

Previously, you reviewed commands such as **cd**, **ls**, and **pwd** that can help you get around Linux filesystems. With commands such as **find** and **locate**, you reviewed how to identify the location of desired files.

Now it's time to start reading and processing the content of files. Most Linux configuration files are text files. Linux editors are text editors. Linux commands are designed to read text files. To identify the types of files in the current directory, try the **file *** command.

cat

The most basic command for reading files is **cat**. The **cat** *filename* command scrolls the text within the *filename* file. It also works with multiple filenames; it concatenates the filenames that you might list as one continuous output to your screen. You can redirect the output to the file of your choice, as described in the earlier section "Standard Streams and Command Redirection."

less and more

Larger files demand command utilities that can help you scroll through the file text at your leisure. These utilities are known as *pagers*, and the most common are **more** and **less**. With the **more** *filename* command, you can scroll through the text of a file, from start to finish, one screen at a time. With the **less** *filename* command, you can scroll in both directions through the same text with the PAGE UP, PAGE DOWN, and arrow keys. Both commands support vi-style searches.

As the **less** and **more** commands do not change files, they're an excellent way to scroll through and search for items in a large text file such as an error log. For example, to search through the basic /var/log/messages file, run the following command:

```
# less /var/log/messages
```

You'll then be able to scroll up and down the log file for important information. You can use the forward slash and question mark to search forward or backward through the file. For example, once you've run the command just shown, you'll be taken to a screen similar to that shown in Figure 2-5.

To search forward in the file for the term "error," type the following in the pager:

```
/error
```

To search in the reverse direction, substitute a **?** for the /.

The **zless** variant of the **less** command has one more feature unavailable to commands such as **more** and **cat**: it can read text files compressed in gzip format, normally shown with the .gz extension. For example, the man pages associated with many standard commands that are run in the shell can be found in the /usr/share/man/man1 directory. All of the files in this directory are compressed in .gz format. Nevertheless, the **zless** command can read those files.

And that points to the operation of the **man** command. In other words, these two commands are functionally equivalent:

```
# man cat
# zless -R /usr/share/man/man1/cat.1.gz
```

FIGURE 2-5 The less pager and /var/log/messages

```
May 29 17:29:26 server1 journal[1213]: Registering session with GDM
May 29 17:29:26 server1 systemd[1]: Received SIGRTMIN+21 from PID 400 (plymouthd).
May 29 17:29:26 server1 systemd[1]: Finished Hold until boot process finishes up.
May 29 17:29:26 server1 systemd[1]: Reached target Multi-User System.
May 29 17:29:26 server1 systemd[1]: Reached target Graphical Interface.
May 29 17:29:26 server1 systemd[1]: Starting Record Runlevel Change in UTMP...
May 29 17:29:26 server1 systemd[1]: systemd-update-utmp-runlevel.service: Deactivated successfully.
May 29 17:29:26 server1 systemd[1]: Finished Record Runlevel Change in UTMP.
May 29 17:29:26 server1 systemd[1]: Startup finished in 1.257s (kernel) + 1.532s (initrd) + 3.855s (userspace) = 6.646s.
May 29 17:29:26 server1 systemd[1]: Created slice Slice /system/dbus-:1.1-org.fedoraproject.SetroubleshootPrivileged.
May 29 17:29:26 server1 systemd[1]: Started dbus-:1.1-org.fedoraproject.SetroubleshootPrivileged@0.service.
May 29 17:29:29 server1 chronyd[812]: Selected source 216.239.35.8 (time.google.com)
May 29 17:29:29 server1 chronyd[812]: System clock TAI offset set to 37 seconds
May 29 17:29:36 server1 systemd[1]: Created slice User Slice of UID 1000.
May 29 17:29:36 server1 systemd[1]: Starting User Runtime Directory /run/user/1000...
May 29 17:29:36 server1 systemd-logind[794]: New session 2 of user alex.
May 29 17:29:36 server1 systemd[1]: Finished User Runtime Directory /run/user/1000.
May 29 17:29:36 server1 systemd[1]: Starting User Manager for UID 1000...
May 29 17:29:36 server1 systemd[1670]: Queued start job for default target Main User Target.
May 29 17:29:36 server1 systemd[1670]: Created slice User Application Slice.
May 29 17:29:36 server1 systemd[1670]: Started Mark boot as successful after the user session has run 2 minutes.
May 29 17:29:36 server1 systemd[1670]: Started Daily Cleanup of User's Temporary Directories.
```

head and tail

The **head** and **tail** commands are separate tools that work in essentially the same way. By default, the **head** *filename* command looks at the first 10 lines of a file; the **tail** *filename* command looks at the last 10 lines of a file. You can specify the number of lines shown with the **-n** *xy* switch. For example, the **tail -n 15 /etc/passwd** command lists the last 15 lines of the /etc/passwd file.

The **tail** command can be especially useful for problems in progress. For example, if there's an ongoing problem with failed login attempts, the following command monitors the noted file and displays new lines on the screen as new log entries are recorded:

```
# tail -f /var/log/secure
```

Commands to Process Text Streams

A text stream is the movement of data. For example, the **cat** *filename* command streams the data from the *filename* file to the terminal. When these files get large, it's convenient to have commands that can filter and otherwise process these streams of text.

Linux includes simple commands to help you search, check, or sort the contents of a file. In addition, there are special files that contain others; some of these container files are known colloquially as "tarballs." We will explore tarballs in Chapter 9.

on the **job**

Tarballs are a common way to distribute Linux packages. Packages are normally distributed in a compressed format, with a .tar.gz or .tgz file extension, consolidated as a package in a single file.

sort

You can sort the contents of a file in a number of ways. By default, the **sort** command sorts the contents in alphabetical order, depending on the first letter in each line. For example, the **sort /etc/passwd** command would sort all users (including those associated with specific services and such) by username.

grep

The **grep** command uses a search term to look through a file. It returns the full line that contains the search term. For example, **grep 'Michael Jang' /etc/passwd** looks for the name of this user in the /etc/passwd file.

You can use regular expressions within a **grep** command. Regular expressions provide a powerful way to specify complex search patterns. Some of the characters that have a special meaning inside a regular expression are shown in Table 2-7. If you want a metacharacter to lose its special meaning and be taken literally, precede it by a blackslash (\).

TABLE 2-7   Special Characters in Regular Expressions

Metacharacter	Description
.	Any single character. Often used with the * multiplier to indicate any number of characters.
[]	Match any single character included within the square brackets. For example, the command **grep 'jo[ah]n' /etc/passwd** would return all lines in /etc/passwd that contain the string *joan* or *john*.
?	Match the preceding element zero or one time. For example, the command **grep -E 'ann?a' /etc/passwd** would return all lines in /etc/passwd that contain the string *ana* or *anna*.
+	Match the preceding element one or more times. For example, the command **grep -E 'j[a-z]+n' /etc/passwd** would return all lines in /etc/passwd that contain the letters *j* and *n*, with one or more lowercase letters in between. Therefore, this regular expression would match strings such as *joan*, *john*, and also *jason* and *jonathan*.
*	Match the preceding element zero or more times. For example, the command **grep 'jo[a-z]*n' /etc/passwd** would return all lines in /etc/passwd that contain the string *jo* followed by zero or more lowercase letters and terminated by the character *n*. Therefore, the previous regular expression would match strings such as *jon*, *joan*, or *john*.
^	Match the beginning of a line. For example, the command **grep '^bin' /etc/passwd** would return all lines in /etc/passwd that start with the sequence of characters *bin*.
$	Match the end of a line. For example, the command **grep '/bin/[kz]sh$' /etc/passwd** would return all lines in /etc/passwd that terminate with the sequence of characters */bin/ksh* or */bin/zsh* (that is, all records corresponding to the users who have set Korn or zsh as their default shells).

The **grep** command supports some useful switches. To make the search case-insensitive, you can pass the **-i** option to the command line. The **-E** option enables the use of extended regular expression syntax. Another interesting switch is **-v**, which reverses the matching logic—that is, it tells **grep** to select only the lines that do *not* match a regular expression.

As an example, suppose you want to select only the lines from /etc/nsswitch.conf that are not blank and do not contain a comment (that is, they do not start with the # character). This can be achieved by running the following command:

```
# grep -v '^$' /etc/nsswitch.conf | grep -v '^#'
```

Note how the first **grep** command selects all the lines that are not blank (the regular expression that matches a blank line is **^$**—that is, start of line and immediate end of line). Then, the output is piped to a second **grep** command, which excludes all the lines that start with a hash character.

The same result can be obtained with a single instance of **grep** and the **-e** switch, which allows you to specify multiple search patterns on the same command:

```
# grep -v -e '^$' -e '^#' /etc/nsswitch.conf
```

For more information on regular expressions, type **man 7 regex**.

diff

One useful option to find the difference between files is the **diff** command. If you've just used a tool such as the Network Manager Connection Editor described in Chapter 3, it'll modify a file such as eth0.nmconnection in the /etc/NetworkManager/system-connections directory.

If you've backed up that eth0.nmconnection file, the **diff** command can identify the differences between the two files. For example, the following command identifies the differences between the eth0.nmconnection file in the /root and the /etc/NetworkManager/system-connections directories:

```
# diff -u /root/eth0.nmconnection /etc/NetworkManager/system-connections/
eth0.nmconnection
```

The -u option in the **diff** command represents the "unified format." This format not only highlights the differences between files but also displays several surrounding lines for context. This contextual view facilitates a clearer understanding of the variations in relation to the adjacent content.

wc

The **wc** command, short for "word count," can return the number of lines, words, and characters in a file. The **wc** options are straightforward; for example, **wc -l** *filename* returns the number of lines in that file.

sed

The **sed** command, short for "stream editor," allows you to search for and change specified words or even text streams in a file. For example, the following command exchanges the first instance of the word "Windows" with "Linux" in each line of the file opsys and writes the result to the file newopsys:

```
# sed 's/Windows/Linux/' opsys > newopsys
```

However, this may not be enough. If there's more than one instance of "Windows" in a line in the opsys file, it does not change the second instance of that word. But you can fix this by adding a "global" suffix:

```
# sed 's/Windows/Linux/g' opsys > newopsys
```

The following example would make sure that all Samba shares configured with the **writable = yes** directive are reversed:

```
# sed 's/writable = yes/writable = no/g' /etc/samba/smb.conf > ~/smb.conf
```

Of course, you should then review the results in the /root/smb.conf file before overwriting the original /etc/samba/smb.conf file.

awk

The **awk** command, named for its developers (Aho, Weinberger, and Kernighan), rather than a command, is more of a full programming language. It can identify lines with a keyword and read out the text from a specified column in that line. A common example is with the /etc/passwd file. For example, the following command will read out the fourth field in /etc/passwd (the group ID) of every user with a listing of "mike":

```
# awk -F : '/mike/ {print $4}' /etc/passwd
```

Edit Text Files at the Console

The original version of the RHCSA objectives specified the use of the Vim editor. Strictly speaking, it doesn't matter what text editor you use to edit text files. However, we believe that you need to know how to use the Vim editor, and apparently most system administrators agree. The Vim editor is short for "vi, improved." When installed, the Vim editor can be started with the **vi** command. Hereafter, we refer to that text editor as vi.

We think every administrator needs at least a basic knowledge of vi. Although emacs would also be a valid choice, vi may help you save a broken system. If you ever have to restore a critical configuration file using emergency boot media, vi may be the only editor you'll have available.

While RHEL 9 also includes access to the more intuitive nano editor, a knowledge of vi commands can help you in searching and editing key sections of text files more quickly.

Although the RHEL boot media supports more console-based editors, vi is one of the most feature-rich and efficient editors available on Linux.

You should know how to use the two basic modes of vi: command and insert. When you use vi to open a file, it opens in command mode. Some of the commands start insert mode. Opening a file is easy: just use the **vi** *filename* command.

The following is only the briefest of introductions to the vi editor. For more information, there are several books available on the topic, as well as a tutorial that you can start through the **vimtutor** command.

vi Command Mode

In command mode, you can do everything to a text file except edit it. The options in command mode are broad and varied, and they are the subject of a number of book-length texts. In summary, options in vi command mode fall into seven categories:

- **Open**   To open a file in the vi editor from the command-line interface, run the **vi** *filename* command.
- **Search**   For a forward search, start with a backslash (/), followed by the search term. Remember, Linux is case sensitive, so if you're searching for "Michael" in /etc/passwd, use the **/Michael** command. For a reverse search, start with a question mark (**?**).
- **Close**   To leave vi, use the **:q** command.
- **Abandon**   If you want to abandon any changes, use the **:q!** command.
- **Write**   To save your changes, use the **w** command. You can combine commands; for example, **:wq** writes the file and exits vi.
- **Edit**   You can use a number of commands to edit files through vi, such as **x**, which deletes the currently highlighted character; **dw**, which deletes the currently highlighted word; and **dd**, which deletes the current line. Remember, **yy** copies the current line into a buffer, **p** places text from a buffer, and **u** restores text from a previous change.
- **Insert**   A number of commands allow you to start insert mode, including **i** to start inserting text at the current position of the editor and **o** to open up a new line immediately below the current position of the cursor. To exit insert mode, press the ESC key.

Basic Text Editing

In modern Linux systems, editing files with vi is easy. Just use the normal navigation keys (arrow keys, PAGE UP, and PAGE DOWN), and then one of the basic commands such as **i** or **o** to start vi's insert mode, and type your changes directly into the file.

When you're finished with insert mode, press the ESC key to return to command mode. You can then save your changes, or abandon them and exit vi.

Table 2-8 summarizes the Vim commands that we have encountered in this section.

TABLE 2-8	Vim Commands	
Category	**Command**	**Description**
Insert mode	i	Enters insert mode at the current position
	o	Enters insert mode one line below the current position
	ESC	Terminates insert mode and returns to command mode
Copy and paste	yy	Copies the current line into the buffer
	p	Pastes the contents of the buffer
Delete text	x	Deletes the current character
	dw	Deletes the current word
	dd	Deletes the current line
Search text	/*text*	Runs a forward search of the word *text*
	?*text*	Runs a reverse search of the word *text*
Save and exit	:w	Saves changes
	:wq	Saves and exits
	:q!	Exits and abandons any changes

on the **Ü o b**

If you find Vim too cryptic, type vimtutor. **This is a short, interactive tutorial that will take you about 25–30 minutes to complete. If, after completing the tutorial, you still don't like Vim, consider an alternative editor, as explained in the next section.**

on the **Ü o b**

There are several specialized variations of the vi **command:** vipw **edits /etc/ passwd,** vigw **edits /etc/group, and** visudo **edits /etc/sudoers. The benefit of these commands is that they set appropriate locks to prevent file corruption.**

EXERCISE 2-1

Using vi to Create a New User

In this exercise, you'll create a new user by editing the /etc/passwd file with the vi text editor. Although there are other ways to create new Linux users, which we will cover in more detail in Chapter 6, this exercise helps you verify your skills with vi and at the command-line interface.

1. Open a Linux command-line interface. Log in as the root user and type the **vipw** command. This command uses the vi editor to open /etc/passwd.

2. Navigate to the end of the file. There are several ways to do this in command mode, including the DOWN ARROW key, the PAGE DOWN key, and the **G** command.

3. Identify a line associated with a regular user. If you've just created a new user, it should be the last line in the file. If a regular user does not yet exist, identify the first line, which should be associated with the root administrative user, with the number 0 in the third and fourth columns.

4. Make one copy of this line. If you're already comfortable with vi, you should know that you can copy an entire line to the buffer with the **yy** command. This "yanks" the line into the buffer. You can then restore or insert that line as many times as desired with the **p** command.

5. Change the username, user ID, group ID, user comment, and home directory for the new user. For detailed information on each entry, see Chapter 6. For example, in the following illustration, this corresponds to tweedle, 1001, 1001, Tweedle Dee, and /home/tweedle. Make sure the username also corresponds to the home directory.

```
rpc:x:32:32:Rpcbind Daemon:/var/lib/rpcbind:/sbin/nologin
gluster:x:995:990:GlusterFS daemons:/run/gluster:/sbin/nologin
chrony:x:994:989::/var/lib/chrony:/sbin/nologin
libstoragemgmt:x:993:987:daemon account for libstoragemgmt:/var/run/lsm:/sbin/no
login
setroubleshoot:x:992:986::/var/lib/setroubleshoot:/sbin/nologin
pipewire:x:991:985:PipeWire System Daemon:/var/run/pipewire:/sbin/nologin
saslauth:x:990:76:Saslauthd user:/run/saslauthd:/sbin/nologin
dnsmasq:x:984:984:Dnsmasq DHCP and DNS server:/var/lib/dnsmasq:/sbin/nologin
radvd:x:75:75:radvd user:/:/sbin/nologin
clevis:x:983:982:Clevis Decryption Framework unprivileged user:/var/cache/clevis
:/sbin/nologin
cockpit-ws:x:982:980:User for cockpit-ws:/nonexisting:/sbin/nologin
sssd:x:981:979:User for sssd:/:/sbin/nologin
colord:x:980:978:User for colord:/var/lib/colord:/sbin/nologin
gdm:x:42:42::/var/lib/gdm:/sbin/nologin
rpcuser:x:29:29:RPC Service User:/var/lib/nfs:/sbin/nologin
gnome-initial-setup:x:979:977::/run/gnome-initial-setup/:/sbin/nologin
sshd:x:74:74:Privilege-separated SSH:/var/empty/sshd:/sbin/nologin
avahi:x:70:70:Avahi mDNS/DNS-SD Stack:/var/run/avahi-daemon:/sbin/nologin
tcpdump:x:72:72::/:/sbin/nologin
michael:x:1000:1000:Michael Jang:/home/michael:/bin/bash
tweedle:x:1001:1001:Tweedle Dee:/home/tweedle:/bin/bash
```

6. Return to command mode by pressing the ESC key. Save the file with the **:w** command, and then exit with the **:q** command. (You can combine the two commands in vi; the next time you make a change and want to save and exit, run the **:wq** command.)

7. You should see the following message:

```
You have modified /etc/passwd.
You may need to modify /etc/shadow for consistency.
Please use the command 'vipw -s' to do so.
```

That message can be ignored because the next step adds appropriate information to the /etc/shadow file. However, you don't need to modify /etc/shadow directly.

8. As the root user, run the **passwd** *newuser* command. Assign the password of your choice to the new user. For this example, the new user is tweedle.

9. The process is not yet complete; every user needs a group. To that end, run the **vigr** command. Repeat the earlier steps that copied an appropriate line from near the end of the file. Note that group names and group ID numbers normally are identical to their usernames and user ID numbers.

10. All you need to change for the new entry is the group name and group ID number. Based on the information shown in the previous illustration, this would be a group name of tweedle and a group number of 1001.

11. Repeat the aforementioned **:wq** command to close vi and save the change.

12. Pay attention to the following message:

    ```
    You have modified /etc/group.
    You may need to modify /etc/gshadow for consistency.
    Please use the command 'vigr -s' to do so.
    ```

13. As suggested, run the **vigr -s** command to open the /etc/gshadow file. You'll note that there's less information in this file. Once a copy is made of an appropriate line, all you'll need to do is change the group name.

14. Repeat the aforementioned **:wq** command to close vi and save the change. Actually, you'll get a message that suggests that the file is read-only. You'd have to run **:wq!** in this case to write to this "read-only" file, overriding current settings.

15. Additional steps are required to properly set up the new user related to that user's home directory and standard files from the /etc/skel directory. However, if you completed this exercise correctly, you should be able to log in with the new username. For more information on users, see Chapter 6.

If You Don't Like vi

If you absolutely hate vi, you can use nano, a small and friendly editor. By default, when you run commands such as **edquota** and **crontab**, they open configuration files using the vi editor. To change the default editor used by system commands to nano, run

```
# export EDITOR=/bin/nano
```

To change the default editor for all users, add the preceding line to the /etc/environment configuration file:

```
# echo 'export EDITOR=/bin/nano' >> /etc/environment
```

Because the nano editor is fairly intuitive, as shown in Figure 2-6, instructions will not be provided in this book. The full manual is available at https://www.nano-editor.org.

Similar changes can be made if you prefer a different editor, such as emacs.

FIGURE 2-6

The /etc/nsswitch
.conf file opened
with the nano
editor

```
  GNU nano 5.6.1                    /etc/nsswitch.conf
# Generated by authselect on Wed Jan 25 21:19:48 2023
# Do not modify this file manually.

# If you want to make changes to nsswitch.conf please modify
# /etc/authselect/user-nsswitch.conf and run 'authselect apply-changes'.
#
# Note that your changes may not be applied as they may be
# overwritten by selected profile. Maps set in the authselect
# profile takes always precedence and overwrites the same maps
# set in the user file. Only maps that are not set by the profile
# are applied from the user file.
#
# For example, if the profile sets:
#     passwd: sss files
# and /etc/authselect/user-nsswitch.conf contains:
#     passwd: files
#     hosts: files dns
# the resulting generated nsswitch.conf will be:
#     passwd: sss files # from profile
#     hosts: files dns  # from user file
                                [ Read 94 lines ]
^G Help        ^O Write Out  ^W Where Is  ^K Cut      ^T Execute   ^C Location
^X Exit        ^R Read File  ^\ Replace   ^U Paste    ^J Justify      Go To Line
```

Edit Text Files in the GUI

No question, the Red Hat exams have become friendlier for users of the GUI. The gedit
text editor was even included for a short time in the RHCSA objectives. More traditional
Linux administrators may have been horrified. (The gedit editor has since been deleted
from the objectives.)

Once gedit is installed, you can start it by choosing Activities | Show Applications | Text
Editor. Because it is an intuitive GUI text editor, its use is trivial. Don't obsess about editors;
they are just tools on exams and in real life.

However, if you're editing configuration files on remote systems, it's possible that you
won't have access to gedit on that system, especially if the GUI hasn't been installed there.
You could start gedit and forward the application display to the GUI on your local machine
using a feature called X forwarding. But many administrators set up VMs without the GUI
to save disk space and system resources.

CERTIFICATION OBJECTIVE 2.05

Accessing the Documentation

Although there's no Internet access allowed during Red Hat exams, there is a lot of
documentation available already installed on a RHEL 9 system. It starts with the man
pages, which document the options and settings associated with most commands and

many configuration files. It continues with the info documents. Although fewer commands and files have such documents, when available, they do provide even more information.

Many packages include extensive documentation in the /usr/share/doc directory. Just apply the **ls** command to that directory. Every subdirectory there includes information about the capabilities of each associated package.

When You Need Help

The first thing we usually do when we need help with a command is to run it by itself. If more information is required, the command prompts with a request for more information, including a variety of options. As an example, look at the output to the following command:

```
$ dnf
```

If that approach doesn't work, generally some amount of help is available with the **-h** or the **--help** switch. Sometimes a mistake leads to some hints; the output to the following command suggests legal options to the **cd** command:

```
$ cd -h
bash: cd: -h: invalid option
cd: usage: cd [-L|[-P [-e]]] [dir]
```

Sometimes the **-h** switch is more helpful; take a look at the output to the **fdisk -h** command. But the **-h** option doesn't always show a help message; in that case, the **--help** switch may serve that purpose. Look at Figure 2-7 as an example, which displays the output to the **ls --help** command.

FIGURE 2-7	`[alex@server1 ~]$ ls --help`
	`Usage: ls [OPTION]... [FILE]...`
Help with the ls	`List information about the FILEs (the current directory by default).`
command	`Sort entries alphabetically if none of -cftuvSUX nor --sort is specified.`

```
Mandatory arguments to long options are mandatory for short options too.
  -a, --all                  do not ignore entries starting with .
  -A, --almost-all           do not list implied . and ..
      --author               with -l, print the author of each file
  -b, --escape               print C-style escapes for nongraphic characters
      --block-size=SIZE      with -l, scale sizes by SIZE when printing them;
                               e.g., '--block-size=M'; see SIZE format below
  -B, --ignore-backups       do not list implied entries ending with ~
  -c                         with -lt: sort by, and show, ctime (time of last
                               modification of file status information);
                               with -l: show ctime and sort by name;
                               otherwise: sort by ctime, newest first
  -C                         list entries by columns
      --color[=WHEN]         colorize the output; WHEN can be 'always' (default
                               if omitted), 'auto', or 'never'; more info below
  -d, --directory            list directories themselves, not their contents
  -D, --dired                generate output designed for Emacs' dired mode
  -f                         do not sort, enable -aU, disable -ls --color
  -F, --classify             append indicator (one of */=>@|) to entries
```

A Variety of man Pages

Few people can remember every switch to every command. That's one reason why command documentation is so important. Most Linux commands are documented in a format known as the man page. If you run the **man** command by itself, RHEL returns the following message:

```
What manual page do you want?
```

For example, say you need to set up a logical volume but have forgotten the switches associated with the **lvextend** command. To browse the man page for that command, run **man lvextend**. As with many other commands, there's an EXAMPLES section, like that shown in Figure 2-8. If you've run the **lvextend** command before, that section may help jog your memory.

Such man pages are available for most configuration files and commands. However, there may be more. So what if you're not sure about the name of the man page? In that case, the **whatis** and **apropos** commands can help. For example, to find the man pages with "nfs" in the title, run the following command:

```
# whatis nfs
```

If you want to find the man pages with nfs in the description, the following command can identify related commands:

```
# apropos nfs
```

However, if you've just installed a service such as httpd, associated with the Apache web server, commands such as **whatis httpd** and **apropos apachectl** probably won't provide any information. These commands work from a database in the /var/cache/man directory.

FIGURE 2-8

Examples from the lvextend man page

```
EXAMPLES
        Extend the size of an LV by 54MiB, using a specific PV.
        lvextend -L +54 vg01/lvol10 /dev/sdk3

        Extend  the  size of an LV by the amount of free space on PV /dev/sdk3.
        This is equivalent to specifying "-l +100%PVS" on the command line.
        lvextend vg01/lvol01 /dev/sdk3

        Extend an LV by 16MiB using specific physical extents.
        lvextend -L+16m vg01/lvol01 /dev/sda:8-9 /dev/sdb:8-9

        Extend an LV to use all remaining free space in volume  group  and  all
        resize its filesystem with fsadm(8).
        lvextend -l+100%FREE -r vg01/lvol01

SEE ALSO
        lvm(8), lvm.conf(5), lvmconfig(8), lvmdevices(8),

        pvchange(8), pvck(8), pvcreate(8), pvdisplay(8), pvmove(8),
        pvremove(8), pvresize(8), pvs(8), pvscan(8),

        vgcfgbackup(8), vgcfgrestore(8), vgchange(8), vgck(8), vgcreate(8),
        vgconvert(8), vgdisplay(8), vgexport(8), vgextend(8), vgimport(8),
Manual page lvextend(8) line 397/433 96% (press h for help or q to quit)
```

You can update that database by starting the man-db-cache-update service. The following command updates the database of man pages:

```
# mandb
```

If you encounter a situation, such as during a Red Hat exam, where the associated man page is not installed, there are at least three possible reasons. The associated functional software package may not be installed. The RPM package named man-pages may also not be installed. In some cases, there is a package specifically dedicated to documentation that must be installed separately. For example, there's an httpd-manual package installed separately from the Apache web server.

In some cases, multiple man pages are available. Take a look at the following output to the **whatis smbpasswd** command:

```
smbpasswd              (5)  - The Samba encrypted password file
smbpasswd              (8)  - change a user's SMB password
```

The numbers (5) and (8) are associated with different sections of man pages. If you're interested in details, they're shown in the output to the **man man** command. The man page shown by default is the man page associated with the **smbpasswd** command. In this case, if you want the man page for the smbpasswd encrypted password file, run the following command:

```
$ man 5 smbpasswd
```

To exit from a man page, press **q**.

The info Manuals

The list of available info manuals is somewhat limited. However, the coverage of some topics (for example, the bash shell) is usually more extensive than a corresponding man page. For a full list of info documents, run the **ls /usr/share/info** command. When an info manual is not available, a request defaults to the associated man page.

To learn more about the bash shell, run the **pinfo bash** command. **pinfo** has a user interface similar to the Lynx web browser and it is a more user-friendly alternative to the traditional **info** command. As shown in Figure 2-9, info manuals are organized into sections. To access a section, move the cursor to the asterisked entry and press ENTER.

To exit from an info page, press **q**.

Detailed Documentation in /usr/share/doc

The list of documentation available in the /usr/share/doc directory seems impressive. But the quality of the documentation depends on the work of its developers. The subdirectories include the name and version number of the installed package. Some of these subdirectories include just one file, normally named COPYING, which specifies the license under which the given software was released.

FIGURE 2-9

A sample info
manual

```
File: dir,      Node: Top,      This is the top of the INFO tree.

This is the Info main menu (aka directory node).
A few useful Info commands:

   'q' quits;
   'H' lists all Info commands;
   'h' starts the Info tutorial;
   'mTexinfo RET' visits the Texinfo manual, etc.

* Menu:

Archiving
* Cpio: (cpio).              Copy-in-copy-out archiver to tape or disk.
* Tar: (tar).                Making tape (or disk) archives.

Basics
* Bash: (bash).              The GNU Bourne-Again SHell.
* Common options: (coreutils)Common options.
* Coreutils: (coreutils).    Core GNU (file, text, shell) utilities.
* Date input formats: (coreutils)Date input formats.
* Ed: (ed).                  The GNU line editor
-----Info: (dir)Top, 332 lines --Top---------------------------------------
Welcome to Info version 6.7.  Type H for help, h for tutorial.
```

Sometimes, the documentation directory includes useful examples. For example, the sudo/ subdirectory includes sample configuration files and directives for administrative control, which can be helpful when you're configuring administrators with different privileges.

The documentation may include entire manuals in HTML format. For an example, if you install the pam-docs package, the pam/ subdirectory includes an entire online manual for the Pluggable Authentication Modules (PAM) system.

CERTIFICATION SUMMARY

The focus of this chapter is on the basic command-line tools, which were formerly associated with Red Hat exam prerequisites. Those prerequisites have now been incorporated into the main body of the RHCSA objectives.

The command line is the interface of a shell, an interpreter that allows you to interact with the operating system using various commands. Although no shell is specified in the objectives, the default shell in most Linux distributions, including RHEL 9, is bash. You can start a command-line prompt at one of the default consoles or at a terminal in the GUI.

At the bash prompt, you can manage the files and directories through which Linux is configured and organized. Linux configuration files are predominantly in text format, allowing for configuration, search, and modification using various commands. It's essential to manage file ownership and permissions with the **chown** and **chmod** commands, ensuring appropriate users and groups have access to files and directories. Text files can be analyzed as streams of data that can be interpreted and processed. To edit a text file, you need a text editor such as Vim, nano, or gedit.

Linux documentation is extensive. It starts with command switches such as **-h** and **--help**, which provide hints on what goes with a command. It continues with man and info pages. Many packages include extensive documentation files in the /usr/share/info directory. In many, perhaps most, cases, you do not need Internet access to find the hints needed.

TWO-MINUTE DRILL

Here are some of the key points from the certification objectives in Chapter 2.

Shells

- ❑ The default Linux shell is bash.
- ❑ Six command-line virtual consoles are available by default; if the GUI is installed, it takes over the first virtual console.
- ❑ You can open multiple command-line terminals in the GUI.
- ❑ Shells work with three data streams: stdin, stdout, and stderr.
- ❑ Command redirection allows you to manage streams of data with operators such as >, >>, <, |, and 2>.

Standard Command-Line Tools

- ❑ Everything in Linux can be reduced to a file.
- ❑ Commands such as **pwd** and **cd** can help navigate directories.
- ❑ Concepts such as directory paths, the PATH, and the tilde (~) can help you understand and use commands at the shell.
- ❑ Basic commands allow you to find needed files and read file contents. These commands include **ls**, **find**, and **locate**.
- ❑ File creation and deletion commands include **touch**, **cp**, **ln**, **mv**, and **rm**; corresponding directory creation and deletion commands are **mkdir** and **rmdir**.
- ❑ Commands can be customized with the **alias** command.

File Permissions

- ❏ Standard Linux file permissions are read, write, and execute, which may vary for the user owner, the group owner, and other users.
- ❏ Special permissions include the SUID, SGID, and sticky bits.
- ❏ Default user permissions are based on the value of the umask.
- ❏ Ownership and permissions can be changed with the **chown**, **chgrp**, and **chmod** commands.
- ❏ Special file attributes can be listed with the **lsattr** command and modified by the **chattr** command.

Managing Text Files

- ❏ Linux is managed through a series of text configuration files.
- ❏ Text files can be read as streams of data with commands such as **cat**, **less**, **more**, **head**, and **tail**.
- ❏ New files can be created, copied, moved, linked, and deleted with the **touch**, **cp**, **mv**, **ln**, and **rm** commands. Commands can be customized with the **alias** command.
- ❏ File filters such as the **sort**, **grep**, **wc**, **sed**, and **awk** commands support the processing of text streams.
- ❏ Understanding text editors is a critical skill. An earlier version of the RHCSA objectives specified the use of Vim and gedit.

Accessing the Documentation

- ❏ If you need a hint for a command, try it by itself; alternatively, try the **-h** and **--help** switches.
- ❏ Command man pages often include examples; **whatis** and **apropos** can search for man pages on different topics.
- ❏ If an info manual is available for a command or file, you'll find it in the /usr/share/info directory.
- ❏ Many packages include extensive documentation and examples in the /usr/share/doc directory.

SELF TEST

The following questions will help you measure your understanding of the material presented in this chapter. As there are no multiple-choice questions on the Red Hat exams, there are no multiple-choice questions in this book. These questions exclusively test your understanding of the chapter. Getting results, not memorizing trivia, is what counts on the Red Hat exams.

Shells

1. What is the name of the default shell in RHEL 9?
2. From the GUI, what key combination moves to virtual console 3?

Standard Command-Line Tools

3. What single command creates the /abc/def/ghi/jkl series of directories?
4. What symbol represents the home directory of the current user?
5. What command lists all the files whose name starts with the letters ab, contains one extra character, and is followed by one of the digits 1, 2, or 3?
6. What command lists all the files whose name ends with .conf in the /etc directory?

File Permissions

7. What single command changes the user owner to professor and group owner to assistants for the local file named question2.txt?

Managing Text Files

8. What command lists the last 10 lines of the /var/log/messages file?
9. What command returns lines with the term Linux from the /var/log/messages file?
10. What sequence of commands extracts all the lines in /etc/passwd that contain the string /bin/bash and sorts them alphabetically?
11. What sequence of commands returns all the users whose default shell is bash?

Accessing the Documentation

12. What command searches the database of man pages for manuals that reference the **passwd** command and configuration file?

13. If there are man pages for the hypothetical **abcde** command and file, in sections 5 and 8, what command is sure to call up the man pages from section 5?

LAB QUESTIONS

Red Hat presents its exams electronically. For that reason, the labs in this chapter are available from the companion website that accompanies the book. In case you haven't yet set up RHEL 9 on a system, refer to Chapter 1 for installation instructions. The answers for each lab follow the Self Test answers.

SELF TEST ANSWERS

Shells

1. The default shell in RHEL 9 is bash, also known as the Bourne-again shell.

2. From the GUI, the key combination that moves to virtual console 3 is CTRL-ALT-F3.

Standard Command-Line Tools

3. The single command that creates the /abc/def/ghi/jkl series of directories is **mkdir -p /abc/def/ghi/jkl**.

4. The symbol that represents the home directory of the current user is the tilde (~).

5. The command **ls ab?[123]** lists all the files whose name starts with ab, contains one extra character, and is followed by one of the digits 1, 2, or 3.

6. The command **find /etc -name '*.conf'** lists all the files whose name ends with .conf in the /etc directory.

File Permissions

7. The single command that changes the user owner to professor and group owner to assistants for the noted file is

```
# chown professor.assistants question2.txt
```

It's acceptable to substitute a colon (:) for the dot (.).

Managing Text Files

8. The command that lists the last 10 lines of the /var/log/messages file is **tail -n 10 /var/log/messages**. Because 10 lines is the default, **tail /var/log/messages** is also a valid solution.

9. The command that returns lines with the term Linux from the /var/log/messages file is **grep Linux /var/log/messages**. Other variations are acceptable, such as **cat /var/log/messages | grep Linux**.

10. The command **grep /bin/bash /etc/passwd | sort** extracts all the lines in /etc/passwd that contain the string /bin/bash and sorts them alphabetically.

11. There are many ways to answer this question. A possible solution is

```
# awk -F: '{print $1" "$7}' /etc/passwd | grep /bin/bash | awk '{print $1}'
```

The first **awk** command in the pipeline extracts the first and seventh fields (the username and shell) from each line of /etc/passwd. The result is piped to **grep**, which keeps only the lines that contain /bin/bash. Finally, the last **awk** command selects the first field (the username) from the output. The overall result is that this pipeline returns all the users whose default shell is bash.

Accessing the Documentation

12. The command that searches the database of man pages for manuals that reference the **passwd** command and configuration file is **whatis passwd**. The **apropos** and **man -k** commands go further because they list man pages with the text "passwd" in the command or the description.

13. The command that calls up the man page from section 5 for the hypothetical **abcde** command and file is **man 5 abcde**.

LAB ANSWERS

Lab 1

This lab is tricky, because it requires you to practice with a bash feature not explained in the chapter. As suggested, type **man bash** and search for the string "brace expansion" (type / followed by the search string, then press the **N** key until you find the relevant section).

1. Create the directory book in your home directory:

```
$ mkdir ~/book
```

Confirm that the directory exists:

```
$ ls -l ~
```

2. Change to the new directory and create the files:

```
$ cd ~/book
$ touch Ch{0,1}{0..9}.txt
$ rm -f Ch00.txt
```

The preceding **touch** command is the quickest way to create all the requested files with one operation. Note that the command also creates a Ch00.txt file, which is not requested, so you need to remove it.

3. Remove the book directory and all its contents with the following command:

```
$ rm -rf ~/book
```

Lab 2

You can create the rhcsa directory and lab.txt file with the following commands:

```
$ mkdir ~/rhcsa
$ cd ~/rhcsa
$ echo "Labs for the RHCSA Exam" > lab.txt
$ date +%F >> lab.txt
```

Next, display the contents of the lab.txt file and count the characters in it:

```
$ cat lab.txt
$ wc -m lab.txt
```

If you didn't know that **-m** is the **wc** command option to display the number of characters in a file, recall that you can type **man wc** to find that information. To create the archive directory and complete the other tasks in the lab, run

```
$ mkdir archive
$ mv lab.txt archive
$ mv ~/rhcsa /tmp/
```

Lab 3

First, create a file that contains a list of filenames in the /etc directory whose names end with "conf":

```
# find /etc -name "*conf" > ~/filelist.txt
```

Note that a normal user would not have permissions to see all the files within the /etc directory. For this reason, you can run the previous command as the root user.

Finally, count the number of lines in the file and display all lines that contain the string "security":

```
# wc -l ~/filelist.txt
# grep security ~/filelist.txt
```

Lab 4

The required commands are shown next:

```
$ awk -F: '{print $3" "$1}' /etc/passwd | grep '^[0-9][0-9] '
```

As you can see, this command line consists of a pipe of two commands:

1. The **awk** command prints the third and first fields for each line of the /etc/passwd file, where fields are separated by a colon (:) character.
2. The output of the **awk** command is redirected to the input of the **grep** command, which selects all lines that start with two digits followed by a space character.

Lab 5

This lab reinforces the practical understanding of Linux file and directory permissions.

1. Start by creating the directory and the file:

```
# mkdir /var/log/rhcsa
# echo "A simple logfile" > /var/log/rhcsa/main.log
```

2. Set the ownership for main.log:

```
# chown root:nobody /var/log/rhcsa/main.log
```

3. Adjust permissions for main.log: here, we want the root user to read and write (rw-), the nobody group to have no permissions (---), and others to only read (r--):

```
# chmod 604 /var/log/rhcsa/main.log
```

4. Set permissions for /var/log/rhcsa directory: we want the root user to have full access (rwx), the owner group to have no permissions (---), and others to access but not list (--x):

```
# chmod 701 /var/log/rhcsa
```

5. To verify your changes, you can use the ls command:

```
# ls -l /var/log/rhcsa
# ls -ld /var/log/rhcsa
```

6. As a regular user, try to read the file and list the contents of the directory. The first command should execute successfully, while the second will produce an error:

```
$ cat /var/log/rhcsa/main.log
$ ls -l /var/log/rhcsa
```

Lab 6

This lab gives you the opportunity to practice with Vim. As explained in this chapter, if you do not like Vim, there are alternatives. However, after completing the tutorial, you should be comfortable enough to use Vim for day-to-day operations and, hopefully, you should be able to appreciate its speed and efficiency.

Chapter 3

Managing Basic Networking

T he RHCSA exam requires that you know how to configure network interfaces and configure hostname resolution. In other words, you need to be prepared to configure IPv4 and IPv6 settings on a network device and to configure your system as a Domain Name Service (DNS) client so that it can resolve hostnames.

Chapter 1 covered the basics of the installation process, and Chapter 2 covered basic command-line tools and file editors. The next step is the network configuration, which is covered in this chapter. Once a system is connected to the network, you can connect to it remotely, install packages from a repository, and configure network services.

After you complete the installation of the systems for your test lab, you'll want to be able to administer them remotely. Understanding SSH connections for remote administration is not only an RHCSA requirement but also an essential skill in the real world.

INSIDE THE EXAM

IPv4 and IPv6

Although excellent GUI tools are available to help you manage network services, you should have a strong understanding of command-line tools and configuration files. Command-line tools can help you understand and manage network services directly or through related configuration files. The associated objectives are

- Configure IPv4 and IPv6 addresses
- Configure network services to start automatically at boot
- Start, stop, and check the status of network services

Of course, these objectives require a basic understanding of IP networking.

Configuration of Name Resolution

Name resolution depends on databases of hostnames or fully qualified domain names (FQDNs) such as server1.example.com and IP addresses such as 172.16.0.100. The sources from which Linux obtains name resolution information are usually the local /etc/hosts database of hostnames and IP addresses, as well as available databases of DNS servers.

That is what you need to learn for the following RHCSA objective:

- Configure hostname resolution

While network troubleshooting is no longer a part of the entry-level Red Hat exam, the way you address problems with respect to network configuration and hostname resolution can help you better understand how networks operate.

Access Remote Systems and Transfer Files Securely

The RHCSA objectives state that you need to know how to

- Access remote systems using SSH
- Securely transfer files between systems

If systems administrators had to be in physical contact with every system, half of their lives would be spent en route from system to system. With tools such as Secure Shell (SSH), administrators can do their work remotely and transfer files securely. Although SSH is automatically installed in a standard configuration in RHEL 9, custom configuration options such as key-based authentication are covered later in the book.

A Networking Primer

TCP/IP is a series of protocols organized in layers, known as a protocol suite. It was developed for Unix and eventually adopted as the standard for communication on the Internet. IP addresses identify a network interface in an IP network, and IP addressing is one of the most important concepts of TCP/IP. A number of TCP/IP tools and configurations are available to help you manage a network.

As with the explanations of command-line skills in Chapter 2, the description of TCP/IP networking in this section is an oversimplification intended to prepare you for the RHCSA exam, rather than a detailed introduction to TCP/IP networking. If you find this section overwhelming or incomplete, refer to Jang's and Soyinka's books listed in the introduction to Chapter 1. Linux is built for networking, and there is no practical way to pass any Red Hat exam unless you understand networking in some detail.

Although the focus of current enterprise networks is still on IP version 4 addressing, some organizations have mandated a move toward IP version 6 (IPv6) networks. The focus of this section is on IPv4, whereas IPv6 is covered in a separate section later in this chapter. However, most of the configuration files and tools that are used for IPv4 also apply to IPv6.

IPv4 Networks

Every network interface that communicates on a network needs its own IP address. Some addresses are assigned permanently to a network interface; these are known as *static* IP addresses. Others are leased from a Dynamic Host Configuration Protocol (DHCP) server for a limited amount of time; these are known as *dynamic* IP addresses.

IPv4 addresses are 32-bit binary numbers and are usually expressed in "dot-decimal" notation (such as 172.16.0.100), with each decimal octet representing 8 bits. An IP address is made up of two parts: a network (or *subnet*) address and a host part. Until the publication of RFC 1517 in 1993 by the Internet Engineering Task Force (https://www.ietf.org), IP addresses were categorized into different classes, which defined the size of the network and the host part of the address.

Today, IP addresses are usually analyzed using a classless logic. That means that the subnet mask, rather than the address class, is used to determine the network and host parts of an IP address. The old classful addressing scheme introduced by RFC 791 is shown in Table 3-1. Some concepts of RFC 791 still remain in practice today; as an example, the IP range 224.0.0.0–239.255.255.255 is used for multicast addresses.

In addition, a number of private IP addresses are not to be assigned to any computer that is directly connected to the Internet. The most common private network ranges are

TABLE 3-1	IP Address Classes	
Class	**IP Range**	**Note**
A	0.0.0.0–127.255.255.255	Allows networks of up to 16,777,214 hosts
B	128.0.0.0–191.255.255.255	Allows networks of up to 65,534 hosts
C	192.0.0.0–223.255.255.255	Allows networks of up to 254 hosts
D	224.0.0.0–239.255.255.255	Reserved for multicasts
E	240.0.0.0–255.255.255.255	Reserved for experimental use

defined in RFC 1918 and are associated with network addresses 10.0.0.0–10.255.255.255, 172.16.0.0–172.31.255.255, and 192.168.0.0–192.168.255.255. In addition, network addresses 127.0.0.0 through 127.255.255.255 are reserved for loopback communication on a local host.

Networks and Routing

As discussed in the previous section, an IP address has two parts: a network part and a host identifier. To determine the network part and the host part, IP addresses are associated with a *subnet mask* (also known as a *netmask* or *prefix*). This is a 32-bit number made of a sequence of binary ones followed by zeros.

The subnet mask can be represented in the same dot-decimal notation used for IPv4 addresses. For example, 255.255.255.0 is a subnet mask made of 24 binary ones and 8 zeros. An alternative notation is known as Classless Inter-Domain Routing (CIDR) notation and consists of a slash character (/) followed by a number that indicates the amount of one bits in the netmask. As an example, the subnet mask 255.255.255.0 can be written as /24 in CIDR notation.

Given an IP address and a subnet mask, all you have to do to determine the network portion of the IP address is provide a logical AND between the IP address and the netmask. For example, given the IP address 172.16.0.100 with netmask /24, the first three bytes of the address (172.16.0) represent the network part, whereas the last byte (100) is the host identifier.

Three key IP components define a network:

- **Network address**   Always the first IP address in a range
- **Broadcast address**   Always the last address in the same range
- **Subnet mask**   Helps your computer define the network portion and the host portion of an IP address

You can assign IP addresses between the network and broadcast addresses (not including these addresses) to any computer on the network. As an example, suppose you are defining the range of addresses for a private network. Start with the private network address 192.168.56.0 and a subnet mask of 255.255.255.0. Based on this information, the broadcast address is 192.168.56.255, and the range of IP addresses that you can assign on that particular network is 192.168.56.1 through 192.168.56.254. That subnet mask is also defined by the number of associated bits, 24. In other words, the given network can be represented by 192.168.56.0/24.

IP addresses are assigned to network interfaces. A host with multiple network interfaces that forwards traffic across different networks is called a *router*. IP hosts separated by other groups of IP hosts by a router must be located in different networks.

Related to networking and routing is the concept of the *default gateway*. It's a host that defines the junction between the local network and all other networks that your machine does not know how to reach. Although the gateway IP address is part of the local network, that address is assigned to a router, which may have an IP address on a different network, such as the public Internet. The default gateway IP address is normally configured in the routing table for the local system, as defined by the **ip route** command described in the following section.

Tools and Commands

Numerous tools are available to manage the TCP/IP protocol suite on your Linux computer. In older versions of Red Hat Enterprise Linux, some of the most important network management commands were **ifconfig**, **arp**, **netstat**, and **route**. Those commands have been deprecated, in favor of the **ip** tool, which supports more advanced features. Table 3-2 provides a list of the deprecated commands along with their equivalent **ip** commands.

TABLE 3-2   The ifconfig, arp, and netstat Commands with Their Equivalent ip Commands

Obsolete Command	Equivalent Command in RHEL 9	Description
ifconfig	ip [-s] link ip addr	Shows the link status and IP address information for all network interfaces
ifconfig eth0 192.168.56.150 ↵ netmask 255.255.255.0	ip addr add 192.168.56.150/24 ↵ dev eth0	Assigns an IP address and netmask to the eth0 interface
arp	ip neigh	Shows the ARP table
route netstat -r	ip route	Displays the routing table
netstat -tulpna	ss -tupna	Shows all listening and non-listening sockets, along with the program to which they belong

e x a m

ⓦatch **Even though they are considered "obsolete," the** ifconfig, arp, **and** netstat **commands are still popular among system engineers. There is no need for you to learn them for the RHCSA exam. However, if you are a longtime Linux user and feel** **more comfortable with** ifconfig, arp, **and** netstat **installed, you can find them in the** *net-tools* **RPM package, which is installed by default as part of the Server with GUI installation (software installation is covered in Chapter 4).**

A Note on Interface Names

By default, Red Hat Enterprise Linux 9 names network interfaces based on their physical location, such as enoX for onboard Ethernet interfaces and enpXsY for PCI slots. Some naming examples are given in Table 3-3. (RHEL 9 uses the traditional enumeration method of eth0, eth1, etc., only as a fallback choice.) Hence, you may find the first onboard network interface to be named *eno1*, while an interface located on PCI bus 3, slot 0, would be named *enp3s0*.

In the examples in this chapter, the network interface in our test system is named eth0. On your RHEL systems, the name may differ. Don't obsess over interface names! It's just a name and does not affect the functionality of any network configuration commands. The old ethX naming had the drawback that it was not always consistent, because it was dependent on the order in which network interfaces were detected at boot. The new naming convention in RHEL 9 helps to solve this problem by referring to the physical location of the interface in its name, such as the PCI slot.

ping and traceroute

The **ping** and **traceroute** commands are often used to diagnose and troubleshoot network problems. The **ping** command allows you to test connectivity. It can be applied to an IP address on the local system, on the local network, or on a different network, such as on the Internet. For the purpose of this section, assume your IP address is 192.168.56.100 and

TABLE 3-3	Interface Name	Description
Ethernet Interface Name Examples	enoN	Nth Ethernet onboard interface
	ensN	Ethernet card in PCI hotplug slot N
	enpXsY	Ethernet card in PCI bus X slot Y
	ethN	Nth Ethernet interface (old naming convention)

the default gateway address on the local network is 192.168.56.1. If you're having problems connecting to a host, try the following **ping** commands in order. The first step is to test the integrity of TCP/IP on your computer:

```
# ping 127.0.0.1
```

Normally, **ping** works continuously on Linux; you'll need to press CTRL-C to stop this command. If you need to verify a proper connection to a LAN, **ping** the IP address of the local network interface:

```
# ping 192.168.56.100
```

If that works, **ping** the address of another computer on your network. Then start tracing the route to the Internet. **ping** the address for the network gateway (in this case, 192.168.56.1). If possible, **ping** the address of the network's connection to the Internet, which would be on the other side of the gateway. It may be the public IP address of your router on the Internet. Finally, **ping** the address of a computer that you know is active on the Internet.

You can substitute hostnames such as www.google.com for an IP address. If the hostname doesn't work, there is likely a problem with the database of hostnames and IP addresses, more commonly known as a Domain Name System (DNS). It could also indicate a problem with the /etc/hosts configuration file.

The **traceroute** command is provided by the traceroute RPM package (see Chapter 4 for information on installing software). **traceroute** automates the process just described by tracking the route path to a destination. For example, the following command finds the path to the IP address 192.168.20.5:

```
# traceroute -n 192.168.20.5
traceroute to 192.168.20.5 (192.168.20.5), 30 hops max, 60 byte packets
 1   192.168.56.1   0.204 ms   0.152 ms   0.148 ms
 2   192.168.1.1    1.826 ms   2.413 ms   4.050 ms
 3   192.168.20.5   2.292 ms   2.630 ms   2.554 ms
```

Look at the **-n** option in this command. This tells **traceroute** to display IP addresses rather than hostnames. The command also shows the round-trip time (RTT) to reach each hop along the path. By default, three different probes are sent for each hop.

Please note that some **traceroute** command options require root privileges. Another command that serves the same purpose and is not subjected to this limitation is **tracepath**.

on the **Job**

By default, traceroute **relies on UDP probe packets with an increasing time-to-live (TTL) value in the IP header in order to find the route path to a given destination. Sometimes, a firewall along the path may block UDP packets. In that case, you may try to run** traceroute **with the** -I **or** -T **option to enable ICMP or TCP probe packets, respectively.**

Review Current Network Adapters with ip

The **ip** command can display the current state of active network adapters. It also can be used to assign network addresses and more. Run the **ip link show** command to review the link status of the active network adapters on the system. Optionally, include the **-s** switch (**ip -s link show**) if you want to display statistics about network performance.

To review IP address information, try the **ip address show** command, which gives the same output of **ip link show**, but it also includes IP addresses and their properties. The **ip address show eth0** command listed next reflects the current configuration of the Ethernet network adapter:

```
# ip address show eth0
2: eth0: <BROADCAST,MULTICAST,UP,LOWER_UP> mtu 1500 qdisc mq state ↵
UP group default qlen 1000
    link/ether 00:0c:29:0c:30:d4 brd ff:ff:ff:ff:ff:ff
    altname enp3s0
    inet 172.16.0.100/24 brd 172.16.0.255 scope global noprefixroute eth0
        valid_lft forever preferred_lft forever
    inet6 fe80::20c:29ff:fe0c:30d4/64 scope link noprefixroute
        valid_lft forever preferred_lft forever
```

The **ip** command is flexible. For example, the **ip a s** command is functionally equivalent to **ip addr show** or **ip address show**.

Configure a Network Adapter with ip

You can also use **ip** to assign IP address information. For example, the following command adds the noted IP address and network mask to the eth0 network adapter:

```
# ip addr add 172.16.0.50/24 dev eth0
```

The first argument, **172.16.0.50/24**, specifies the new IP address and netmask. The next argument, **dev eth0**, tells you which device is being configured. To make sure the change worked, run the **ip addr show eth0** command again.

With the right options, the **ip** command can modify additional network settings. Some of these options are shown in Table 3-4.

However, you'll want to make sure the changes survive a reboot, whether it be for the RHCSA exam or for a server that you want to administer remotely. The **ip** command is useful for troubleshooting or to temporarily configure an IP address for troubleshooting a network problem. It is not the appropriate tool to make changes that persist after a system reboot, because any changes made with the **ip** command are, by definition, temporary. To configure permanent changes to the network configuration, use **nmcli** or manually modify the configuration files in the /etc/NetworkManager/system-connections directory, described shortly.

TABLE 3-4	ip Command Options

Command	Description
ip link set *device* up	Activates the specified interface.
ip link set *device* down	Deactivates the specified interface.
ip addr flush dev *device*	Removes all IP addresses from the specified interface.
ip link set *device* txqlen *N*	Changes the length of the transmit queue for the specified interface.
ip link set *device* mtu *N*	Sets the maximum transmission unit as *N*, in bytes.
ip link set *device* promisc on	Activates promiscuous mode. This allows the network adapter to read all packets received, not just the packets addressed to the host. Can be used to analyze the network for problems or to try to decipher messages between other hosts.
ip link set *device* promisc off	Deactivates promiscuous mode.

Activate and Deactivate Network Adapters

It's possible to use the **ip** command to activate and deactivate network adapters. For example, the following commands deactivate and reactivate the first Ethernet adapter:

```
# ip link set eth0 down
# ip link set eth0 up
```

ip as a Diagnostic Tool

The Address Resolution Protocol (ARP) associates the hardware address of a network interface (MAC) with an IP address. The **ip neigh** command displays a table of hardware and IP addresses on the local computer. This command can help detect problems such as duplicate addresses on the network. Such problems may happen with improperly configured systems or cloned virtual machines. If needed, you can use the **ip neigh** command to set or modify ARP table entries manually. As hardware addresses are not routable, an ARP table is limited to the local network. Here's sample output from the command, showing all ARP entries in the local database:

```
# ip neigh show
172.16.0.50 dev eth0 lladdr 00:0c:29:e4:d3:2f STALE
172.16.0.2 dev eth0 lladdr 00:50:56:e3:ca:bb REACHABLE
```

The first column in the output lists known IP addresses on the LAN, followed by the interface to which the neighbor is attached and its link layer address (MAC address). The last entry shows whether or not the neighbor's hardware address is reachable. A STALE entry may indicate that its ARP cache timeout has expired since a packet was last seen from that host. If the ARP table is empty, no recent connections exist to other systems on the local network.

Routing Tables with ip route

The **ip** command is versatile. One important version of this command, **ip route**, displays routing tables. It's functionally equivalent to the deprecated **route** command. When run with the **-r** switch (**ip -r route**), this command looks to /etc/hosts files and DNS servers to display hostnames rather than numeric IP addresses.

The routing table for the local system normally includes a reference to the default gateway address. For example, look at the following output to the **ip route** command:

```
default via 172.16.0.2 dev eth0  proto static  metric 100
172.16.0.0/24 dev eth0  proto kernel  scope link  src 172.16.0.100 metric 100
```

The deprecated **netstat -nr** command should display the same table. For this routing table, the gateway IP address is 172.16.0.2. Any network packets with a destination other than the 172.16.0.0/24 network range are sent through the gateway address (in other words, the layer 2 address for this gateway is looked up and put in the frame as the destination MAC address). The system at the gateway address, usually a router, forwards that packet to the next router according to its routing table until it gets to a router that is directly connected to the destination.

Display Network Connections with ss

The **ss** command replaces the deprecated **netstat** tool to display network connections. With the right combination of command switches, it can show listening and nonlistening TCP and UDP sockets. One command we like to use is

```
# ss -tuna4
```

which shows all (**-a**) network sockets using IPv4 (**-4**) and both the TCP (**-t**) and UDP (**-u**) protocols in numeric (**-n**) format. If the **-p** switch is specified, **ss** also shows the process ID (PID) of the process using each socket. Figure 3-1 illustrates a sample output.

FIGURE 3-1   Output from the ss -tuna4 command

```
[root@server1 ~]# ss -tuna4
Netid State   Recv-Q  Send-Q      Local Address:Port      Peer Address:Port
udp   UNCONN  0       0              0.0.0.0:5353           0.0.0.0:*
udp   UNCONN  0       0         192.168.124.1:53           0.0.0.0:*
udp   UNCONN  0       0       0.0.0.0%virbr0:67            0.0.0.0:*
udp   UNCONN  0       0              0.0.0.0:111            0.0.0.0:*
udp   UNCONN  0       0              0.0.0.0:37060          0.0.0.0:*
tcp   LISTEN  0       128            0.0.0.0:111            0.0.0.0:*
tcp   LISTEN  0       32        192.168.124.1:53           0.0.0.0:*
tcp   LISTEN  0       128            0.0.0.0:22             0.0.0.0:*
tcp   LISTEN  0       5            127.0.0.1:631            0.0.0.0:*
tcp   ESTAB   0       0       192.168.122.100:22      192.168.122.1:47068
[root@server1 ~]#
```

At the end of the output, note the peer address of 192.168.122.1:47068. The 47068 port number is just the source port on the remote server. The corresponding local address of 192.168.122.100:22 specifies a port number of 22 (the local SSH service) for a connection from 192.168.122.1. You may also see a second entry with the same port number, which identifies the associated SSH daemon listening for connections. Other lines in this output identify other listening services.

CERTIFICATION OBJECTIVE 3.02

Network Configuration and Troubleshooting

Now that you've reviewed the basics of IP addressing and associated commands, it's time to look at the configuration files. These configuration files determine whether networking is started during the boot process. If networking is activated, these files also determine whether addresses and routes are configured statically as documented or dynamically with a DHCP client.

Basic network configuration only confirms that systems can communicate through their IP addresses. But that is not enough. Whether you're pointing to systems such as server1 .example.com or URLs such as www.mheducation.com, network configuration is not enough if hostname resolution is not working.

on the **job**

Some of the most common causes of network problems are physical in nature. This section assumes you've checked all network connections. On a VM, that means making sure the virtual network interface wasn't accidentally deleted or deactivated on the VM or on the physical host.

Network Configuration Services

If there's trouble with a network configuration, one thing to check is the current status of the network. To do so, run the following command:

```
# systemctl status NetworkManager
```

RHEL 9 uses a service known as Network Manager to monitor and manage network settings. Using the **nmcli** command-line tool, you can interact with Network Manager and display the current status of network devices:

```
# nmcli dev status
```

The command should list configured and active devices. If a key device such as eth0 is not listed as connected, your network connection is probably down or the device is not configured. Key configuration files are located in the /etc/NetworkManager/system-connections directory.

Sometimes mistakes happen. If you've deactivated an adapter or just lost a wireless connection, try something simple: restart networking. The following command restarts networking with current configuration files:

```
# systemctl restart NetworkManager
```

If a simple restart of networking services doesn't work, then it's time to get into the files. The /etc/NetworkManager/system-connections directory is where Red Hat Enterprise Linux stores and retrieves networking information. With available Red Hat configuration tools, you don't have to touch these files, but it's good to know they're there. Each installed network adapter, such as ens3, gets its own *name*.nmconnection configuration file, where *name* is the name of the device or the name of the connection. For example, eth0 is given file eth0.nmconnection. This file includes the IP address information required to identify this adapter on a network.

What you see in the *.nmconnection files depends on how an Ethernet network adapter was configured. For example, look at the situation where networking was set up only for the purposes of installation. If you did not configure networking when setting the hostname during the GUI installation process, the network interface would have retrieved its IP settings from a DHCP server.

Generally, the network options configured through a DHCP server include the IP address, the network mask, the gateway address for access to external networks, and the IP address of any DNS servers for that network.

When a network interface is configured to get its IP settings from a DHCP server, the corresponding nmconnection file would contain at least the following directives:

```
[connection]
id=eth0
type=ethernet
[ipv4]
method=auto
```

Network Manager includes **nmcli** to control the status of the service and apply network configuration changes. Rather than modifying the configuration via **nmcli**, you can change a device configuration file directly. For that purpose, the configuration file shown in Figure 3-2 provides a guide.

Most of these directives are straightforward. They define a configuration for an Ethernet network interface with name eth0, using a defined IP address, a netmask, a default gateway, and a DNS server.

After saving the file, you still have to notify Network Manager of the changes. This is achieved by running the following commands (**con** is short for **connection**):

```
# nmcli con reload
# nmcli con down eth0
# nmcli con up eth0
```

Shortly, you'll see how to use Network Manager's command-line tool to modify the configuration of a network device.

FIGURE 3-2

A manual
configuration
of eth0

```
[root@server1 ~]# cat /etc/NetworkManager/system-connections/eth0.nmconnection
[connection]
id=eth0
uuid=8c996298-43c9-3395-97b5-3d3182f27e9c
type=ethernet
autoconnect-priority=-999
interface-name=eth0
timestamp=1678906972

[ethernet]

[ipv4]
address1=172.16.0.100/24,172.16.0.2
dns=172.16.0.2;
method=manual

[ipv6]
addr-gen-mode=eui64
method=auto
```

Network Configuration Tools

Red Hat includes several tools that can be used to configure network devices in RHEL 9. The first is the Network Manager command-line tool, **nmcli**, introduced in the prior section. If you prefer a text-based graphical tool, you can start **nmtui** from a virtual terminal. As an alternative, the Network Manager Connection Editor is a GTK+ 3 application that you can start from a GNOME terminal with the **nm-connection-editor** command.

All the tools mentioned interact with the Network Manager system service.

The nmcli Configuration Tool

Network Manager can store different profiles, also known as *connections*, for the same network interface. This allows you to switch from one profile to another. For example, you may have a home profile and a work profile for a laptop Ethernet adapter and switch between the two depending on the network to which you are attached.

You can display all the configured connections in Network Manager by running the following command:

```
# nmcli con show
NAME   UUID                                    TYPE       DEVICE
eth0   394f6436-5524-4154-b26e-6649b4d29027    ethernet   eth0
```

To show how **nmcli** can be used to set up a different connection profile, the following command creates a new connection for eth0:

```
# nmcli con add con-name "eth0-work" type ethernet ifname eth0
```

Then, a static IP address and default gateway can be configured, as shown here:

```
# nmcli con mod "eth0-work" ipv4.addresses ↵
192.168.20.100/24 ipv4.gateway 192.168.20.1
```

You can run **nmcli con show** *connection-id* to display the current settings for a connection. You can also modify additional properties from **nmcli**. For example, to add a DNS server to the eth-work connection, run

```
# nmcli con mod "eth0-work" +ipv4.dns 192.168.20.1
```

Finally, to switch to the new connection profile, run

```
# nmcli con up "eth0-work"
```

You can prevent a connection from starting automatically at boot with the following command:

```
# nmcli con mod "eth0-work" connection.autoconnect no
```

The nmtui Configuration Tool

As suggested by the name, this tool provides a text-based user interface and can be started from a command-line terminal. Just run the **nmtui** command. With a console tool, you'd need to press TAB to switch between options and press the SPACEBAR or the ENTER key to select the highlighted option.

Press the DOWN ARROW key until Quit is highlighted, and then press ENTER. For now, make a backup of the file from the /etc/NetworkManager/system-connections directory. Based on the **diff** command, Figure 3-3 compares the contents of an eth0 interface that uses the DHCP protocol, as configured during the installation process, with an interface that uses static IP addressing, configured with the **nmtui** tool.

The directives shown in Figure 3-3 are described in Table 3-5, along with some other configuration directives that you may find in the system-connections directory.

FIGURE 3-3   The differences between static and dynamic network configuration

```
[root@server1 system-connections]# diff -u eth0.nmconnection.orig  eth0.nmconnection
--- eth0.nmconnection.orig      2023-03-28 19:53:00.766673689 -0400
+++ eth0.nmconnection   2023-03-28 19:56:47.803190988 -0400
@@ -4,12 +4,14 @@
 type=ethernet
 autoconnect-priority=-999
 interface-name=eth0
-timestamp=1678906972
+timestamp=1678914265

 [ethernet]

 [ipv4]
-method=auto
+address1=172.16.0.100/24,172.16.0.2
+dns=172.16.0.2;
+method=manual

 [ipv6]
 addr-gen-mode=eui64
[root@server1 system-connections]# 
```

TABLE 3-5   Network Configuration Directives in the /etc/NetworkManager/system-connections Directory

Directive	Description
[connection] interface-name=*ifname*	The name of the network interface.
[connection] id=*name*	Name of the interface connection profile used by Network Manager.
[connection] timestamp=*value*	The date and time of the last configuration change in Unix format, expressed as number of seconds since 00:00:00 UTC on January 1, 1970.
[connection] uuid=*identifier*	Universal Unique Identifier for the device.
[connection] type=ethernet	Network type; should be set to "ethernet" for an Ethernet device.
[connection] autoconnect=*bool*	Directive that can take the Boolean values true or false to specify whether the network device is started during the boot process.
[ipv4] method=*string*	May be set to "manual" for static configuration or "auto" to acquire IP addresses from a DHCP server.
[ipv4] address1=172.16.0.100/24	Static IP address and network mask in CIDR format (i.e., /24).
[ipv4] gateway=172.16.0.2	IP address of the default gateway.
[ipv4] dns=8.8.8.8	IP address of the first DNS server, which is configured in /etc/resolv.conf.
[ipv4] dns-search=example.com	Specifies the domain search list in /etc/resolv.conf.
[ipv4] ignore-auto-dns=*bool*	If set to true, ignores DNS server information passed by a DHCP server.

EXERCISE 3-1

Configure IPv4 Settings on a Network Interface

In this exercise, you'll configure the first Ethernet network interface with the Network Manager text-based user interface tool. All you need is a command-line interface. Take the following steps:

1. Back up a copy of the current configuration file for the Ethernet interface. This would be the *.nmconnection file in the /etc/NetworkManager/system-connections directory (the filename may vary, depending on the interface name). (Hint: use the **cp** command, not the **mv** command.)

2. Run the **nmtui** command.

3. In the menu that appears, Edit a Connection should be highlighted. If necessary, press the ARROW or TAB key until it is. Then press ENTER.

4. In the screen that appears, make sure the first Ethernet network interface is highlighted and press ENTER.

5. In the Edit Connection window shown here, the Automatic option may be selected under IPv4 Configuration. If so, highlight it and press ENTER; then select Manual.

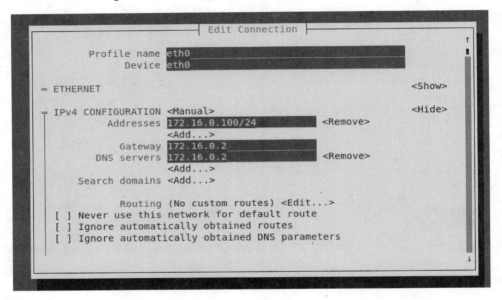

6. If the IPv4 settings are not shown, highlight the Show option at the right of IPv4 Configuration and press ENTER. This expands the current IPv4 settings.

7. Enter the IP address information for the system. The settings shown in the window are based on the settings described in Chapter 1 for the server1.example.com system. When complete, highlight OK and press ENTER.

8. You're taken back to the device screen. Make sure Quit is highlighted and press ENTER.

9. Check the result with the **ip addr show** and **ip route** commands. The configuration of the network interface and the associated routing table should reflect the new settings.

10. To restore the original configuration, restore the *.nmconnection file to the /etc/NetworkManager/system-connections directory and run **nmcli conn reload**.

Network Manager Connection Editor

Now you'll work with the default graphical network management tool for RHEL 9, the Network Manager Connection Editor tool. When connecting to different networks, Network Manager is designed to make that switching between, say, a wireless and an Ethernet connection as seamless as possible. But that's something more applicable to portable systems as opposed to servers. For the scope of the RHCSA exam, all you need to know is how to configure a network interface with that tool.

The Network Manager Connection Editor is not really new, because it has been in use in Fedora for several years. It only runs in the GUI. To start it, run the **nm-connection-editor** command. This opens the Network Connections tool shown in Figure 3-4.

As you can see from the figure, the tool lists the connection profile for the first Ethernet network interface. It also supports the configuration of other types of networks, including wireless, mobile broadband cards (such as those used to connect to 4G and 5G networks), and Digital Subscriber Line (DSL) connections. On a regular server, the focus is on reliable connections, and that is still based on a standard wired Ethernet device.

Highlight the connection profile of the first Ethernet device (eth0) and click the gear icon; then click the IPv4 Settings tab, as shown in Figure 3-5. Unless previously configured, the default Method setting assumes that the network interface will receive its configuration settings automatically from a DHCP server.

FIGURE 3-4

Network Manager Connection Editor

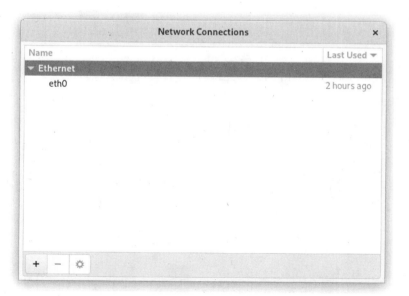

FIGURE 3-5 Editing an Ethernet connection in the Network Manager Connection Editor

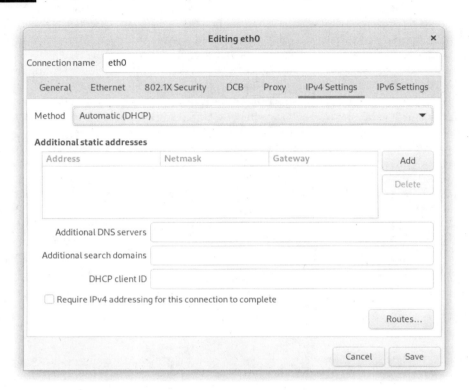

Click the Method drop-down text box. Although Connection Editor supports the configuration of a network interface in several different ways, the only one of interest in this case is Manual. Select that option, and the Additional Static Addresses section of the window should no longer be blanked out. Now add the IP address information for the system. Based on the server1.example.com system described in Chapter 1, here are the appropriate options:

- **Address**   172.16.0.100
- **Netmask**   255.255.255.0 (24 in CIDR notation is an acceptable equivalent in this field)
- **Gateway**   172.16.0.2
- **Additional DNS Servers**   172.16.0.2
- **Additional Search Domains**   example.com
- **DHCP Client ID**
- **Require IPv4 Addressing for This Connection to Complete**   Deselected

If properly entered, the configuration associated with the first Ethernet interface is titled with the connection name listed in Figure 3-5. For that configuration, the settings are saved in the eth0.nmconnection file in the /etc/NetworkManager/system-connections directory.

Configure Name Resolution

The final piece in network configuration is typically name resolution. In other words, does the local system have the information required to translate domain names such as mheducation.com to IP addresses such as 52.7.41.60?

Name resolution was easy when Unix was first being developed. When the predecessor to the Internet was first put into use, the worldwide computer network had four hosts, one computer at each of four different universities. It was easy to set up a static file with a list of each of their names and corresponding addresses. That file has evolved into what is known in Linux as /etc/hosts.

But now the Internet is more complex. Although you could try to set up a database of every domain name and IP address on the Internet in the /etc/hosts file, that would take almost forever and would not be a scalable solution. That's why most users set up connections to DNS servers. On RHEL 9, that's still documented in the /etc/resolv.conf configuration file.

On smaller networks, some administrators set up the /etc/hosts file as a database for the name of each system and IP address on the local network. If desired, administrators could even set up a few IP addresses of domains on the Internet, although this setup would break if any of those Internet domains made DNS changes on their own.

But if you've configured a connection to a DNS server and systems in /etc/hosts, what's searched first? That's the purpose of the /etc/nsswitch.conf configuration file, which specifies the search order for various name-service databases, including hostnames.

Hostname Configuration Files

RHEL 9 includes at least four hostname configuration files of interest: /etc/hostname, /etc/hosts, /etc/resolv.conf, and /etc/nsswitch.conf. These four files, taken together, contain the local hostname, the local database of hostnames and IP addresses, the IP address of one or more DNS servers, and the order in which these databases are searched.

/etc/nsswitch.conf

The /etc/nsswitch.conf file specifies database search priorities for everything from authentication to name services. As the name server switch file, it includes the following entry, which determines what database is searched first:

```
hosts: files dns myhostname
```

When a system gets a request to search for a hostname such as tester1.example.com, the preceding directive means the /etc/hosts file is searched first. If that name is not found in /etc/hosts, the next step is to search available configured DNS servers, normally using those configured in the /etc/resolv.conf file. If the name is still not found, the system looks at its hostname.

The resolver library also uses information in the /etc/host.conf file. The entry in this file is simply

```
multi on
```

which tells the system to return all IP addresses in /etc/hosts that are mapped to the same hostname, instead of returning only the first entry.

/etc/hosts

The /etc/hosts file is a static database of hostnames/FQDNs and IP addresses. It's suitable for small, relatively static networks. However, using it for networks where there are frequent changes can be a pain. Every time a system is added or removed, you'll have to change this file—not only on the local system but also on every other system on that network.

The /etc/hosts file is well suited to the local virtual machines created in Chapter 1. A simple version of the file might include the following entries:

```
127.0.0.1 localhost localhost.localdomain localhost4 localhost4.localdomain4
::1 localhost localhost.localdomain localhost6 localhost6.localdomain6
172.16.0.100 server1.example.com server1
172.16.0.50 tester1.example.com tester1
```

In some cases, you may want to set up multiple entries for an IP address. For example, the following entries could be added to specify the IP addresses for web and FTP servers:

```
172.16.0.50 www.example.com
172.16.0.100 ftp.example.com
```

/etc/resolv.conf

The standard file for documenting the location of DNS servers is still /etc/resolv.conf. Typically, it'll have one or two entries, similar to the following:

```
search example.com
nameserver 172.16.0.2
```

The **search** directive appends the example.com domain name to searches for simple hostnames. The **nameserver** directive specifies the IP address of the configured DNS server. If in doubt about whether the DNS server is operational, run one of the following commands:

```
# dig @172.16.0.2 mheducation.com
# host mheducation.com 172.16.0.2
```

In the preceding commands, substitute the IP address associated with the DNS server that you want to test, which could be one of the servers listed in the **nameserver** directive in your /etc/resolv.conf file. You can specify up to three **nameserver** directives in this file.

on the !ⓄⓄb **It may not be wise to edit the /etc/resolv.conf file directly. If you have configured DNS servers with another tool such as** nmcli, **Network Manager will overwrite any changes you make when directly editing that file unless you override this behavior with** ignore-auto-dns **in the connection file.**

/etc/hostname

During the boot process, the network service looks to the /etc/hostname file to define the value of the local hostname. The hostname should be set as an FQDN such as tester1.example.com. As suggested earlier, it's a simple file, where the hostname is documented with a directive such as the following:

```
tester1.example.com
```

Of course, you can modify the value of the hostname with the **hostname** *newname* command. However, this change is only temporary and is not reflected in the /etc/hostname file. To make the change persistent, use the **hostnamectl set-hostname** *newname* command.

CERTIFICATION OBJECTIVE 3.03

An Introduction to IPv6

One of the special challenges of the RHCSA exam is IPv6 networking. While most current networks are configured with IPv4 addresses, several regions have run out of public IPv4 addresses.

Internet Protocol Version 6 (IPv6) was introduced in the late 1990s as a replacement for IPv4. It turns out that the 4 billion (2^{32}) IPv4 addresses are not enough. IPv6 supports many more addresses, potentially up to 2^{128}, or 3.4×10^{38} (340 undecillion) addresses.

Basic IPv6 Addressing

The first section of this chapter introduced the "dot-decimal" notation for IPv4 addresses, where each decimal octet represents 8 bits of the 32-bit address (for example, 192.168.56.100). IPv6 addresses are made of 128 bits and are set up in hexadecimal notation, also known as base 16. In other words, an IPv6 address may include the following "digits":

```
0, 1, 2, 3, 4, 5, 6, 7, 8, 9, a, b, c, d, e, f
```

An IPv6 address is normally organized in eight groups of four hexadecimal numbers each, called "nibbles" since each character represents half a byte, in the following format:

```
2001:0db8:3dab:0001:0000:0000:0000:0072
```

You can simplify IPv6 addressing further:

- Remove any leading zeros in a nibble. For example, you can write 0db8 as db8, 0072 as 72, 0000 as 0, and so on.
- Replace any sequence of 0000 nibbles with a pair of colons (::). As an example, you can abbreviate 0000:0000:0000 with a pair of colons. However, to avoid ambiguity, you can apply this rule only once in an IPv6 address.

Hence, you can rewrite the previous address in a much more compact form:

```
2001:db8:3dab:1::72
```

Similar to IPv4, IPv6 addresses are made of two parts: a host and a network address. The host portion of an IPv6 address is known as the *interface identifier*. In IPv6, subnet masks are typically specified in prefix notation (such as /48).

As an example, assume that the IPv6 address 2001:db8:3dab:1::72 has a network prefix of /64. In other words, the network part of that IPv6 address includes the first 64 bits of that address. In this case, that network prefix is 2001:db8:3dab:1. The interface identifier includes the last 64 bits, shown as the hexadecimal number 72.

IPv6 addresses are classified in several categories. First, there are three address formats:

- **Unicast**   A unicast address is associated with a single network adapter.
- **Anycast**   An anycast address can be assigned to multiple hosts simultaneously. It can be used for load balancing and redundancy. Anycast addresses are organized in the same way as unicast addresses.
- **Multicast**   A multicast address is used to send a message to multiple destinations simultaneously.

With that diversity of address formats, IPv4-style broadcast addresses aren't needed. If you want to send a message to multiple systems, use IPv6 multicast addresses.

IPv6 addresses are also organized in several different ranges, as described in Table 3-6. The default route in IPv4 (0.0.0.0/0) is shown as ::/0 in IPv6.

The link-local address range requires explanation. Every interface in an IPv6 network is automatically configured with a link-local address. These addresses are not routable; as such, communication is limited to the local network segment. Link-local addresses are needed for various IPv6 operations.

TABLE 3-6   IPv6 Address Types

IPv6 Address Type	Address Range	Description
Global unicast	2000::/3	Used for host-to-host communications
Anycast	Same as unicast	Assigned to any number of hosts
Multicast	ff00::/8	Used for one-to-many and many-to-many communications
Link-local	fe80::/10	Reserved for link-local communications
Unique local	fd00::/8	The equivalent of RFC 1918 private addresses in IPv4

Even if you haven't configured IPv6 in your servers, each network interface is automatically assigned a link-local address, as shown in the following output:

```
# ip addr show eth0
eth0: <BROADCAST,MULTICAST,UP,LOWER_UP> mtu 1500 qdisc mq state ↵
UP group default qlen 1000
    link/ether 00:0c:29:0c:30:d4 brd ff:ff:ff:ff:ff:ff
    altname enp3s0
    inet 172.16.0.100/24 brd 172.16.0.255 scope global noprefixroute eth0
       valid_lft forever preferred_lft forever
    inet6 fe80::20c:29ff:fe0c:30d4/64 scope link noprefixroute
       valid_lft forever preferred_lft forever
```

To identify a link-local address, look for an address that starts with fe80. Note the "scope link" entry. As you can see, interface eth0 has the following IPv6 link-local address: fe80::20c:29ff:fe0c:30d4/64.

Troubleshooting Tools

Most of the network tools introduced in this chapter work seamlessly with both IPv4 and IPv6 addresses. There are two notable exceptions: the **ping** and **tracepath** commands. For IPv6 networking, you would use the **ping6** and **tracepath6** commands.

The **ping6** command works in a similar way to **ping**. Even before you configure an IPv6 address, you can run the **ping6** command on the Linux system hosting your server1 .example.com virtual machine:

```
# ping6 -I vmnet8 fe80::20c:29ff:fe0c:30d4/64
```

Since link-local addresses are not routable, you must specify the outbound interface (**-I**) in the **ping6** command when you ping a remote link-local address.

Configure IPv6 Addresses

As with IPv4 networking, you can configure an IPv6 address with the Network Manager command-line tool **nmcli**, the text-based graphical tool **nmtui**, or the Network Manager Connection Editor.

Start the Network Manager Connection Editor from the GUI with the **nm-connection-editor** command. Select the connection profile of the first Ethernet device (eth0 in our system), click the gear icon, then click the IPv6 Settings tab, shown in Figure 3-6.

Click the Method drop-down text box and select Manual. You can now add IP address information for the system. For example, on server1.example.com we added the following settings:

- **Address**   2001:db8:3dab::2
- **Prefix**   64
- **Gateway**   2001:db8:3dab::1

FIGURE 3-6   Editing an IPv6 address in the Network Manager Connection Editor

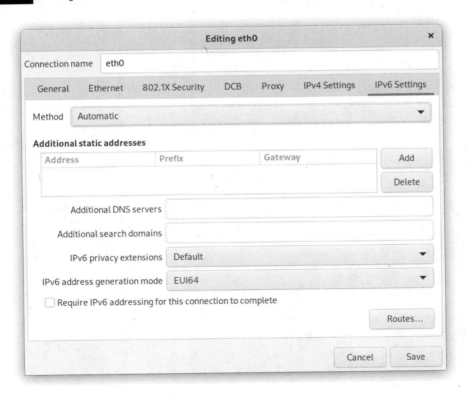

Similarly, we have associated the IPv6 address 2001:db8:3dab:1 with the vmnet8 interface on our physical system. You can verify the configuration with the following command:

```
# ip addr show eth0

eth0: <BROADCAST,MULTICAST,UP,LOWER_UP> mtu 1500 qdisc mq state ↵
UP group default qlen 1000
    link/ether 00:0c:29:0c:30:d4 brd ff:ff:ff:ff:ff:ff
    altname enp3s0
    inet 172.16.0.100/24 brd 172.16.0.255 scope global noprefixroute eth0
        valid_lft forever preferred_lft forever
    inet6 2001:db8:3dab::2/64 scope global noprefixroute
        valid_lft forever preferred_lft forever
    inet6 fe80::20c:29ff:fe0c:30d4/64 scope link noprefixroute
        valid_lft forever preferred_lft forever
```

The configuration is saved in the eth0.nmconnection file in the /etc/NetworkManager/system-connections directory. Open that file. You will notice that the Network Manager Connection Editor added the following configuration lines:

```
[ipv6]
addr-gen-mode=eui64
address1=2001:db8:3dab::2
gateway=2001:db8:3dab::1
method=manual
```

The **addr-gen-mode** directive is used to auto-generate an IPv6 address derived from the hardware address of the network interface and requires **method** to be set to **auto** to be effective. The next variables, **address1** and **gateway**, set the IP addresses of the interface and the default gateway, respectively.

CERTIFICATION OBJECTIVE 3.04

Administration with Secure Shell and Secure Copy

Red Hat Enterprise Linux installs the Secure Shell (SSH) packages by default. The RHCSA requirement with respect to SSH is simple: you need to know how to use it to access remote systems. In addition, you need to know how to securely transfer files between systems. Therefore, this section examines how to use the **ssh** and **scp** commands to access remote systems and transfer files.

As suggested earlier, the stage is already set by the default installation of SSH on standard installations of RHEL 9. Although firewalls are enabled by default, the standard RHEL 9 firewall leaves TCP port 22 open for SSH access. Related configuration files are stored in the /etc/ssh directory.

The Secure Shell daemon is secure because it encrypts messages. In other words, malicious users who are listening to traffic on a network can't read the data sent between SSH clients and servers. And that's important on a public network such as the Internet. RHEL incorporates SSH version 2, which supports multiple key-exchange methods and is incompatible with the older SSH version 1. Client commands such as **ssh**, **scp**, and **sftp** are covered in this section, while key-based authentication for SSH is covered in Chapter 8.

Command-Line Access

To access a remote system with **ssh**, you need a username and password on that remote system. By default, direct **ssh**-based access to the root account is not enabled. For example, the following command opens a shell on the noted server1 system and authenticates with the username michael:

```
$ ssh michael@server1.example.com
```

on the
ⓘob

If you get an error such as "Name or service not known" when you attempt to access a remote host via ssh, **that indicates that the system cannot resolve the hostname to an IP address. You will configure name resolution in one of this chapter's labs. In the meantime, to log in to server1.example.com via** ssh, **use the IP address that you configured in Chapter 1.**

The following command works in the same way:

```
$ ssh -l michael server1.example.com
```

Without the username, the **ssh** command assumes that you're logging in remotely as the username on the local system. For example, if you were to run the command

```
$ ssh server1.example.com
```

from the user michael account, the **ssh** command would assume that you're trying to log in to the server1.example.com system as user michael.

The first time the **ssh** command is run between systems, it presents something similar to the following message:

```
$ ssh server1.example.com
The authenticity of host 'server1.example.com (172.16.0.100)' can't be
established.
ED25519 key fingerprint is SHA256:DGKRTlWNwnQ2c7GroUFaG8XogUZLbEteVsHA2YI4YG8.
This key is not known by any other names
Are you sure you want to continue connecting (yes/no/[fingerprint])? Yes
Warning: Permanently added 'server1.example.com' (ED25519) to the list of
known hosts.
michael@server1.example.com's password:
```

Once connected via **ssh**, you can do anything on the remote system that's supported by your user privileges on that machine. For example, you can even shut down the remote system gracefully with the **poweroff** command if you have privileges to do so. After executing that command, you'll typically have a couple of seconds to exit the remote system with the **exit** command.

More SSH Command-Line Tools

If you prefer to access the remote system with an FTP-like client, the **sftp** command is for you. Although the **-l** switch doesn't have the same meaning of the **ssh** command, it still can be used to log in to the account of any user on the remote system. Whereas regular FTP communication proceeds in clear text, communication with the **sftp** command can be used to transfer files in encrypted format.

Alternatively, if you just want to transfer files over an encrypted connection, the **scp** command can help. For example, we created some of the screenshots for this book on the test VMs configured in Chapter 1. To transmit one of those screenshots to one of our systems, we used a command similar to the following, which copied the F02-07.tif file from the local directory to the remote system with the noted hostname, in the /home/michael/RHbook/Chapter2 directory:

```
# scp F02-07.tif michael@server1:/home/michael/RHbook/Chapter2/
```

Unless key-based authentication has been configured (as discussed in Chapter 8), the command prompts for the password of the user michael on the system named server1. Once the password is confirmed, the **scp** command transfers the F02-07.tif file in encrypted format to the noted directory on the remote system named server1.

Graphical Secure Shell Access

You can use the **ssh** command to forward the output of a GUI application over a network. As strange as it sounds, it works if the local system runs an X server while you call remote GUI client applications from remote systems.

By default, both the SSH server and client configuration files are set up to support X11 communication over a network. All you need to do is connect to the remote system with the **-X** switch (or **-Y** to use trusted X11 forwarding, which bypasses some security extension controls). For example, you could use the command sequence shown in Figure 3-7 to monitor the remote system.

FIGURE 3-7 Remote GUI access via SSH

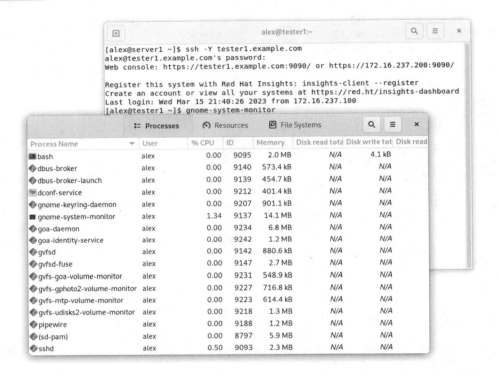

SCENARIO & SOLUTION

Networking is down.	Check physical connections. Run **ip link show** to check active interfaces. Run the **systemctl status NetworkManager** command. Check IP settings by running **ip addr show**.
Unable to access remote systems.	Use the **ping** and **traceroute** commands to test access to local and then remote IP addresses. On an IPv6 network, use **ping6** and **tracepath6**.
Current network settings lead to conflicts.	Check network device configuration in the /etc/NetworkManager/system-connections files. Review settings with the Network Manager Connection Editor.

(continued)

Hostname not recognized.	Review /etc/hostname, run the **hostname** command, and review /etc/hosts for consistency. Configure the hostname with **hostnamectl** if needed.
Remote hostnames not recognized.	Review /etc/hosts and /etc/nsswitch.conf. Check /etc/resolv.conf for an appropriate DNS server IP address. Run the **dig** command to test the DNS resolution.
You need to transfer a file to a remote system.	Use **scp** or **sftp**. You need an account on the remote server.

CERTIFICATION SUMMARY

Linux is inherently a network operating system. Network devices such as eth0 can be configured with both IPv4 and IPv6 addresses. Network review and configuration commands include **ip link show** and **ip addr show**. Additional related commands include **ss**, **ping**, and **tracepath**. Individual devices are configured in the /etc/NetworkManager/system-connections directory. Network devices can also be configured with the **nmcli** and **nmtui** commands at the console and the Network Manager Connection Editor.

Configuring hostname and name resolution is an essential skill. If you have not set a hostname at installation, run the **hostnamectl** command. While the RHCSA objectives do not cover the configuration of a DNS server, you must know how to configure a DNS client. The **nmcli** and **nmtui** commands and the Network Manager Connection Editor that you used to configure network interfaces also enable you to specify the IP address of a DNS server.

Once the network is configured, you do not need to access a system from its console, but you can access it remotely. The SSH service can help set up remote encrypted sessions between Linux systems. The RHCSA exam requires that you know how to use an SSH client and to securely transfer files between systems. You can use the **ssh** command to log in to remote systems; use the **ssh -Y** command to access trusted remote GUI applications; and use the **scp** command to copy files remotely over an encrypted connection.

TWO-MINUTE DRILL

Here are some of the key points from the certification objectives in Chapter 3.

A Networking Primer

❑ IPv4 addresses have 32 bits. There are five classes of IPv4 addresses and three different sets of private IPv4 addresses suitable for setting up TCP/IP on a private LAN.

❑ The subnet mask (also known as netmask or prefix) is used to find the network and host parts of an IP address.

❑ Tools such as **ping**, **traceroute**, **tracepath**, **ip**, and **ss** can help you diagnose problems on the LAN.

❑ Name resolution configuration files such as /etc/resolv.conf determine how a system finds the right IP address; the /etc/resolv.conf file may be configured from a DHCP server by Network Manager.

Network Configuration and Troubleshooting

❑ Individual network devices are configured in the /etc/NetworkManager/system-connections directory.

❑ Network configuration tools include the console-based **nmcli** and **nmtui** commands and the Network Manager Connection Editor.

❑ Name resolution configuration files include /etc/nsswitch.conf, /etc/hosts, and /etc/resolv.conf.

An Introduction to IPv6

❑ IPv6 addresses have 128 bits organized in groups of four nibbles (16 bits).

❑ The three different types of IPv6 addresses are unicast, anycast, and multicast.

❑ IPv6 addresses can be limited to local network segments (link-local) or routable.

Administration with Secure Shell and Secure Copy

❑ SSH is installed by default on RHEL 9. It's even accessible through default firewalls.

❑ The **ssh** command can be used to access remote systems securely. It can even enable access to remote GUI utilities.

❑ Related commands include **sftp** and **scp**.

SELF TEST

The following questions will help you measure your understanding of the material presented in this chapter. Because there are no multiple-choice questions on the Red Hat exams, there are no multiple-choice questions in this book. These questions exclusively test your understanding of the chapter. Getting results, not memorizing trivia, is what counts on the Red Hat exams.

A Networking Primer

1. In IPv4 addressing, with a network address of 192.168.100.0 and a broadcast address of 192.168.100.255, what is the range of assignable IP addresses?

2. Given the addresses described in Question 1, what **ip** command assigns the IPv4 address 192.168.100.100 to network device eth0?

3. What tools are available in RHEL 9 to configure the settings on a network device so that they persist after a system reboot?

4. What **nmcli** command creates a connection profile named "home" for the network interface eth0, with IP address 192.168.100.20/24, default gateway 192.168.100.254, and DNS server 192.168.100.254?

5. After configuring the connection profile as described in Question 4, what command brings up the new connection profile?

Network Configuration and Troubleshooting

6. What is the full path to the configuration file with the hostname of the local system?

7. What is the default full path to the configuration file associated with the connection profile of the eth0 Ethernet adapter for the local system?

An Introduction to IPv6

8. What is the shortest representation of the 2001:0db8:00aa:0000:04ba:0000:0000:00cd IPv6 address?

9. What command can you use to ping an IPv6 address?

Administration with Secure Shell and Secure Copy

10. What **ssh** command switch enables access to remote GUI utilities via X11 forwarding?

11. What command initiates a secure copy of the file /etc/hosts from the system server1.example.com to the /tmp directory on the local host?

LAB QUESTIONS

Red Hat presents its exams electronically. For that reason, the labs in this chapter are available from the companion website that accompanies the book. In case you haven't yet set up RHEL 9 on a system, refer to Chapter 1 for installation instructions. The answers for each lab follow the Self Test answers.

SELF TEST ANSWERS

A Networking Primer

1. The range of assignable IP addresses in the noted IPv4 network is 192.168.100.1 through 192.168.100.254.

2. Given the addresses described in Question 1, the **ip** command that assigns IPv4 address 192.168.100.100 to network device eth0 is **ip addr add 192.168.100.100/24 dev eth0**. Note that the settings configured with this command do not persist after a system reboot.

3. You can configure the settings on a network device so that they persist after a reboot using either **nmcli**, **nmtui**, or the Network Manager Connection Editor.

4. The following **nmcli** command creates a connection profile named "home" for the network interface eth0, with IP address 192.168.100.20/24, default gateway 192.168.100.254, and DNS server 192.168.100.254:

    ```
    # nmcli con add con-name home type ethernet ifname eth0 ipv4.addresses ↵
    192.168.100.20/24 ipv4.gateway 192.168.100.254 ipv4.dns 192.168.100.254
    ```

5. The following command brings up the network profile:

    ```
    nmcli con up home
    ```

Network Configuration and Troubleshooting

6. The full path to the configuration file with the hostname of the local system is /etc/hostname.

7. The default full path to the configuration file associated with the connection profile of the eth0 Ethernet adapter for the local system is /etc/NetworkManager/system-connections/eth0 .nmconnection. If you use different connection profiles in Network Manager, you would find a file for each connection profile within the /etc/NetworkManager/system-connections directory.

An Introduction to IPv6

8. The shortest representation of the 2001:0db8:00aa:0000:04ba:0000:0000:00cd IPv6 address is 2001:db8:aa:0:4ba::cd.

9. You can use the **ping6** command to ping an IPv6 address. If this is a link-local address, you need to specify the outbound interface with the **-I** switch.

Administration with Secure Shell and Secure Copy

10. The **ssh** command switch that enables access to trusted remote GUI utilities via X11 forwarding is -Y. The -X switch is also an acceptable answer.

11. The required command to securely copy /etc/hosts from server1 to /tmp on the local host is **scp server1.example.com:/etc/hosts /tmp/**.

LAB ANSWERS

Lab 1

This lab sets up an invalid IP address configuration for all connections present on the system.

1. Test connections to local and remote systems, such as the hostname or FQDN for the local system and the IP address of the nameserver in /etc/resolv.conf:

```
# ping server1.example.com
# ping 172.16.0.2
```

2. Check the link status and IP settings:

```
# ip addr show
```

3. Review applicable network configuration files. Can you identify the problem yet?

```
# cat /etc/NetworkManager/system-connections/*.nmconnection
```

4. If you can't identify the problem, open the Network Manager Connection Editor and review the information in the IPv4 settings of the connection profile:

```
# nm-connection-editor
```

5. The network configuration was altered by setting the wrong IP address and removing the default gateway settings. Open the Network Manager Connection Editor and manually restore the original configuration.

6. If you still have problems, restore the configuration from the backup files:

```
# cp /root/backup/*.nmconnection /etc/NetworkManager/system-connections/
# reboot
```

Lab 2

This lab deactivates all active network connection profiles on the system and reconfigures them to not connect after a reboot.

1. Test connections to local and remote systems, such as the hostname or FQDN for the local system and the IP address of the nameserver in /etc/resolv.conf:

```
# ping server1.example.com
# ping 172.16.0.2
```

2. Check the link status and IP settings:

```
# ip addr show
```

You should see that the network interface has no IP settings.

3. Open the Network Manager Connection Editor and check the connection IP settings:

```
# nm-connection-editor
```

4. List the active connections. The output of the commands should be blank:

```
# nmcli conn show --active
```

5. Using Network Manager Connection Editor, edit the connection profile and ensure that in the General tab the option "Connect automatically with priority" is selected. This should restore network connectivity.

6. If you still have problems, restore the configuration from the backup files:

```
# cp /root/backup/*.nmconnection /etc/NetworkManager/system-connections/
# reboot
```

Lab 3

This lab removes the DNS client configuration. You should find that IP connectivity works fine but name resolution fails.

1. Try pinging www.google.com. The command should fail.

```
# ping www.google.com
```

2. This indicates an issue with network resolution. If you check the contents of /etc/resolv.conf, you will find that the file is empty:

```
# cat /etc/resolv.conf
```

3. Open the Network Manager Connection Editor and manually restore the original configuration by editing the DNS server and search domains settings in the IPv4 Settings tab.

4. If you still have problems, restore the configuration from the backup files:

```
# cp /root/backup/*.nmconnection /etc/NetworkManager/system-connections/
# reboot
```

Lab 4

In this lab, you set up the /etc/hosts file on each of the systems described in Chapter 1. Except for the local system settings added by Network Manager, the data in /etc/hosts on the two systems may be identical. Specifically, that file should include the following entries:

```
172.16.0.100   server1.example.com server1
172.16.0.50   tester1.example.com tester1
```

Your IP addresses may differ, depending on the virtual network set up by your hypervisor, as discussed in Chapter 1.

Duplication with data inserted by Network Manager is not a problem, as long as the data is consistent. In fact, it's possible to set up multiple names for an IP address; for example, if you set up a web server on the 172.16.0.50 system, you could add the following entry to /etc/hosts:

```
172.16.0.50   www.example.com
```

Once you have completed the configuration, try pinging tester1.example.com from server1.example .com (and vice versa). Name resolution in /etc/hosts should work:

```
# ping server1.example.com
# ping tester1.example.com
```

Labs 5 and 6

These labs are guided exercises to let you become familiar with **nmtui** and the Network Manager Connection Editor. You should be able to follow all the steps and make configuration changes.

1. Once you have modified the IP configuration, test connectivity between the two virtual machines using the **ping** command (your IP address may differ):

   ```
   # ping 172.16.0.101
   ```

2. As a bonus task, try configuring IPv6 addresses on your test systems. For instance, configure the IPv6 address fd00::1/64 on server1.example.com and fd00::2/64 on tester1.example.com, and ensure that you can ping each other's IP address with **ping6** from each host:

   ```
   # ping6 fd00::1
   # ping6 fd00::2
   ```

3. If something goes wrong, you can restore the original configuration from the backup files:

   ```
   # cp /root/backup/*.nmconnection /etc/NetworkManager/system-connections/
   # reboot
   ```

Chapter 4

Software Management

CERTIFICATION OBJECTIVES

After installation is complete, systems are secured, filesystems are configured, and other initial setup tasks are completed, you still have work to do. Almost certainly before your system is in the state you desire, you will be required to install or remove packages. To make sure the right updates are installed, you need to know how to get a system working with Red Hat Subscription Management (RHSM) or the repository associated with a rebuild distribution.

To accomplish these tasks, you need to understand how to use the **rpm** and **dnf** commands in detail. Although these are "just" two commands, they are rich in detail. Entire books have been dedicated to the **rpm** command, such as the *Red Hat RPM Guide* by Eric Foster-Johnson. For many, that degree of in-depth knowledge of the **rpm** command is no longer necessary, given the capabilities of the **dnf** command and the additional package management tools provided in RHEL 9.

INSIDE THE EXAM

Administrative Skills

As the management of RPM packages is a fundamental skill for Red Hat administrators, you should expect to use the **rpm**, **dnf**, and related commands on the RHCSA exam. The RHCSA objectives include one specific requirement addressed in this chapter:

- Install and update software packages from Red Hat Network, a remote repository, or from the local filesystem

The RHCSA exam for RHEL 8 also included the following objective:

- Work with package module streams

Although this objective is no longer included in the RHCSA exam objectives for RHEL 9, working with package module streams is still an important topic and might be restored in future revisions of the exam objectives. For this reason, we have included an optional section in this chapter to explain how module streams work. However, feel free to skip this section or return to it later, assuming that it still is not relevant for your exam preparation after this book is published.

Another closely related objective requires knowledge of the **tar** archiving utility, which is covered in Chapter 9. Before Red Hat introduced RPM packages, tar archives were the standard method for distributing software.

Now let's break down these skills a bit. First, we will introduce the **rpm** command. This is a very powerful software management tool, but lacks two important features that are provided by **dnf**: the management and installation of dependencies, which is software that is required by another software package; and the ability to work with repositories, which are collections of software packages accessible on a local filesystem or over the network. To work with **dnf**, you will configure access to Red Hat Subscription Management (RHSM) to download software packages. You can also use the same **dnf** commands to install and update packages from a remote third-party repository. Since RHEL 8, Red Hat also offers a new concept to support the distribution of different versions of the same application: this is the purpose of module streams.

CERTIFICATION OBJECTIVE 4.01

The RPM Package Manager

One of the major duties of a system administrator is software management. This includes installing new applications, updating services, and patching kernels. Without the right tools, it can be difficult to figure out what software is on a system, what is the latest update, and what applications depend on other software. Worse, you may install a new software package only to find it has overwritten a crucial file from a currently installed package.

on the
ⓘob
As previously indicated, since RHEL 8, Red Hat introduced a new default package manager, dnf, also known as "Dandified YUM" or DNF. The yum command, which was the default package manager in RHEL 7, is simply a symbolic link to dnf in RHEL 9. However, you do not need to know all the differences between dnf and yum to pass the RHCSA exam. For more information about the changes between dnf and yum, go to https://dnf.readthedocs.io.

RPM is a recursive acronym for RPM Package Manager (formerly Red Hat Package Manager). RPM was designed to alleviate the software management problems just discussed. With RPM, software is managed in discrete *packages*. An RPM package includes the software with instructions for adding, removing, and upgrading those files. When properly used, the RPM tool can back up key configuration files before proceeding with upgrades and removals. It can also help you identify the currently installed version of any RPM-based application.

RPMs and the **rpm** command are very focused on individual packages, which in many cases is far from ideal and is why **rpm** has been supplemented with the **dnf** command. With a connection to a repository such as that available from RHSM you'll be able to use **dnf** to satisfy dependencies automatically.

What Is a Package?

In the generic sense, an RPM package is a container of files. It includes the group of files associated with a specific program or application, which normally contains binary files, installation scripts, and configuration and documentation files. It also includes instructions on how and where these files should be installed and uninstalled.

An RPM package name usually consists of the version, the release, and the architecture for which it was built. For example, the fictional penguin-3.4.5-26.el9.x86_64.rpm package is version 3.4.5, release 26.el9. The x86_64 indicates that it is suitable for computers built to the AMD/Intel 64-bit architecture.

Many RPM packages include software compiled for a specific CPU type (for example, x86_64). You can identify the CPU type for the system with the uname -i **or** uname -p **command. More information about your processor can be found in /proc/cpuinfo.**

What Is the RPM Database?

At the heart of this system is the RPM database, which is stored locally on each machine in the /var/lib/rpm directory. Among other things, this database tracks the version and location of every file in each RPM. The RPM database also maintains an MD5 checksum of each file. With the checksum, you can use the **rpm -V** *package* command to determine whether any file from that RPM package has changed. The RPM database makes it easy to add, remove, and upgrade individual packages because it's configured to know which files to handle and where to put them.

RPM also manages conflicts between packages. For example, assume you have a package that installs a configuration file, and you want to update from an older to a newer version of the software. Call the original configuration file /etc/*someconfig*.conf. You've already installed package X. If you then try to install a more recent version of package X, the RPM package can be configured to preserve the original configuration file and install the new one as /etc/*someconfig*.conf.rpmnew.

Alternatively, the RPM creator can build the RPM in such a way that it will back up the original /etc/*someconfig*.conf file (with a filename such as /etc/*someconfig*.conf.rpmsave) before upgrading package X and then replace the configuration file with a new version. This may occur if the format of the old configuration file is incompatible with the new release of the software.

Although RPM upgrades are supposed to preserve or save existing configuration files, there are no guarantees, especially if the RPM is created by someone other than Red Hat. It's best to back up all applicable configuration files before upgrading any associated RPM package.

What Is a Repository?

RPM packages are frequently organized into repositories. Generally, such repositories include groups of packages with different functions. For example, the Red Hat Customer Portal gives access to the following RHEL 9 Server repositories:

- **BaseOS**   The main repository, which includes the packages associated with the core RHEL 9 system, along with updates
- **AppStream**   A large group of open-source applications, which includes databases and run-time languages

Each repository includes a database of packages in a repodata/ subdirectory. That database includes information on each package and allows installation requests to include all dependencies. If you have a subscription to RHSM, access to the Red Hat repositories is enabled in the product-id.conf and subscription-manager.conf files, in the /etc/dnf/plugins directory. Those files are discussed later in this chapter.

on the
() o b

A dependency is a package that needs to be installed to make sure all the features of a target package work as designed.

Install an RPM Package

There are three basic commands that *may* install an RPM. They won't work if the RPM to install requires any dependencies. For example, if you haven't installed the SELinux policy DBUS (policycoreutils-dbus) and development tool package (policycoreutils-devel) and try to install the SELinux configuration GUI (policycoreutils-gui), you'll get the following message (version numbers may vary):

```
# rpm -i policycoreutils-gui-3.4-4.el9.noarch.rpm
error: Failed dependencies:
        policycoreutils-dbus = 3.4-4.el9 is needed by↵
policycoreutils-gui-3.4-4.el9.noarch
        policycoreutils-devel = 3.4-4.el9 is needed by↵
policycoreutils-gui-3.4-4.el9.noarch
```

One way to test this is to mount the RHEL 9 DVD with the **mount /dev/cdrom /media** command. Next, find the noted policycoreutils-gui package in the AppStream/Packages/ subdirectory. Alternatively, you could download that package directly from the Red Hat Customer Portal or a configured repository with the **dnf download policycoreutils-gui** command. This and other **dnf** commands are discussed later in this chapter. Be aware that some Linux GUI desktop environments automatically mount a CD/DVD media that is inserted into an associated drive. If so, you'll see the mount directory in the output to the **mount** command.

When dependency messages are shown, **rpm** does not install the given package. Note the dependency messages: policycoreutils-gui requires the policycoreutils-dbus and policycoreutils-devel packages of the same version number.

on the
() o b

Sure, you can use the --nodeps **option to make** rpm **ignore dependencies, but that can lead to other problems, unless you install those dependencies as soon as possible. The best option is to use an appropriate** dnf **command, described later in this chapter. In this case, a** dnf install policycoreutils-gui **command would automatically install the other dependent RPM as well.**

If you're not stopped by dependencies, the following three basic commands can install RPM packages:

```
# rpm -i packagename
# rpm -U packagename
# rpm -F packagename
```

The **rpm -i** option installs the package, if it isn't already installed. The **rpm -U** option upgrades any existing package or installs it if an earlier version isn't already installed. The **rpm -F** option upgrades only existing packages. It does not install a package if it wasn't previously installed.

We like to add the **-vh** options with the **rpm** command. These options add verbose mode and use hash marks that can help monitor the progress of the installation. So when we use **rpm** to install a package, we run the following command:

```
# rpm -ivh packagename-version.arch.rpm
```

There's one more thing associated with a properly designed RPM package. When unpacking a package, the **rpm** command checks to see whether it would overwrite any configuration files. The **rpm** command tries to make intelligent decisions about what to do in this situation. As suggested earlier, if the **rpm** command chooses to replace an existing configuration file, it provides a warning (in most cases) similar to this:

```
# rpm -U penguin-3.4.5-26.el9.x86_64.rpm
warning: /etc/someconfig.conf saved as /etc/someconfig.conf.rpmsave
```

The **rpm** command normally works in the same fashion when a package is erased with the **-e** switch. If a configuration file has been changed, it's also saved with an .rpmsave extension in the same directory.

It's up to you to look at both files and determine what modifications, if any, need to be made. Of course, as not every RPM package is perfect, there's always a risk that such an update would overwrite that critical customized configuration file. In that case, backups are important.

In general, the **rpm** commands to upgrade a package work only if the package being installed is of a newer version. Sometimes, an older version of a package is desirable. As long as there are no security issues with the older package, administrators may be more comfortable with slightly older releases. Bugs that may be a problem on a newer package may not exist in an older version of that package. So if you want to "downgrade" a package with the **rpm -i**, **-U**, or **-F** command, the **--force** switch can help.

on the job **If you've already customized a package and then upgraded it with** rpm, **check if there is a saved configuration file ending with an .rpmnew extension. Use it as a guide to change the settings in the new configuration file. But remember, with upgrades, there may be additional required changes. Therefore, you should test the result for every conceivable production environment.**

Uninstall an RPM Package

The **rpm -e** command uninstalls a package. But first, RPM checks a few things. It performs a dependency check to make sure no other packages need what you're trying to uninstall. If dependent packages are found, **rpm -e** fails with an error message identifying these packages. With properly configured RPMs, if you have modified related configuration files, RPM makes a copy of the file, adds an .rpmsave extension to the end of the filename, and then erases the original. It can then proceed with the uninstallation. When the process is complete, it removes the package from the database.

on the **Job**

Be very careful about which packages you remove from a system. Like many other Linux utilities, rpm may silently let you shoot yourself in the foot. For example, if you were to remove the packages that include the running kernel, it could render that system unusable at the next boot.

Install RPMs from Remote Systems

With the RPM system, you can even specify package locations similar to an Internet address, in URL format. For example, if you want to apply the **rpm** command to the foo.rpm package on the /pub directory of the ftp.rpmdownloads.com FTP server, you can install this package with a command such as the following:

```
# rpm -ivh ftp://ftp.rpmdownloads.com/pub/foo.rpm
```

Assuming you have a network connection to that remote server, this particular **rpm** command logs on to the FTP server anonymously and downloads the file. Unfortunately, an attempt to use wildcards in the package name with this command leads to an error message associated with "file not found." The complete package name is required, which can be an annoyance.

If the FTP server requires a username and password, you can include them in the following format:

```
ftp://username:password@hostname:port/path/to/remote/package.rpm
```

where *username* and *password* are the username and password you need to log on to this system, and *port*, if required, specifies a nonstandard port used on the remote FTP server.

Based on the preceding example, if the username is **mjang** and the password is **Ila451MS**, you could install an RPM directly from a remote server with the following command:

```
# rpm -ivh ftp://mjang:Ila451MS@192.168.122.1/pub/inst/ ↵
policycoreutils-gui-3.4-4.el9.x86_64.rpm
```

RPM Installation Security

Security can be a concern, especially with RPM packages downloaded over the Internet. If a "black hat" hacker were to somehow be able to modify the content of a third-party repository, how would you know that packages from those sources were genuine? The key is GNU Privacy Guard (GPG), which is the open-source implementation of Pretty Good Privacy (PGP). If an RPM file is signed using a private GPG key, the integrity of the package can be verified with the corresponding public GPG key. A valid signature also ensures that the package has been signed by an authorized party and does not come from a malicious hacker.

If you haven't imported or installed the Red Hat public GPG keys, you might have noticed something similar to the following message when packages are installed:

```
warning: vsftpd-3.0.3-49.el9.x86_64.rpm: Header V3 RSA/SHA256 ↵
Signature, key ID fd431d51: NOKEY
```

If you're concerned about security, this warning should raise alarm bells. During the RHEL 9 installation process, GPG keys are stored in the /etc/pki/rpm-gpg directory. Take a look at the contents of this directory. You'll find files such as RPM-GPG-KEY-redhat-release. To actually use the key to verify packages, it has to be imported—and the command to import the GPG key is fairly simple:

```
# rpm --import /etc/pki/rpm-gpg/RPM-GPG-KEY-redhat-release
```

If there's no output, the **rpm** command probably successfully imported the GPG key. The GPG key is now included in the RPM database, which can be verified with the **rpm -qa gpg-pubkey** command.

In the /etc/pki/rpm-gpg directory, there are normally two GPG keys available, as described in Table 4-1.

Later in this chapter, you'll see how GPG keys are imported automatically from remote repositories when new packages are installed.

Updating the Kernel

Kernel updates incorporate new features, address security issues, and generally help Linux systems work better. However, kernel updates can go wrong and prevent systems booting or cause applications to break; this is particularly common if specialized packages that depend on an existing version of a kernel have been installed.

TABLE 4-1	GPG Key	Description
GPG Keys to Verify Software Updates	RPM-GPG-KEY-redhat-beta	Packages built for the RHEL 9 beta
	RPM-GPG-KEY-redhat-release	Released packages for RHEL 9

If you are aware of any software that relies on a custom kernel module, don't upgrade a kernel if you're not ready to repeat every step taken to customize software with the existing kernel, whether that be obtaining new closed-source kernel modules from the vendor for the new version, rebuilding specialized modules for the new kernel, or performing other manual work. For example, the drivers for a few wireless network cards and printers without in-tree open-source drivers may be tied to a specific version of a kernel. Some virtual machine software components (not including KVM) may be installed against a specific version of a kernel.

If you see an available update for a kernel RPM, the temptation is to run the **rpm -U** *newkernel* command. Don't do it! It overwrites your existing kernel, and if the updated kernel doesn't work with the system, you're out of luck. (Well, not completely out of luck, but if you reboot and have problems, you'll have to use rescue mode, discussed in Chapter 5, to boot the system and reinstall the existing kernel. In the days when there were separate Troubleshooting and System Maintenance sections on the RHCE exam, that might have made for an interesting test scenario.) The best option for upgrading to a new kernel is to install it, specifically with a command such as this:

```
# rpm -ivh newkernel
```

If you're connected to an appropriate repository, the following command works equally well:

```
# dnf install kernel
```

This installs the new kernel, along with related files, side by side with the current working kernel. One example of the result is shown in Figure 4-1, in the output to the **ls /boot** command.

on the
Ĵob

It is also safe to install a new kernel by running dnf update kernel. **In fact, by default, dnf is configured to always install a kernel package and leave any old kernel in place. This applies to a maximum of three kernels installed at the same time.**

FIGURE 4-1

New and existing kernel files in the /boot directory

```
[root@server1 ~]# ls /boot
config-5.14.0-162.6.1.el9_1.x86_64
config-5.14.0-284.11.1.el9_2.x86_64
efi
grub2
initramfs-0-rescue-5cf7267e8cbd4ed6951e03a7e0e357d4.img
initramfs-5.14.0-162.6.1.el9_1.x86_64.img
initramfs-5.14.0-162.6.1.el9_1.x86_64kdump.img
initramfs-5.14.0-284.11.1.el9_2.x86_64.img
loader
symvers-5.14.0-162.6.1.el9_1.x86_64.gz
symvers-5.14.0-284.11.1.el9_2.x86_64.gz
System.map-5.14.0-162.6.1.el9_1.x86_64
System.map-5.14.0-284.11.1.el9_2.x86_64
vmlinuz-0-rescue-5cf7267e8cbd4ed6951e03a7e0e357d4
vmlinuz-5.14.0-162.6.1.el9_1.x86_64
vmlinuz-5.14.0-284.11.1.el9_2.x86_64
[root@server1 ~]# 
```

File	Description
config-*	Kernel configuration settings; a text file
efi/	Files required at boot by the UEFI firmware
grub2/	Directory with GRUB configuration files
initramfs-*	The initial RAM disk filesystem, a root filesystem called during the boot process to help load other kernel components, such as block device modules
loader/	Boot configuration options for each kernel that is installed on the system
System.map-*	Map of system names for variables and functions, with their locations in memory
vmlinuz-*	The actual Linux kernel

Table 4-2 briefly describes the different files for the various parts of the boot process in the /boot directory.

The installation of a new kernel adds options to boot the new kernel in the GRUB configuration file (/boot/grub2/grub.cfg), without erasing existing options. By default, the system will boot with the newly installed kernel. Therefore, if that kernel does not work, you can restart the system, access the GRUB menu, and then boot from the older, previously working kernel.

CERTIFICATION OBJECTIVE 4.02

More RPM Commands

The **rpm** command is rich with details. All this book can do is cover some of the basic ways **rpm** can help you manage RHEL. You've already read about how **rpm** can install and upgrade packages in various ways. Queries can help you identify what's installed in detail. Verification tools can help you check the integrity of packages and individual files. You can use related tools to help identify the purpose of different RPMs and to compile a full list of RPMs already installed.

| TABLE 4-3 | rpm --query Options |

rpm Query Command	Meaning
rpm -qa	Lists all installed packages.
rpm -qf /path/to/file	Identifies the package associated with /path/to/file.
rpm -qc *packagename*	Lists only configuration files from *packagename*.
rpm -qd *packagename*	Lists only documentation files from *packagename*.
rpm -qi *packagename*	Displays basic information for *packagename*.
rpm -ql *packagename*	Lists all files from *packagename*.
rpm -qR *packagename*	Notes all dependencies; you can't install *packagename* without them.
rpm -q --changelog *packagename*	Displays change information for *packagename*.

Package Queries

The simplest **rpm** query verifies whether a specific package is installed. The following command verifies the installation of the systemd package (the version number may vary):

```
# rpm -q systemd
systemd-250-12.el9_1.x86_64
```

You can do more with **rpm** queries, as described in Table 4-3. Note how queries can be performed either with **-q** or **--query**; full-word switches such as **--query** are usually associated with a double-dash.

If you want to query an RPM package file rather than the local RPM database, all you have to do is add the **-p** switch and specify the path or URL of the package file. As an example, the following command lists all files of the RPM package epel-release-latest-9.noarch.rpm:

```
# rpm -qlp epel-release-latest-9.noarch.rpm
```

Package Signatures

RPM uses several methods for checking the integrity of a package. You've seen how to import the GPG key. Some of the available methods are shown when you verify a package with the **rpm --checksig** *pkg.rpm* command. (The -K switch is equivalent to **--checksig**.)

For example, if you've downloaded a package from a third party such as the hypothetical pkg-1.2.3-4.noarch.rpm package and want to check it against the imported GPG keys, run the following command (**-v** makes the output verbose):

```
# rpm --checksig -v pkg-1.2.3-4.noarch.rpm
```

If successful, you'll see output similar to the following:

```
pkg-1.2.3-4.noarch.rpm:
    Header V3 RSA/SHA256 Signature, key ID fd431d51: OK
    Header SHA256 digest: OK
    Header SHA1 digest: OK
    Payload SHA256 digest: OK
    V3 RSA/SHA256 Signature, key ID fd431d51: OK
    MD5 digest: OK
```

This guarantees that the package is authentic and the RPM file was not modified by a third party. You may already recognize the algorithms used to verify package integrity:

- **rsa** Named for its creators, Rivest, Shamir, and Adleman, it's a public key encryption algorithm.
- **sha1** Secure Hash Algorithm-1, a cryptographic hash function that produces a 160-bit hash value.
- **sha256** A cryptographic hash function that produces a 256-bit hash value.
- **md5** Message Digest 5, a cryptographic hash function that produces a 128-bit hash value.

File Verification

The verification of an installed package compares information about that package with information from the RPM database on a system. The **--verify** (or **-V**) switch checks the size, MD5 checksum, permissions, type, owner, and group of each file in the package. Verification can be done in a number of ways. Here are a few examples:

- Verify all files. Naturally, this may take a long time on your system. (Of course, the **rpm -Va** command performs the same function.)
  ```
  # rpm --verify -a
  ```
- Verify all files within a package against a downloaded RPM.
  ```
  # rpm --verify -p vsftpd-3.0.3-49.el9.x86_64.rpm
  ```
- Verify a file associated with a particular package.
  ```
  # rpm --verify --file /bin/ls
  ```

	Failure Code	Meaning
TABLE 4-4	S	File size
rpm --verify Codes	M	Mode (permissions)
	5	MD5 Digest
	D	Device file
	L	Symbolic link
	U	User ownership
	G	Group ownership
	T	File modification time
	P	Capabilities

If the integrity of the files or packages is verified, you will see no output. Any output means that a file or package is different from the original. There's no need to panic if certain changes appear; after all, administrators do edit configuration files. There are nine tests. If there has been a change, the output is a string of up to eight failure code characters, each of which tells you what happened during each test.

If you see a dot (.), that test passed. The following example shows /bin/vi with an incorrect group ID assignment:

```
# rpm --verify --file /bin/vi
......G..   /bin/vi
```

Table 4-4 lists the failure codes and their meanings.

Now here's an interesting experiment: When you have one version of a package installed, use the **rpm --verify -p** command with a second version of the same package. Finding such a package should not be too difficult because Red Hat updates packages for feature updates, security patches, and, yes, bug fixes frequently. For example, when we wrote this book for RHEL 9, we had access to both sssd-client-2.7.3-4.el9.x86_64.rpm and sssd-client-2.8.2-2 .el9.x86_64.rpm. When the latter version was installed, we ran the command

```
# rpm --verify -p sssd-client-2.7.3-4.el9.x86_64.rpm
```

and got a whole list of changed files, as shown in Figure 4-2. This command provides information on what was changed between different versions of the sssd-client package.

FIGURE 4-2

Verifying changes
between packages

```
[root@server1 ~]# rpm --verify -p sssd-client-2.7.3-4.el9.x86_64.rpm
..5....T.   /usr/lib64/cifs-utils/cifs_idmap_sss.so
S.5....T.   /usr/lib64/krb5/plugins/authdata/sssd_pac_plugin.so
..5....T.   /usr/lib64/krb5/plugins/libkrb5/sssd_krb5_locator_plugin.so
S.5....T.   /usr/lib64/libnss_sss.so.2
S.5....T.   /usr/lib64/libsubid_sss.so
S.5....T.   /usr/lib64/security/pam_sss.so
S.5....T.   /usr/lib64/security/pam_sss_gss.so
..5....T.   /usr/lib64/sssd/modules/sssd_krb5_localauth_plugin.so
.......T. l /usr/share/licenses/sssd-client/COPYING
.......T. l /usr/share/licenses/sssd-client/COPYING.LESSER
S.5....T. d /usr/share/man/es/man8/sssd_krb5_locator_plugin.8.gz
S.5....T. d /usr/share/man/man8/pam_sss.8.gz
S.5....T. d /usr/share/man/man8/pam_sss_gss.8.gz
S.5....T. d /usr/share/man/man8/sssd_krb5_localauth_plugin.8.gz
S.5....T. d /usr/share/man/man8/sssd_krb5_locator_plugin.8.gz
S.5....T. d /usr/share/man/ru/man8/pam_sss.8.gz
S.5....T. d /usr/share/man/ru/man8/pam_sss_gss.8.gz
S.5....T. d /usr/share/man/ru/man8/sssd_krb5_locator_plugin.8.gz
S.5....T. d /usr/share/man/sv/man8/pam_sss.8.gz
S.5....T. d /usr/share/man/sv/man8/pam_sss_gss.8.gz
S.5....T. d /usr/share/man/sv/man8/sssd_krb5_locator_plugin.8.gz
S.5....T. d /usr/share/man/uk/man8/pam_sss.8.gz
S.5....T. d /usr/share/man/uk/man8/pam_sss_gss.8.gz
S.5....T. d /usr/share/man/uk/man8/sssd_krb5_locator_plugin.8.gz
[root@server1 ~]# ▮
```

EXERCISE 4-1

Practice with rpm Commands

In this exercise, you'll practice with some of the **rpm** command options that we have
described so far.

1. In VMware Workstation (or the hosted hypervisor application that you are using),
   select your server1 VM and click Edit Virtual Machine Settings.

2. Mount the RHEL 9 ISO file that you downloaded in Chapter 1. To do so, in the
   Settings window select CD/DVD (SATA) and click Use ISO Image. Browse and select
   the path of the RHEL 9 ISO image. Ensure that the option Connected is selected.

3. Log in to the system and type the **df** command. If the DVD was automounted,
   you should see an entry in the **df** output that shows that the DVD is available at a
   directory path such as /run/media/*yourusername*/RHEL-9-1-0-BaseOS-x86_64. If
   for some reason you do not see the DVD being mounted, you can mount it manually
   by entering the following command (as root):

```
# mount /dev/cdrom /media
```

4. Change the directory to the directory where the DVD is mounted by entering either

```
# cd /run/media/yourusername/RHEL-9-1-0-BaseOS-x86_64
```

or, if you mounted the DVD manually,

```
# cd /media
```

5. List the content of this directory. You should notice that there are two directories, BaseOS and AppStream, which include the RPM packages of the BaseOS and AppStream repositories.

```
# ls
```

6. Change to the BaseOS/Packages/ directory and list its contents:

```
# cd BaseOS/Packages
# ls
```

7. Find information about the RPM package tmux (the exact version of the package may differ, depending on which version of the RHEL 9 DVD you have mounted):

```
# rpm -qpi tmux-3.2a-4.el9.x86_64.rpm
```

8. Check if the tmux package is installed by entering the following command. In a typical Red Hat installation, you should find that this package is not present.

```
# rpm -q tmux
```

9. Install the tmux RPM package:

```
# rpm -ivh tmux-3.2a-4.el9.x86_64.rpm
```

10. List the files that have been created after the installation of the tmux package:

```
# rpm -ql tmux
```

CERTIFICATION OBJECTIVE 4.03

Dependencies and the dnf Command

The **dnf** command makes it easy to add and remove software packages to and from a system. It maintains a database regarding the proper way to add, upgrade, and remove packages. This makes it relatively simple to add and remove software with a single command. That single command overcame what was known as "dependency hell."

The **dnf** command extends the capabilities of **yum**, which was originally developed for an old Linux distribution now discontinued, Yellow Dog Linux. The name of the command is based on the Yellowdog Updater, Modified (YUM). Given the trouble associated with dependency hell, Linux users were motivated to find a solution. The **yum** command was adapted for Red Hat distributions with the help of developers from Duke University.

The configuration of **dnf** depends on package libraries known as repositories. Red Hat repositories are available through Red Hat Subscription Management, while repositories of third-party rebuild distributions use their own publicly available servers. In either case, it's important to know the workings of the **dnf** command as well as how it installs and updates individual packages and package groups.

An Example of Dependency Hell

To understand more about the need for the **dnf** command, examine Figure 4-3. This **rpm** command tries to install the **gcc** compiler, but fails because some dependencies are missing. Although how to use a compiler is not an exam requirement, the associated package dependencies will illustrate the need for **dnf**.

You could try to use the **rpm** command to install each of these packages. To do so, take the following steps:

1. Include the RHEL 9 DVD. Insert it into its drive, or make sure it's included in the configuration for the target virtual machine.

2. Unless it's already mounted, mount that DVD with the following command. Of course, a different empty directory can be substituted for /media.

   ```
   # mount /dev/cdrom /media
   ```

3. Navigate to the directory where the DVD is mounted (that is, /media or some subdirectory of /media).

4. The RPM packages on the RHEL 9 DVD can be found in the BaseOS/Packages/ and AppStream/Packages/ subdirectories of the DVD. Navigate to the AppStream/Packages directory of the DVD.

FIGURE 4-3   Excerpt of the packages required to install the gcc RPM

```
[root@server1 Packages]# rpm -ivh gcc-11.3.1-2.1.el9.x86_64.rpm
error: Failed dependencies:
        glibc-devel >= 2.2.90-12 is needed by gcc-11.3.1-2.1.el9.x86_64
        (annobin if (gcc or clang)) is needed by (installed) redhat-rpm-config-1
99-1.el9.noarch
        (gcc-plugin-annobin if gcc) is needed by (installed) redhat-rpm-config-1
99-1.el9.noarch
[root@server1 Packages]# █
```

FIGURE 4-4   These packages have dependencies.

```
[root@server1 Packages]# rpm -ivh gcc-11.3.1-2.1.el9.x86_64.rpm glibc-devel-2.34
-40.el9_64.x86_64.rpm annobin-10.73-3.el9.x86_64.rpm gcc-plugin-annobin-11.3.1-2.1.
el9.x86_64.rpm
error: Failed dependencies:
        glibc-headers = 2.34-40.el9 is needed by glibc-devel-2.34-40.el9.x86_64
        kernel-headers >= 3.2 is needed by glibc-devel-2.34-40.el9.x86_64
        libxcrypt-devel(x86-64) >= 4.0.0 is needed by glibc-devel-2.34-40.el9.x8
6_64
[root@server1 Packages]# █
```

FIGURE 4-5   There are even more dependencies.

```
[root@server1 Packages]# rpm -ivh gcc-11.3.1-2.1.el9.x86_64.rpm glibc-devel-2.34
-40.el9.x86_64.rpm annobin-10.73-3.el9.x86_64.rpm gcc-plugin-annobin-11.3.1-2.1.
el9.x86_64.rpm glibc-headers-2.34-40.el9.x86_64.rpm kernel-headers-5.14.0-162.6.
1.el9_1.x86_64.rpm libxcrypt-devel-4.4.18-3.el9.x86_64.rpm
```

5. Enter the **rpm -ivh** command, and then type in the names of the packages listed in Figure 4-3. It may be easiest to use command completion for this purpose; for example, if you were to type in

   ```
   # rpm -ivh glibc-devel-
   ```

   you could then press the TAB key twice and review available packages that start with **glibc-devel-**. You could then enter additional letters and press the TAB key again to complete the name of the package.

6. After a bit of work, you'd end up with something similar to the command and results shown in Figure 4-4. What actually appears depends on the current revision level of each package, as well as what's already installed on the local system.

7. The next step is to try to include the missing dependencies in the list of packages to be installed. When we try this step, it leads to the command and results shown in Figure 4-5.

At this point, we do not have more dependencies to install, but for some RPM packages there could be even more levels of dependent packages to include. This pain is known as dependency hell.

Relief from Dependency Hell

Before **yum** and **dnf**, some attempts to use the **rpm** command were stopped by the dependencies described earlier. Sure, you could install those dependent packages with the same command, but what if those dependencies themselves have dependencies? That perhaps is the biggest advantage of the **yum** and **dnf** commands.

Before **yum**, RHEL incorporated dependency resolution into the update process. Through RHEL 4, this was done with **up2date**. Red Hat incorporated **yum** starting with RHEL 5. Since RHEL 8, **yum** is a symbolic link to **dnf**, the next-generation package manager, which supports all the **yum** command options and more.

With **dnf**, all you need to do to install the packages listed in Figure 4-4 is run the following command:

```
# dnf install gcc
```

If so prompted, accept the request to install additional dependent packages, and then all of the noted dependencies are installed automatically. (Yes, the -**y** switch would perform the same function.) If updates are available from connected repositories, the latest available version of each package is installed. The **dnf** command is described in more detail later in this chapter.

But if you're running RHEL 9 without a connection to Red Hat Subscription Management, nothing happens. Shortly, you'll see how to do so.

A number of third-party repositories are available for RHEL. They include several popular applications that are not supported by Red Hat. For example, one of the authors of this book uses an external repository to install packages associated with his laptop wireless network card.

Although the owners of these repositories work closely with some Red Hat developers, there are some reports where dependencies required from one repository are unavailable from other repositories, leading to a different form of "dependency hell." However, the more popular third-party repositories are excellent; we have never encountered dependency hell when using these repositories.

on the
ⓘob
There are two main reasons why Red Hat does not include most proven and popular packages available from third-party repositories. Some are not released under open-source licenses, and others are packages that Red Hat simply chooses not to support.

Red Hat Subscription Management

Relief from dependency hell depends on the proper configuration of **dnf**. You need to know not only how to configure **dnf** to connect to repositories over the Internet but also how to configure **dnf** to connect to repositories on a local network.

The RHCSA exam objectives require candidates to be able to "install and update software packages from Red Hat Network." As previously mentioned, while the Red Hat Network has been succeeded by Red Hat Subscription Management, the exam objective continues to refer to this service by its legacy name. Access to Red Hat Subscription Management is provided over the Internet or over a local Red Hat Satellite server.

Perhaps the key benefit of Red Hat Satellite (or an alternative such as Spacewalk or Katello) is the ability to store software packages on a local system on the network. Once an appropriate connection is configured from the client systems, Satellite Server can even run remote commands on any schedule. If you're administering a whole bunch of systems, Red Hat Satellite supports configuration of systems in groups. For example, if there are 10 systems configured as RHEL 9–based web servers, you can configure those systems as a single group. You can then schedule a single command that's applied to all of those systems remotely. For more information on Red Hat Satellite, see the latest version of the documentation, available from https://access.redhat.com/products/. However, this is out of scope for the RHCSA exam.

If you have enrolled in the Red Hat Developer Program, as explained in Chapter 1, you are entitled to use a Red Hat Developer subscription. Exercise 4-2 explains how to subscribe your system to the RHSM.

EXERCISE 4-2

Subscribe a System to Red Hat Subscription Management

1. If you haven't done so already, join the Red Hat Developer Program and register at https://developers.redhat.com. If you do not have an account, create a new one.

2. Point the browser to https://access.redhat.com/management/subscriptions/. You should see a Red Hat Developer Subscription for Individuals in your inventory. This subscription allows you to register a RHEL system and download updates from RHSM.

3. Log in to the server1.example.com system that you installed in Chapter 1. Run the following command to register this system with RHSM. You will be prompted to type your Red Hat account username and password. If the system is already registered, use the --**force** command option to re-register the machine.

    ```
    # subscription-manager register
    ```

4. Subscribe the system to a Red Hat product. In the following command, the --auto option finds the most appropriate subscription (which will be the Red Hat Developer subscription, if you don't have any others):

    ```
    # subscription-manager attach --auto
    ```

5. Alternatively, list all available subscriptions. Take note of the pool IDs.

    ```
    # subscription-manager list --available
    ```

    Then, use the pool ID that you have retrieved from the last command to attach a system to a subscription:

    ```
    # subscription-manager attach ↵
    --pool= 2c946b9b880c497b0188123f741671eb
    ```

6. Review current settings. Run the following command to list the subscriptions attached to the system:

```
# subscription-manager list
```

The command output should be similar to that shown here:

```
[root@server1 ~]# subscription-manager list
+----------------------------------------------+
      Installed Product Status
+----------------------------------------------+
Product Name:   Red Hat Enterprise Linux for x86_64
Product ID:     479
Version:        9.2
Arch:           x86_64
Status:         Subscribed
Status Details:
Starts:         05/11/2023
Ends:           05/10/2024

[root@server1 ~]# █
```

7. Show all available repositories available for the system:

```
# subscription-manager repos
```

8. Show the repositories currently enabled:

```
# subscription-manager repos --list-enabled
```

The command output should be similar to the following:

```
[root@server1 ~]# subscription-manager repos --list-enabled
+----------------------------------------------------------+
      Available Repositories in /etc/yum.repos.d/redhat.repo
+----------------------------------------------------------+
Repo ID:   rhel-9-for-x86_64-baseos-rpms
Repo Name: Red Hat Enterprise Linux 9 for x86_64 - BaseOS (RPMs)
Repo URL:  https://cdn.redhat.com/content/dist/rhel9/$releasever/x86_64/baseos/os
Enabled:   1

Repo ID:   rhel-9-for-x86_64-appstream-rpms
Repo Name: Red Hat Enterprise Linux 9 for x86_64 - AppStream (RPMs)
Repo URL:  https://cdn.redhat.com/content/dist/rhel9/$releasever/x86_64/appstream/os
Enabled:   1

[root@server1 ~]# █
```

9. You can enable additional repositories with the following command:

```
# subscription-manager repos --enable=REPOID
```

10. Confirm with the following **dnf** command that the system is subscribed to the BaseOS and AppStream repositories:

```
# dnf repolist
```

The command output should be similar to the following:

```
[root@server1 ~]# dnf repolist
Updating Subscription Management repositories.
repo id                        repo name
rhel-9-for-x86_64-appstream-rpms Red Hat Enterprise Linux 9 for x86_64 - AppStream (RPMs)
rhel-9-for-x86_64-baseos-rpms  Red Hat Enterprise Linux 9 for x86_64 - BaseOS (RPMs)
[root@server1 ~]#
```

11. The system is now ready for the installation of new packages. Try running the following command to install a software package:

```
# dnf install wireshark
```

The result should be similar to what's shown below. As you see, in this example the **dnf** command not only downloads and installs the wireshark RPM but also installs the dependent packages to make sure that all software dependencies are satisfied.

```
[root@server1 ~]# yum install wireshark
Updating Subscription Management repositories.
Last metadata expiration check: 2:15:00 ago on Mon 15 May 2023 01:45:27 AM CDT.
Dependencies resolved.
================================================================================
 Package           Arch    Version        Repository                       Size
================================================================================
Installing:
 wireshark         x86_64  1:3.4.10-4.el9  rhel-9-for-x86_64-appstream-rpms 3.9 M
Installing dependencies:
 libsmi            x86_64  0.4.8-30.el9    rhel-9-for-x86_64-appstream-rpms 2.2 M
 openal-soft       x86_64  1.19.1-16.el9   rhel-9-for-x86_64-appstream-rpms 539 k
 pcre2-utf16       x86_64  10.40-2.el9     rhel-9-for-x86_64-appstream-rpms 218 k
 qt5-qtbase        x86_64  5.15.3-1.el9    rhel-9-for-x86_64-appstream-rpms 3.7 M
 qt5-qtbase-common noarch  5.15.3-1.el9    rhel-9-for-x86_64-appstream-rpms  13 k
 qt5-qtbase-gui    x86_64  5.15.3-1.el9    rhel-9-for-x86_64-appstream-rpms 6.3 M
 qt5-qtdeclarative x86_64  5.15.3-1.el9    rhel-9-for-x86_64-appstream-rpms 4.2 M
 qt5-qtmultimedia  x86_64  5.15.3-1.el9    rhel-9-for-x86_64-appstream-rpms 822 k
 wireshark-cli     x86_64  1:3.4.10-4.el9  rhel-9-for-x86_64-appstream-rpms  20 M
 xcb-util-image    x86_64  0.4.0-19.el9    rhel-9-for-x86_64-appstream-rpms  22 k
 xcb-util-keysyms  x86_64  0.4.0-17.el9    rhel-9-for-x86_64-appstream-rpms  16 k
 xcb-util-renderutil x86_64 0.3.9-20.el9   rhel-9-for-x86_64-appstream-rpms  20 k
 xcb-util-wm       x86_64  0.4.1-22.el9    rhel-9-for-x86_64-appstream-rpms  35 k

Transaction Summary
================================================================================
Install  14 Packages

Total download size: 42 M
Installed size: 179 M
Is this ok [y/N]:
```

Basic dnf Configuration

Now that you are subscribed to repositories on the RHSM, you have to understand how **dnf** is configured in some detail. It starts with the /etc/dnf/dnf.conf configuration file and continues with files in the /etc/dnf and /etc/yum.repos.d directories. As you can see, even though **dnf** is the current tool, directory names still feature the term **yum**. To get the full list of **dnf** configuration directives and their current values, run the following command:

```
# dnf config-manager --dump
```

The Basic dnf Configuration File: dnf.conf

This section analyzes the default version of the /etc/dnf/dnf.conf file, line by line. Although you won't make changes to this file in most cases, you need to understand at least the standard directives in this file if something goes wrong. The following lines are straight excerpts from the default version of this file. The first directive is a header; the **[main]** header suggests that all directives that follow apply globally to **dnf**:

```
[main]
```

The **gpgcheck** boolean directive makes sure the **dnf** command actually checks the GPG signature of downloaded packages:

```
gpgcheck=1
```

The **installonly_limit** directive specifies how many of the packages listed in the **installonlypkgs** option (usually the kernel) can be installed at the same time:

```
installonly_limit=3
```

The **clean_requirements_on_remove** boolean directive instructs **dnf** to go through each package dependency when removing packages. If this configuration option is set to True, any dependencies that are not required by other packages will also be removed.

```
clean_requirements_on_remove=True
```

If enabled, the **best** directive tells **dnf** to always try to install the highest version available of a package during an upgrade:

```
best=True
```

Configuration Files in the /etc/dnf/plugins Directory

The default files in the /etc/dnf/plugins directory configure a connection between **dnf** and the Red Hat Portal or a local Satellite server. If you're studying from a RHEL rebuild distribution such as AlmaLinux, you'll see a different set of files in this directory. This is a Red Hat book, however, so the focus will be on the two basic files in the RHEL 9 installation.

Spacewalk Plugin   If you have a subscription to the RHSM via an old version of Red Hat Satellite Server, the spacewalkplugin.conf file in this directory is especially important. The directives, shown next, enable the plugin and check GPG signatures of RPM packages:

```
[main]
enabled = 1
gpgcheck = 1
timeout = 120
```

Red Hat Subscription Management Plugins   The subscription-manager.conf and product-id.conf files are designed to connect the **dnf** system to the Red Hat Portal using Subscription Management. As discussed in this chapter, Subscription Management is used to subscribe a system to RHSM for system updates. The file subscription-manager.conf is straightforward. The first directive enables the plugin. The last directive, if set to 1, disables all repositories that are not managed by Subscription Management. This is useful when the system runs Fedora and you do not want to use the default system repositories because the system is managed by Red Hat Satellite or Katello.

```
[main]
enabled=1
disable_system_repos=0
```

Configuration Files in the /etc/yum.repos.d Directory

The configuration files in the /etc/yum.repos.d directory are designed to connect systems to actual **dnf** repositories. If you're running a rebuild distribution such as AlmaLinux, you'll see files with the .repo extension in this directory, which configure access to public repositories on the Internet. If you're running RHEL 9 and registered the system with Red Hat Subscription Management, you'll see a redhat.repo file, which lists all the repositories available for the system on the Red Hat Portal.

A couple of elements in common for configuration files in the /etc/yum.repos.d directory are the file extension (.repo) and the documentation, available with the **man dnf.conf** command.

A properly configured .repo file in the /etc/yum.repos.d directory can be a terrific convenience to enable the installation of groups of packages with the **dnf** command. As the /etc/yum.repos.d directory might be empty on a new RHEL 9 system, you should know how to create that file from scratch, using data for the installation server and information available in the dnf.conf man page.

Understand the Default redhat.repo Configuration File   If you have subscribed the system to Red Hat Subscription Management, you should see a redhat.repo file in the /etc/yum.repos.d directory, with content similar to that shown in Figure 4-6. Although it includes a number of different repositories, you can learn from the pattern of directives configured for each repository.

FIGURE 4-6   Several repositories configured in one file

```
[rhel-9-for-x86_64-baseos-rpms]
name = Red Hat Enterprise Linux 9 for x86_64 - BaseOS (RPMs)
baseurl = https://cdn.redhat.com/content/dist/rhel9/$releasever/x86_64/baseos/os
enabled = 1
gpgcheck = 1
gpgkey = file:///etc/pki/rpm-gpg/RPM-GPG-KEY-redhat-release
sslverify = 1
sslcacert = /etc/rhsm/ca/redhat-uep.pem
sslclientkey = /etc/pki/entitlement/3082478711287883002-key.pem
sslclientcert = /etc/pki/entitlement/3082478711287883002.pem
sslverifystatus = 1
metadata_expire = 86400
enabled_metadata = 1

[rhel-atomic-7-cdk-3.16-rpms]
name = Red Hat Container Development Kit 3.16 /(RPMs)
baseurl = https://cdn.redhat.com/content/dist/rhel/atomic/7/7Server/$basearch/cdk/3.16/os
enabled = 0
gpgcheck = 1
gpgkey = http://
sslverify = 1
sslcacert = /etc/rhsm/ca/redhat-uep.pem
sslclientkey = /etc/pki/entitlement/3082478711287883002-key.pem
sslclientcert = /etc/pki/entitlement/3082478711287883002.pem
sslverifystatus = 1
metadata_expire = 86400
enabled_metadata = 0
```

There are several stanzas in the redhat.repo file, one for each Red Hat repository. For example, the first stanza shown in Figure 4-6 defines the configuration settings for the BaseOS repository. The first line, in brackets, provides a name for the repository. In this case, **[rhel-9-for-x86_64-baseos-rpms]** just stands for the name of the base repository used by RHEL 9. It doesn't represent the directory where the associated packages are installed.

Although the name of the repository follows, it's just for documentation purposes and does not affect how packages or package databases are read or downloaded. In fact, the inclusion of the **name** directive is optional.

```
name=Red Hat Enterprise Linux 9 for x86_64 - BaseOS (RPMs)
```

The **baseurl** directive specifies the URL that contains the actual repository of packages. It commonly works with either the HTTP/HTTPS or FTP protocol. It can even work with local directories or mounted Network File System shares.

```
baseurl=https://cdn.redhat.com/content/dist/rhel9/$releasever/x86_64 ↵
/baseos/os
```

The **enabled** directive specifies if a repository is enabled or not:

```
enabled=1
```

When you run the **dnf repolist** command, the name of all the enabled repositories will be shown in output similar to the following.

```
repo id                          repo name
rhel-9-for-x86_64-baseos-rpms Red Hat Enterprise Linux 9 - BaseOS
```

If you want to disable checking the GPG signatures of each package to be downloaded (a bad idea!), the following command puts that wish into effect:

```
gpgcheck=0
```

Of course, if you enable **gpgcheck**, any GPG check requires a GPG key; the following directive specifies one key from the local /etc/pki/rpm-gpg directory for that purpose:

```
gpgkey=file:///etc/pki/rpm-gpg/RPM-GPG-KEY-redhat-release
```

Create Your Own /etc/yum.repos.d Configuration File   You need to learn how to create a local configuration file in the /etc/yum.repos.d directory, to allow the installation of packages from repositories other than the Red Hat ones. To do so, you'll need to set up a text file with a .repo extension in the /etc/yum.repos.d directory. That file needs only three lines.

On RHEL 9, especially during an exam, the /etc/yum.repos.d directory may be empty. So you may not have access to an existing configuration file to use as a template. The man page of the dnf.conf file may look overwhelming if you need to find information during the RHCSA exam.

Fortunately, the **dnf config-manager** command allows you to easily configure a repository. To configure a new repository, the only thing you need is to pass to **dnf config-manager** the URL of the repo:

```
# dnf config-manager --add-repo=https://myrepo.example.com
```

This command will create a file named myrepo.example.com.repo with the same content as shown in Figure 4-7.

Next, you can open the file and customize the settings. The identifier for the repository is shown in brackets. Unless specified by the RHCSA exam, it doesn't matter what single word you put between the brackets as the identifier.

Alternatively, you can create the .repo file manually. For example, create a new file named whatever.repo in the /etc/yum.repos.d directory. (To some extent, the filename of the .repo

FIGURE 4-7

Excerpt from a .repo file

```
[root@server1 ~]# cat /etc/yum.repos.d/myrepo.example.com.repo
[myrepo.example.com]
name=created by dnf config-manager from https://myrepo.example.com
baseurl=https://myrepo.example.com
enabled=1
[root@server1 ~]#
```

file does not matter, as long as it has a .repo extension in the /etc/yum.repos.d directory.) In that file, add the following identifier:

```
[test]
```

Next comes the **name** directive for the repository. This should be human readable and does not affect the functionality of the repository. To demonstrate, we add the following directive:

```
name=somebody likes Linux
```

e x a m

ⓦ a t c h You should learn how to create a working .repo file in the /etc/yum .repos.d directory during Red Hat exams. It can be a big timesaver when you need to install additional packages.

Finally, there's the **baseurl** directive, which can be configured to point to an installation server. The RHCSA requirements imply that you need to know how to install software from the Red Hat Network. They also suggest that you need to know how to install and update packages from a remote repository. To meet this objective, you need to know the URL of that remote server or repository. It's reasonable to expect that URL to be provided during the exam.

For example, in a classroom environment, a **baseurl** directive may look like this:

```
baseurl=http://192.168.122.1/inst
```

Next, add the following line:

```
gpgcheck=0
```

That's all you need. Of course, security is important in real life, and for this reason you should enable **gpgcheck** and specify where the GPG key is found with the **gpgkey** directive. But if your focus is on the exam, the best advice is often to keep things as simple as possible.

EXERCISE 4-3

Create a dnf Repository from the RHEL 9 DVD

This exercise requires access to the RHEL 9 DVD. You'll be using the tester1.example.com system that you installed in Chapter 1. Because this system is not subscribed to the Red Hat Subscription Management (if it is, run **subscription-manager unregister**), you will create a **dnf** repository to install packages locally from the RHEL 9 DVD.

1. In VMWare Workstation (or your hosted hypervisor), select your tester1 VM and click Settings.
2. Mount the RHEL 9 ISO file that you downloaded in Chapter 1. To do so, in the Settings window select CD/DVD (SATA) and click Use ISO Image. Browse and select the path of the RHEL 9 ISO image. Ensure that the option Connected is selected.

3. Log in to the system and type the **df** command. If the DVD was automounted, you should see an entry in the **df** output that shows that the DVD is available at a directory path such as /run/media/*yourusername*/RHEL-9-1-0-BaseOS-x86_64. If for some reason you do not see the DVD being mounted, you can mount it manually by entering the following command (as root):

```
# mount /dev/cdrom /media
```

In this exercise we assume that the DVD is mounted to /run/media/*yourusername*/ RHEL-9-1-0-BaseOS-x86_64. Change your commands accordingly if this is not the case.

4. Navigate to the /etc/yum.repos.d directory.
5. Open a new file in a text editor and name it (for example) **rhel9.repo**.
6. Edit the rhel9.repo file. Create a new stanza of directives. Use an appropriate stanza title such as [**rhel**].
7. Specify BaseOS as a **name** directive for the repository.
8. Include a **baseurl** directive set to **file:///run/media/*yourusername*/RHEL-9-1-0-BaseOS-x86_64/BaseOS/**.
9. Include an **enabled=1** directive.
10. Add **gpgkey=0**.
11. Save and close the file.
12. Run the **dnf clean all** and **dnf update** commands.
13. Next, try the following command:

```
# dnf install tmux
```

14. If successful, you should see the following output:

```
==================================================================================
 Package            Architecture      Version                Repository      Size
==================================================================================
Installing:
 tmux               x86_64            3.2a-4.el9             rhel            476 k

Transaction Summary
==================================================================================
Install  1 Package

Total size: 476 k
Installed size: 1.1 M
Is this ok [y/N]: █
```

You've now set up a repository on the local DVD.

15. Restore the original configuration by deleting the rhel9.repo file from the /etc/yum.repos.d directory.

Third-Party Repositories

Other groups of third-party developers create packages for RHEL 9. They include packages for some popular software not supported by Red Hat. The website for one of these third parties can be found at https://docs.fedoraproject.org/en-US/epel/.

To add third-party repositories to a system, you'd create a custom .repo file in the /etc/yum.repos.d directory.

Some repositories, such as EPEL (Extra Packages for Enterprise Linux), simplify the configuration by providing an RPM package that includes a .repo configuration file and a GPG key to verify the packages. To configure the repository, all you have to do is install that RPM file:

```
# rpm -ivh https://dl.fedoraproject.org/pub/epel/ ↵
epel-release-latest-9.noarch.rpm
```

If you want to disable any repository in the /etc/yum.repos.d directory, add the following directive to the applicable repository file:

```
enabled=0
```

EXERCISE 4-4

Configure Access to the EPEL Repository

In this exercise, you will configure access to the EPEL repository. Rather than installing the epel-release-latest-9.noarch.rpm package, as just described, you will configure the repository manually. This will provide you a great opportunity to practice with the configuration of a repository.

1. Log in to the server1.example.com system.
2. Run the following command:
   ```
   # dnf install https://dl.fedoraproject.org/pub/epel/ ↵
   epel-release-latest-9.noarch.rpm
   ```
3. The command has created a file named epel.repo in the /etc/yum.repos.d/ directory.
4. Install the calc RPM package, which comes from the EPEL repository:
   ```
   # dnf install calc
   ```

Basic dnf Commands

If you want to learn more about the intricacies of the **dnf** command, run the command by itself. You'll see the following output scroll by, probably far too fast. Of course, you can pipe the output to the **less** command pager with the **dnf | less** command.

```
# dnf
Updating Subscription Management repositories.
usage: dnf [options] COMMAND

List of Main Commands:
...
```

You'll examine how a few of these commands and options work in the following sections. Although you might not have Internet access during a Red Hat exam, you may have a network connection to a locally configured repository, which you should be ready to configure via the appropriate file in the /etc/yum.repos.d directory, as described earlier. As well as during the exam, **dnf** is an excellent tool for administering Red Hat systems.

Start with a simple command: **dnf list**. It'll return a list of all packages, whether they're installed or available, along with their version numbers and repositories. **dnf list | grep** *packagename* tells you what version of a package you will get with a **dnf install**. If you want to show all the configured repositories, you can do this with **dnf repolist all**. More information about a specific package can be obtained via the **dnf info** command. For example, the following command is functionally equivalent to **rpm -qi samba**:

```
# dnf info samba
```

The **rpm -qi** command works if the queried package is already installed, because it retrieves information directly from the RPM database on the local system. Conversely, the **dnf info** command is not subject to that limitation, because it retrieves information from the upstream software repositories. It queries the repository metadata and displays information about the specified package.

Installation Mode

There are two basic installation commands. If you haven't installed a package before, or you want to update it to the latest stable version, run the **dnf install** *packagename* command. You don't need to specify the version or release number. Only the package name is required. For example, if you're checking for the latest version of the Samba RPM, the following command will update it or add it if it isn't already installed on the target system:

```
# dnf install samba
```

If you just want to keep the packages on a system up to date, run the **dnf update** *packagename* command. For example, if you already have the Samba RPM installed, the following command makes sure it's updated to the latest version:

```
# dnf update samba
```

If you haven't installed Samba, this command doesn't add it to your installed packages. In that way, the **dnf update** command is analogous to the **rpm -F** command.

Of course, the **dnf** command is not complete without options that can remove a package. The first one is straightforward because it uninstalls the Samba package along with any dependencies:

```
# dnf remove samba
```

The **dnf update** command by itself is powerful; if you want to make sure that all installed packages are updated to the latest stable versions, run the following command:

```
# dnf update
```

The **dnf update** command may take some time as it communicates with the Red Hat Portal or other repositories. It may need to download the current database of packages with all dependencies. It then finds all packages with available updates and adds them to the list of packages to be updated. It finds all dependent packages if they're not already included in the list of updates.

What if you just want a list of available updates? The **dnf list updates** command can help there. It's functionally equivalent to the **dnf check-update** command.

But what if you aren't quite sure what to install? For example, if you want to install the Evince document reader and think the operational command includes the term "evince," then the **dnf provides "*/evince*"** command can help.

Alternatively, to search for all instances of files with the .repo extension, run the following command:

```
# dnf provides "*/*.repo"
```

It lists all instances of the packages with files that end with the .repo extension, with the associated RPM package. The wildcard is required because the **provides** option requires the full path to the file. It accepts partial filenames; for example, the **dnf provides "/etc/systemd/*"** command returns the RPM associated with files in the /etc/systemd directory. Once the needed package is known, you can proceed with the **dnf install** *packagename* command.

on the **job**

In many cases, problems with dnf **can be solved with the** dnf clean all **command. If there are recent updates to Red Hat packages (or third-party repositories), this command flushes the current cache of metadata, allowing you to synchronize metadata with configured repositories, without having to wait the default 24 hours before the cache is automatically flushed.**

Security and dnf

GPG digital signatures can verify the integrity and authenticity of **dnf** updates. It's the same system described earlier in this chapter for RPM packages. As an example, look at the output the first time a new package is installed over a network on RHEL 9:

```
# dnf install samba
```

After packages are downloaded, you'll see something similar to the following messages:

```
Importing GPG key 0xFD431D51:
 Userid     : "Red Hat, Inc. (release key 2) <security@redhat.com>"
 Fingerprint: 567E 347A D004 4ADE 55BA 8A5F 199E 2F91 FD43 1D51
 From       : /etc/pki/rpm-gpg/RPM-GPG-KEY-redhat-release
Is this ok [y/N]: y
Key imported successfully
Importing GPG key 0x5A6340B3:
 Userid     : "Red Hat, Inc. (auxiliary key 3) <security@redhat.com>"
 Fingerprint: 7E46 2425 8C40 6535 D56D 6F13 5054 E4A4 5A63 40B3
 From       : /etc/pki/rpm-gpg/RPM-GPG-KEY-redhat-release
Is this ok [y/N]: y
```

If you're simultaneously downloading packages from other repositories, additional GPG keys may be presented for approval. As suggested by the last line, **N** is the default response; you actually have to type in **y** to proceed with the download and installation—not only of the GPG key but also of the package in question.

You may notice that the GPG key used is from the same directory of keys associated with the **rpm** command earlier in this chapter.

Updates and Security Fixes

Red Hat maintains a public list of errata, classified by RHEL release, at https://access.redhat .com/errata-search/. If you have a RHEL subscription, affected packages are normally made available through the Red Hat Portal; for RHSM-connected machines, all you need to do is run the **dnf update** command periodically. This list is useful for those third parties who use RHEL source code, such as AlmaLinux and even Oracle Linux; typically RHEL rebuilds provide similar errata shortly after Red Hat.

Package Groups and dnf

The **dnf** command can do more. It can install and remove packages in groups. With the following command, you can identify available package groups from configured repositories:

```
# dnf group list
```

FIGURE 4-8

Packages in the
Virtualization
Host group

```
[root@server1 ~]# dnf group info "Virtualization Host"
Updating Subscription Management repositories.
Last metadata expiration check: 0:08:33 ago on Mon 15 May 2023 05:31:39 AM CDT.
Environment Group: Virtualization Host
 Description: Minimal virtualization host.
 Mandatory Groups:
   Base
   Core
   Standard
   Virtualization Hypervisor
   Virtualization Tools
 Optional Groups:
   Debugging Tools
   Network File System Client
   Remote Management for Linux
   Virtualization Platform
[root@server1 ~]#
```

Note how the groups are divided into installed and available groups. Some of the groups listed may be of particular interest, such as "Virtualization Host," which installs the KVM hypervisor. To find out more about this group, run the following command. The output is shown in Figure 4-8.

```
# dnf group info "Virtualization Host"
```

There are two types of groups in **dnf**: regular groups, which include standard RPM packages, and environment groups, which are made of other groups. "Virtualization Host" in Figure 4-8 is identified as an "Environment Group" and is in fact a collection of regular groups.

To list all groups, you can type

```
# dnf group list hidden
```

Let's get some information about one of the regular groups:

```
# dnf group info "Remote Desktop Clients"
```

Note how the packages are all listed as "Optional Packages," as shown in Figure 4-9.

In other words, they're not normally installed with the package group. Thus, suppose you were to run the following command:

```
# dnf group install "Remote Desktop Clients"
```

Nothing would be installed. Optional packages from this package group can be installed with the following command option:

```
# dnf group install --with-optional "Remote Desktop Clients"
```

FIGURE 4-9

Packages in the
Remote Desktop
Clients group

```
[root@server1 ~]# dnf group info "Remote Desktop Clients"
Updating Subscription Management repositories.
Last metadata expiration check: 0:11:08 ago on Mon 15 May 2023 05:31:39 AM CDT.
Group: Remote Desktop Clients
 Optional Packages:
   freerdp
   tigervnc
[root@server1 ~]#
```

But Optional Packages is not the only category. The following command lists all packages in the "Printing Client" package group. The output is shown in Figure 4-10.

```
# dnf group info "Printing Client"
```

Packages in the Printing Client group are classified in two other categories. Mandatory packages are always installed with the package group. Default packages are normally installed with the package group; however, specific packages from this group can be excluded with the **-x** switch. For example, the following command installs the three mandatory and seven default packages:

```
# dnf group install "Printing Client"
```

In contrast, the following command excludes the paps and the gutenprint-cups packages from the list of those to be installed:

```
# dnf group install "Printing Client" -x paps -x gutenprint-cups
```

The options to the **dnf** command are not complete unless there's a command that can reverse the process. As suggested by the name, the **dnf group remove** command uninstalls all packages from the noted package group:

```
# dnf group remove "Printing Client"
```

Exclusions are not possible with the **dnf group remove** command. If you don't want to remove all packages listed in the output to the command, it may be best to remove target packages individually.

FIGURE 4-10

Packages in the Printing Client group

```
[root@server1 ~]# dnf group info "Printing Client"
Updating Subscription Management repositories.
Last metadata expiration check: 0:14:37 ago on Mon 15 May 2023 05:31:39 AM CDT.
Group: Printing Client
 Description: Tools for printing to a local printer or a remote print server.
 Mandatory Packages:
   cups
   cups-pk-helper
   enscript
 Default Packages:
   colord
   gutenprint
   gutenprint-cups
   gutenprint-doc
   paps
   pnm2ppa
   system-config-printer-udev
 Optional Packages:
   bluez-cups
   hplip
[root@server1 ~]# 
```

More dnf Commands

A number of additional **dnf**-related commands are available. Two of them may be of particular interest to those studying for the Red Hat exams: **dnf config-manager** and **dnf download** can, respectively, display all current configuration settings and download individual RPM packages. One more related command is **createrepo**, which can help you set up a local repository.

View All Directives with dnf config-manager

To some extent, the directives listed in the dnf.conf and related configuration files provide only a small snapshot of available directives. To review the full list of directives, run the **dnf config-manager --dump** command. Pipe it to the **less** command as a pager. It includes nearly 100 lines. The excerpt from the [**main**] section shown in Figure 4-11 includes settings that apply to all the configured repositories.

FIGURE 4-11

A partial list of dnf directives

```
color_update_remote = bold,green
config_file_path = /etc/dnf/dnf.conf
countme = 0
debug_solver = 0
debuglevel = 2
defaultyes = 0
deltarpm = 1
deltarpm_percentage = 75
disable_excludes =
diskspacecheck = 1
enabled = 1
enablegroups = 1
errorlevel = 3
exclude =
exclude_from_weak =
exclude_from_weak_autodetect = 1
excludepkgs =
exit_on_lock = 0
fastestmirror = 0
gpgcheck = 1
gpgkey_dns_verification = 0
group_package_types = mandatory, default, conditional
history_list_view = commands
history_record = 1
history_record_packages = dnf, rpm
ignorearch = 0
includepkgs =
install_weak_deps = 1
installonly_limit = 3
installonlypkgs = kernel, kernel-PAE, installonlypkg(kernel), installonlypkg(ke
rnel-module), installonlypkg(vm), multiversion(kernel)
installroot = /
ip_resolve = whatever
keepcache = 0
localpkg_gpgcheck = 0
log_compress = 0
```

| TABLE 4-5 | Configuration Parameters from yum-config-manager |

Configuration Directive in dnf	Description
assumeyes	Set to no by default; if set to 1, **dnf** proceeds automatically with package installation and removal.
cachedir	Set to the directory for metadata and downloaded package files.
enablegroups	Supports **dnf group** commands.
installonlypkgs	Lists packages that should never be updated in addition to the default ones, which normally includes Linux kernel packages.
installonly_limit	Identifies the maximum number of packages listed by installonlypkgs that can be installed concurrently. The default is 3.
logdir	Specifies the name of the directory where logs are stored, normally /var/log/.
pluginconfpath	Identifies the directory with plugins, normally /etc/dnf/plugins.
reposdir	Specifies the directory with repository configuration files.
sslverify	If set to 1, remote SSL certificates are verified.

Some of the directives do not have any default values, such as **exclude**; some don't really matter, such as the color directives. Some of the most significant directives are shown in Table 4-5. It is not a comprehensive list. If you're interested in a directive not shown, it's defined in the man page for the dnf.conf file.

Package Downloads with dnf download

As suggested by the name, the **dnf download** command can be used to download packages from **yum**-based repositories. It's a fairly simple command. For example, the following command reviews the contents of configured repositories for a package named cups:

```
# dnf download cups
```

Either the RPM package is downloaded to the local directory or the command returns the following error messages:

```
No package cups available.
```

Sometimes, more specifics are required. If there are multiple versions of a package stored on a repository, the default is to download the latest version of that package. That may not always be what you want. For example, if you want to use a specific version of the RHEL 9 kernel, use the following command:

```
# dnf download kernel-5.14.0-284.11.1.el9_2
```

Create Your Own Repository with createrepo

An earlier version of the exam objectives for RHEL 6 suggested that you should know how to "create a private yum repository." Although that objective has since been removed, it's a necessary job skill for a Red Hat system engineer.

Custom repositories can provide additional control. Enterprises that want to control the packages installed on their Linux systems can create their own customized repository. Although this can be based on the standard repositories developed for a distribution, it can include additional packages such as custom software unique to an organization. Just as easily, it can omit packages that may violate organizational policies such as games. Limits on the choices for certain functions such as browsers can minimize related support requirements.

To create a customized repository, you need to collect desired packages in a specific directory. The **createrepo** command can process all packages in that directory. The database is created in XML files in a repodata/ subdirectory. An example of this package database already exists in the BaseOS/repodata/ subdirectory of the RHEL 9 DVD.

The Red Hat Portal enables support of customized repositories with related products, such as Red Hat Satellite Server. For more information on repository management, see *Linux Patch Management*, written by Michael Jang and published by Prentice Hall.

CERTIFICATION OBJECTIVE 4.04

Module Streams (*)

Suppose you need to install a service, or an application runtime, such as Apache, Perl, or NodeJS, and you need a specific release of that software. With **rpm** or **dnf**, you can specify in the command line the exact version of the package that you want to install. Assuming that this is available in your software repositories, everything will work, until you run **dnf update**. What if a newer major release of that package is available? The package manager will automatically update it to the latest release.

Here's where *modularity* comes in handy. With module streams, a vendor can distribute multiple releases of the same application, and a system administrator can pin to a specific release when installing the software.

As an example, suppose that you need to install NodeJS 18. As of this writing, RHEL 9 software repositories include both NodeJS 16 and NodeJS 18. A command such as **dnf install nodejs** would install version 16. You could specify the exact version of the package to install, such as **dnf install nodejs-16.***, but the next time that you run **dnf update**, NodeJS may be upgraded to a new major version, if available, which is not what you want.

> **NOTE: * Please note that this section will not be on the exam, but contains useful information.**

Fortunately, Red Hat distributes NodeJS 18 as module streams. This way, you can pin to the release that you need and still get patches for that release, but you will never be upgraded to the latest major release when you run **dnf update**.

Some of the more experienced readers may have noticed that module streams try to solve the same problem addressed by software collections in RHEL 7. In fact, software collections provide the ability to distribute multiple versions of the same application and to install them in a separate root tree. However, there is a major difference with module streams: while software collections allow installation of multiple releases of the same application *concurrently*, module streams only permit installation of one version of an application on a system.

Getting Information About Module Streams

As described earlier in this chapter, RHEL 9 comes with two repositories: BaseOS and AppStream. While BaseOS includes the core operating system software, AppStream contains user-level applications, some of which are packaged as modules.

The **dnf module** command has been introduced in RHEL 9 to manage module streams. To familiarize yourself with some of the concepts of modules, list all modules with the **dnf module list** command. An excerpt of the output is shown in Figure 4-12.

The first column in Figure 4-12, Name, displays the module name, such as nodejs. The second column, Stream, shows the module stream, which is the specific version of that application that we can install.

The next column, Profiles, includes, for each module stream, a list of available profiles. This is a way of grouping RPM packages within module streams. For example, the postgresql 15 module stream has two profiles, client and server. That means that we can choose to install PostgreSQL for a server installation or for a client by specifying the profile that we wish to install.

Note that some profiles are marked as default, [**d**]. That means that if we do not pass the name of a profile at installation, by default **dnf** will install the server RPM packages for the default profile.

FIGURE 4-12   Listing module streams

```
[root@server1 ~]# dnf module list
Updating Subscription Management repositories.
Last metadata expiration check: 1:26:54 ago on Mon 15 May 2023 05:31:39 AM CDT.
Red Hat Enterprise Linux 9 for x86_64 - AppStream (RPMs)
Name        Stream  Profiles                              Summary
maven       3.8     common [d]                            Java project management and project comprehension tool
nginx       1.22    common [d]                            nginx webserver
nodejs      18 [e]  common [d] [i], development, minimal, s2  Javascript runtime
                    i
php         8.1     common [d], devel, minimal            PHP scripting language
postgresql  15      client, server                        PostgreSQL server and client module
ruby        3.1     common [d]                            An interpreter of object-oriented scripting language

Hint: [d]efault, [e]nabled, [x]disabled, [i]nstalled
[root@server1 ~]#
```

To get the list of RPM packages that are installed by the PostgreSQL module, type

```
# dnf module info postgresql
```

You can even be more specific by indicating the module name and the stream, separated by a colon:

```
# dnf module info nodejs:18
```

The --**profile** command option shows the RPM packages that will be installed on each profile:

```
# dnf module info --profile nodejs:18
```

Installing and Removing Module Streams

At the bottom of Figure 4-12, you can see that a stream or a profile can be marked as default, [**d**], enabled, [**e**], disabled, [**x**], or installed, [**i**]. We have already seen that "default" can refer to which profile of a module stream is installed by default, if none is specified. It can also refer to a stream if a module has more than one, or to indicate which stream will be installed if none is specified.

To install a module stream, the corresponding module stream must be enabled first. This can be done by running the **dnf module enable** command. For example, to enable the nodejs 18 stream, run

```
# dnf module enable nodejs:18
```

Next, install the module:

```
# dnf module install nodejs
```

However, the **dnf module install** command automatically enables a module, so you can replace the previous two commands with the following one:

```
# dnf module install nodejs:18
```

Optionally, you can specify a profile (for example, the "minimal" profile) with this syntax:

```
# dnf module install nodejs:18/minimal
```

Removing a module requires one command:

```
# dnf module remove nodejs:18
```

Next, you can "reset" the stream, which disables the stream and resets the configuration to the default settings:

```
# dnf module reset nodejs
```

CERTIFICATION SUMMARY

This chapter focuses on the management of RPM packages. With different command options, you also saw how the **rpm** tool installs, removes, and upgrade packages, as well as how it works locally and remotely. When presented with a new version of a kernel, it's important to never replace the existing kernel with **rpm**. A properly configured installation of a later kernel version does not overwrite the existing kernel, but brings the kernels together, side by side. You'll then be able to boot into either kernel.

With the **rpm** command, you also learned how to query packages, to examine to which package a file belongs, to validate a package signature, and to find the current list of installed RPMs. You also saw the difficulties associated with dependencies that drove users to the **dnf** command.

The **dnf** command is much more powerful than the **rpm** command. When there are dependencies, it installs those packages simultaneously. You learned how to configure Red Hat and other repositories to work with the **dnf** command. You should now be able to configure your own repositories and subscribe a system to the Red Hat Portal using the **subscription-manager** command. As you saw, the **dnf** command can also install or remove package groups.

Module streams provide a way to distribute multiple versions of the same application, and to pin to a specific release when installing it. The **dnf module** command can be used to list, install, and uninstall module streams.

 TWO-MINUTE DRILL

Here are some of the key points from the certification objectives in Chapter 4.

The RPM Package Manager

❏ The RPM database tracks where each file in a package is located, its version number, and much more.

❏ The **rpm -i** command installs RPM packages.

❏ The **rpm -e** command uninstalls RPM packages.

❏ The **rpm** command can even install RPMs directly from remote servers.

❏ RPM package verification is supported by the GPG keys in the /etc/pki/rpm-gpg directory.

❏ Kernel RPMs should always be installed, never upgraded.

❏ The upgrade mode of RPM replaces the old version of the package with the new one.

More RPM Commands

❏ The **rpm -q** command determines whether packages are installed on a system; with additional switches, it can list more about a package and identify the package for a specific file.

❏ Package signatures can be checked with the **rpm --checksig** (or **-K**) command.

❏ The **rpm -V** command can identify files that have changed from the original installation of the package before the RPM is installed.

❏ The **rpm -qa** command lists all currently installed packages.

Dependencies and the dnf Command

❏ By including additional required packages, the **dnf** command can help avoid "dependency hell."

❏ The behavior of the **dnf** command is configured in the /etc/dnf/dnf.conf file, plugins in the /etc/dnf/plugins directory, and repositories configured in the /etc/yum.repos.d directory.

❏ Red Hat organizes packages in two main repositories for RHEL 9, BaseOS and AppStream.

❏ Repositories for rebuild distributions and from third parties are accessible online.

❏ The **dnf** command can install, erase, and update packages. It also can be used to search in different ways.

❏ The **dnf** command uses GPG signatures to validate RPM packages.

❏ The **dnf** command can install, remove, and list package groups.

❏ Module streams are a way to distribute multiple versions of the same application in a single repository.

❏ A stream is a collection of RPM packages that are required by a specific version of an application.

SELF TEST

The following questions will help measure your understanding of the material presented in this chapter. As no multiple-choice questions appear on the Red Hat exams, no multiple-choice questions appear in this book. These questions exclusively test your understanding of the chapter. It is okay if you have another way of performing a task. Getting results, not memorizing trivia, is what counts on the Red Hat exams. There may be more than one answer to many of these questions.

The RPM Package Manager

1.   What command would you use to install the penguin-3.26.x86_64.rpm package, with verbose messages in case of errors? The package is on the current directory.

2.   What command would you use to upgrade the penguin RPM with the penguin-3.27.x86_64.rpm package? The package is on the ftp.remotemj02.abc server.

3.   If you've downloaded a later version of the Linux kernel to the local directory and the package filename is kernel-5.14.0-284.11.1.el9_2.x86_64.rpm, what's the best command to make it a part of your system?

4.   What directory contains RPM GPG keys on an installed system?

More RPM Commands

5.   What command lists all currently installed RPMs?

6.   What command lists all the files in the package penguin-3.26.x86_64.rpm?

7.   If you've downloaded from a third party an RPM called third.i686.rpm, how can you validate the associated package signature?

Dependencies and the dnf Command

8.   What is the full path to the directory where **dnf** repositories are normally configured?

9.   What command from the console starts the process of registration to Red Hat Subscription Management?

10.   What command searches **dnf** repositories for the package associated with the /etc/passwd file?

11.   What directive specifies a **dnf** repository URL in a .repo file?

12.   How do you enable and install the module nodejs, stream version 18, profile development?

LAB QUESTIONS

Red Hat presents its exams electronically. For that reason, the labs in this chapter are available from the companion website that accompanies the book. In case you haven't yet set up RHEL 9 on a system, refer to Chapter 1 for installation instructions. The answers for the labs follow the Self Test answers.

SELF TEST ANSWERS

The RPM Package Manager

1. The command that installs the penguin-3.26.x86_64.rpm package, with verbose messages in case of errors, is

   ```
   # rpm -iv penguin-3.26.x86_64.rpm
   ```

   Additional switches that don't change the functionality of the command, such as **-h** for hash marks, are acceptable. This applies to subsequent questions as well.

2. The command that upgrades the aforementioned penguin RPM with the penguin-3.27.x86_64.rpm package from the ftp.remotemj02.abc server is

   ```
   # rpm -Uv ftp://ftp.remotemj02.abc/penguin-3.27.x86_64.rpm
   ```

3. If you've downloaded a later version of the Linux kernel to the local directory and the package filename is kernel-5.14.0-284.11.1.el9_2.x86_64.rpm, the best way to make it a part of your system is to install it—and not upgrade the current kernel. Kernel upgrades overwrite existing kernels. Kernel installations allow kernels to exist side by side; if the new kernel doesn't work, you can still boot into the working kernel. As the desired package is already downloaded, you'd use a command similar to the following:

   ```
   # rpm -iv kernel-5.14.0-284.11.1.el9_2.x86_64.rpm
   ```

   Variations of the **rpm** command, such as **rpm -i** and **rpm -ivh**, are acceptable. However, variations that upgrade, with the -**U** or -**F** switch, are incorrect.

4. The directory with RPM GPG keys on an installed system is /etc/pki/rpm-gpg.

More RPM Commands

5. The command that lists all installed RPMs is

```
# rpm -qa
```

6. The command that lists all the files in the package penguin-3.26.x86_64.rpm is

```
# rpm -ql penguin-3.26.x86_64.rpm
```

7. If you've downloaded from a third party an RPM called third.i686.rpm, you'll first need to download and install the RPM-GPG-KEY file associated with that repository. You can then validate the associated package signature with a command like the following (note the uppercase -K; --checksig is equivalent to -K):

```
# rpm -K third.i386.rpm
```

Dependencies and the dnf Command

8. The **dnf** command repositories are normally configured in files in the /etc/yum.repos.d directory. Technically, **yum** command repositories can also be configured directly in the /etc/dnf/dnf.conf file.

9. The **subscription-manager** command starts the process of registering a system to Red Hat Subscription Management.

10. The **dnf provides /etc/passwd** command identifies packages associated with that file.

11. The **baseurl** directive specifies the URL of a **dnf** repository.

12. To install the module nodejs, stream version 18, profile development, run the following command:

```
# dnf module install nodejs:18/development
```

Note that this command automatically enables the stream, so you do not need to run **dnf module enable** first.

LAB ANSWERS

Lab 1

1. Run the following command to create a list of all the packages installed on the system and save it to the /root/pkgs.txt file:

```
# rpm -qa > /root/pkgs.txt
```

2. To answer this question, you can count the lines of the /root/pkgs.txt file or run the following command:

```
# rpm -qa | wc -l
```

3. To identify which package the file /etc/sestatus.conf belongs to, run

```
# rpm -qf /etc/sestatus.conf
```

4. You should notice that zlib is already installed (**rpm -q zlib**). To find information and the list of files provided by the zlib RPM package, run

```
# rpm -qil zlib
```

5. This question is slightly different from the previous one, in that the tmux package is not installed by default. Assuming that the RHEL 9 DVD is mounted at /run/media/*yourusername*/RHEL-9-1-0-BaseOS-x86_64, run the following commands to answer the question:

```
# cd /run/media/yourusername/RHEL-9-1-0-BaseOS-x86_64/BaseOS/Packages
# rpm -qpil tmux-*
```

Lab 2

Create a file named /etc/yum.repos.d/sql.repo with the following content:

```
[sql-tools]
name=sql-tools
baseurl=https://packages.microsoft.com/rhel/9/prod/
enabled=1
gpgcheck=1
gpgkey=https://packages.microsoft.com/keys/microsoft.asc
```

Run the following commands to search for and install the package:

```
# dnf search mssql-tools
# dnf -y install mssql-tools
```

Lab 3

One way to check all the files in the /usr/sbin directory is to run the following command:

```
# rpm -aV | grep /usr/sbin
```

If successful, the command should provide the following output, indicating that the timestamp of the file is different from that of the original file:

```
# .......T.    /usr./sbin/sshd
```

To reinstall the package, type

```
# dnf reinstall openssh-server
```

The **dnf remove openssh-server** command followed by **dnf install openssh-server** would achieve the same result.

Lab 4

This lab is intended to help you examine what the **dnf update** command can do. As you can see from the update.txt file created in this lab, the messages display how **dnf** searches for all newer packages from configured repositories or the Red Hat Portal, downloads their metadata, and uses them to check for dependencies that also need to be downloaded and installed.

Lab 5

To find information about the "Graphical Administration Tools" group, type

```
# dnf group info "Graphical Administration Tools"
```

You should find that this group consists of five optional packages.
To install the wireshark package, type

```
# dnf install -y wireshark
```

Lab 6

First, list the existing postgresql module streams:

```
# dnf module list postgresql
```

You will find that there is one stream, version 15.
To install PostgreSQL from the 15 stream and the client profile, run

```
# dnf module install postgresql:15/client
```

Note that this command will automatically enable the stream, so it is not necessary to run **dnf module enable** first.
Finally, confirm that the stream is enabled and installed:

```
# dnf module list postgresql
```

Chapter 5

systemd and
the Boot Process

T his chapter is focused on what happens from the moment a system is powered up to the time a login prompt is available. This is called the boot process. When the system powers on, the BIOS/UEFI firmware searches for a bootable device. Assuming this is a local hard drive, the GUID Partition Table (GPT) or Master Boot Record (MBR) of that device points to the GRUB 2 bootloader. Once an option to boot RHEL 9 is selected in GRUB 2, the bootloader loads a special file, initramfs, and gives control to the Linux kernel, which then starts **systemd**, the first Linux process. The **systemd** process then initializes the system and activates appropriate system units. When Linux boots into a specific target, it starts a series of "units," including the SSH daemon and the service associated with the Network Time Protocol (NTP). You can customize this process.

INSIDE THE EXAM

Understanding the Boot Process

Objectives related to the boot process have been consolidated into the RHCSA exam. Perhaps the most basic skill related to the boot process is an understanding of the commands that start and stop the boot process, such as **systemctl poweroff** and **systemctl reboot**:

- Boot, reboot, and shut down a system normally

In this chapter, you'll be introduced to systemd targets, which replace the traditional runlevels in RHEL 6 and other older Linux distributions. From the standard RHEL 9 boot menu, you need to know how to

- Boot systems into different targets manually

Closely related to this objective is this one:

- Interrupt the boot process in order to gain access to a system

You should be able to gain access to a system to recover a lost root password or to troubleshoot issues during the boot process.

Also, you must know how to automatically boot the system into different "targets," such as nongraphical multi-user mode or a GUI desktop:

- Configure systems to boot into a specific target automatically

As Linux is a network operating system, and as most users can't do much without network services, it's important to know how to

- Start and stop services and configure services to start automatically at boot

You'll also learn how to

- Modify the system bootloader

Closely related to these objectives, and part of the boot process, are objectives related to how filesystems are mounted, as covered in Chapter 7.

The Network Time Service

This chapter covers the configuration of a client that syncs the time using NTP. The corresponding exam objective is

- Configure time service clients

The Boot Process

Although not officially a Red Hat exam prerequisite or requirement, a basic understanding of the BIOS and the UEFI firmware is a fundamental skill for all serious computer users. The Unified Extensible Firmware Interface (UEFI) is a newer standard and has replaced the Basic Input/Output System (BIOS) on many modern systems. But for our purposes, their functionalities are the same.

Because of the variety of BIOS/UEFI firmware available, this discussion is general. It's not possible to provide any sort of step-by-step instructions for modifying the wide array of available BIOS/UEFI menus. In any case, such instructions are not directly relevant either to the administration of Linux or to any of the Red Hat exams. However, these skills can help you boot from different Linux installation media, access default virtualization settings, and more.

Basic System Configuration

When a computer is powered up, the first thing that starts is the BIOS/UEFI firmware. Based on settings stored in stable, read-only memory, the BIOS/UEFI system performs a series of diagnostics to detect and connect the CPU and key controllers. This is known as the Power On Self Test (POST). If you hear beeps during this process, there may be a hardware problem such as an improperly connected drive controller. The BIOS/UEFI system then looks for attached devices such as the graphics card. After the graphics hardware is detected, you may see a screen similar to Figure 5-1, which displays other hardware as detected, tested, and verified.

FIGURE 5-1	

The BIOS Initialization menu

```
F2  = System Setup
F10 = Lifecycle Controller
F11 = Boot Manager
Force PXE Boot Requested via Attribute

Initializing Serial ATA devices...
 Port J: PLDS DVD+/-RW DS-8ABSH

Initializing Intel(R) Boot Agent XE v2.3.27
PXE 2.1 Build 092 (WfM 2.0)



PowerEdge Expandable RAID Controller BIOS
Copyright(c) 2014 LSI Corporation
Press <Ctrl><R> to Run Configuration Utility
F/W Initializing Devices 26%
```

If your system has a UEFI menu, it may include a Trusted Platform Module (TPM). Although TPM technology is built to enhance security on a system, it has caused controversy within the open-source community due to privacy and vendor lock-in issues. Many open-source professionals worked to minimize any such problems through the Open Trusted Computing (OpenTC) group of the European Union. RHEL 9 can take advantage of TPM hardware features to enhance system security.

Once complete, the BIOS/UEFI passes control to the boot device, typically the first drive. The first stage of the GRUB 2 bootloader is normally copied to the MBR or GPT. It serves as a pointer to the other information from the GRUB 2 menu. At that point, you should see a bootloader screen.

Startup Menus

Generally, one of the reasons to access the BIOS/UEFI firmware menu is to boot from different media, such as a CD or USB key. In many cases, you can bypass this process.

Sometimes, all you see after POST is a blank screen. The BIOS/UEFI is often configured in this way. In that case, you'll need to do some guessing based on your experience on how to access the boot or BIOS menu.

In many cases, boot menus are directly accessible by pressing a key such as ESC, DEL, F1, F2, or F12. Such boot menus may have entries similar to the following:

```
    Boot Menu
 1. Removable Devices
 2. Hard Drive
 3. CD-ROM Drive
 4. USB Drive
 5. Built-In LAN
```

From that or similar menus, you should be able to select the desired boot device using the ARROW and ENTER keys.

Access to Linux Bootloaders

As noted in Chapter 1, the standard Linux bootloader is GRUB 2, and the first part of it (known as stage 1) is installed in the MBR or GUID table of the default drive. Normally, the BIOS should automatically start the bootloader, with a message similar to

```
Red Hat Enterprise Linux (5.14.0-162.6.1.el9_1.x86_64) 9.1 (Plow)
Red Hat Enterprise Linux (0-rescue-5cf7267e8cbd4ed6951e03a7e0e357
...
The selected entry will be started automatically in 5s.
```

FIGURE 5-2   The GRUB 2 menu

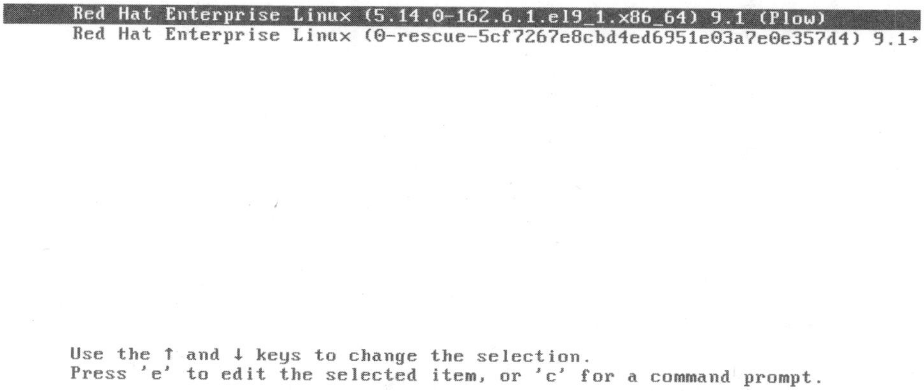

```
Red Hat Enterprise Linux (5.14.0-162.6.1.el9_1.x86_64) 9.1 (Plow)
Red Hat Enterprise Linux (0-rescue-5cf7267e8cbd4ed6951e03a7e0e357d4) 9.1→




     Use the ↑ and ↓ keys to change the selection.
     Press 'e' to edit the selected item, or 'c' for a command prompt.
```

If you press a key before those five seconds are complete, GRUB 2 will present a menu similar to that shown in Figure 5-2.

If the system includes more than one Linux kernel, or more than one operating system, there may be multiple choices available, which you can highlight with the UP ARROW and DOWN ARROW keys. To boot Linux from the highlighted option, press ENTER.

On old PCs (pre-21st century), some BIOSes could not find your bootloader unless it was located within the first 1024 cylinders of the hard disk. For that reason, the partition where the /boot directory is configured is normally the first available primary partition.

RHEL 9 supports the traditional MBR partitioning layout and the newer GPT format. Whereas the MBR partitioning scheme supports a maximum size of 2TB per disk, GPT does not have such limitation. However, to boot RHEL from a disk with a GPT partition layout, you need a system with the UEFI firmware interface rather than a traditional BIOS firmware. You should check with your hardware vendor if UEFI is supported by your system.

CERTIFICATION OBJECTIVE 5.02

Bootloaders and GRUB 2

The standard bootloader associated with Red Hat Enterprise Linux is GRUB 2, the GRand Unified Bootloader version 2. As suggested by the Red Hat exam requirements, for the RHCSA exam you need to know how to use the GRUB 2 menu to boot into different targets and diagnose and correct boot failures arising from bootloader errors. In GRUB version 1, which was the default in RHEL 6, the associated configuration file was relatively easy to understand and customize. However, although the GRUB 2 menu is similar to what's seen on RHEL 6, the steps required to configure that bootloader are quite different, as you'll see later in this chapter.

GRUB, the GRand Unified Bootloader

Red Hat has implemented GRUB 2 as the only bootloader for its Linux distributions. It's normally configured to boot into a configured default kernel. GRUB 2 finds the configuration in the /boot directory and displays a menu, which will look similar to Figure 5-2. You can use the GRUB 2 menu to boot any operating system detected during the Linux installation process, or any other operating system added to appropriate configuration files.

GRUB 2 is flexible. Not only can the configuration be easily generated from the CLI, but also it can be edited directly from the GRUB 2 menu. From the menu shown in Figure 5-2, you can press E to temporarily edit the selected item, or press c to open a GRUB 2 command prompt. This section is focused on booting into different systemd targets.

Boot into an Emergency Shell

To pass a parameter to the kernel through GRUB 2, press E at the first GRUB 2 menu. This allows you to edit the boot parameters sent to the kernel. Locate the line that starts with the directive **linux**. Scroll down with the DOWN ARROW key if necessary. You might then see a configuration line similar to the following:

```
linux ($root)/vmlinuz-5.14.0-162.6.1.el9_1.x86_64 root=/dev/mapper/rhel-root
ro crashkernel=1G-4G:192M,4G-64G:256M,64G-:512M resume=/dev/mapper/rhel-swap
rd.lvm.lv=rhel/root rd.lvm.lv=rhel/swap rhgb quiet
```

Yeah, that's a lot of stuff, which will be explained later in this chapter. What matters for the RHCSA exam is that you understand how to add more kernel parameters to the end of this line. For example, if you add the string **systemd.unit=emergency.target** to the end of this line and press CTRL-X, Linux starts in a mode of operation called *emergency target*, which runs a rescue shell.

From the emergency target, type the root password and then type **exit**. The system will go into the default target, which normally is either the multi-user target or the graphical target. If you have made changes or repairs to any partitions, the next step is to reboot the computer with the **systemctl reboot** command. At some point during a Red Hat exam, you should test the changes that you've made with a reboot.

On RHEL 9, the shutdown, reboot, **and** halt **commands are symbolic links to** systemctl. **They have the same effect as the** systemctl poweroff, systemctl reboot, **and** systemctl halt **commands, respectively.**

e x a m
ⓦatch

Changes must survive a reboot during the RHCSA exam, so you'll want to restart your system at least once to verify each of the requirements is met even after a reboot.

To a certain extent, the concept of the systemd targets is similar to that of runlevels in older Linux distributions and is detailed later in this chapter. For now, all you need to know is that when RHEL 9 is configured to boot into a GUI, it's configured to boot into the graphical target by default. That target can be changed by appending a **systemd.unit=***name***.target** string to the end of the kernel command line.

If you need direct access into a recovery shell, add the string **systemd.unit=rescue.target** to the end of the kernel command line. In rare cases, some systems are so troubled, they don't boot into the rescue target. In that case, you can boot the system into the emergency target by appending the string **systemd.unit=emergency.target** to the kernel command line. The difference between rescue and emergency targets is that the former mounts the filesystems in read-write mode, while the latter does not mount any filesystems, apart from the root filesystem in read-only mode.

The emergency and rescue targets require the root password to log in and get full root administrative privileges. If you have lost the root password, you will need to add the string **rd.break** to the end of the kernel command line and follow the procedure illustrated later in Exercise 5-2. As that supports full administrative privileges, including changes to the root administrative password, you may want to password-protect the GRUB 2 menu. Somebody who can change the boot order can achieve the same thing with a bootable USB drive, so it is also important to protect your BIOS or UEFI firmware to ensure the system only boots the local disk without a password. However, this is out of the scope of the RHCSA exam.

Now you should understand how to boot into different targets during the boot process. Table 5-1 summarizes the boot options described so far.

TABLE 5-1	How to Start an Emergency Shell

Boot Option	Description
systemd.unit=emergency.target	Emergency shell; only the / filesystem is mounted in read-only mode. The root password is required to log in.
system.unit=rescue.target	Emergency shell; all filesystems are mounted. The root password is required to log in.
rd.break	Emergency shell; used to recover the root password.

exam

watch

Red Hat exams are "closed book." Although you are allowed to use all documentation that can be found on your RHEL installation, during recovery or emergency procedures you may not have access to man pages or other documentation resources. Therefore, it is extremely important that you practice the exercises

in this chapter without the help of any documentation. You should memorize the steps to boot into an emergency shell or to recover a root password; otherwise, you may be in trouble, not just during the RHCSA exam, but also in real life when performing your job duties as a Linux sysadmin.

EXERCISE 5-1

Boot into a Different Target

One key skill is knowing how to boot into a different systemd target. This exercise assumes you've configured RHEL 9 per Chapter 1, which sets the graphical target as the default. Run the **ls -l /etc/systemd/system/default.target** command to verify. If the current system reflects the defaults, this file should be a symbolic link to the graphical.target file within the directory /usr/lib/systemd/system. As an alternative, run the following command:

```
# systemctl get-default
```

It should return the string "graphical.target." Now you can start the exercise.

1. Reboot your system using the **reboot** command.
2. When you see the following message, make sure to press any key to access the GRUB 2 menu:

   ```
   The selected entry will be started automatically in 5s.
   ```

3. Press E to edit the current menu entry.
4. Scroll down with the DOWN ARROW key to locate the line starting with **linux**. First, delete the kernel options **rhgb quiet**. Then, at the end of the line, type **systemd .unit=multi-user.target** and press CTRL-X to boot this kernel.
5. Watch the boot messages. What kind of login screen do you see?
6. Log in to this system. You can use any existing user account.

7. Run the **reboot** command to restart this system.

8. Repeat Steps 2 through 4, but boot this system into the rescue target by passing the option **systemd.unit=rescue.target** to the kernel.

9. Watch the boot messages. What kind of login screen do you see? Which filesystems are mounted?

10. Repeat Steps 2 through 4, but boot this system into the emergency target by passing the option **systemd.unit=emergency.target** to the kernel.

11. Watch the boot messages. What kind of login screen do you see? Do you have to log in at all? Which filesystems are mounted?

12. Repeat Steps 2 through 4, but this time append **rd.break** to the kernel command line.

13. Watch the boot messages. What kind of login screen do you see? Do you have to log in at all? Is the root filesystem mounted from the hard drive?

14. Type **reboot** to log out and restart the system.

EXERCISE 5-2

Recover the Root Password

If you boot a RHEL 9 system into the rescue or emergency target, you are prompted for the root password. But what if you have forgotten the password? This exercise shows the steps required to reset a lost password for the root user. During the password-recovery process, you probably won't have access to documentation. Hence, you should practice the following procedure until you are fully prepared to use it in a crisis:

1. Use the following command to change the root password to a random string. This command hides the random password from you:

```
# openssl rand -base64 15 | passwd --stdin root
```

2. Log out from your session. Try to log in again as the root user. You shouldn't be able to log in to the system with the old known root password.

3. Reboot the server.

4. When you see the following message, press a key to access the GRUB 2 menu:

```
The selected entry will be started automatically in 5s.
```

5. Press E to edit the current menu entry.

6. Scroll down with the DOWN ARROW key to locate the line starting with **linux**. Press CTRL-E or END to move to the end of the line, and then type the string **rd.break**.

7. Press CTRL-X to boot the system.

8. The **rd.break** directive interrupts the boot sequence before the root filesystem is properly mounted. Confirm this by running **ls /sysroot**. If you know the contents of the root filesystem, the output should look familiar.

9. Remount the root /sysroot filesystem as read-write and change the root directory to /sysroot (you will learn more about the **mount** command in Chapter 7):

```
# mount -o remount,rw /sysroot
# chroot /sysroot
```

10. Change the root password:

```
# passwd
```

11. Because SELinux is not running, the **passwd** command does not preserve the context of the /etc/passwd file. To ensure that the /etc/passwd file is labeled with the correct SELinux context, instruct Linux to relabel all files at the next boot with the following command:

```
# touch /.autorelabel
```

12. Type **exit** to close the chroot jail, and then type **exit** again to reboot the system.

13. It may take a few minutes for SELinux to relabel all files. Once you get a login prompt, confirm that you are able to log in as the root user.

Modify the System Bootloader

The RHCSA specifically requires that you need to know how to "modify the system bootloader." That means you need to know how to configure GRUB 2 in detail. The configuration is available in the file /etc/grub2.cfg, which is a symbolic link that points to /boot/grub2/grub.cfg on systems configured in BIOS mode, or /boot/efi/EFI/redhat/grub.cfg for servers that use an UEFI boot manager. See Figure 5-3 to see an excerpt of the grub.cfg file. In the rest of this chapter, we will assume that you run a traditional BIOS-based system or a UEFI-capable system in BIOS mode. We'll refer to /boot/grub2/grub.cfg as the standard path of the configuration file.

Although the number of options and directives in the grub.cfg file may seem overwhelming, don't panic. You never need to touch this file directly. The right approach is to generate a new version of this file with the **grub2-mkconfig** tool, based on the /etc/default/grub configuration file and on the scripts in the /etc/grub.d/ directory. The /etc/default/grub file is much simpler to understand, safer, and more convenient to edit than

FIGURE 5-3 An excerpt of the grub.cfg file

```
### BEGIN /etc/grub.d/10_linux ###
insmod part_msdos
insmod xfs
set root='hd0,msdos1'
if [ x$feature_platform_search_hint = xy ]; then
  search --no-floppy --fs-uuid --set=root --hint='hd0,msdos1'  d812e0fb-87c7-49d5-89d5-3453fb415838
else
  search --no-floppy --fs-uuid --set=root d812e0fb-87c7-49d5-89d5-3453fb415838
fi
insmod part_msdos
insmod xfs
set boot='hd0,msdos1'
if [ x$feature_platform_search_hint = xy ]; then
  search --no-floppy --fs-uuid --set=boot --hint='hd0,msdos1'  d812e0fb-87c7-49d5-89d5-3453fb415838
else
  search --no-floppy --fs-uuid --set=boot d812e0fb-87c7-49d5-89d5-3453fb415838
fi

# This section was generated by a script. Do not modify the generated file - all changes
# will be lost the next time file is regenerated. Instead edit the BootLoaderSpec files.
#
# The blscfg command parses the BootLoaderSpec files stored in /boot/loader/entries and
# populates the boot menu. Please refer to the Boot Loader Specification documentation
# for the files format: https://systemd.io/BOOT_LOADER_SPECIFICATION/.

# The kernelopts variable should be defined in the grubenv file. But to ensure that menu
# entries populated from BootLoaderSpec files that use this variable work correctly even
# without a grubenv file, define a fallback kernelopts variable if this has not been set.
```

grub.cfg. Once you have made a modification to /etc/default/grub, generate the new GRUB configuration file by running

```
# grub2-mkconfig -o /boot/grub2/grub.cfg
```

Do not manually edit the /boot/grub2/grub.cfg file. Use grub2-mkconfig **and the /etc/default/grub file to make modifications to grub.cfg.**

The following is a detailed analysis of a typical version of the /etc/default/grub file:

```
GRUB_TIMEOUT=5
GRUB_DISTRIBUTOR="$(sed 's, release .*$,,g' /etc/system-release)"
GRUB_DEFAULT=saved
GRUB_DISABLE_SUBMENU=true
GRUB_TERMINAL_OUTPUT="console"
GRUB_CMDLINE_LINUX="crashkernel=1G-4G:192M,4G-64G:256M,↵
64G-:512M resume=/dev/mapper/rhel-swap rd.lvm.lv=rhel/↵
root rd.lvm.lv=rhel/swap rhgb quiet"
GRUB_DISABLE_RECOVERY="true"
GRUB_ENABLE_BLSCFG=true
```

In the first line, the GRUB_TIMEOUT variable specifies the time in seconds before GRUB 2 automatically boots the default operating system. You can interrupt the countdown by pressing any key on the keyboard. If this variable is set to 0, GRUB 2 will not display a list of bootable kernels, unless you press and hold an alphanumeric key during the BIOS initial screen.

The value of the GRUB_DISTRIBUTOR variable returns "Red Hat Enterprise Linux" on a standard RHEL installation, and is displayed before each kernel-bootable entry. You can modify this entry to any string of your choice if you wish.

The next variable is GRUB_DEFAULT and is related to the default kernel that GRUB 2 loads at boot. The value "saved" instructs GRUB 2 to look at the saved_entry variable in the file /boot/grub2/grubenv. This variable is updated with the name of the latest kernel every time that a new kernel is installed.

You can update the saved_entry variable and instruct GRUB 2 to boot a different default kernel via the **grub2-set-default** command. As an example,

```
# grub2-set-default 1
```

sets the second menu entry as the default kernel. This may be slightly confusing because GRUB 2 starts counting from 0. Hence, **grub2-set-default 0** points to the first available menu. Similarly, the command **grub2-set-default 1** points to the second kernel entry, and so on.

The next configuration line in /etc/default/grub defines the variable GRUB_DISABLE_SUBMENU. This is set to "true" by default to disable any submenu entries at boot. Then follows the variable GRUB_TERMINAL_OUTPUT, which tells GRUB 2 to use a text console as the default output terminal. The last two variables defined in the file are GRUB_DISABLE_RECOVERY, which disables the generation of recovery menu entries, and GRUB_ENABLE_BLSCFG, which tells GRUB 2 to use a special file format, the Boot Loader Specification (BLS).

The variable GRUB_CMDLINE_LINUX is more interesting. It specifies the options to pass to the Linux kernel. For example, **rd.lvm.lv** tells the name of the logical volumes where the root filesystem and swap partition are located. The **crashkernel** option is used to reserve some memory for **kdump**, which is invoked to capture a kernel core dump if the system crashes. Finally, at the end of the line, the **rhgb quiet** directives enable the Red Hat graphical boot and hide the boot messages by default. If you want to enable verbose boot messages, remove the **quiet** option from this line.

How to Update GRUB 2

If you need to reinstall the GRUB 2 bootloader, just run the **grub2-install** command. If it doesn't automatically write the GRUB 2 pointer to the MBR, or if multiple hard drives are available, you may need to include the hard drive device, such as /dev/vda. It's also possible to set up GRUB 2 on a portable drive; just specify the device with the command.

When the GRUB 2 configuration file is generated using **grub2-mkconfig**, no additional commands are required. The pointer from the MBR automatically reads the current version of the /boot/grub2/grub.cfg file.

The GRUB 2 Command Line

An error in grub.cfg can result in an unbootable system. For example, if GRUB 2 identifies the wrong volume as the root partition (/), Linux will hang during the boot process. Other configuration errors in /boot/grub2/grub.cfg can lead to a kernel panic during the boot process.

Now that you've analyzed the GRUB 2 configuration file, you can probably visualize some of the effects of errors in this file. If some of the filenames or partitions are wrong, GRUB 2 won't be able to find critical files such as the Linux kernel. If the GRUB 2 configuration file is completely missing, you'll see a prompt similar to this:

```
grub>
```

You can access a GRUB 2 command line by pressing the c key when the menu is displayed. To see a list of available commands, press the TAB key at the grub> prompt, or type the **help** command.

Command completion is also available. For example, if you don't remember the name of the kernel file, type **linux** / and then press the TAB key to review the available files in the /boot directory.

You should be able to find all detected hard drives on a standard PC from the BIOS/UEFI menus with the **ls** command. As an example, let's find the /boot partition and grub.cfg file on this particular system. By default, the /boot directory is mounted on a separate partition. First, run **ls** at the grub> command line:

```
grub> ls
(hd0) (hd0,msdos1) (hd0,msdos2)
```

The string **hd0** denotes the first hard drive, whereas **msdos1** is the first partition, created with the MBR format (msdos). If a server was partitioned using the newer GPT partition format, GRUB 2 would identify the first partition as **gpt1** rather than **msdos1**. Similarly, **hd0,msdos2** denotes the second partition on the first hard drive.

Next, use that information to find the grub.cfg file:

```
grub> ls (hd0,msdos1)/grub2/grub.cfg
grub.cfg
```

If the file is not on the noted partition, you'll see an "error: file '/grub2/grub.cfg' not found" error message. You may also see "error: unknown filesystem" if the noted partition does not contain a valid filesystem.

We know that the /boot directory is on (**hd0,msdos1**). To confirm the location of grub.cfg, run the following command:

```
grub> cat (hd0,msdos1)/grub2/grub.cfg
```

You should see the contents of the grub.cfg file in the output. Press a key to scroll through the content of the file until you are back to the GRUB 2 command line.

There's one more way to identify the partition with the /boot directory. Run the **search.file** command to find grub.cfg:

```
grub> search.file /grub2/grub.cfg
```

GRUB 2 should return the partition with the /boot directory. In this case, it's the first partition on the first hard drive:

```
hd0,msdos1
```

Now you can use these commands from the GRUB 2 configuration file to boot Linux from the grub> prompt. If the top-level root filesystem is located on a partition, you may even confirm the contents of the /etc/fstab file with a command like the following:

```
grub> cat (hd0,msdos2)/etc/fstab
```

If the root filesystem resides on an LVM volume, the preceding command might return an "error: unknown filesystem" message. If you encounter this problem, load the LVM module using the following command:

```
grub> insmod lvm
```

Now, the **ls** command should also include logical volumes in its output:

```
grub> ls
(hd0) (hd0,msdos2) (hd0,msdos1) (lvm/rhel-root) (lvm/rhel-swap)
```

Finally, to print the content of /etc/fstab, run the following command:

```
grub> cat (lvm/rhel-root)/etc/fstab
```

EXERCISE 5-3

Using the GRUB 2 Command Line

In this exercise, you'll boot RHEL 9 manually. Follow these steps:

1. Boot the system. When you see the following line at the top of the screen, press any key to access the GRUB 2 menu:

   ```
   The selected entry will be started automatically in 5s.
   ```

2. Press c for a GRUB-based command-line interface. You should see the grub> prompt.
3. Load the LVM module:

   ```
   grub> insmod lvm
   ```

4. List all partitions and logical volumes:

```
grub> ls
```

5. Identify the root partition. This may be named something like "lvm/rhel-root." You may need to use some trial and error to find out (for example, by trying to display the /etc/fstab file from all the device names previously listed by GRUB 2).

```
grub> cat (lvm/rhel-root)/etc/fstab
```

6. Set the root variable to the device that you have identified as that containing the root filesystem:

```
grub> set root=(lvm/rhel-root)
```

7. Enter the **linux** command, which specifies the kernel and root directory partition. Yes, this is a long line; however, you can use command completion (press the TAB key) to make it faster. In addition, the only important parts of the line are the kernel file and the location of the top-level root directory.

```
linux (hd0,msdos1)/vmlinuz-5.14.0-162.6.1.el9_1.x86_64↵
root=/dev/mapper/rhel-root
```

8. Enter the **initrd** command, which specifies the initial RAM disk command and file location. Again, you can use the TAB key for filename completion.

```
initrd (hd0,msdos1)/initramfs-5.14.0-162.6.1.el9_1.x86_64.img
```

9. Now enter the **boot** command. If this command is successful, Linux should now boot the selected kernel and initial RAM disk just as if you selected that option from the GRUB 2 configuration menu.

An Option for Booting from GRUB 2: Rescue Mode

The troubleshooting objectives associated with a previous version of the RHCSA exam prep guide suggested that you needed to be able to recover from a complete boot failure, such as if the GRUB 2 configuration file were corrupt or missing. In other words, if you've tried to boot directly from the grub> prompt described earlier and failed, you might need to resort to the option known as rescue mode. That requires access to the installation DVD or the network boot disk.

The RHCSA objectives no longer include a requirement associated with rescue mode. However, because the rescue of unbootable systems is an important skill, it may be included in future versions of the exam.

To that end, boot from one of those media options. You should see the installation screen with the following options:

```
Install Red Hat Enterprise Linux 9.1
Test this media & install Red Hat Enterprise Linux 9.1
Troubleshooting
```

Select the Troubleshooting option and press ENTER. You will see a second screen with the following options:

```
Install Red Hat Enterprise Linux 9.1 using text mode
Rescue a Red Hat Enterprise Linux system
Run a memory test
Boot from local drive
Return to main menu
```

Select the Rescue a Red Hat Enterprise Linux system option and press ENTER. Rescue mode runs a stable minimal version of the RHEL 9 operating system on the local machine. It's in essence a text-only version of the "Live DVD" media available on other Linux distributions such as Knoppix or Ubuntu distributions.

on the **For RHEL 9, it's best to use RHEL 9 rescue media. Such media uses a kernel compiled by Red Hat, customized for supported hardware. Nevertheless, options such as Knoppix are also good.**

You can use the rescue environment to recover unbootable systems. In most cases, the next step you see is shown in Figure 5-4.

FIGURE 5-4

Options for
the rescue
environment

```
Starting installer, one moment...
anaconda 34.25.1.14-1.e19 for Red Hat Enterprise Linux 9.1 started.
 * installation log files are stored in /tmp during the installation
 * shell is available on TTY2
 * when reporting a bug add logs from /tmp as separate text/plain attachments
================================================================================
================================================================================
Rescue

The rescue environment will now attempt to find your Linux installation and
mount it under the directory : /mnt/sysroot.  You can then make any changes
required to your system.  Choose '1' to proceed with this step.
You can choose to mount your file systems read-only instead of read-write by
choosing '2'.
If for some reason this process does not work choose '3' to skip directly to a
shell.


1) Continue
2) Read-only mount
3) Skip to shell
4) Quit (Reboot)

Please make a selection from the above: _
```

FIGURE 5-5

Mounting the
root filesystem
in the rescue
environment

```
Your system has been mounted under /mnt/sysroot.

If you would like to make the root of your system the root of the active system,
run the command:

        chroot /mnt/sysroot

When finished, please exit from the shell and your system will reboot.

Please press ENTER to get a shell:
```

The *Continue* option, as shown in Figure 5-5, mounts all detected volumes as subdirectories of the /mnt/sysroot directory. The *Read-Only Mount* option mounts detected volumes in read-only mode. The *Skip to Shell* option moves straight to a command-line interface. Select Continue. After confirmation, you'll be presented with a shell prompt.

From the shell prompt, enter the **chroot /mnt/sysroot** command. As the regular top-level root directory for the system is mounted on the /mnt/sysroot directory, the **chroot** command changes the root directory, as if the /mnt/sysroot filesystem was mounted under /.

Do practice what you've learned about GRUB 2 in this section. It could help you recover from a real-world problem—and Red Hat does say that their exams are filled with "real-world tasks." However, don't assume that you have access to a CD or a DVD during a Red Hat exam. If a rescue media is not available, that should mean that there's at least one alternative method you can use to address the problem.

CERTIFICATION OBJECTIVE 5.03

Between GRUB 2 and Login

This section provides a basic overview of the boot process after the GRUB 2 bootloader finds the kernel. If you understand this process, you can diagnose a wide variety of boot problems. The messages associated with the kernel provide a step-by-step view of the process.

The loading of Linux depends on a temporary filesystem, known as the initial RAM disk. Once the boot process is complete, control is given to systemd, known as the first process. This section will describe the contents of systemd in detail, through the configuration of units and targets.

on the Job

Most Linux distributions, including RHEL 9, have replaced Upstart and SysVinit with the systemd service manager.

In this section, you'll also review the commands that allow you to reboot and shut down a system normally.

In systemd, the Unix philosophy that "everything is a file" can be paraphrased as "everything is a unit." Units are the basic building blocks of systemd.

Kernels and the Initial RAM Disk

After you select a kernel from the GRUB 2 configuration menu, Linux hands over boot responsibilities to the kernel with the help of the initial RAM disk, also known by its filename in the /boot directory, initramfs. As suggested by its name, it is actually a filesystem, but it is saved in a file rather than on a disk partition.

During the boot process, Linux loads that temporary filesystem into your RAM. Linux then loads hardware drivers and starts the first process, **systemd**.

Next, **systemd** activates all the system units for the initrd.target and mounts the root filesystem under /sysroot. Finally, **systemd** restarts itself in the new root directory and activates all units for the default target (we will look in more detail at units and targets in the next section).

To learn more, disable the **quiet** directive for the desired kernel in the GRUB configuration file. Boot your system. Watch as the messages pass quickly through the screen. After logging in, you can review these messages by running the **dmesg** command.

You can find more log information in the systemd journal. Display its contents with the **journalctl** command. What you see depends on the hardware and configuration of the local system. Key messages include the following:

- The version of the kernel
- SELinux status, if active. By default, SELinux first starts in permissive mode, until the configured policy (enforcing) is loaded near the end of the boot process.
- The amount of recognized RAM (which does not necessarily match the actual amount of installed RAM)
- CPUs
- Kernel command line, specifying the logical volume or root filesystem
- Freeing of memory associated with the initial RAM disk (initramfs)
- Hard drives and partitions (as defined by their device filenames, such as /dev/sda or /dev/vda1)
- Active filesystems
- Swap partitions

The log file is filled with excellent information. If the system is loading the wrong kernel, you'll see evidence of that here. If Linux isn't using a partition that you've configured, you'll also see it here (indirectly). If SELinux isn't loading properly, you'll see it in messages toward the end of the file.

a t c h   Remember that the Red | cannot be solved by some Linux command),
Hat exams are not hardware exams. If you | inform your instructor/exam proctor. Don't
identify a problem with a key hardware | be surprised, however, if she responds that
component, such as a network card (which | it's not a hardware problem.

The First Process, Targets, and Units

The Linux kernel continues the boot process by calling the first process, **systemd**. In RHEL 9, the legacy **init** process is configured with a symbolic link to **systemd**.

Units are the basic building blocks of systemd. The most common are *service units*, which have a **.service** extension and activate a system service. To show a list of all service units, type the following command:

```
# systemctl list-units --type=service --all
```

The **--all** flag includes all units, not just the active ones. There are other types of units, such as mount and automount units, which manage mount points; path units, which activate a service when there is a change on a filesystem path (such as a spool directory); socket units, which start a service only when a client connection is made (if you have used the **xinetd** daemon, this is similar to how **xinetd** starts services on demand); and many, many more.

A special type of unit is a *target unit*, which is used to group together other system units and to transition the system into a different state. To list all target units, type the following command:

```
# systemctl list-units --type=target --all
```

The most important target units are described in Table 5-2.

In systemd, targets serve the same function as runlevels in previous RHEL distributions. In RHEL 6, seven runlevels, 0 through 6, were available. Linux services were organized by runlevel. Each runlevel was associated with a level of functionality.

TABLE 5-2	Target Unit	Description
The systemd Target Units	emergency.target	Emergency shell; only the / filesystem is mounted in read-only mode.
	graphical.target	The default target for multi-user graphical systems.
	multi-user.target	Nongraphical multi-user system.
	rescue.target	Emergency shell; all filesystems are mounted.

Runlevel	systemd Target	Description
0	poweroff.target	Halt the system
1	rescue.target	Single-user mode for maintenance and repair
2	multi-user.target	Multi-user, without NFS
3	multi-user.target	Full multi-user mode
4	multi-user.target	Not used in RHEL 6
5	graphical.target	X11 GUI with networking
6	reboot.target	Reboot the system

For example, in runlevel 1, only one user was allowed to log in to that Linux system. X11 mode, also known as runlevel 5, was used to start Linux with a GUI login screen, if appropriate packages were installed. Table 5-3 compares systemd targets and the runlevels defined in RHEL 6.

Run the following command:

```
# ls -l /usr/lib/systemd/system/runlevel?.target
```

Note the symbolic links in the output. See how files such as runlevel0.target, runlevel1 .target, and so on are linked to systemd targets such as poweroff.target and rescue.target? These links provide backward compatibility with the old SysV runlevels. You can even refer to graphical.target as runlevel5.target and multi-user.target as runlevel3.target.

Targets are controlled by units, organized in unit files. Although the default target is defined in /etc/systemd/system, you can override the default during the boot process from the GRUB 2 menu.

Each target may be associated with several systemd units. Each unit can start or stop Linux services such as printing (**cupsd**), scheduling (**crond**), the Apache web server (**httpd**), the Samba file server (**smbd**), and more. When configured, the boot process starts and stops the systemd units of your choice. These units are known as dependencies. To list all dependencies of the default graphical.target unit, run the following command:

```
# systemctl list-dependencies graphical.target
```

The default target is specified as a symbolic link from the /etc/systemd/system/default.target file to either multi-user.target or graphical.target. You can also use the **systemctl** command to retrieve the current default target or to change the current settings, as shown here:

```
# systemctl get-default
graphical.target
# systemctl set-default multi-user.target
Removed "/etc/systemd/system/default.target".
Created symlink /etc/systemd/system/default.target → ↵
/usr/lib/systemd/system/multi-user.target.
```

As you can see from this output, the **systemctl set-default multi-user.target** command creates a symbolic link named /etc/systemd/system/default.target, which points to the corresponding multi-user.target configuration file.

Switch Between Targets

Now that you've examined the different targets available on RHEL 9, it's time to explore how to switch between targets. On earlier versions of RHEL, this is functionally equivalent to switching runlevels. First, establish the default target with the following command:

```
# systemctl get-default
graphical.target
```

RHEL 9 normally boots to either graphical.target or multi-user.target. After logging in as the administrative user, you can move to a different target with the **systemctl isolate** command. For example, the following command moves the system to the multi-user target:

```
# systemctl isolate multi-user.target
```

After that command is complete, rerun the **systemctl get-default** command. The output confirms that the default target has not changed:

```
graphical.target
```

Now try something else. What do you think happens when the following command is executed?

```
# systemctl isolate poweroff.target
```

Reboot and Shut Down a System Normally

The commands required to reboot and shut down a system are straightforward. As just suggested in the previous section, the following commands provide one way to shut down and reboot a system, respectively:

```
# systemctl poweroff
# systemctl reboot
```

For legacy purposes, Red Hat has created symbolic links from the following commands to **systemctl**. These commands work just as they did in earlier versions of RHEL.

```
# shutdown
# reboot
```

systemd Replaces Upstart and SysVinit

The **systemd** process is the first process started at boot. It takes charge of activating all services. It replaces the traditional **init** daemon and the Upstart system, which is also a substitute for **init** and was the default **init** daemon on RHEL 6. The design and philosophy of Upstart are very similar to the old SysVinit system, which relies on init scripts to activate services, and on the concept of runlevels, which was introduced in the previous sections.

In contrast, systemd introduces a lot of new tools and can do much more, while maintaining compatibility with SysVinit. The design of systemd is based on optimal efficiency. First, at boot, systemd activates only the services that are strictly required, whereas others are started on demand. As an example, systemd starts the CUPS printing service only when a print job is sent to the /var/spool/cups queue. In addition, systemd parallelizes the initialization of services.

As a result, the boot process under systemd is faster. To display the time required to boot your system, run the following command:

```
# systemd-analyze time
Startup finished in 1.187s (kernel) + 1.246s↵
(initrd) + 2.898s (userspace) = 5.332s.
```

This output shows the time required to initialize the kernel, plus the time to load the initial RAM disk (initrd) and the time to activate systemd units (userspace). The total time is 5.332 seconds. But there's more. You can display a detailed account of the time required to activate each systemd unit by running **systemd-analyze blame**. An example is shown in Figure 5-6.

The numbers in Figure 5-6 don't equal the total userspace time reported by **systemd-analyze time**. That happens because systemd starts multiple services simultaneously.

FIGURE 5-6

Initialization time of systemd units

```
[root@server1 ~]# systemd-analyze blame
1.706s plymouth-quit-wait.service
 811ms dracut-initqueue.service
 476ms kdump.service
 324ms rhsm.service
 322ms systemd-udev-settle.service
 271ms NetworkManager-wait-online.service
 204ms initrd-switch-root.service
 138ms firewalld.service
 130ms fwupd.service
 125ms udisks2.service
  92ms packagekit.service
  85ms systemd-vconsole-setup.service
  85ms power-profiles-daemon.service
  84ms accounts-daemon.service
  82ms polkit.service
  70ms upower.service
  65ms systemd-logind.service
  60ms user@1000.service
  55ms chronyd.service
  54ms switcheroo-control.service
  51ms systemd-udev-trigger.service
  51ms initrd-parse-etc.service
  41ms ModemManager.service
  35ms lvm2-monitor.service
```

But there's even more. Although an in-depth knowledge of all the features of systemd is outside of the scope of the RHCSA exam, systems administrators can take advantage of some of its capabilities.

Some Linux developers have argued that systemd does too much and breaks the Unix philosophy of writing programs that "do one thing and do it well." However, as of today, systemd has been adopted by most of the major Linux distributions.

Logging

The **systemd** process includes a powerful logging system. You can display all collected logs with the **journalctl** command. By default, the journal log files are temporarily stored in RAM in a ring buffer in the /run/log/journal directory. To get Linux to write journal log files persistently on disk, run the following commands:

```
# mkdir /var/log/journal
# journalctl --flush
```

Once persistent logging is enabled, you can show log messages from a specific boot with the **-b** switch: **journalctl -b 0** displays the log messages since the last boot, **journalctl -b 1** from the boot before the last one, and so on. You don't have to switch through different log files because **journactl** automatically aggregates available data from the current and all rotated log files.

You can also filter log messages based on their priority using the **-p** command option. As an example, **journalctl -p warning** displays all messages with a priority level of "warning" or higher. Log messages of a "warning" priority level are displayed in yellow, whereas messages with priority levels of "err" and higher are shown in red.

Control Groups

Control groups (or cgroups) are a feature of the Linux kernel to group processes together and control or limit their resource usage (such as CPU, memory, and so on). In systemd, cgroups are primarily used to track processes and to ensure that all processes that belong to a service are terminated when a service is stopped.

Under the traditional SysVinit system, it is difficult to identify the service associated with a process. In fact, services often start multiple processes. When you stop a SysVinit service, that service may not be able to terminate all dependent (child) processes. You're stuck with either stopping all dependent processes manually (with the **ps** and **kill** commands) or accepting a system with orphaned processes in an unknown state until the next reboot.

FIGURE 5-7

The cgroup
hierarchy

```
├─NetworkManager.service (#3304)
│ → trusted.invocation_id: 3103e35838664499961c113fe3f1bb14
│ └─889 /usr/sbin/NetworkManager --no-daemon
├─gdm.service (#3808)
│ → trusted.invocation_id: 838b9a32228247549bad8053e8589c64
│ └─1150 /usr/sbin/gdm
├─switcheroo-control.service (#2977)
│ → trusted.invocation_id: 2d606f119ba542139de5f665c477d42c
│ └─783 /usr/libexec/switcheroo-control
├─rsyslog.service (#2851)
│ → trusted.invocation_id: dc1c42c41edc474d9b57c794a37dafdb
│ └─780 /usr/sbin/rsyslogd -n
├─firewalld.service (#3262)
│ → trusted.invocation_id: 5fbefb9cda5948ff90a2a86a23a1da38
│ └─823 /usr/bin/python3 -s /usr/sbin/firewalld --nofork --nopid
├─qemu-guest-agent.service (#2809)
│ → trusted.invocation_id: 40cec57353c941d19aabd983805805cc
│ └─779 /usr/bin/qemu-ga --method=virtio-serial --path=/dev/virtio-ports/org.>
├─alsa-state.service (#3145)
│ → trusted.invocation_id: 7cf34ed6e10643d998a802779a2ed72f
│ └─815 /usr/sbin/alsactl -s -n 19 -c -E ALSA_CONFIG_PATH=/etc/alsa/alsactl.c>
├─spice-vdagentd.service (#4657)
│ → trusted.invocation_id: b251a178ac2d471f9f5da664eb7ca6ea
lines 208-230
```

To address this limitation, systemd labels processes associated with a service using cgroups. In this way, systemd uses cgroups to kill all processes in a group, if required.

The command **systemd-cgls** displays the cgroup hierarchy in a tree format, as shown in Figure 5-7. From the excerpt in Figure 5-7, you can identify cgroups such as Network Manager and rsyslog.service, along with the processes they have spawned. Note the one-to-one correspondence between cgroups and systemd service units.

Dependencies

The traditional SysVinit system starts services sequentially. In contrast, systemd can activate services in parallel by keeping track of all dependencies between units. The **systemctl list-dependencies** command displays a tree with all dependencies between units.

You can show the dependencies for any available unit. Dependent units must be started first. For example, the following command shows the units that must be started before the **rsyslog** service:

```
# systemctl list-dependencies rsyslog.service
```

An excerpt of the command output is shown in Figure 5-8.

FIGURE 5-8

Dependencies
between systemd
units

```
rsyslog.service
  ● ┌─system.slice
  ● └─sysinit.target
  ●     ┌─dev-hugepages.mount
  ●     ├─dev-mqueue.mount
  ●     ├─dracut-shutdown.service
  ○     ├─iscsi-onboot.service
  ●     ├─kmod-static-nodes.service
  ○     ├─ldconfig.service
  ●     ├─lvm2-lvmpolld.socket
  ●     ├─lvm2-monitor.service
  ○     ├─multipathd.service
  ●     ├─nis-domainname.service
  ●     ├─plymouth-read-write.service
  ●     ├─plymouth-start.service
  ●     ├─proc-sys-fs-binfmt_misc.automount
  ○     ├─selinux-autorelabel-mark.service
  ●     ├─sys-fs-fuse-connections.mount
  ●     ├─sys-kernel-config.mount
  ●     ├─sys-kernel-debug.mount
  ●     ├─sys-kernel-tracing.mount
  ○     ├─systemd-ask-password-console.path
  ○     ├─systemd-binfmt.service
lines 1-23
```

systemd Units

The **systemd** process uses various configuration files to start other processes. You can find these configuration files in the following directories: /etc/systemd/system and /usr/lib/systemd/system.

The default configuration files are stored in /usr/lib/systemd/system. Custom files, stored in /etc/systemd/system, supersede these files. Don't change files in the /usr/lib/systemd/system directory. Any software updates may overwrite those files.

We have already discussed *service* and *target* units, but there are more. Table 5-4 gives a brief description of all available unit types.

Examine the contents of the /usr/lib/systemd/system directory. Each file contains the configuration of a systemd unit whose type matches the filename extension. As an example, the file graphical.target defines the configuration for the graphical login target unit, whereas the file rsyslog.service includes the configuration for the rsyslog service unit.

You can list all active systemd units using the following command:

```
# systemctl list-units
```

The **list-units** keyword is optional because it is the default. If you want to include inactive, maintenance, and failed units, add the **--all** command switch. An excerpt of the output of the command is shown in Figure 5-9.

The first column lists the unit name, while the second column (not shown in Figure 5-9) tells whether or not the unit was properly loaded. The third column displays the state of the unit: active, inactive, failed, or maintenance. The next column includes more detail. Finally, the last column shows a brief description of the unit.

TABLE 5-4 The systemd Unit Types

Unit Type	Description
Target	A group of units. It is used as a synchronization point at startup to define a set of units to be activated.
Service	A service, such as a daemon like the Apache web server.
Socket	An IPC or network socket, used to activate a service when traffic is received on a listening socket (similar to the activation of services on demand performed by the **xinetd** daemon).
Device	A device unit, such as a drive or partition.
Mount	A filesystem mount point controlled by systemd.
Automount	A filesystem automount point controlled by systemd.
Swap	A swap partition to be activated by systemd.
Path	A path monitored by systemd, used to activate a service when the path changes.
Timer	A timer controlled by systemd, used to activate a service when the timer elapses.
Snapshot	Used to create a snapshot of the systemd run-time state.
Slice	A group of system resources (such as CPU, memory, and so on) that can be assigned to a unit via the cgroup interface.
Scope	A unit for organizing and managing resource utilization of a set of system processes.

FIGURE 5-9

systemd units

```
lvm2-lvmpolld.socket
spice-vdagentd.socket
sssd-kcm.socket
systemd-coredump.socket
systemd-initctl.socket
systemd-journald-dev-log.socket
systemd-journald.socket
systemd-rfkill.socket
systemd-udevd-control.socket
systemd-udevd-kernel.socket
dev-mapper-rhel\x2dswap.swap
basic.target
cryptsetup.target
getty.target
graphical.target
integritysetup.target
local-fs-pre.target
local-fs.target
multi-user.target
network-online.target
network-pre.target
network.target
nss-user-lookup.target
lines 111-133
```

FIGURE 5-10	UNIT FILE	STATE	VENDOR PRESET
	proc-sys-fs-binfmt_misc.automount	static	-
	-.mount	generated	-
Installed unit files	boot.mount	generated	-
	dev-hugepages.mount	static	-
	dev-mqueue.mount	static	-
	proc-sys-fs-binfmt_misc.mount	disabled	disabled
	run-vmblock\x2dfuse.mount	disabled	disabled
	sys-fs-fuse-connections.mount	static	-
	sys-kernel-config.mount	static	-
	sys-kernel-debug.mount	static	-
	sys-kernel-tracing.mount	static	-
	tmp.mount	disabled	disabled
	cups.path	enabled	enabled
	insights-client-results.path	disabled	disabled
	ostree-finalize-staged.path	disabled	disabled
	systemd-ask-password-console.path	static	-
	systemd-ask-password-plymouth.path	static	-
	systemd-ask-password-wall.path	static	-
	session-2.scope	transient	-
	accounts-daemon.service	enabled	enabled
	alsa-restore.service	static	-
	alsa-state.service	static	-
	lines 1-23		

Whereas the **systemctl list-units** command gives a run-time snapshot of the state of each unit, the following command shows whether a unit is enabled or disabled at startup:

```
# systemctl list-unit-files
```

An example of the output is shown in Figure 5-10. As you can see, units can be "enabled" or "disabled." There is also another state, named "static," which means that a unit is enabled and it cannot be manually disabled.

Virtual Consoles and Login Screens

The login terminals in Linux are virtual terminals. Most Linux systems, including RHEL 9, are configured with six standard command-line virtual terminals. These consoles are numbered from 1 to 6. When configured with a GUI and a login manager, RHEL 9 substitutes the graphical login screen for the first and second virtual consoles.

What does that all mean? In Linux, you can switch between virtual consoles with an ALT-function key combination. For example, ALT-F2 brings you to the second virtual console. You can switch between adjacent virtual terminals by pressing ALT-RIGHT ARROW or ALT-LEFT ARROW. For example, to move from virtual console 2 to 3, press ALT-RIGHT ARROW. If you're in a GUI, add the CTRL key. So in RHEL 9, if the GUI is installed, you'd press CTRL-ALT-F3 to get to the third virtual console.

When you log in to a regular virtual console, Linux returns a command-line shell. The default shell for a user is defined in the /etc/passwd file described in Chapter 6. When you log in to a GUI, Linux returns the configured GUI desktop.

CERTIFICATION OBJECTIVE 5.04

Control by Target

With systemd, Red Hat Enterprise Linux service management is customized by target. Since systemd includes links to runlevels for backward compatibility with SysVinit, you can still refer to the runlevels listed in Table 5-3 with commands such as **init** and **telinit**. However, you should get familiar with targets because this is the standard method of activating services at boot.

Linux is highly customizable. Therefore, it makes sense that the systemd units that start in each target can be customized. Although GUI tools are available to customize systemd units, configuring them from the command-line interface is generally a lot faster.

Functionality by Target

As described earlier, the basic functionality of each target is listed in the configuration files in the directories /etc/systemd/systemd and /usr/lib/systemd/system. For example, let's start with the default target, which in a RHEL 9 system with graphical login is

```
# systemctl get-default
graphical.target
```

The system knows that graphical.target is the default thanks to a symbolic link from the /etc/systemd/system/default.target file to the graphical.target file in /usr/lib/system/system. Take a look at one of those files. An excerpt is shown here:

```
[Unit]
Description=Graphical Interface
Documentation=man:systemd.special(7)
Requires=multi-user.target
Wants=display-manager.service
Conflicts=rescue.service rescue.target
After=multi-user.target rescue.service rescue.target ↵
display-manager.service
AllowIsolate=yes
```

on the

ⓙob

You may also use the systemctl cat *unitname* **command to display the content of a system unit file.**

This means that a target can include another target. In this case, graphical.target is a superset of multi-user.target. After all systemd units in multi-user.target have started, graphical.target activates display-manager.service, as indicated by the Wants directive in the graphical.target configuration file.

Other services started by graphical.target may be listed in the graphical.target.wants subdirectory in /etc/systemd/system or /usr/lib/systemd/system. In a default RHEL 9 installation, we see the following file:

```
# ls /usr/lib/systemd/system/graphical.target.wants
systemd-updated-utmp-runlevel.service
```

The Innards of systemd Units

The systemd units are activated whenever a system moves to a different target. Therefore, the units associated with the default target are executed during the boot process. Appropriate units are also started when you change targets; for example, when you run the **systemctl isolate multi-user.target** command from the graphical.target, Linux stops all service units that were started by the graphical target.

But you can control systemd units directly. For example, examine the content of the file rsyslog.service from the /usr/lib/systemd/system directory, as shown in Figure 5-11.

FIGURE 5-11

The configuration file of the rsyslog service unit

```
[root@server1 ~]# cat /usr/lib/systemd/system/rsyslog.service
[Unit]
Description=System Logging Service
;Requires=syslog.socket
Documentation=man:rsyslogd(8)
Documentation=https://www.rsyslog.com/doc/

[Service]
Type=notify
EnvironmentFile=-/etc/sysconfig/rsyslog
ExecStart=/usr/sbin/rsyslogd -n $SYSLOGD_OPTIONS
ExecReload=/usr/bin/kill -HUP $MAINPID
UMask=0066
StandardOutput=null
Restart=on-failure

# Increase the default a bit in order to allow many simultaneous
# files to be monitored, we might need a lot of fds.
LimitNOFILE=16384

[Install]
WantedBy=multi-user.target
;Alias=syslog.service
[root@server1 ~]# █
```

FIGURE 5-12   Displaying the status of a service

```
[root@server1 ~]# systemctl status rsyslog
● rsyslog.service - System Logging Service
     Loaded: loaded (/usr/lib/systemd/system/rsyslog.service; enabled; vendor p>
     Active: active (running) since Wed 2023-04-12 15:54:56 BST; 7h ago
       Docs: man:rsyslogd(8)
             https://www.rsyslog.com/doc/
   Main PID: 780 (rsyslogd)
      Tasks: 3 (limit: 22988)
     Memory: 5.8M
        CPU: 1.013s
     CGroup: /system.slice/rsyslog.service
             └─780 /usr/sbin/rsyslogd -n

Apr 12 15:54:56 localhost systemd[1]: Starting System Logging Service...
Apr 12 15:54:56 localhost systemd[1]: Started System Logging Service.
Apr 12 15:54:56 localhost rsyslogd[780]: [origin software="rsyslogd" swVersion=>
Apr 12 15:54:56 localhost rsyslogd[780]: imjournal: journal files changed, relo>
[root@server1 ~]#
```

The configuration starts with the Unit section, which contains a description of the service. Then comes the service configuration, which includes the type of the service, a pointer to a file with some environment variables that configure the service behavior, the main executable to run to activate the service, and a directive that sends all standard output from the service to /dev/null.

Finally, the WantedBy directive tells us that this service will be activated at boot when the system enters into the multi-user target.

Now, run the following command:

```
# systemctl status rsyslog.service
```

If you specify a unit name without an extension, by default systemd assumes that it is a service unit. Hence, a short version of the previous command is

```
# systemctl status rsyslog
```

This command should return an output similar to that shown in Figure 5-12, including the status of the service unit, its main process ID, and up to the 10 most recent log lines. If some of the log lines are truncated, use the -l switch to display them in full.

You can stop a service by running a command such as this:

```
# systemctl stop rsyslog.service
```

Alternatively, the **systemctl** command can be used with the options shown in Table 5-5; for example, the following command reloads the SSH configuration file without stopping or starting the service:

```
# systemctl reload sshd.service
```

	Command	Description
TABLE 5-5 systemctl Service Control Commands	start	Starts the service if it's currently not running.
	stop	Stops the service if it's currently running.
	restart	Stops and then starts the service.
	reload	If supported, it loads the current version of the configuration file(s). The service is not stopped, and clients that have previously connected are not kicked off.
	try-restart	Stops and then restarts the service only if it is already running.
	condrestart	Same as **try-restart**.
	status	Lists the current operational status of the service.

Service Configuration

The **systemctl** command gives you a simple way to enable a service for the default target. First, try the following command:

```
# systemctl list-unit-files --type=service
```

This gives an output similar to Figure 5-10, but limited to service units. You'll see the whole list of installed services in the system, along with their activation status at boot.

The **systemctl** command can do more. With that command, you can change the boot state of a particular service. For example, in a system with the Postfix e-mail server installed, the following command checks if the Postfix service is configured to start at boot:

```
# systemctl list-unit-files | grep postfix.service
postfix.service                              enabled
```

An equivalent command is

```
# systemctl is-enabled postfix.service
enabled
```

This indicates that the Postfix e-mail server is configured to start in the default target. If you want to make sure the Postfix service does not start in the default target, execute the following command:

```
# systemctl disable postfix.service
```

Run the **systemctl list-unit-files** command again to confirm the change. To turn it back on for the default target, run the same command, substituting **enable** for **disable**, as shown here:

```
# systemctl enable postfix.service
```

When you enable a service, the **systemctl enable** command creates a symbolic link in the directory /etc/systemd/system/multi-user.target.wants that points to the corresponding unit configuration file in /usr/lib/systemd/system. If you wish, you can enable or disable services manually by creating symbolic links in the appropriate systemd directories. However, using **systemctl** is the preferred way because it is less error-prone.

When a service is disabled, you can still start and stop it manually via the **systemctl start** and **stop** commands. This means that the **systemctl disable** command does not prevent a user from accidentally starting a service by mistake. If you want to disable a service unit at boot and ensure that it cannot be started anymore, you should use the **mask** command, as illustrated here:

```
# systemctl mask postfix.service
Created symlink /etc/systemd/system/postfix.service → /dev/null
```

As shown, this command creates a symbolic link in /etc/systemd/system named postfix .service, which points to /dev/null. A configuration file in /etc/systemd/system always takes precedence over a corresponding file in /usr/lib/systemd/system. Hence, the result is that the default postfix.service file in /usr/lib/systemd/system is "masked" by the symbolic link in /etc/systemd/system to /dev/null.

CERTIFICATION OBJECTIVE 5.05

Time Synchronization

The configuration of a Network Time Protocol (NTP) client is straightforward. This section provides an overview of the configuration files and the associated command tools.

There are good reasons to keep different systems running on the same clock. For example, a web server and a client logging in different times would make troubleshooting extremely difficult. Several services rely on accurate timestamps. As an example, a time drift of more than five minutes would cause a Kerberos client to fail authentication.

The time synchronization daemon included with RHEL 9 is **chronyd**. This replaces **ntpd**, which was included with RHEL releases up to version 7. **chronyd** has some unique features compared to **ntpd** and keeps accurate time in a variety of conditions, whether it is installed on systems that are always connected to the network, such as servers, or on virtual or mobile systems. Before we describe the configuration of **chronyd**, we will explain how to configure the time zone.

Time Zone Configuration

Every system, real or virtual, has an internal clock. The installation process on RHEL 9 normally sets the hardware clock to local time rather than UTC. However, UTC (which is essentially identical to Greenwich Mean Time, or GMT) is usually the best setting for servers to avoid issues when switching to daylight saving time.

Every RHEL 9 system includes a time zone configured in the /etc/localtime file. This is a symbolic link that points to one of the time zones files in /usr/share/zoneinfo. As an example, /etc/localtime should point to /usr/share/zoneinfo/America/Los_Angeles if you are based in California.

Rather than manually setting a symbolic link to a time zone file, you can use the **timedatectl** utility. If you run the command alone with no arguments, it will show a summary of the current time settings, including the current time, time zone, and NTP status. Some sample output is shown in Figure 5-13.

You can display a list of the available time zones by running the following command:

```
# timedatectl list-timezones
```

Then, to switch to a different time zone, run **timedatectl** with the **set-timezone** command. Here's an example:

```
# timedatectl set-timezone America/Los_Angeles
```

FIGURE 5-13

Date and time settings

```
[root@server1 ~]# timedatectl
               Local time: Wed 2023-04-12 22:53:34 BST
          Universal time: Wed 2023-04-12 21:53:34 UTC
                RTC time: Wed 2023-04-12 21:53:34
               Time zone: Europe/London (BST, +0100)
System clock synchronized: yes
             NTP service: active
           RTC in local TZ: no
[root@server1 ~]# 
```

Sync the Time with chronyd

The default **chronyd** configuration file, /etc/chrony.conf, is set up to connect to a pool of public servers from the NTP pool project. When used collectively, the **chronyd** daemon minimizes time errors.

```
pool 2.rhel.pool.ntp.org iburst
```

Some versions of RHEL, such as those deployed in cloud environments, may use different NTP servers. The **iburst** configuration option shown here speeds the initial synchronization when the **chronyd** service is started.

To configure **chronyd** to synchronize with a different NTP server, just modify the **server** directives in /etc/chrony.conf and restart **chronyd**:

```
# systemctl restart chronyd
```

Don't forget to configure **chronyd** to start automatically at boot:

```
# systemctl enable chronyd
```

You can display information about the current time sources using the **chronyc sources -v** command. An example is shown in Figure 5-14.

A quick way to enable and start chronyd **using the default configuration**	**is by running the command** timedatectl set-ntp true**.**

FIGURE 5-14

NTP server statistics

```
[root@server1 ~]# chronyc sources -v
210 Number of sources = 4

  .-- Source mode  '^' = server, '=' = peer, '#' = local clock.
 / .- Source state '*' = current synced, '+' = combined , '-' = not combined,
| /   '?' = unreachable, 'x' = time may be in error, '~' = time too variable.
||                                         .- xxxx [ yyyy ] +/- zzzz
||                                        /   xxxx = adjusted offset,
||         Log2(Polling interval) -.      |   yyyy = measured offset,
||                                   \     |   zzzz = estimated error.
||                                    |    |
MS Name/IP address         Stratum Poll Reach LastRx Last sample
===============================================================================
^* kvm1.websters-computers.c      2   6    77    33  +717us[ -992us] +/-   26ms
^+ static.132.14.76.144.clie      2   6    37    97 +3483us[+1774us] +/-   67ms
^+ ntp-ext.cosng.net              2   6    77    31 -2928us[-2928us] +/-   42ms
^+ ghost-networks.de              2   6    77    32 -1419us[-1419us] +/-   51ms
[root@server1 ~]#
```

CERTIFICATION SUMMARY

This chapter covered the basic boot process of a RHEL system. It starts with the hardware POST and continues with the BIOS or UEFI system. Once boot media is found, the process moves to the first stage of the GRUB 2 bootloader. The GRUB 2 menu allows you to select and customize the kernel to be booted.

Once you've selected an option, GRUB 2 hands control to the kernel. The kernel loads a temporary filesystem known as the initial RAM disk. Then essential drivers and filesystems are loaded, and the kernel executes the first process, also known as **systemd**.

Linux services are controlled by systemd targets, which group together other systemd units. The default target is configured as a symbolic link in the directory /etc/systemd/ system, and the unit configuration files are stored in this directory and in /usr/lib/systemd/ system. The status of those systemd units can be configured and queried using the **systemctl** command. The systemd targets are linked to other targets and to unit configuration files. **systemctl** can also be used to start, stop, restart, reload systemd units, and more.

You may need to set up local systems as NTP clients. The default NTP service in RHEL 9 is **chronyd**.

 ## TWO-MINUTE DRILL

Here are some of the key points from the certification objectives in Chapter 5.

The Boot Process

❑ Although not strictly a part of the exam, it's important to know the basics of the BIOS and the UEFI.

❑ You can change the boot sequence from the BIOS/UEFI menu.

❑ Once the BIOS/UEFI detects the designated boot drive(s), it hands control to GRUB 2 via the Master Boot Record (MBR) or GUID Partition Table (GPT) of the appropriate drive.

Bootloaders and GRUB 2

❑ RHEL 9 uses GRUB 2.

❑ The GRUB 2 configuration file is organized into sections.

❏ From the GRUB 2 menu, you can boot into a systemd target other than the default.

❏ You can even boot from a GRUB 2 menu into a rescue shell that provides root administrative access without an account password.

❏ The GRUB 2 configuration file specifies a kernel, a root directory volume, and an initial RAM disk for each operating system.

❏ If the GRUB 2 configuration file is missing, you may be able to boot from the grub> prompt with information on the /boot directory partition, the Linux kernel file, the top-level root directory, and the initial RAM disk file.

Between GRUB 2 and Login

❏ You can analyze boot messages through the **journalctl** command.

❏ Default system targets are configured as a symbolic link from the /etc/systemd/ system directory.

❏ The **systemd** process has replaced Upstart and SysVinit, which were part of older RHEL distributions. **systemd** has configuration files in the /etc/systemd/system and /usr/lib/systemd/system directories.

❏ Once the kernel boots, it hands control to systemd, also known as the first process.

Control by Target

❏ The default target configured in /etc/systemd/system activates systemd units in the /usr/lib/systemd/system directory.

❏ Target units can include other targets and units to be activated.

❏ You can use **systemctl** to control a service with the **start**, **stop**, **restart**, **reload**, and other commands.

❏ The services that start in each target can also be controlled with **systemctl** and the **enable/disable** commands.

Time Synchronization

❏ The **timedatectl** tool can be used to check the current time, date, time zone, and NTP service status.

❏ The default NTP service in RHEL 9 is **chronyd**. It keeps time in sync with servers configured in the /etc/chrony.conf file.

SELF TEST

The following questions will help measure your understanding of the material presented in this chapter. As no multiple-choice questions appear on the Red Hat exams, no multiple-choice questions appear in this book. These questions exclusively test your understanding of the chapter. It is okay if you have another way of performing a task. Getting results, not memorizing trivia, is what counts on the Red Hat exams. There may be more than one answer for many of these questions.

The Boot Process

1. On what part of the boot hard drive is the first stage of the GRUB 2 bootloader typically located?

Bootloaders and GRUB 2

2. When you see the GRUB 2 configuration menu, what command would you use to modify the configuration?
3. What string would you add to the **linux** command line to boot into the emergency target?
4. If you see the **set root=(hd0,msdos1)** directive in the GRUB 2 configuration file, on what partition is the /boot directory? Assume the GRUB 2 configuration file is properly configured.

Between GRUB 2 and Login

5. What temporary filesystem is loaded directly from the GRUB 2 menu?
6. What one-word command can you use to read systemd log messages?
7. In what directories can you find the configuration files associated with the first process?
8. How do you switch from the graphical target to the multi-user target?

Control by Target

9. What command lists the default target?
10. Name three commands that can be typically run from **systemctl** to control the status of systemd units.
11. What command lists the state of all systemd units currently available on the local system, including those that are not active?

Time Synchronization

12. What command lists the current time, time zone, and status of the time synchronization service?

13. Which configuration file is used by **chronyd**?

LAB QUESTIONS

Red Hat presents its exams electronically. For that reason, the labs in this chapter are available from the companion website that accompanies the book. In case you haven't yet set up RHEL 9 on a system, refer to Chapter 1 for installation instructions. The answers for the labs follow the Self Test answers.

SELF TEST ANSWERS

The Boot Process

1. For the BIOS/UEFI to hand control over to Linux, it needs to identify the Master Boot Record (MBR) or the GUID Partition Table (GPT) of the boot hard drive.

Bootloaders and GRUB 2

2. From the GRUB 2 menu, the command that modifies the configuration is **e**, which stands for "edit."

3. To boot into the emergency target from the GRUB 2 **linux** command line, you'd append the string **systemd.unit=emergency.target**.

4. The **set root=(hd0,msdos1)** directive implies that the /boot directory is on the first partition on the first hard drive.

Between GRUB 2 and Login

5. The temporary filesystem loaded from the GRUB 2 menu is the initial RAM disk filesystem, also known by its filename, initramfs.

6. The one-word command that you can use to read systemd log messages is **journalctl**.

7. The configuration files associated with the first process are located in the /etc/systemd/system and /usr/lib/systemd/system directories.

8. The command to switch from the graphical target to the multi-user target is **systemctl isolate multi-user.target**.

Control by Target

9. The command that lists the default target is **systemctl get-default**.

10. Typical commands that can be run from **systemctl** include **start**, **stop**, **restart**, **reload**, **enable**, **disable**, and more.

11. The **systemctl list-units --all** command (or just **systemctl --all**) lists the state of all units, including inactive ones.

Time Synchronization

12. The **timedatectl** command lists the current time, time zone, and status of the time synchronization service.

13. The **chronyd** configuration file is /etc/chrony.conf.

LAB ANSWERS

Yes, there are many Linux systems that run for years at a time without a reboot. But reboots are sometimes required, such as when newer kernels are installed. So when configuring a Linux system, make sure any changes survive a reboot. On a Red Hat exam, you won't get credit unless your changes survive a reboot.

Lab 1

If successful, this lab will show you how to change the default target, along with the relative importance of the options in the GRUB bootloader. Remember, you can modify the default target via the **systemctl** command:

```
# systemctl set-default multi-user.target
```

or manually by modifying the /etc/systemd/system/default.target symbolic link:

```
# rm -f /etc/systemd/system/default.target
# ln -s /usr/lib/systemd/system/multi-user.target ↵
/etc/systemd/system/default.target
```

To confirm that the changes worked, run

```
# systemctl get-default
```

Then, you can set again the graphical target to be the default by running

```
# systemctl set-default graphical.target
```

Lab 2

This lab is the same as Exercise 5-2. Practice with the root password recovery procedure until you are familiar with all the steps and you don't need to rely on the documentation. Remember, Red Hat exams are "closed book."

Lab 3

After completing this lab, you should have modified the variables GRUB_TIMEOUT and GRUB_CMDLINE_LINUX in /etc/default/grub, as shown here:

```
GRUB_TIMEOUT=10
GRUB_CMDLINE_LINUX="crashkernel=1G-4G:192M,4G-64G:256M,64G-:512M
resume=/dev/mapper/rhel-swap rd.lvm.lv=rhel/root rd.lvm.lv=rhel/swap rhgb"
```

Note that the **quiet** keyword has been removed from GRUB_CMDLINE_LINUX to enable verbose messages at boot.

Then, run the **grub2-mkconfig** command to generate a new GRUB configuration file:

```
# grub2-mkconfig -o /boot/grub2/grub.cfg
```

To really test the result, reboot the system. What happens? Finally, revert your changes.

Lab 4

The initial command executed in this lab moved the grub.cfg configuration file to the /root directory. If you understand GRUB 2 well, you should have been able to boot the system from the grub> prompt.

Otherwise, follow the steps in Exercise 5-3 to boot the system. You should have run the following commands to the grub> prompt (some details may vary, such as the version of the kernel installed):

```
grub> insmod lvm
grub> set root=(lvm/rhel-root)
grub> linux (hd0,msdos1)/vmlinuz-5.14.0-162.6.1.el9_1.x86_64↵
root=/dev/mapper/rhel-root
grub> initrd (hd0,msdos1)/initramfs-5.14.0-162.6.1.el9_1.x86_64.img
grub> boot
```

Next, restore the original grub.cfg file:

```
# mv /root/grub.cfg /boot/grub2/grub.cfg
```

Alternatively, generate a new grub.cfg configuration file with the **grub2-mkconfig** command. If unsuccessful, you can recover the grub.cfg file by booting into the rescue target described in this chapter. From the rescue mode command-line prompt, you should be able to restore the original configuration with the following commands:

```
# chroot /mnt/sysroot
# cp /root/grub.cfg /boot/grub2/
```

Lab 5

One way to accomplish the tasks in this lab is with the following steps:

1. Run the following:

   ```
   timedatectl set-timezone America/Chicago
   ```

2. Edit the /etc/chrony.conf file and change the pool directive to

   ```
   pool time.google.com iburst
   ```

   Then, restart the **chronyd** daemon:

   ```
   systemctl restart chronyd
   ```

3. To confirm your changes, run **timedatectl** to check the current time zone. Then, check that the **chornyd** daemon is running and syncing the time from time.google.com:

   ```
   # systemctl status chronyd
   # chronyc sources -v
   ```

Lab 6

To complete this lab, log in to tester1.example.com:

1. Run the following commands to enable persistent journal logs on disk:

```
# mkdir /var/log/journal
# journalctl --flush
```

2. Reboot the system and save the journal log messages from the boot before the last one to the file /root/journal-beforelast.log:

```
# journalctl -b 1 /root/journal-beforelast.log
```

Lab 7

On tester1.example.com, follow these steps to complete the lab:

1. Confirm the current status of the kdump and rhcd services:

```
# systemctl status kdump
# systemctl status rhcd
```

2. Stop **kdump** and configure the service so that it does not start at boot:

```
# systemctl stop kdump
# systemctl disable kdump
```

3. Configure **rhcd** to start at boot:

```
# systemctl enable kdump
```

4. Reboot the system and check the status of the services. You can list more than one service on the same command line:

```
# systemctl status kdump rhcd
# systemctl is-enabled kdump rhcd
```

Chapter 6

User Administration

F undamental to Linux administration is the management of users and groups. In this chapter, you'll examine different ways to manage the variety of users and groups available to Linux. Important skills in this area range from the simple login to user account management, group membership, and group collaboration. The configuration of administrative privileges for Linux users can help the master administrator distribute responsibilities to others.

You'll see how to manage these tasks from the command line, with the help of the files of the shadow password suite. You'll also use tools such as the Cockpit web console to set up some of these tasks. As you should expect, Red Hat GUI tools can't do it all, which emphasizes the importance of understanding user management from the command line.

INSIDE THE EXAM

This chapter addresses several RHCSA objectives. Briefly explained, these objectives include the following:

- Log in and switch users in multiuser targets

That means you need to know how to log in with regular accounts when RHEL 9 is running in the multiuser or graphical targets. To switch users, you need to know how to switch to a different account using the **su** command.

- Create, delete, and modify local user accounts
- Change passwords and adjust password aging for local user accounts
- Create, delete, and modify local groups and group memberships

You could use commands such as **useradd**, **usermod**, **groupadd**, **groupmod**, and **chage** as well as Cockpit to accomplish these tasks. While this chapter explains how you can use both types of tools, there is no guarantee that Cockpit will be available during an exam.

- Configure superuser access

You must be able to assign root privileges using the /etc/sudoers file and the wheel group.

- Create and configure set-GID directories for collaboration

This objective refers to how to set one or more directories for collaboration among a group of users.

CERTIFICATION OBJECTIVE 6.01

User Account Management

You need to know how to create and configure users. This means knowing how to configure and modify accounts, work with passwords, and organize users in groups. You also need to know how to configure the environment associated with each user account: in configuration files and in user settings.

If you've installed RHEL 9 following the instructions in Chapter 1, the default Red Hat installation should include a regular user account in addition to the root administrative account. Although no regular user accounts except root are required, it's important to set up some regular user accounts. Even if you're going to be the only user on the system, do create at least one non-administrative account for day-to-day work. Then you can use the root account only when it's necessary to administer the system. You can add accounts to Red Hat Enterprise Linux systems using various utilities, including direct editing of password configuration files (the manual method), the **useradd** command (the command-line method), and the Cockpit web console (the graphical method).

Different Kinds of Users

There are three basic types of Linux user accounts: superuser (root), regular, and system. The superuser root account is automatically created when Linux is installed, and it has administrative privileges for all services on a Linux system. A "black hat" hacker who has a chance to take control of this account can take full control of that system.

For the times when you do log in as an administrator, RHEL builds in safeguards for root users. Log in as the root user, and then run the **alias** command. You'll see entries such as the following:

```
alias rm='rm -i'
```

Due to this particular alias, when the root user runs the **rm** command, the shell actually executes the **rm -i** command, which prompts for confirmation before the **rm** command deletes a file. Note that the **-f** option in **rm**, such as **rm -f** *filename*, supersedes this safety setting.

Regular users have the necessary privileges to perform standard tasks on a Linux computer. They can access programs such as bash, a database, or a web browser. They can store files in their own home directories. Since regular users do not normally have administrative privileges, they cannot accidentally delete critical operating system configuration files. You can assign a regular account to most users, safe in the knowledge that they can't disrupt a system with the privileges they have on that account.

Services such as Apache, mail, and printing have their own individual system accounts. These accounts exist to allow each of these services to interact with Linux systems, and are not allowed to log in interactively on a system. Normally, you won't need to change any system account, but if you see that someone is running a command shell through one of these accounts, be wary. Someone may have broken into your system.

on the
Job

To review recent logins, run the last | less **command. If the login is from a remote location, it will be associated with a specific IP address outside your network.**

To show the identity of a user, type the **id** command followed by the username, or just **id** to show the identity of the current user. An example of the information displayed by the **id** command is shown next:

```
$ id
uid=1000(mj) gid=1000(mj) groups=1000(mj),10(wheel) ↵
context=unconfined_u:unconfined_r:unconfined_t:s0-s0:c0.c1023
```

Ignore the last line in the output, which defines the SELinux context. The **id** command shows the numeric user ID (UID) of the user along with its name inside parentheses. Every user belongs to a primary group, which is displayed with its group ID (GID) and name. The command shows all the groups the user is part of, with their GIDs and name.

The Shadow Password Suite

When Unix was first developed back in the 1970s, security was not a serious concern. Everything required for user and group management was contained in the /etc/passwd and /etc/group files. As suggested by the name, passwords were originally in the /etc/passwd file. The problem is that file is "world readable." Anyone with a copy of that file, before the shadow password suite was introduced, would have a copy of the encrypted password for every user. Even though passwords are not saved in clear text, they may be vulnerable to brute-force attacks. For example, a dictionary attack can usually decipher a password in a few seconds, if the password is based on a common dictionary word. That was the main motivation behind the development of the shadow password suite, which moves more sensitive information to other files that are readable only by the root administrative user.

The four configuration files of the shadow password suite are /etc/passwd, /etc/group, /etc/shadow, and /etc/gshadow. Default settings for user accounts are stored in the /etc/login.defs file.

The /etc/passwd File

The /etc/passwd file contains basic information about every user. Open that file in a text editor and browse around a bit. At the top of the file, the first line defines the root login account (the superuser). Other users in this file may relate to services such as mail, ftp, and sshd. There may be regular users designed for logging in to the system. An excerpt of the /etc/passwd file is shown in Figure 6-1.

There are seven columns of information in the /etc/passwd file, delineated by colons. Each column in /etc/passwd includes specific information. For example, the user account defined by the following line has seven fields, described in Table 6-1:

```
mj:x:1000:1000:Michael Jang:/home/mj:/bin/bash
```

The RHEL 9 version of /etc/passwd includes more secure features for user accounts when compared to some other Linux distributions. The only accounts with a real login shell are user accounts. Service accounts such as mail or nobody are assigned the false /sbin/nologin shell.

The /etc/group File

Every Linux user is assigned to a *primary group*, which is the group corresponding to the GID defined in /etc/passwd. By default, in RHEL 9 every user gets his own private group, with the same name as their username. A user may also be a member of other groups, which are usually referred to as *supplementary groups* to distinguish them from a user's primary group.

FIGURE 6-1   The /etc/passwd file

```
[root@server1 ~]# cat /etc/passwd
root:x:0:0:root:/root:/bin/bash
bin:x:1:1:bin:/bin:/sbin/nologin
daemon:x:2:2:daemon:/sbin:/sbin/nologin
adm:x:3:4:adm:/var/adm:/sbin/nologin
lp:x:4:7:lp:/var/spool/lpd:/sbin/nologin
sync:x:5:0:sync:/sbin:/bin/sync
shutdown:x:6:0:shutdown:/sbin:/sbin/shutdown
halt:x:7:0:halt:/sbin:/sbin/halt
mail:x:8:12:mail:/var/spool/mail:/sbin/nologin
operator:x:11:0:operator:/root:/sbin/nologin
games:x:12:100:games:/usr/games:/sbin/nologin
ftp:x:14:50:FTP User:/var/ftp:/sbin/nologin
nobody:x:65534:65534:Kernel Overflow User:/:/sbin/nologin
systemd-coredump:x:999:997:systemd Core Dumper:/:/sbin/nologin
dbus:x:81:81:System message bus:/:/sbin/nologin
polkitd:x:998:996:User for polkitd:/:/sbin/nologin
avahi:x:70:70:Avahi mDNS/DNS-SD Stack:/var/run/avahi-daemon:/sbin/nologin
tss:x:59:59:Account used for TPM access:/dev/null:/sbin/nologin
colord:x:997:993:User for colord:/var/lib/colord:/sbin/nologin
clevis:x:996:992:Clevis Decryption Framework unprivileged user:/var/cache/clevis
rtkit:x:172:172:RealtimeKit:/proc:/sbin/nologin
sssd:x:995:991:User for sssd:/:/sbin/nologin
geoclue:x:994:990:User for geoclue:/var/lib/geoclue:/sbin/nologin
```

TABLE 6-1   The Anatomy of /etc/passwd

Field	Example	Description
Username	mj	The user logs in with this name. Usernames can include digits, hyphens (-), dots (.), and underscores (_). However, they should not start with a hyphen or be longer than 32 characters.
Password	x	The password. You should normally see an *x*, which means that the actual encrypted password is stored in /etc/shadow. An asterisk means that the user will not able to log in.
User ID	1000	The unique numeric UID for that user. By default, Red Hat starts regular UIDs at 1000.
Group ID	1000	The primary GID associated with that user. By default, RHEL creates a new group for every new user, and the number matches the UID, if the corresponding GID is available. Some other Linux and Unix systems assign all users to a default users group.
User info	Michael Jang	You can enter any information of your choice in this field. Standard options include the user's full name, telephone number, e-mail address, and physical location. You can leave this blank.
Home directory	/home/mj	By default, RHEL places new home directories in /home/*username*.
Login shell	/bin/bash	By default, RHEL assigns users to bash as the default shell. You can change this to any available shell you have installed.

FIGURE 6-2

The /etc/group file

```
[root@server1 ~]# cat /etc/group
root:x:0:
bin:x:1:
daemon:x:2:
sys:x:3:
adm:x:4:
tty:x:5:
disk:x:6:
lp:x:7:
mem:x:8:
kmem:x:9:
wheel:x:10:alex
cdrom:x:11:
mail:x:12:
man:x:15:
dialout:x:18:
floppy:x:19:
games:x:20:
tape:x:33:
video:x:39:
ftp:x:50:
lock:x:54:
audio:x:63:
users:x:100:
nobody:x:65534:
dbus:x:81:
utmp:x:22:
utempter:x:35:
input:x:999:
```

The main purpose of a primary group is to assign a group owner to a new file. All files are owned by the UID and primary group GID of the user who created them.

Open /etc/group in a text editor. Browse around a bit. The first line in this file specifies information for the root administrative user's group. Some groups have a special purpose. For example, being a member of the wheel group gives the privilege to run administrative commands via sudo, as explained later in the chapter. An excerpt of the /etc/group file is shown in Figure 6-2.

There are four columns of information in the /etc/group file, delineated by colons. As an example, the group defined in the following line has four fields, described in Table 6-2:

```
reviewers:x:2000:mj,ao,sd
```

The /etc/shadow File

The /etc/shadow file is a supplement to /etc/passwd. It contains eight columns of information, and the first column contains the same list of usernames as documented in /etc/passwd. As long as there's an *x* in the second column of each /etc/passwd entry, Linux knows to look at /etc/shadow for more information. Open that file in a text editor

TABLE 6-2 The Anatomy of /etc/group

Field	Example	Description
Group name	reviewers	Each user gets his own primary group, with the same name as his username. You can also create supplementary groups.
Group password	x	The password. You should see an *x*, which points to /etc/gshadow for the actual password.
Group ID	2000	The numeric GID associated with the group. By default, RHEL creates a new group for every new user. If you want to create a supplementary group, you should assign a GID number outside the standard range; otherwise, Red Hat GIDs and UIDs would probably get out of sequence.
Group members	mj,ao,sd	Lists the usernames that are members of the group. If there is a username that lists the GID of the group as its primary group in /etc/passwd, that username is also a member of the group.

and browse around a bit. You'll see the same pattern of information, starting with the root administrative user. An excerpt of the /etc/shadow file is shown in Figure 6-3.

As shown in Table 6-3, /etc/shadow includes the encrypted password in the second column, and the remaining information relates to the way passwords are managed. The first two characters of the second column specify the encryption hash for the password. If you see a $1, the password is hashed to the Message Digest 5 (MD5) algorithm, the standard through RHEL 5. If you see a $6, the password is protected with the 512-bit Secure Hash Algorithm (SHA-512), the standard since RHEL 6.

FIGURE 6-3 The /etc/shadow file

```
[root@server1 ~]# cat /etc/shadow
root:$6$SO0TUSunspd6x.ny$j9kMsDzp.xnlPZtNofai6ZIv0Cvh9TDlS3.jJkGkNpXOXGqi3Sn1XkgtpyV4QtbUV2pKcmk6k6Rue7xA
Zm1KC.::0:99999:7:::
bin:*:17988:0:99999:7:::
daemon:*:17988:0:99999:7:::
adm:*:17988:0:99999:7:::
lp:*:17988:0:99999:7:::
sync:*:17988:0:99999:7:::
shutdown:*:17988:0:99999:7:::
halt:*:17988:0:99999:7:::
mail:*:17988:0:99999:7:::
operator:*:17988:0:99999:7:::
games:*:17988:0:99999:7:::
ftp:*:17988:0:99999:7:::
nobody:*:17988:0:99999:7:::
dbus:!!:18223::::::
systemd-coredump:!!:18223::::::
systemd-resolve:!!:18223::::::
tss:!!:18223::::::
polkitd:!!:18223::::::
geoclue:!!:18223::::::
rtkit:!!:18223::::::
pulse:!!:18223::::::
qemu:!!:18223::::::
usbmuxd:!!:18223::::::
unbound:!!:18223::::::
rpc:!!:18223:0:99999:7:::
gluster:!!:18223::::::
chrony:!!:18223::::::
```

TABLE 6-3	The Anatomy of /etc/shadow	

Column	Field	Description
1	Username	Username
2	Password	Encrypted password; requires an *x* in the second column of /etc/passwd
3	Date of last password change	Date of the last password change, in number of days after January 1, 1970
4	Minimum password age	Minimum number of days that a user must keep a password before she can change it
5	Maximum password age	Maximum number of days after which a password must be changed
6	Password warning period	Number of days before password expiration when a warning is given
7	Password inactivity period	Number of days after password expiration during which the password is still accepted, but the user is prompted to change her password
8	Account expiration date	Number of days since January 1, 1970, after which the password will expire
9	Reserved	Reserved for future use

Note that some users in Figure 6-3 have * or !! characters in the password field. That means that the user will not be able to use a password to log in. This is a standard configuration for system user accounts.

The /etc/gshadow File

The /etc/gshadow file is the group configuration file in the shadow password suite. It includes the group administrators, which can add other group members using the **gpasswd** command. If desired, you can even configure a hashed password. Once a password is set, the group administrators can add or remove members to the group by using the **gpasswd** command and typing the required password. An excerpt of the /etc/gshadow file is shown in Figure 6-4. For example, the group defined by the following line has four fields, described in Table 6-4:

```
reviewers:!:mj:mj,ao,sd
```

ⓦ a t c h **If you do not remember the meaning of a field in the files described in this section, open the corresponding man page. Note that** man passwd **shows the man page of the** passwd **command, while** man 5 passwd **is the correct command to display the man page for the /etc/passwd file.**

FIGURE 6-4

FIGURE 6-4

The /etc/gshadow
file

```
[root@server1 ~]# cat /etc/gshadow
root:::
bin:::
daemon:::
sys:::
adm:::
tty:::
disk:::
lp:::
mem:::
kmem:::
wheel:::alex
cdrom:::
mail:::
man:::
dialout:::
floppy:::
games:::
tape:::
video:::
ftp:::
lock:::
audio:::
users:::
nobody:::
dbus:!::
utmp:!::
utempter:!::
input:!::
```

TABLE 6-4   The Anatomy of /etc/gshadow

Field	Example	Description
Group name	reviewers	The group name.
Password	!	Most groups have a !, which indicates no password; some groups may have a hashed password similar to that shown in the /etc/shadow file.
Administrators	mj	A comma-separated list of users who can change the members or the password of the group using the **gpasswd** command.
Group members	mj,ao,sd	A comma-delineated list of usernames that are members of the group.

The /etc/login.defs File

The /etc/login.defs file provides the baseline for a number of parameters in the shadow password suite. This section provides a brief analysis of some of the active directives in the default version of this file. As you'll see, the configuration options go somewhat beyond authentication. Keep in mind that if you change any settings, those are effective only for new users, not for existing ones.

| TABLE 6-5 | /etc/login.defs Password-Aging Configuration Parameters |

Configuration Parameter	Description
PASS_MAX_DAYS	After this number of days, the password must be changed.
PASS_MIN_DAYS	Passwords must be kept for at least this number of days.
PASS_WARN_AGE	Users are warned this number of days before PASS_MAX_DAYS.

The first configuration parameter in the /etc/login.defs file specifies the directory where mailboxes are located:

```
MAIL_DIR /var/spool/mail
```

In the file, there are three directives related to default password aging information. The directives are explained in the comments inside the file and in Table 6-5.

As suggested earlier, user ID (UID) and group ID (GID) numbers for regular users and groups start at 1000. Since Linux supports UID and GID numbers above 4 billion (actually, up to $2^{32} - 1$), the maximum UID and GID numbers of 60000, as defined in the /etc/login.defs file, may seem strange. However, this leaves higher numbers available for other user databases, such as those associated with OpenLDAP or Microsoft Active Directory. In the following lines, **UID_MIN** specifies the minimum UID to assign when a new regular user is created, **UID_MAX** specifies the maximum UID, and so on:

```
UID_MIN   1000
UID_MAX   60000
GID_MIN   1000
GID_MAX   60000
```

Similarly, the **useradd** and **groupadd** commands with the **-r** switch create a system user or system group, respectively, whose ID is chosen within the following range:

```
SYS_UID_MIN 201
SYS_UID_MAX 999
SYS_GID_MIN 201
SYS_GID_MAX 999
```

Normally, when the **useradd** command is run to create a new user, it automatically creates home directories as well, which is confirmed by the following directive:

```
CREATE_HOME yes
```

As described later in this chapter, other files set the value of the umask. But if those other files did not exist, this directive would govern the default umask for regular users:

```
UMASK     022
```

The following directive is critical in the implementation of the *user private group scheme*. In this configuration scheme, users are made members of their own private group, normally with the same UID and GID numbers. The following directive means that the umask group bits will be the same as the owner bits for non-root users. Additionally, the group will be deleted if all the users in that group are also deleted.

```
USERGROUPS_ENAB yes
```

Finally, the following directive was used to determine the algorithm used to encrypt passwords, by default SHA 512:

```
ENCRYPT_METHOD SHA512
```

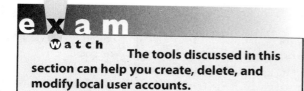

ⓦatch The tools discussed in this section can help you create, delete, and modify local user accounts.

Command-Line Tools

There are two basic ways to add users through the command-line interface. As the root user, you can add users directly by editing the /etc/passwd file in a text editor such as vi. To this end, both **vipw** and **vigr** were described in Chapter 2. Alternatively, you can use text commands customized for the purpose.

Add Users Directly

Open the /etc/passwd file in the text editor of your choice. As described in Chapter 2, you can do so with the **vipw** command. However, if you add users by directly editing the files of the shadow password suite, you'll have to do two more things:

- *Add a user home directory.* For example, for user donna, you'd have to add the /home/donna home directory, making sure that user donna and group donna both have ownership of that directory.
- *Populate the user home directory.* The default option is to copy the files from the /etc/skel directory, discussed later in this chapter. You'd also have to make sure that user donna and group donna have ownership of those files copied to the /home/donna directory.

Add Users to a Group Directly

Every Linux user is assigned to a group, at least his own private group. The GID number listed in the /etc/group file for a user's primary group must match that shown for that user in the /etc/passwd file. The user is usually the only member of that group.

Of course, users can be members of other groups as well. For example, to create a group named project, you could add the entries to the /etc/group and /etc/gshadow files. One way to do so in a text editor is with the **vigr** command. As an example, the following entry might be appropriate for a group named project:

```
project:x:60001:
```

The number 60001 is used, as that is beyond the limit of the **GID_MAX** directive from the /etc/login.defs file described earlier. But that's just an arbitrary limit used by the **groupadd** command. There's no prohibition against a higher number, as long as it does not duplicate existing GIDs. However, it is convenient when the UID and GID numbers of regular users match.

Of course, for a group to be useful, you'd have to add users already configured in the /etc/passwd file at the end of the line. The following example assumes these users already exist:

```
project:x:60001:michael,elizabeth,stephanie,tim
```

You'd also have to add this group to the /etc/gshadow file. You could do so directly with the **vigr -s** command. Alternatively, to set up a group administrator with a password, you could run the **gpasswd** command. For example, the **gpasswd project** command would set up a password for administering the group, as described later in this chapter. It would automatically add the encrypted password with the given group name to the /etc/gshadow file.

Add Users at the Command Line

Alternatively, you can simplify this process with the **useradd** command. The **useradd michael** command would add user michael to the /etc/passwd file. In addition, the **useradd** command creates the /home/michael home directory, adds the standard files from the /etc/skel directory, and assigns the default shell, /bin/bash. The **useradd** command is the recommended way to add users on RHEL. It includes a number of command options. The most common are shown in Table 6-6.

Assign a Password

Once a new user is created, you can use the **passwd** *username* command to assign a password to that user. For example, the **passwd pm** command prompts you to assign a new password to user pm. For security reasons, RHEL is configured to avoid passwords that are based on dictionary words, shorter than eight characters, too simple, based on palindromes, and other, similar criteria. Nevertheless, such passwords are legal and accepted if the **passwd** command is run by the root user.

TABLE 6-6	useradd Command Options

Option	Description
-u *UID*	Overrides the default assigned *UID*. By default, in RHEL this starts at 1000 for regular users and can continue sequentially to the maximum number of user IDs supported by the Linux kernel, which is $2^{32} - 1$, something over 4 billion users.
-g *GID*	Overrides the default assigned *GID*. If available, RHEL uses the same GID and UID numbers for each user. If you specify a GID, the corresponding group must already exist.
-c *info*	Enters the comment of your choice about the user, such as her name.
-d *dir*	Overrides the default home directory for the user, /home/*username*.
-e *YYYY-MM-DD*	Sets an expiration date for the user account.
-f *num*	Specifies the number of days after password expiration that the account will be permanently disabled.
-G *group1, group2*	Makes the user a member of the supplementary groups *group1* and *group2*, based on their current names as defined in the /etc/group file. A space between *group1* and *group2* would lead to an error.
-s *shell*	Overrides the default shell for the user, /bin/bash.

Add or Delete a Group at the Command Line

When it's appropriate to add a special group to the shadow password suite, you may want to use the **groupadd** command. Generally, you'll want to use it with the **-g** option. For example, the following command would set up a special project group with a GID of 60001:

```
# groupadd -g 60001 project
```

If you don't use the **-g** option, the **groupadd** command takes the next available GID number. For example, if two regular users are configured on a system, they each have UID and GID numbers of 1000 and 1001, respectively. If you've run the **groupadd project** command without specifying a GID number, the project group is assigned a GID of 1002. The next regular user that's created would get a UID of 1002 and a GID of 1003, which could lead to confusion.

Fortunately, the command to delete a group is simpler. If the project group has completed its work, you can delete that group from the shadow password suite database with the following command:

```
# groupdel project
```

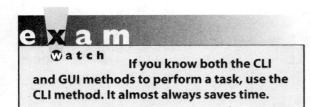

watch If you know both the CLI and GUI methods to perform a task, use the CLI method. It almost always saves time.

Delete a User

The removal of a user account is a straightforward process. The easiest way to delete a user account is with the **userdel** command. By default, this command does not delete that user's home directory, so administrators can transfer files from that user, perhaps to an employee who has taken over the tasks of the deleted user. Alternatively, the **userdel -r** *username* command deletes that user's home directory along with all of the files stored in that home directory.

This is a lot faster than the GUI method, for which you open the Cockpit web console, select the user, and then click Delete. Although it's probably easier for a less experienced user to remember the GUI method, text commands can save you time.

EXERCISE 6-1

Add a User with Cockpit Web Console

One alternative to user management commands such as **useradd** and **usermod** is the Red Hat Cockpit web console.

1. Install the cockpit RPM package if it is not present:

   ```
   # rpm -q cockpit || dnf install cockpit
   ```

2. Permit the Cockpit service through the firewall:

   ```
   # firewall-cmd --add-service=cockpit --permanent
   # firewall-cmd --reload
   ```

3. Start the Cockpit service:

   ```
   # systemctl enable --now cockpit.socket
   ```

4. Open Firefox and point to the URL https://localhost:9090. Accept the server's certificate, log in with the root account credentials, select the Accounts page, and click Create New Account. This opens a new window, as shown here:

Create new account

Full name	Michael Jang
User name	mjang
Password	••••••••••••••••

Excellent password

Confirm	••••••••••••••••
Authentication	⦿ Use password ☐ Require password change on first login ○ Disallow password authentication ⑦

[Create]   Cancel

5. Complete the form. All entries are required, except Full Name. The entries are fairly self-explanatory. The password should be at least eight characters and should ideally contain a mix of upper- and lowercase letters, numbers, and punctuation to keep it more secure from the standard password-cracking programs.

6. Enter the identical password in the Confirm field and click Create when you are done.

7. Select the account that you have just created. You will see the screen shown below. Select the Server Administrator check box to give the user administrative privileges.

Michael Jang

[Terminate session] [Delete]

Full name	Michael Jang
User name	mjang
Roles	☑ Server administrator ⑦
Last login	Never
Options	☐ Disallow interactive password ⑦ Never expire account edit
Password	[Set password] [Force change] Never expire password edit

8. Repeat the process as desired for any additional new users that may be required. Make sure to create at least one new user prior to running Exercise 6-2.

EXERCISE 6-2

Real and Fake Shells

Do not run this exercise unless a regular user has already been created on the local system. If desired, run Exercise 6-1 first, as that allows you to create a new regular user on the target system.

1. Open the /etc/passwd file. Find a current regular user with a UID of 1000 or above.
2. Identify the default shell. It's specified in the last column, normally /bin/bash for regular users.
3. Change the default shell to /sbin/nologin, and save the changes to the /etc/passwd file.
4. Open a different virtual console. Press the CTRL-ALT-F2 keys to open a different console. (If you're already in the second virtual console, substitute F3, F4, F5, or F6 for F2.)
5. Try logging in as the modified user. What happens?
6. Return to the original console. If it's the GUI, it should be accessible with the CTRL-ALT-F1 key combination. If that is not possible (such as when the GUI is not installed), you should still be able to log in as the root administrative user.
7. Reopen the /etc/passwd file. Restore the /bin/bash shell to the target regular user.

Modify an Account

As a Linux administrator, you may want to modify an existing user account. While the Cockpit web console is straightforward to use and convenient to create or delete users, command-line interface options offer more features.

We've described some of these commands, such as **useradd**, **userdel**, **groupadd**, and **groupdel**. A few other key user administration commands are **usermod**, **groupmod**, and **chage**.

usermod

The **usermod** command modifies various settings in /etc/passwd. In addition, it allows you to change the settings in /etc/shadow, such as the expiration date for an account, or to add a user to a supplementary group in /etc/group. For example, the following command sets the account associated with user test1 to expire on June 8, 2023:

```
# usermod -e 2023-06-08 test1
```

| TABLE 6-7 | usermod Command Options |

Option	Description
-a -G *group1*	Appends to existing group memberships; multiple groups may be specified, split with a comma, with no spaces.
-l *newlogin*	Changes the username to *newlogin*, without changing the home directory.
-L	Locks a user's password.
-U	Unlocks a user's password.

The following command makes user test1 a member of a group named accounting:

```
# usermod -G accounting test1
```

The **usermod** command is closely related to the **useradd** command; in fact, the **usermod** command supports all of the **useradd** command options listed earlier in Table 6-6. The **usermod** command includes several additional options, some of which are listed in Table 6-7.

When a user password is locked, an exclamation mark (!) is added before the user's encrypted password in /etc/shadow.

groupmod

The **groupmod** command is relatively simple. It has two practical uses. The following command changes the GID number of the group named project (in this case, to 60002):

```
# groupmod -g 60002 project
```

In contrast, the following command changes the name of the group named project to secret:

```
# groupmod -n secret project
```

watch The chage **command is an excellent way to address the RHCSA objective to "adjust password aging for local user accounts."**

chage

The **chage** command is primarily used to manage aging information for a password, by modifying the corresponding fields in the /etc/shadow file. While some of the parameters can also be set with the **useradd** and **usermod** commands, most of the command options are different, as described in Table 6-8.

TABLE 6-8	chage Command Options

Option	Description
-d YYYY-MM-DD	Sets the last change date for a password; the output is shown in /etc/shadow as the number of days after January 1, 1970.
-E YYYY-MM-DD	Assigns the expiration date for an account; the output is shown in /etc/shadow as the number of days after January 1, 1970.
-I *num*	Locks an account *num* days after a password has expired; can be set to -1 to make the account permanent.
-l	Lists all aging information.
-m *num*	Sets a minimum number of days that a user must keep a password.
-M *num*	Sets a maximum number of days that a user is allowed to keep a password; can be set to -1 to remove that limit.
-W *num*	Specifies when a user is warned to change her password, in number of days before the password expiration date.

CERTIFICATION OBJECTIVE 6.02

Administrative Control

It's important for administrators to execute most actions as regular users because the root administrative user has full privileges on a system. Limits on regular users can help protect Linux systems from accidents. Regular users who have the root administrative password can temporarily take root privileges with the **su** command. The **su** command can also allow a user to become another user, provided that the correct password for the target user is specified.

Both the **su** and **sudo** commands allow running commands as another user, as well as opening a shell as another user. For administrative tasks, **sudo** offers more flexibility, because the configuration can tell exactly which commands a user is allowed to run. With **sudo** and the help of the /etc/sudoers file, it's possible to set up dedicated administrators with partial or complete root administrative privileges or to execute a command as another user.

The Ability to Log In

The file /etc/security/access.conf regulates access by all users. Although this topic is not explicitly listed in the RHCSA exam objectives, it is an important skill that you should master as a system administrator.

By default, in RHEL 9 the file /etc/security/access.conf does not have any effect. To enable access.conf, add the following line to /etc/pam.d/password-auth and /etc/pam.d/system-auth:

```
account required pam_access.so
```

The default version of this file is completely commented out, but the comments provide useful examples. The first example shows how to disallow (with the -) logins to the first virtual console (tty1) to *all* users but root:

```
-:ALL EXCEPT root:tty1
```

Scroll down further in the file. The following lines (with the +) show how to allow the root user to access the system from three specific remote IP addresses and from the localhost address:

```
+:root:192.168.200.1 192.168.200.4 192.168.200.9
+:root:127.0.0.1
```

If you're protecting a system from outside networks, this type of limitation on direct root administrative access makes sense. As long as the **su** or **sudo** command allows it, users who log in remotely as regular users can still elevate their privileges accordingly.

Be aware that the directives in this file are considered in order. So, if directives that allow access (with the +) come first, then the following directive denies access to all other users from all other local and remote logins:

```
-:ALL:ALL
```

The su Command

In some cases, such as Red Hat exams, it's appropriate to log in as the root administrative user. But in real production systems, it's best to log in as a regular user. As a regular user, you can temporarily open a shell with root administrative privileges with the **su** command. Normally, that command prompts for the password of the root administrative user. After you've completed administrative tasks, it's best to log out of the root administrative account; the **exit** command would return to the regular account of that user.

The **su -l** command is slightly different because it opens a *login shell* for the root administrative account. That means **su -l** changes the current directory to the root user's home directory, /root, and sets the user's environment as if the root user had logged in directly.

If you have the password of a second user, you can use the **su -l** *username* command to log in directly to that account. For example, if you wanted to switch to user dickens' account, you'd run the **su -l dickens** command. When you enter her password successfully, the command takes you to the /home/dickens directory.

Finally, the **su -c** command can be used to assume administrative privileges for one command. For example, the following command can be used to modify the first virtual drive on a system (assuming the root administrative password is successfully entered in response to the prompt):

```
$ su -c '/sbin/fdisk /dev/sda'
```

Limit Access to su

As discussed earlier, the ability to log in directly as the root administrative user can be regulated. Further limitations on administrative access are possible. For example, you can limit the users who are allowed to run the **su** command. This requires two basic steps.

First, you'll need to list the users who should have access to the **su** command. Make them a part of the wheel group. By default, here is what this line in /etc/group looks like:

```
wheel:x:10:
```

You can add selected users to the end of this line directly with the **usermod -G wheel** *username* command or with the Cockpit web console.

Second, this requires a change to the configuration of Pluggable Authentication Modules (PAM). While PAM is not an RHCE objective, there's a commented directive available in the /etc/pam.d/su file ready for this purpose:

```
# auth    required pam_wheel.so use_uid
```

If this line is activated, only users who are members of the wheel group are allowed to use the **su** command.

The sg Command

With the **sg** command, you can execute a command as another group. Assume you're a member of the project group. Then the command **sg project -c** *command* allows you to run commands with the identity of the group named project. For example, the following command copies the important.doc file to the noted directory:

```
$ sg project -c 'cp important.doc /home/project'
```

The file important.doc in the directory /home/project is owned by the group project, because the **cp** command was run under the project group.

Superuser Access with the sudo Command

You can limit access to the **sudo** command. Regular users who are authorized in /etc/sudoers can access administrative commands with their own password. Unlike **su**, typically the **sudo** command requires you to type your own user account's password, rather than the password of the user that you are trying to access.

To access /etc/sudoers run the **visudo** command. The **visudo** command locks the /etc/sudoers file against simultaneous edits and checks the syntax of the file before exiting. The following directive is active in the default version of the file. This allows the root user to run any command as any user:

```
root        ALL=(ALL)  ALL
```

The **root** keyword indicates that this configuration applies to the root user. Thanks to this configuration, the root user can run any command (due to the last ALL on the line), from any host (thanks to the first ALL), as any user (the second ALL).

Other users can be given administrative access. For example, if you want to allow user boris full administrative access, add the following directive to /etc/sudoers:

```
boris       ALL=(ALL)  ALL
```

In this case, all boris needs to do to run an administrative command is to preface it with the **sudo** command. For example, if boris runs the following command, he's prompted for his own regular user password before the noted service is started:

```
$ sudo systemctl start vsftpd
Password:
```

Alternatively, you can allow special users administrative access without a password. As suggested by the comments in the file, the following directive in /etc/sudoers would allow all users who are members of the wheel group to run administrative commands without a password:

```
%wheel    ALL=(ALL)  NOPASSWD: ALL
```

But you don't have to allow full administrative access. For example, if you want to allow users who are members of the %users group to shut down the local system, activate the following directive:

```
%users  localhost=/sbin/shutdown -h now
```

In many Linux configuration files, the % sign in front of a directive specifies a group. For example, another directive shown in comments specifies a group of commands that can be run by users who are members of the %sys group:

```
%sys ALL = NETWORKING, SOFTWARE, SERVICES, STORAGE, DELEGATING, ↵
PROCESSES, LOCATE, DRIVERS
```

Each of the directives can be associated with a set of commands. For example, users in the sys group, who are allowed to run PROCESSES directives, can run the commands associated with the following configuration line:

```
Cmnd_Alias PROCESSES = /bin/nice, /bin/kill, /usr/bin/kill, ↵
/usr/bin/killall
```

In a similar fashion, you could set up an admin group of users who are allowed to run these commands with the following directive:

```
%admin ALL = PROCESSES
```

This assumes that groups such as admin exist in the /etc/group and /etc/gshadow files.

User and Shell Configuration

Each user on any Red Hat Enterprise Linux system has an *environment* when logged on to the system. The environment defines directories where Linux looks for programs to run, the look of the login prompt, the terminal type, and more. This section explains how you can configure the default environment for local users. All system-wide shell configuration files are kept in the /etc directory. These files are bashrc, profile, and the scripts in the /etc/profile.d directory. These files and scripts are supplemented by hidden files in each user's home directory, as just described. Let's take a look at these files.

Home Directories and /etc/skel

When a new user is created with standard commands such as **useradd** or with the Cockpit web console, a default set of configuration files is copied to the user's home directory from the /etc/skel directory.

Home Directory

The home directory is where a user starts when logging in to a RHEL system. The home directory for most users is /home/*username*, where *username* is the user's login name. Every user should normally have write permission in his own home directory, so each user is free to read and write his own files.

/etc/skel

The /etc/skel directory contains default environment files for new accounts. The **useradd** command copies these files to the home directory for new users. The contents of /etc/skel may vary. While the standard files in this directory are hidden, administrators are free to add more files for new users. Standard files from one copy of /etc/skel are described in Table 6-9.

| TABLE 6-9 | Standard Files in the /etc/skel Directory |

File	Description
.bashrc	This basic bash configuration file may include a reference to the general /etc/bashrc configuration file. It can include commands to run when the bash shell is started. One example is an alias such as **rm='rm -i'**.
.bash_logout	This file is executed when you exit a bash shell, and it can include commands appropriate for this purpose, such as commands for clearing a screen.
.bash_profile	This file is sourced only when invoking a bash login shell, and it configures the bash startup environment. This is the appropriate place to add environment variables or modify the directories in your user account PATH.
.mozilla/	This directory includes options associated with the Firefox web browser, developed by the Mozilla project.

ⓦatch

Linux includes many hidden files that start with a dot (.). To list these files, run the ls -a command. For example, if you want to list all the files in the /etc/skel directory, run the ls -a /etc/skel command.

If you've installed more than a standard set of software packages on RHEL, additional configuration files and subdirectories may appear in the /etc/skel directory. For example, the installation of certain packages may include configuration files associated with emacs and the Z shell (zsh) in this directory.

As the system administrator, you can edit these files or place custom files in /etc/skel. When new users are created, these files are copied to the new users' home directories.

on the ⓘob

/etc/profile and ~/.bash_profile are executed before starting an interactive shell, while /etc/bashrc and ~/.bashrc are run for both interactive and noninteractive shells (such as scripts).

/etc/bashrc

The /etc/bashrc file is used for aliases and functions on a system-wide basis. Open this file in the text editor of your choice. Read each line in this file. Even if you don't understand the script commands, you can see that this file sets the following bash shell parameters for each user:

■ It assigns a value of **umask**, which sets the default permissions for newly created files. It supports one set of permissions for root and system users (with user IDs below 200) and another for regular users.

■ It assigns and defines a prompt, which is what you see just before the cursor at the command prompt.

■ It includes settings from *.sh files in the /etc/profile.d/ directory.

The settings here are supplemented by the .bashrc file in each user's home directory and, for login shells, by the /etc/profile, .bash_profile, and .bash_logout files.

/etc/profile and /etc/profile.d

The /etc/profile file is used for system-wide environments and startup files, and is sourced when bash is invoked as an interactive shell.

The first part of the file sets the PATH for searching for commands. Additional directories are added to the PATH with the **pathmunge** function. Then it exports the PATH, USER, LOGNAME, MAIL, HOSTNAME, HISTSIZE, and HISTCONTROL variables and finally runs the scripts in the /etc/profile.d directory. You can check the current value of any of these variables with the **echo $*variable*** command.

/etc/profile.d

The /etc/profile.d directory is designed to contain scripts to be executed in a login or interactive shell (that is, not in a script or a command that is run as **bash -c *command***). If you performed a "Server with GUI" installation, the following is a partial listing of the files; those with .sh extensions apply to the default bash shell:

```
bash_completion.sh    csh.local         less.sh
colorgrep.csh         debuginfod.csh    PackageKit.sh
colorgrep.sh          flatpak.sh        sh.local
colorls.csh           gawk.csh          vte.csh
colorxzgrep.csh       gawk.sh           which2.csh
colorxzgrep.sh        lang.csh          which2.sh
```

In most cases, there are two versions of a script, customized for different shell environments. Look at the files in the /etc/profile.d script directory. You can see that any script in this directory that ends with .sh is included as part of the configuration sourced by /etc/profile. Scripts with other extensions, such as .csh, relate to the C shell.

EXERCISE 6-3

Another Way to Secure a System

One more way to help secure a system is to change the default permissions for new files and directories. In this exercise, you'll reconfigure a system to remove access permissions for default files from other users or groups.

1. Back up the current version of the /etc/bashrc and /etc/login.defs.

2. Open the /etc/bashrc file in a text editor. Two lines in the file set the umask. One of the two lines is selected, depending on the **if** statement above them. See if you can determine which value of umask is assigned to a regular user.

3. The **if** statement tests to see whether the username and group name are the same and that the UID is greater than 199. In other words, the umask value of 002 is given to non-login shells run by regular users. A umask value of 022 is given to system users.

4. Change the first **umask** statement to exclude all permissions for groups and others. In other words, replace the umask of 002 with a umask of 077.

5. Save and exit the file.

6. In the /etc/login.defs file, find the UMASK directive and change its value to 077. This umask value is used by a login shell.

7. Log in as a regular, nonprivileged user. Use the **touch** command to make a new empty file. Use **ls -l** to verify the permissions on that file.

8. Open a non-login shell (i.e., type **bash**). Again, use the **touch** command to make a new empty file and use **ls -l** to verify the permissions on that new file.

    You have just changed the default umask for login and non-login shells. While this is an excellent option for security, it would affect the steps used in other chapters. Therefore, the final step is important.

9. Restore the original versions of /etc/bashrc and /etc/profile from the backup created in Step 1.

Shell Configuration Files in User Home Directories

As described earlier, each user gets a copy of all files from the /etc/skel directory, typically when the account is created. Most of them are hidden, revealed only with commands such as **ls -a**. As users start working with their accounts, more configuration files may be added to their home directories. Some users may work primarily with the default bash shell, whereas others will have additional configuration files related to their GUI desktop environments, such as GNOME.

The default Linux shell is bash, and until recently it was specifically included as the only shell described in associated Red Hat exam objectives. Although bash is no longer specifically included in the objectives, it is the default for RHEL 9.

Login, Logout, and User Switching

While this may seem like a "no-brainer" topic for Linux users with even a couple of days of experience, one of the RHCSA topics is "Log in and switch users in multiuser targets." It includes concepts from different chapters. As discussed in Chapter 5, the multi-user targets are multi-user.target and graphical.target. Virtual terminals are available at all of these targets. In the RHEL 9.1 release, a text login prompt appears as follows:

```
Red Hat Enterprise Linux Server 9.1 (Plow)
Kernel 5.14.0-162.6.1.el9_1.x86_64 on an x86_64

server1 login:
```

The hostname, as well as the versions of RHEL 9 and the kernel, will vary. But that's irrelevant to actual logins; all you need to do is type in a username, press ENTER, and type in a password when prompted.

Logouts from the command line are even simpler; the **exit**, **logout**, and CTRL-D commands all perform logouts from the command line. Of course, once you've logged out from a system, the login prompt just shown will appear.

As discussed earlier in this chapter, there's a different way to switch user accounts. For example, to switch from the current account to user donna's account, run the following command:

```
$ su -l donna
```

The same **exit**, **logout**, and CTRL-D commands can be used to exit from user donna's account. Of course, users can log in to and log out of the GUI. Although the steps vary a bit by desktop environment, they are as simple as the steps required to log in to and log out of any other operating system.

CERTIFICATION OBJECTIVE 6.04

Special Groups

In the past, many Linux distributions would typically assign all users to the same primary group, making it easier for them to share files. However, this approach had a security downside: if permissions weren't carefully configured, all members of that primary group could access each other's files and directories. This was often undesirable, as users might not want to share their data with everyone in the group. Red Hat has addressed this issue by assigning unique group ID (GID) numbers to each user, enhancing both security and user privacy.

As previously mentioned, this is known as the user private group scheme. Users get exclusive access to their own primary groups and don't have to worry about other users reading the files in their directories.

Standard and Red Hat Groups

In RHEL, each user gets her own special private group by default. As noted earlier, UIDs and GIDs normally start at 1000, are assigned matching numbers, and proceed in ascending order. In addition, you can set up special groups of dedicated users, ideally with higher GIDs. For example, an administrator might configure a group for the accounting department, perhaps with a GID of 70000.

Shared Directories

Most people work in groups, and they may want to share files. However, there may be good reasons for people in those groups to keep their information hidden from others. To support such groups, you can set up a shared directory, with access limited to the members of the group.

Assume you want to set up a shared directory, /home/accshared, for a group of accountants. To that end, you can set up a shared directory with the following basic steps:

1. Create the shared directory:

   ```
   # mkdir /home/accshared
   ```

2. Create a group for the accountants. Call it accgrp. Give it a group ID that doesn't interfere with existing group or user IDs. One way to do this is to add a line such as the following to the /etc/group file. Substitute the desired usernames.

   ```
   accgrp:x:70000:robertc,alanm,victorb,roberta,alano,charliew
   ```

3. Set up appropriate ownership for the new shared directory. The following commands prevent any specific user from taking control of the directory and assign group ownership to accgrp:

   ```
   # chown nobody:accgrp /home/accshared
   # chmod 2770 /home/accshared
   ```

Any user who is a member of the accgrp group can now create files in and copy files to the /home/accshared directory. Any files generated within or copied to that directory will be owned by the accgrp group.

This is made possible by the 2770 permissions assigned to the /home/accshared directory. Let's break that down into its component parts. The first digit (2) is the *set group ID bit*, also known as the *SGID bit*. When an SGID bit is set on a directory, any files created in that directory automatically have their group ownership set to be the same as the group owner of the directory. In addition, group ownership of files copied from other directories is reassigned (in this case, to the group named accgrp). There is a second way to set the SGID bit for the /home/accshared directory:

```
chmod g+s /home/accshared
```

The remaining digits are basic knowledge for any experienced Linux or Unix user. The 770 sets read, write, and execute permissions for the user and group that own the directory. Other users get no permissions to that directory.

Recall from Chapter 2 that the read permission on a directory allows the user to list its contents, while the write permission gives the ability to create new files in it. The execute permission on a directory is perhaps the most misunderstood, because there is nothing to execute: it just gives permission to access the contents of the directory (i.e., **cd** into it).

EXERCISE 6-4

Control Group Ownership with the SGID Bit

In this exercise, you will create new files in a directory designed to be shared by a group of users. You'll also see the difference in what happens before and after the SGID bit is set.

1. Add users called test1, test2, and test3. Specify passwords when prompted. Check the /etc/passwd and /etc/group files to verify that each user's private group was created.

   ```
   # useradd test1; echo changeme | passwd --stdin test1
   # useradd test2; echo changeme | passwd --stdin test2
   # useradd test3; echo changeme | passwd --stdin test3
   ```

2. Edit the /etc/group file and add a group called tg1. Make the test1 and test2 accounts members of this group. You could add the following line to /etc/group directly:

   ```
   tg1:x:99999:test1,test2
   ```

   Before you proceed, make sure the group ID assigned to group tg1 (in this case, 99999) is not already in use. Make sure to add the following line to /etc/gshadow. A group password is not required.

   ```
   tg1:!::test1,test2
   ```

3. Create a directory intended for use by the tg1 group:

   ```
   # mkdir   /home/testshared
   ```

4. Change the user and group ownership of the shared directory:

   ```
   # chown   nobody:tg1   /home/testshared
   ```

5. Log in as user test1. Navigate to the /home/test1 directory. Run the **umask** command to confirm that files created from this account will have the appropriate permissions. (The output of the **umask** command for regular users such as test1 should be 0022.) If there's a problem with the home directory or the umask output, you may have made an error earlier in this chapter with user settings. If so, check the **umask** settings in /etc/profile and /etc/bashrc, and repeat Steps 1–5.

6. Run the **cd /home/testshared** command. What happens?

7. Now as the root user, set group write permissions on the testshared directory:

```
# chmod 770 /home/testshared
```

8. As user test1, navigate back to the /home/testshared directory, and then try to create a file in the new directory. So far, so good.

```
$ cd /home/testshared
$ date >> test.txt
$ ls -l test.txt
```

9. As the root user, remove all permissions for other users on new files in the /home/testshared directory:

```
# chmod o-rwx /home/testshared/*
```

10. Now with the following command, check the ownership on the new file. Do you think other users in the tg1 group can access this file? If in doubt, log in as user test2 and see for yourself.

```
$ ls -l
```

11. From the root account, set the SGID bit on the directory:

```
# chmod g+s /home/testshared
```

(Yes, if you are efficiency minded, you may know that the **chmod 2770 /home/testshared** command combines the effect of this and the previous **chmod** commands.)

12. Switch back to the test1 account, navigate back to the /home/testshared directory, and create another file. Remove permissions for other users on the newly created file. Check the ownership on the newly created file. Do you think that user test2 can now access this file? (To see for yourself, try it from the test2 account.)

```
$ date >> testb.txt
$ chmod o-rwx /home/testshared/testb.txt
$ ls -l
```

13. Now log in as the test2 account. Go into the /home/testshared directory. Try accessing the testb.txt file. Create a different file and then use ls -l to check permissions and ownership again. (To see that it worked, try accessing this file from the test1 account.)

14. Switch to the test3 account and check whether that user can or cannot create files in this directory and whether that user can or cannot view the files in this directory. As expected, the user cannot access the /home/testshared directory because it is not part of the tg1 group.

CERTIFICATION SUMMARY

You can manage users and groups with the files of the shadow password suite. These files can be modified directly, with the help of commands such as **useradd** and **groupadd** or the Cockpit web console. The way users are configured is based on the /etc/login.defs file. Any variables or system-wide settings are defined in /etc/bashrc, /etc/profile, and the files in /etc/profile.d/. They can be modified by the .bashrc and .bash_profile files in user home directories.

There are several ways to limit the use of administrative privileges. The ability to log in can be regulated by the file /etc/security/access.conf. Access to the **su** command can be limited with the help of PAM. Partial and complete administrative privileges can be configured for the **sudo** command in the /etc/sudoers file.

By default, Red Hat Enterprise Linux assigns unique user and group ID numbers to each new user. This user private group scheme supports the configuration of special groups for a specific set of users. The users in the group can share and modify each other's files in a dedicated directory, courtesy of the SGID bit.

TWO-MINUTE DRILL

Here are some of the key points from the certification objectives in Chapter 6.

User Account Management

❑ After installation, a system may have only a single login account: root. For everyday operation, it's best to create one or more regular accounts.

❑ The shadow password suite is configured in the /etc/passwd, /etc/shadow, /etc/group, and /etc/gshadow files.

❑ Administrators can add user and group accounts by directly editing the files of the shadow password suite or with commands such as **useradd** and **groupadd**. The way user accounts are configured is defined by the /etc/login.defs file.

❑ Accounts can be added with the Cockpit web console.

Administrative Control

❑ Logins can be regulated by the /etc/security/access.conf file.

❑ Access to the **su** command can be restricted through the /etc/pam.d/su file.

❑ Custom administrative privileges can be configured in the /etc/sudoers file.

User and Shell Configuration

❑ The home directory for new login accounts is populated from the /etc/skel directory.
❑ Each user has an environment when logged on to the system, based on /etc/bashrc, /etc/profile, and the scripts in /etc/profile.d/.
❑ All users have hidden shell configuration files in their home directories, such as .bash_profile and .bashrc.

Special Groups

❑ Red Hat's user private group scheme configures users with their own unique user and group ID numbers.
❑ With appropriate SGID permissions, you can configure a shared directory for a specific group of users.
❑ Setting the SGID bit is easy: run the **chmod g+s** command on the shared directory.

SELF TEST

The following questions will help measure your understanding of the material presented in this chapter. As no multiple-choice questions appear on the Red Hat exams, no multiple-choice questions appear in this book. These questions exclusively test your understanding of the chapter. It is okay if you have another way of performing a task. Getting results, not memorizing trivia, is what counts on the Red Hat exams. There may be more than one answer to many of these questions.

User Account Management

1. What's the standard minimum user ID number for regular users on Red Hat distributions?
2. What command creates the user mike with /sbin/nologin as a shell?

Administrative Control

3. What file restricts users' access?
4. Which file controls the commands that a user can run with the privileges of root or of another user?
5. When a regular user uses the **sudo** command to run an administrative command, what password is required?

User and Shell Configuration

6. If you want to add files to every new user account, what directory should you use?

7. What are the system-wide configuration files associated with the bash shell?

Special Groups

8. What command would set the SGID bit on the /home/developer directory?

9. What command would set up ownership of the developer group on the /home/developer directory?

10. What command would add user alpha to the developer group? (This question assumes the alpha user and the developer group already exist and that alpha may belong to groups other than his primary group.)

LAB QUESTIONS

Red Hat presents its exams electronically. For that reason, the labs in this chapter are available from the companion website that accompanies the book. In case you haven't yet set up RHEL 9 on a system, refer to Chapter 1 for installation instructions. The answers for these labs follow the Self Test answers.

SELF TEST ANSWERS

User Account Management

1. The minimum user ID number for regular users on Red Hat distributions is 1000.

2. The command **useradd -s /sbin/nologin** creates the user mike with /sbin/nologin as a shell.

Administrative Control

3. The file that restricts users' access is /etc/security/access.conf.

4. The file that controls which commands a user can run with the privileges of root or of another user is /etc/sudoers.

5. When a regular user uses the **sudo** command to run an administrative command, the regular password of that user is required, unless the NOPASSWD directive was specified in /etc/sudoers.

User and Shell Configuration

6. To automatically add files to every new user account, you should use the /etc/skel directory.

7. The system-wide configuration files associated with the bash shell are /etc/bashrc, /etc/profile, and the scripts in /etc/profile.d/.

Special Groups

8. The command that would set the SGID bit on the /home/developer directory is **chmod g+s /home/developer**. Numeric options such as **chmod 2770 /home/developer** may not be correct, as they go beyond just setting the SGID bit.

9. The command that sets up ownership of the developer group on the /home/developer directory is **chown :developer /home/developer**. Another command (not covered in this chapter) that achieves the same result is **chgrp developer /home/developer**.

10. The command that adds user alpha to the developer group is **usermod -aG developer alpha**. Note that the **-a** command option is required to prevent the user being removed from other supplementary groups not listed in the **usermod** command.

LAB ANSWERS

Lab 1

While there are several methods available to create new users and groups, they should all come to the same result. In the following steps, you will use the **useradd** and **groupadd** commands to complete the lab tasks.

1. Create the user newguy and make newguy a member of the users group (note that the users group already exists in /etc/group, so there is no need to create this group):

```
# useradd -G users newguy
```

2. Create the user intern:

```
# useradd intern
```

3. Set the password of both users to changeme:

```
# echo changeme | passwd --stdin newguy
# echo changeme | passwd --stdin intern
```

4. Create a new group named peons with GID 12345, and make both users members of that group:

```
# groupadd -g 12345 peons
# usermod -a -G peons newguy
# usermod -G peons intern
```

Note the **-a** command option with **usermod**. This is required because newguy is a member of the users group. If you don't pass the **-a** option (append), newguy will be removed from the users group. Alternatively, you can specify all the supplementary groups that newguy is a member of:

```
# usemod -G peons,users newguy
```

Lab 2

1. First, create the new user senioradm and assign a password:

```
# useradd senioradm
# echo changeme | passwd --stdin senioradm
```

2. With respect to **sudo** privileges, you should add the following line in the /etc/sudoers file:

```
senioradm    ALL=(ALL)         ALL
```

As an alternative to editing the sudoers file (preferably with **visudo**), you could create a new file in the /etc/sudoers.d/ directory and add the new configuration there.

Another valid solution is to make the user a member of the wheel group. In fact, the members of the wheel group can run any command via **sudo**, as configured in this line of /etc/sudoers:

```
%wheel    ALL=(ALL)         ALL
```

3. To test the result, log in as the senioradm user and run an administrative command, prefaced by **sudo**. For example, try the following command:

```
# sudo firewall-cmd --list-all-zones
```

Unless you've run the **sudo** command in the last few minutes, this action will prompt for a password. Enter the password created for user senioradm. It should list all the firewall zones and their configuration.

Lab 3

1. Create the new user junioradm and assign a password:

```
# useradd junioradm
# echo changeme | passwd --stdin junioradm
```

2. With respect to **sudo** privileges, you should add the following line in the /etc/sudoers file:

```
junioradm    ALL=(root) NOPASSWD: /sbin/fdisk
```

As an alternative to editing the sudoers file (preferably with **visudo**), you could create a new file in the /etc/sudoers.d/ directory and add the new configuration there.

3. Run the **fdisk** command via **sudo**:

```
$ sudo fdisk -l
```

If successful, you should see a list of partitions for connected drives in the output.

4. Try to run the same command without **sudo**, and notice the difference:

```
$ fdisk -l
```

You should get some permission errors.

Lab 4

1. This lab specifies "new users," which implies that you should add the directory to /etc/skel, rather than copying to the home directory of every single user:

```
# cp -a /usr/share/doc/bash /etc/skel/
```

2. Test the result by adding a new user named infouser with the **useradd** command:

```
# useradd infouser
# echo changeme | passwd --stdin infouser
```

3. You should find that a /home/infouser directory has been created, with the content of /usr/share/doc/bash in it:

```
# ls -lR /home/infouser
```

Lab 5

1. Create the user account:

```
# useradd mike
# echo changeme | passwd --stdin mike
```

2. Run the following command to check when the password for this user account expires:

```
# chage -l mike
```

3. Set the last day that the password was changed to 0 since January 1, 1970. This will force a password change at the next logon.

```
# chage -d 0 mike
```

4. Set the minimum number of days between password changes and the maximum number of days during which a password is valid for user mike:

```
# chage -m 7 -M 30 mike
```

5. Again, confirm the new settings for user mike.

6. For the last lab requirement, edit the file /etc/login.defs and set PASS_MAX_DAYS to 30 days:

```
PASS_MAX_DAYS 30
```

Lab 6

1. Create the testlock user account and lock the password:

    ```
    # useradd testlock
    # echo changeme | passwd -stdin testlock
    # usermod -L testlock
    ```

    In /etc/shadow, you should see an extra single exclamation mark (!) prepended to the password field of user testlock.

2. Test if you can log in as user testlock from a terminal. If you can, open a shell by running **su** as a normal user or as root. From tester1, check if you can open an SSH session as user testlock.

3. Unlock the user's password and disable the user account by, for instance, setting the expiration date of the account to January 1, 2000:

    ```
    # usermod -U testlock
    # usermod -e 2000-01-01 testlock
    ```

4. Repeat Step 2.

5. Reenable the user account by setting an empty expiring date, and set user testlock's login shell to /sbin//nologin:

    ```
    # usermod -e "" testlock
    # usermod -s /sbin/nologin testlock
    ```

6. Repeat Step 2.

You should have found that when the user's password is locked and when the account is disabled, you cannot log in from a terminal or via SSH. Access via **su** is permitted only as root. Therefore, the two methods may seem equivalent. However, when the user's password is locked, you can still log in to the user account via a password-less authentication method—for example, with SSH key authentication (which is covered in Chapter 8).

Conversely, setting the user's shell to /sbin/nologin disables SSH access (with password and key authentication), as well as access from a terminal or via **su**. However, the user may still be able to authenticate through a web application, if present, or via other programs that rely on password authentication.

In conclusion, which is the most secure method to disable a user account and ensure that access to the system is disabled? If you do not want to delete the user account, use all of them: lock the user's password, disable the account, and set the login shell to /sbin/nologin.

Lab 7

1. Create user accounts for mike, rick, terri, and maryam by using the **useradd** command:

```
# useradd mike
# useradd rick
# useradd terri
# useradd maryam
# echo changeme | passwd -stdin mike
# echo changeme | passwd -stdin rick
# echo changeme | passwd -stdin terri
# echo changeme | passwd -stdin maryam
```

2. Set up a group for these users. Configure a group ID outside the range of regular users in /etc/group with a line such as this:

```
groupadd -G 88888 -a mike,rick,terri,maryam galley
```

3. Create the /home/galley directory. Give it proper ownership and permissions with the following commands:

```
# mkdir /home/galley
# chown nobody:galley
# chmod 2770 /home/galley
```

Chapter 7

Storage and Filesystem Administration

L inux installation is easy, at least for anyone serious about Red Hat certification. Perhaps the most difficult part during the installation of a system is partitioning and formatting your disk drives. However, most administrators have to maintain existing systems. Hence, disk and filesystem management does not end after the installation of a system.

Critical skills related to storage management include adding new partitions, creating logical volumes, mounting and expanding filesystems, and more. In many cases, you'll want to make sure these filesystems are mounted automatically during the boot process, and that requires a detailed knowledge of the /etc/fstab configuration file.

INSIDE THE EXAM

Some of the RHCSA objectives listed in this chapter overlap and may be covered in multiple sections. The objectives all relate in some way to filesystem management and should be considered as a whole in this chapter.

Partition Management

As in the real world, it is the results that matter. It doesn't matter whether you use **fdisk** or **parted** to create an MBR-style partition. However, you should know that the Red Hat implementation of **fdisk** now supports GPT partitions, just as **gdisk** and **parted** do. Make sure that appropriate partitions meet the requirements of the exam.

The current RHCSA objectives include the following related requirements:

- List, create, delete partitions on MBR and GPT disks
- Add new partitions and logical volumes, and swap to a system non-destructively

Logical Volumes

The Logical Volume Manager (LVM) provides a level of abstraction to group and manage partitions and disks in special entities called *volume groups*. On top of a volume group you can create logical volumes, which can be formatted with a filesystem like normal disk partitions. The following RHCSA objectives describe the skills required:

- Create and remove physical volumes

- Assign physical volumes to volume groups
- Create and delete logical volumes

Of course, a logical volume isn't fulfilling its full potential unless you can increase its size, as suggested by the following objective:

- Extend existing logical volumes

Filesystem Management

Partitions and logical volumes must be formatted before they're ready to store files. To that end, you need to know how to meet the following RHCSA objectives:

- Create, mount, unmount, and use vfat, ext4, and xfs file systems
- Configure systems to mount file systems at boot by universally unique ID (UUID) or label
- Mount and unmount network file systems using NFS

The Automounter

The automounter service, known as autofs, is a tool that initiates automatic mounting of filesystems when they're accessed and dismounts them after they've been inactive for a certain duration. This functionality proves invaluable for network-based file systems, detachable storage mediums, and other assets that aren't required to be constantly mounted.

The associated RHCSA objective is

- Configure autofs

CERTIFICATION OBJECTIVE 7.01

Storage Management and Partitions

While it's easier to create partitions and logical volumes during the installation process, not every administrator has that privilege. Therefore, you must learn how to create and manage partitions on installed systems. Once configured, a partition or a logical volume can be referred to generically as a *volume*. In Linux, three tools still predominate for administrators who need to create and manage partitions: **fdisk**, **gdisk**, and **parted**. While these tools are primarily applied to local hard disks, they can also be used for other media such as drives attached over a network.

Current System State

Before using the **fdisk**, **gdisk**, or **parted** utility to create or modify a partition, do check currently available free space along with currently mounted filesystems. The **df** and **mount** commands make it easy. The example shown in Figure 7-1 illustrates how the **df** command displays the total, used, and available free space on all currently mounted filesystems.

The terms *filesystem* and *file system* are interchangeable. Both are used in official Linux documentation.

Note the numbers under the "1K-blocks" column. In this case (except for the temporary filesystems, tmpfs, and devtmpfs), they add up to about 17GiB of allocated space. If the hard drive is larger, unallocated space may be used for another partition. Partitions can be combined with others to configure additional space in volume groups and logical volumes, and that can be useful when you need to expand the space available to appropriate filesystems, such as /home, /tmp, and /var.

Because tmpfs and devtmpfs are temporary filesystems stored in RAM, their contents are removed after a system reboot.

FIGURE 7-1

Disk space usage shown by the df command

```
[root@server1 ~]# df
Filesystem              1K-blocks     Used Available Use% Mounted on
devtmpfs                     4096        0      4096   0% /dev
tmpfs                      892780        0    892780   0% /dev/shm
tmpfs                      357112    10016    347096   3% /run
/dev/mapper/rhel-root    15718400  4084240  11634160  26% /
/dev/mapper/rhel-home     1038336    44652    993684   5% /home
/dev/nvme0n1p1            1038336   291436    746900  29% /boot
tmpfs                      178556      104    178452   1% /run/user/1000
[root@server1 ~]#
```

FIGURE 7-2

Output of the
df command in
human-readable
format

```
[root@server1 ~]# df -h
Filesystem                Size Used Avail Use% Mounted on
devtmpfs                  4.0M    0  4.0M   0% /dev
tmpfs                     872M    0  872M   0% /dev/shm
tmpfs                     349M 9.8M  339M   3% /run
/dev/mapper/rhel-root      15G 3.9G   12G  26% /
/dev/mapper/rhel-home    1014M  44M  971M   5% /home
/dev/nvme0n1p1           1014M 285M  730M  29% /boot
tmpfs                     175M 104K  175M   1% /run/user/1000
[root@server1 ~]# █
```

To print the partition sizes in a more readable format, you can use the **-h** command option, as shown in Figure 7-2. The **-H** command option displays output similar to that of **-h**, but whereas **-H** prints the volume sizes in international units such as KB, MB, and GB, **-h** prints the sizes in KiB (kibibyte), MiB (mebibyte), and GiB (gibibyte).

This difference in notation was briefly explained in Chapter 1. In international units, multiples are expressed in powers of ten. Hence, 1KB = 1000 bytes, 1MB = 1,000,000 bytes, and so on. Conversely, the KiB, MiB, and GiB notation uses powers of two. Therefore, 1KiB = 1024 bytes, 1MiB = 1,048,576 bytes, and so on.

e x a m

ⓦatch You must recognize which units of measure to use depending on the context. For example, if you are asked to create a partition of 1GB, that means 1 billion bytes. However, if you are required to create a partition of 1GiB, that is equivalent to 1024 × 1024 × 1024 bytes, or equivalently 1024 × 1024KiB, or 1024MiB, or 1GiB.

The second command, **mount**, lists the format and mount options for each filesystem. Examine the following output of the partition represented by device /dev/mapper/rhel-home. Note that it is mounted on the /home directory with the xfs file type. The purpose of this filesystem is to separate the home directories of regular users in a dedicated volume.

```
[root@server1 ~]# mount | grep home
/dev/mapper/rhel-home on /home type xfs ↵
(rw,relatime,seclabel,attr2,inode64,logbufs=8,logbsize=32k,noquota)
```

If the output of the **mount** command confuses you, consider the **findmnt** command, which prints all mounted filesystems in a tree-like format, as shown in Figure 7-3.

In the output, note the presence of "special filesystems" such as proc and sysfs, which we cover later in this chapter.

FIGURE 7-3   Output of the findmnt command

```
[root@server1 ~]# findmnt
TARGET                            SOURCE          FSTYPE    OPTIONS
/                                 /dev/mapper/rhel-root
                                                  xfs       rw,relatime,seclabel,attr2,inode64,logbuf
├─/proc                           proc            proc      rw,nosuid,nodev,noexec,relatime
│ └─/proc/sys/fs/binfmt_misc      systemd-1       autofs    rw,relatime,fd=31,pgrp=1,timeout=0,minpro
├─/sys                            sysfs           sysfs     rw,nosuid,nodev,noexec,relatime,seclabel
│ ├─/sys/kernel/security          securityfs      security  rw,nosuid,nodev,noexec,relatime
│ ├─/sys/fs/cgroup                cgroup2         cgroup2   rw,nosuid,nodev,noexec,relatime,seclabel,
│ ├─/sys/fs/pstore                pstore          pstore    rw,nosuid,nodev,noexec,relatime,seclabel
│ ├─/sys/fs/bpf                   none            bpf       rw,nosuid,nodev,noexec,relatime,mode=700
│ ├─/sys/fs/selinux               selinuxfs       selinuxf  rw,nosuid,noexec,relatime
│ ├─/sys/kernel/debug             debugfs         debugfs   rw,nosuid,nodev,noexec,relatime,seclabel
│ ├─/sys/kernel/tracing           tracefs         tracefs   rw,nosuid,nodev,noexec,relatime,seclabel
│ ├─/sys/fs/fuse/connections      fusectl         fusectl   rw,nosuid,nodev,noexec,relatime
│ └─/sys/kernel/config            configfs        configfs  rw,nosuid,nodev,noexec,relatime
├─/dev                            devtmpfs        devtmpfs  rw,nosuid,seclabel,size=4096k,nr_inodes=1
│ ├─/dev/shm                      tmpfs           tmpfs     rw,nosuid,nodev,seclabel,inode64
│ ├─/dev/pts                      devpts          devpts    rw,nosuid,noexec,relatime,seclabel,gid=5,
│ ├─/dev/hugepages                hugetlbfs       hugetlbf  rw,relatime,seclabel,pagesize=2M
│ └─/dev/mqueue                   mqueue          mqueue    rw,nosuid,nodev,noexec,relatime,seclabel
├─/run                            tmpfs           tmpfs     rw,nosuid,nodev,seclabel,size=357112k,nr_
│ ├─/run/credentials/systemd-sysusers.service
│ │                               none            ramfs     ro,nosuid,nodev,noexec,relatime,mode=700
│ ├─/run/vmblock-fuse             vmware-vmblock  fuse.vmw  rw,relatime,user_id=0,group_id=0,default_
│ └─/run/user/1000                tmpfs           tmpfs     rw,nosuid,nodev,relatime,seclabel,size=17
│   └─/run/user/1000/gvfs         gvfsd-fuse      fuse.gvf  rw,nosuid,nodev,relatime,user_id=1000,gro
├─/home                           /dev/mapper/rhel-home
│                                                 xfs       rw,relatime,seclabel,attr2,inode64,logbuf
└─/boot                           /dev/nvme0n1p1  xfs       rw,relatime,seclabel,attr2,inode64,logbuf
[root@server1 ~]# ▊
```

The fdisk Utility

The **fdisk** utility is common to many operating systems. macOS has a fully featured version of **fdisk**. Older versions of Microsoft Windows have a simplified version of **fdisk**.

Although the Linux implementation of **fdisk** includes a wide variety of commands, you need to know only the few discussed here.

fdisk works with partitions created using the traditional Master Boot Record (MBR) partitioning scheme. On newer systems that run UEFI firmware rather than a traditional BIOS, you may see a different partitioning standard: the GUID Partition Table (GPT). Although in earlier releases of RHEL 8 **fdisk** support for GPT was considered experimental, today **fdisk** can handle GPT partitions. Nevertheless, in this chapter, we will demonstrate how to use **gdisk** and **parted** to manage them.

Start fdisk: Help and More

The following screen output lists commands that show how to start **fdisk**, how to get help, and how to quit the program. The /dev/sda drive is associated with the first drive on a Linux system, but the name may be different on your machine, such as /dev/nvme0n1 if you have an NVMe drive. As other systems may be configured with different hard drive device files, you may need to check the output from the **df** and **fdisk -l** commands for clues.

on the
job

An NVMe drive is a type of solid-state drive (SSD) that uses the Non-Volatile Memory Express interface protocol to connect to a computer's motherboard. NVMe is designed to take advantage of the high-speed capabilities of solid-state storage.

When you start **fdisk**, type **m** to list basic **fdisk** commands:

```
# fdisk /dev/sda

Welcome to fdisk (util-linux 2.37.4).
Changes will remain in memory only, until you decide to write them.
Be careful before using the write command.

Command (m for help): m

Help:

  DOS (MBR)
   a   toggle a bootable flag
   b   edit nested BSD disklabel
   c   toggle the dos compatibility flag

  Generic
   d   delete a partition
   F   list free unpartitioned space
   l   list known partition types
   n   add a new partition
   p   print the partition table
   t   change a partition type
   v   verify the partition table
   i   print information about a partition

  Misc
   m   print this menu
   u   change display/entry units
   x   extra functionality (experts only)
[...]
  Save & Exit
   w   write table to disk and exit
   q   quit without saving changes
[...]

Command (m for help): q
#
```

A wide variety of commands are associated with **fdisk**—and more if you run the **x** command to access **fdisk**'s extra functionality.

Using fdisk: A New Drive with No Partitions

After a new drive is installed on Linux, that drive normally isn't configured with partitions. The **fdisk** utility can be used to configure partitions on physical or virtual disks attached to the system. For example, the baseline virtual system for this book includes one drive, which may be named /dev/nvme0n1, /dev/sda, or /dev/vda on your system.

on the **job**

> **SATA, PATA, and SAS SCSI drives are all represented by device files such as /dev/sda, /dev/sdb, and so on.**

If a newly added drive hasn't been used by the RHEL installation program (or some other disk management program), **fdisk** will return the following message the first time it tries to access the drive:

```
Device does not contain a recognized partition table
Building a new DOS disklabel with disk identifier 0xcb0a51f1.
```

In other words, even if you don't create a partition, **fdisk** will automatically write a DOS disk label to the drive if you save your changes.

If you need more than four partitions on the new physical disk, configure the first three partitions as primary partitions, and then configure the fourth partition as an extended partition. That extended partition should typically be large enough to fill the rest of the disk; all logical partitions must fit in that space.

Using fdisk: In a Nutshell

At the **fdisk** command-line prompt, start with the print command (**p**) to examine the partition table. This allows you to review the current entries in the partition table. Assuming free space is available, you can then create a new (**n**) partition.

Generally, partitions are either primary (**p**) or logical (**l**). If it doesn't already exist, you can also create an extended partition (**e**) to contain logical partitions. Remember that in a drive formatted with the MBR scheme, you can have up to four primary partitions, which would correspond to numbers 1 through 4. One of the primary partitions can be configured as an extended partition. The remaining partitions are logical partitions, numbered 5 and above. With an extended partition, you can create a maximum of 12 logical partitions on a drive.

If free space is available, **fdisk** normally starts the new partition at the first available sector or cylinder. The actual size of the partition depends on disk geometry.

Using fdisk: Create a Partition

The following screen output sample shows the steps used to create a new (**n**) partition (**p**), make it bootable (**a**), and then finally write (**w**) the partition information to the disk. (Note that although you may specify a 500MiB partition, the geometry of the disk may not allow that precise size.)

```
# fdisk /dev/sdb

Command (m for help): n
Partition type
   p   primary partition (0 primary, 0 extended, 4 free)
   e   extended (container for logical partitions)
Select (default p): p
Partition number (1-4, default 1): 1
First sector (2048-2097151, default 2048):
Using default value 2048
Last sector, +sectors or +size{K,M,G} (2048-2097151, default 2097151): +500M
Created a new partition 1 of type 'Linux' and of size 500 MiB.

Command (m for help): a
Selected partition 1

Command (m for help): p
Disk /dev/sdb: 1 GiB, 1073741824 bytes, 2097152 sectors
...
   Device Boot     Start       End    Sectors   Size Id  Type
/dev/sdb1    *      2048   1026047   1024000   500M 83  Linux

Command (m for help): w
```

Note how the number of sectors matches the binary representation of 500MiB. Repeat the commands to create any other partitions you might need.

When partitions are added or changed, you generally don't have to reboot to get Linux to read the new partition table, unless another partition on that drive has been formatted and mounted. If so, an attempt to write the partition table with the **w** command fails temporarily with the following message:

```
WARNING: Re-reading the partition table failed with error 16:
 Device or resource busy.
 The kernel still uses the old table. The new table will be used at
 the next reboot or after you run partprobe(8) or kpartx(8)
```

If you run **partprobe /dev/sdb**, the kernel will read the new partition table and you'll be able to use the newly created partition.

Using fdisk: Many Partition Types

One feature of special interest is based on the **t** command to change the partition system identifier. If you need space for logical volumes or even swap space, the **t** command is important. After pressing **t**, you're prompted to enter the partition number (if there's more than one configured). You can then list available partition types with the **L** command, as shown here. (If there's only one partition on the drive, it is selected automatically.)

```
Command (m for help): t
Selected partition 1
Hex code or alias (type L to list all): L
```

The list of available partition identifiers, as shown in Figure 7-4, is impressive. Note how it's not limited to Linux partitions. However, as this book covers Linux, Table 7-1 lists associated partition types.

Unless you're making a change, type in identifier **83**. You'll be returned to the **fdisk** command prompt.

Using fdisk: Delete a Partition

The following example removes the only configured partition. The sample output screen first starts **fdisk**. Then you can print (**p**) the current partition table, delete (**d**) the partition by number (**1** in this case), write (**w**) the changes to the disk, and quit (**q**) from the program. Needless to say, *do not perform this action on any partition where you need the data.*

FIGURE 7-4   Linux partition types in fdisk

```
00 Empty              24 NEC DOS            81 Minix / old Lin  bf Solaris
01 FAT12              27 Hidden NTFS Win    82 Linux swap / So  c1 DRDOS/sec (FAT-
02 XENIX root         39 Plan 9             83 Linux            c4 DRDOS/sec (FAT-
03 XENIX usr          3c PartitionMagic     84 OS/2 hidden or   c6 DRDOS/sec (FAT-
04 FAT16 <32M         40 Venix 80286        85 Linux extended   c7 Syrinx
05 Extended           41 PPC PReP Boot      86 NTFS volume set  da Non-FS data
06 FAT16              42 SFS                87 NTFS volume set  db CP/M / CTOS / .
07 HPFS/NTFS/exFAT    4d QNX4.x             88 Linux plaintext  de Dell Utility
08 AIX                4e QNX4.x 2nd part    8e Linux LVM        df BootIt
09 AIX bootable       4f QNX4.x 3rd part    93 Amoeba           e1 DOS access
0a OS/2 Boot Manag    50 OnTrack DM         94 Amoeba BBT       e3 DOS R/O
0b W95 FAT32          51 OnTrack DM6 Aux    9f BSD/OS           e4 SpeedStor
0c W95 FAT32 (LBA)    52 CP/M               a0 IBM Thinkpad hi  ea Linux extended
0e W95 FAT16 (LBA)    53 OnTrack DM6 Aux    a5 FreeBSD          eb BeOS fs
0f W95 Ext'd (LBA)    54 OnTrackDM6         a6 OpenBSD          ee GPT
10 OPUS               55 EZ-Drive           a7 NeXTSTEP         ef EFI (FAT-12/16/
11 Hidden FAT12       56 Golden Bow         a8 Darwin UFS       f0 Linux/PA-RISC b
12 Compaq diagnost    5c Priam Edisk        a9 NetBSD           f1 SpeedStor
14 Hidden FAT16 <3    61 SpeedStor          ab Darwin boot      f4 SpeedStor
16 Hidden FAT16       63 GNU HURD or Sys    af HFS / HFS+       f2 DOS secondary
17 Hidden HPFS/NTF    64 Novell Netware     b7 BSDI fs          fb VMware VMFS
18 AST SmartSleep     65 Novell Netware     b8 BSDI swap        fc VMware VMKCORE
1b Hidden W95 FAT3    70 DiskSecure Mult    bb Boot Wizard hid  fd Linux raid auto
1c Hidden W95 FAT3    75 PC/IX              bc Acronis FAT32 L  fe LANstep
1e Hidden W95 FAT1    80 Old Minix          be Solaris boot     ff BBT
```

TABLE 7-1	Linux Partition Types in fdisk

Partition Identifier	Description
05	Extended partition; while not a Linux partition type, such partitions are a prerequisite for logical partitions. Also see 85.
82	Linux swap.
83	Linux; applicable for all standard Linux partition formats.
85	Linux extended partition; may not be recognized by other operating systems.
88	Linux plaintext partition table; rarely used.
8e	Linux LVM for partitions used as physical volumes.
fd	Linux RAID; for partitions used as components of a RAID array.

Assuming only one partition exists on this drive, it is selected automatically after you run the **d** command.

```
# fdisk /dev/sdb
Command (m for help): p

Disk /dev/sdb: 1 GiB, 1073741824 bytes, 2097152 sectors
Units = sectors of 1 * 512 = 512 bytes
Sector size (logical/physical): 512 bytes / 512 bytes
I/O size (minimum/optimal): 512 bytes / 512 bytes
Disk label type: dos
Disk identifier: 0x2e3c116d

   Device Boot    Start      End   Sectors   Size Id  Type
/dev/sdb1               2048  1026047   1024000   500M 83  Linux
Command (m for help): d
Selected partition 1
Partition 1 has been deleted.
```

This is the last chance to change your mind before deleting the current partition. To avoid writing the change, exit from **fdisk** with the **q** command. If you're pleased with the changes that you've made and want to make them permanent, proceed with the **w** command:

```
Command (m for help): w
```

You should now have an empty hard drive.

on the **!**
i) o b

If you remove a partition, the partition table on disk is modified to reflect the change, but the actual data on the partition isn't removed. This means that if you re-create the partition using the same layout (same start/end sectors), your data will still be there. It's worth trying this procedure in case you accidentally delete a partition by mistake.

Using fdisk: Create a Swap Partition

Now that you know how to create partitions with **fdisk**, just one additional step is required to set up that partition for swap space. Once you have a swap partition of the desired size, run the **t** command to select a partition, and then run the **l** command to show the partition ID types listed in Figure 7-4.

In this case, at the following prompt, type in **82** for a Linux swap partition:

```
Hex code or alias (type L to list all): 82
```

For example, you could run the following sequence of commands to set up a new swap partition on the second hard drive. The details of what you see depend on the partitions you may have created. It'll be a 900MiB swap space on the first primary partition (/dev/sdb1).

```
Command (m for help): n
Partition type
     p   primary partition (0 primary, 0 extended, 4 free)
     e   extended (container for logical partitions)
Select (default p): p
Partition number (1-4, default 1): 1
First sector (2048-2097151, default 2048): 2048
Last sector, +sectors or +size{K,M,G} (2048-2097151, default 2097151): +900M
Created a new partition 1 of type 'Linux' and of size 900 MiB

Command (m for help): p

Disk /dev/sdb: 1 GiB, 1073741824 bytes, 2097152 sectors
...

    Device Boot     Start      End    Sectors   Size Id  Type
/dev/sdb1               2048  1845247   1843200   900M 83  Linux


Command (m for help): t
Selected partition 1
Hex code or alias (type L to list all): 82
Changed system type of partition 'Linux' to 'Linux swap / Solaris'.

Command (m for help): w
The partition table has been altered.

Calling ioctl() to re-read partition table.
Syncing disks.
```

The **fdisk** utility doesn't actually write the changes to disk until you run the write (**w**) command. Alternatively, you can cancel these changes with the quit (**q**) command. If you don't see any error messages, the changes are written to disk. As described later in this chapter, additional work is required to configure RHEL to use that newly created swap partition.

The gdisk Utility

As illustrated in the previous section, the MBR partitioning scheme supports a maximum of 15 partitions for data (3 primary and 12 logical), plus an extended partition, which is simply a "container" for logical partitions. In contrast, the GPT partitioning scheme can hold up to 128 partitions.

Another limitation of MBR is the disk size. The MBR scheme uses 32-bit logical addresses, which support disk drives up to 2TB. On the other hand, the GPT format relies on 64-bit addresses, which support drives of up to 8 million terabytes!

Although you could use **fdisk** and select the **g** command to switch to a GPT partition table format, the **gdisk** utility was specifically designed for GPT partitions. If you're familiar with **fdisk**, **gdisk** should seem familiar too. When you start **gdisk** on a disk with an MBR partition table, you will see the following warning:

```
[root@server1 ~]# gdisk /dev/sdb
...
******************************************************************
Found invalid GPT and valid MBR; converting MBR to GPT format
in memory. THIS OPERATION IS POTENTIALLY DESTRUCTIVE! Exit by
typing 'q' if you don't want to convert your MBR partitions
to GPT format!
******************************************************************
```

As suggested by the message, type **q** to exit; otherwise, you may lose any data on your drive. In this case, **gdisk** warned us that our disk was formatted using the MBR partition table, and hence we should rather use **fdisk** to modify the partition layout.

Once started, **gdisk** works in a similar way to **fdisk**. Type the question mark (**?**) to get a list of commands:

```
Command (? for help): ?
b       back up GPT data to a file
c       change a partition's name
d       delete a partition
i       show detailed information on a partition
l       list known partition types
n       add a new partition
o       create a new empty GUID partition table (GPT)
p       print the partition table
q       quit without saving changes
r       recovery and transformation options (experts only)
```

```
s          sort partitions
t          change a partition's type code
v          verify disk
w          write table to disk and exit
x          extra functionality (experts only)
?          print this menu

Command (? for help):
```

The next screen output shows the steps used to create a new 500MiB partition (**n**) on an empty disk device /dev/sdc:

```
[root@server1 ~]# gdisk /dev/sdc
GPT fdisk (gdisk) version 1.0.7

Partition table scan:
  MBR: not present
  BSD: not present
  APM: not present
  GPT: not present

Creating new GPT entries in memory.

Command (? for help): n
Partition number (1-128, default 1): 1
First sector (34-2097118, default = 2048) or {+-}size{KMGTP}: 2048
Last sector (2048-2097118, default = 2097118) or {+-}size{KMGTP}: +500M
Current type is 8300 (Linux filesystem)
Hex code or GUID (L to show codes, Enter = 8300):
Changed type of partition to 'Linux filesystem'

Command (? for help): w
```

As with **fdisk**, the **gdisk** tool doesn't write the changes to disk until you type the write (**w**) command. At any time, you can quit the utility without saving any changes with the quit (**q**) command.

The parted Utility

The **parted** command is included in GNU Parted and is becoming increasingly popular. It's an excellent tool developed by the Free Software Foundation. As with **fdisk**, you can use it to create, check, and destroy partitions, but it can do more. You can also use it to resize and copy partitions, as well as the filesystems contained therein. It's the foundation for multiple GUI-based partition management tools, including GParted and QtParted. For more information, see www.gnu.org/software/parted.

In some ways, using the parted **utility may be riskier than using** fdisk. **For example, one of the authors of this book accidentally ran the** mklabel **command from the (parted) prompt on an existing RHEL system. It deleted all existing partitions. Changes were written immediately while** parted **was still running. Fortunately, there was a backup of this virtual system and it could be restored with little trouble.**

During our discussion of **parted**, we'll proceed from section to section, assuming that **parted** is still open with the following prompt:

```
(parted)
```

Using parted: Starting, Getting Help, and Quitting

The screen output shown in Figure 7-5 lists commands that show how to start the **parted** utility, how to get help, and how to quit the program. In this case, the /dev/sdb drive is associated with the second disk on a Linux system. Your computer may have a different drive name; you can check the output from the **df** and **fdisk -l** commands for clues.

As you can see in Figure 7-5, when **parted** is run, it opens its own command-line prompt. Enter **help** for a list of available commands.

A wide variety of commands are available at the **parted** interface. When compared to **fdisk** and **gdisk**, **parted** can do more in some ways, as you will see in the next sections.

FIGURE 7-5   The parted command options

```
(parted) help
  align-check TYPE N                        check partition N for TYPE(min|opt) alignment
  help [COMMAND]                            print general help, or help on COMMAND
  mklabel,mktable LABEL-TYPE                create a new disklabel (partition table)
  mkpart PART-TYPE [FS-TYPE] START END      make a partition
  name NUMBER NAME                          name partition NUMBER as NAME
  print [devices|free|list,all]             display the partition table, or available devices, or
          free space, or all found partitions
  quit                                      exit program
  rescue START END                          rescue a lost partition near START and END
  resizepart NUMBER END                     resize partition NUMBER
  rm NUMBER                                 delete partition NUMBER
  select DEVICE                             choose the device to edit
  disk_set FLAG STATE                       change the FLAG on selected device
  disk_toggle [FLAG]                        toggle the state of FLAG on selected device
  set NUMBER FLAG STATE                     change the FLAG on partition NUMBER
  toggle [NUMBER [FLAG]]                    toggle the state of FLAG on partition NUMBER
  type NUMBER TYPE-ID or TYPE-UUID          type set TYPE-ID or TYPE-UUID of partition NUMBER
  unit UNIT                                 set the default unit to UNIT
  version                                   display the version number and copyright information of
          GNU Parted
(parted) 
```

Using parted: In a Nutshell

At the **parted** command-line prompt, start with the **print** command to list the current partition table. Assuming sufficient unallocated space is available, you can then make a new (**mkpart**) partition. For more information about **parted** command options, use the **help** command; for example, the following command provides more information about **mkpart**:

```
(parted) help mkpart
  mkpart PART-TYPE [FS-TYPE] START END      make a partition

        PART-TYPE is one of: primary, logical, extended
        FS-TYPE is one of: udf, btrfs, nilfs2, ext4, ext3, ext2, f2fs, fat32, fat16, hfsx, hfs+,
        hfs, jfs, swsusp, linux-swap(v1), linux-swap(v0), ntfs, reiserfs, hp-ufs, sun-ufs, xfs,
        apfs2, apfs1, asfs, amufs5, amufs4, amufs3, amufs2, amufs1, amufs0, amufs, affs7, affs6,
        affs5, affs4, affs3, affs2, affs1, affs0, linux-swap, linux-swap(new), linux-swap(old)
        START and END are disk locations, such as 4GB or 10%.  Negative values count from the end
        of the disk.  For example, -1s specifies exactly the last sector.

        'mkpart' makes a partition without creating a new file system on the partition.  FS-TYPE
        may be specified to set an appropriate partition ID.
(parted) █
```

If that's too much information, just run the command. You'll be prompted for the necessary information.

Using parted: A New PC (or Hard Drive) with No Partitions

The first step with any truly new hard drive is to create a partition table. For example, after you add a new hard drive to your virtual RHEL system, just about any command you run in **parted** leads to the following message:

```
Error: /dev/sdb: unrecognised disk label
```

Before you can do anything else with this drive, you need to create a label. As shown from the list of available commands, you can do so with the **mklabel** command. If you type **msdos**, the MBR-style partition scheme will be used. To use the GTP format, type **gpt** at the command prompt:

```
(parted) mklabel
New disk label type? msdos
```

Using parted: Create a New Partition

Now you can create a new partition in **parted** with the **mkpart** command. Naturally, if you have selected the MBR partition scheme, you need to specify the partition type:

```
(parted) mkpart
Partition type?  primary/extended? primary
File system type?  [ext2]? xfs
Start? 1MiB
End? 501MiB
```

For **parted**, we used 1MiB to start the partition at sector 2048. Although we could have used "0MiB" as the starting point, that would have generated a warning because the partition would have not been properly aligned at the 1MiB boundary for best performance. Note also that we ended the partition at 501MiB, so that its size is exactly 500MiB. Now review the results with the **print** command:

```
(parted) print
Model: ATA QEMU HARDDISK (scsi)
Disk /dev/sdb: 1074MB
Sector size (logical/physical): 512B/512B
Partition Table: msdos
Disk Flags:

Number  Start    End    Size   Type     File system  Flags
1       1049kB   525MB  524MB  primary  xfs
```

Note that **parted** displays the sizes in the International System of Units; that is, in kB, MB, GB, and so on. To change the default units, run the **unit** command:

```
(parted) help unit
  unit UNIT                                set the default unit to UNIT

        UNIT is one of: s, B, kB, MB, GB, TB, compact, cyl, chs, %, kiB, MiB,
        GiB, TiB
(parted) unit MiB
```

on the job The GUI-based tool GParted does support formatting to a wider variety of filesystem formats, even though it is just a "front end" to parted. It is available from the EPEL repository, described in Chapter 4.

Using parted: Delete a Partition

It's easy to delete a partition in **parted**. From the (parted) prompt, use the **rm** command to delete the target partition by number.

Of course, before deleting any partition, you should do the following:

- Save any data you need from that partition.
- Unmount the partition.
- Make sure the partition isn't configured in /etc/fstab, so that Linux doesn't try to mount it the next time you boot.
- After starting **parted**, run the **print** command to identify the partition you want to delete, as well as its ID number.

For example, to delete partition /dev/sdb10 from the (parted) prompt, run the following command:

```
(parted) rm 10
```

Using parted: Create a Swap Partition

Now repeat the process to create a swap partition. If necessary, delete the previously created partition to make room. Make the start of the new partition 1MiB after the end of the previous partition. You can still use the same commands, just substitute the **linux-swap** filesystem type as appropriate:

```
(parted) mkpart
Partition type?  primary/extended? primary
File system type?  [ext2]? linux-swap
Start? 501MiB
End? 1001MiB
```

Review the result with the **print** command:

```
(parted) print
Model: ATA QEMU HARDDISK (scsi)
Disk /dev/sdb: 1074MB
Sector size (logical/physical): 512B/512B
Partition Table: msdos
Disk Flags:

Number  Start    End      Size    Type     File system    Flags
  1     1.00MiB  501MiB   500MiB  primary  xfs
  2     501MiB   1001MiB  500MiB  primary  linux-swap(v1)
```

Now exit from **parted**. To use the swap partition, you need to run **mkswap** and **swapon**:

```
(parted) quit

# mkswap /dev/sdb2
# swapon /dev/sdb2
```

Now you can format the new regular Linux partition with the **mkfs.xfs** command:

```
# mkfs.xfs /dev/sdb1
```

We'll cover these commands in detail later in this chapter.

Using parted: Set Up a Different Partition Type

When a partition is created in **parted**, you can change its type with the **set** command. If you have a hard drive with unused partitions, open it with the **parted** command. For example, the following command opens the second virtual hard drive:

```
# parted /dev/sdb
```

Run the **print** command. The Flags column for existing partitions should be empty. Now you'll set that flag with the **set** command. From the commands shown here, the flags are set to use that first partition of the second drive as an LVM partition:

```
(parted) set
Partition number? 1
Flag to Invert? lvm
New state? [on]/off on
```

Now review the result with the **print** command:

```
(parted) print
Model: ATA QEMU HARDDISK (scsi)
Disk /dev/sdb: 1074MB
Sector size (logical/physical): 512B/512B
Partition Table: msdos
Disk Flags:

Number  Start    End      Size     Type     File system      Flags
 1      1.00MiB  501MiB   500MiB   primary  xfs              lvm
 2      501MiB   1001MiB  500MiB   primary  linux-swap(v1)
```

You can use similar steps to configure a partition or a component of a RAID array. It's also a flag; just substitute **raid** for **lvm** in response to the Flag to Invert prompt just shown. If you're following along with a RHEL 9 system, first confirm the result. Exit from **parted** and then run the following commands:

```
# parted /dev/sdb print
# fdisk -l /dev/sdb
```

You'll see the **lvm** flag as shown previously from the **parted** command; you'll see the following confirmation in the output to the **fdisk** command:

```
Device     Boot  Start       End    Sectors   Size Id  Type
/dev/sdb1         2048    1026047   1024000   500M 8e  Linux LVM
/dev/sdb2      1026048    2050047   1024000   500M 82  Linux swap / Solaris
```

If you've set up the baseline virtual system described in Chapter 1, this is an excellent opportunity to set up partitions as components of LVM volumes. Now that you have the tools, it does not matter whether you use **fdisk**, **gdisk**, or **parted** for this purpose. You can choose to use all the free space. Just be sure to create a partition on more than one hard disk for this purpose to help illustrate the power of logical volumes.

Graphical Options

As suggested earlier, excellent graphical front ends are available for disk partitions. The GParted and QtParted options are based on **parted** and are designed for the GNOME and KDE desktop environments, respectively. As they are not available from the Red Hat Network, they are not supported by Red Hat and therefore won't be available for any Red Hat exams.

One graphical option available for RHEL 9 is known simply as Disk Utility, available from the gnome-disk-utility package. Once appropriate packages are installed, you can open Disk Utility from the command-line interface with the **gnome-disks** command.

The Disk Utility screen shown in Figure 7-6 depicts the baseline virtual machine created in Chapter 1; it lists the virtual hard drive, device /dev/nvme0n1, as well as its root and home partitions and the DVD drive.

FIGURE 7-6 The Disk Utility

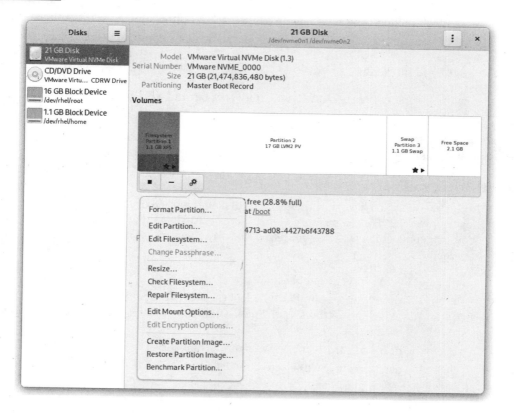

The functionality includes some of the following clickable options from the Settings menu ("gear" icon):

- **Format Partition**   On a drive, sets the MBR- or GPT-style partition formats. On a partition, formats a partition for a number of filesystem formats.
- **Edit Partition**   Sets the partition type, such as Linux swap or Linux LVM.
- **Edit Filesystem**   Sets the filesystem label; labels were commonly used on RHEL 5.
- **Edit Mount Options**   Configures the filesystem mount options, such as mount points and filesystem type.
- **Create Partition Image**   Creates an image file with the content of a drive or partition.
- **Restore Partition Image**   Restores the content of a drive from a partition image.
- **Benchmark Partition**   Allows measurements of read and write performance.
- **Unmount the Filesystem**   Unmounts a filesystem. (This option appears as the "stop" icon.)
- **Delete Partition**   Deletes a partition. (This option appears as the "minus" icon.)
- **Create Partition**   Creates a new partition. (This option appears as the "plus" icon.)

Not all of these options appear in Figure 7-6; for example, the Create Partition option does not appear unless you've selected a "free" area of the target hard drive. In addition, you may note that the functionality of the Disk Utility goes beyond mere partitioning.

EXERCISE 7-1

Work with fdisk and parted

In this exercise, you'll work with both the **fdisk** and **parted** utilities. You will work with a new empty drive. For the purpose of this exercise, **fdisk** and **parted** will be used on drive /dev/nvme0n2. Do save the result of this work. You'll use it for exercises that follow later in this chapter.

1. Shut down server1.example.com.
2. In VMware Workstation Player, select the server1.example.com VM and click Edit Virtual Machine Settings. In the new window that opens, select Add | Hard Disk and click Next.
3. In the next screen, select NVMe as the Virtual Disk Type and click Next.
4. In the next screen, leave selected the default setting Create A New Virtual Disk and click Next.

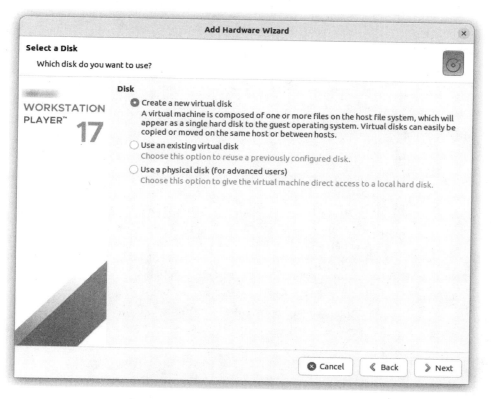

5. A new screen to specify the disk capacity will appear. Select 8.000 in the Maximum Disk Size field to create a new 8GB hard drive, and click Next.

6. In the next screen, leave the default settings and click Finish, then click Save.

7. Power on server1.example.com and open a terminal as the root user.

8. Run the **fdisk -l /dev/nvme0n2** command to review the current status of the /dev/nvme0n2 drive (if your first disk drive has a different device name, substitute with the correct name, such as /dev/sdb or /dev/vdb).

9. Run the **fdisk /dev/nvme0n2** command.

10. Run the **p** command to display any previously configured partitions. The drive should be empty.

11. Create a new partition with the **n** command. Create a primary partition with the **p** command and enter **1** for the partition number.

12. When presented with a request similar to the following, accept the default of 2048 sectors. It is common to start the first partition at 1MiB (= 2048 sectors) to align the partition with the disk geometry:

```
First sector (2048-16777215, default 2048): 2048
```

13. When presented with a request similar to the following, type +2G to create a partition of size 2GiB:

```
Last sector, +/-sectors or +/-size{K,M,G,T,P} (2048-16777215, default 16777215):
+2G
```

14. Run the **p** command again to review the result. Run the **w** command to write the result to disk.

15. Review the result on the /dev/nvme0n2 disk with the **parted /dev/nvme0n2 print** command.

16. Run **parted** in interactive mode with the **parted /dev/nvme0n2** command.

17. From the (parted) prompt, run the **print** command to review the current status of partitions.

18. Type **unit MiB**, then run **print** again. How has the output changed?

19. Create a new partition with the **mkpart** command. Follow the prompts. Enter **primary** as the partition type and **xfs** as a filesystem type; start the partition at **2049MiB** and end it at **4097MiB**, to create a partition of 2048MiB (4097MiB – 2049MiB = 2048MiB). Run the **print** command to confirm the new partition, and identify the partition number.

20. Run the **quit** command to exit from **parted**.

21. Run the **fdisk -l /dev/nvme0n2** command to review the result.

exam

ⓦ a t c h   During the RHCSA exam, you may need to perform simple calculations to find where a partition should end. If your   math is rusty, use the bc calculator or a Python command line to do math operations.

CERTIFICATION OBJECTIVE 7.02

Filesystem Formats

The number of filesystem types may exceed the number of operating systems. While RHEL can work with many of these formats, the default is XFS. Although many users enable other filesystems such as Btrfs, Red Hat may not support them.

Linux supports a rich variety of filesystems. Except for some old filesystems such as ext2, most filesystems incorporate features such as journal-based transactions, large storage support, delayed allocation, and complex algorithms to optimize read and write performance.

In the following sections we split filesystems into two broad categories: standard and journaling. While this is an oversimplification, it is sufficient to categorize the filesystems that are important to Linux.

The filesystems described in this book are just a subset of those that can be configured on a RHEL system. The Linux kernel makes it possible to set up more.

Standard Filesystems

Linux is a clone of Unix. The Linux filesystems were developed to mimic the functionality of Unix filesystems available at the time. The first versions of the Linux operating systems used the Extended Filesystem (ext). In the twentieth century, the default filesystem on Red Hat Linux was the Second Extended Filesystem (ext2). Starting with RHEL 5, Red Hat moved to the Third Extended Filesystem (ext3). For RHEL 6, Red Hat progressed to the Fourth Extended Filesystem (ext4). Both ext3 and ext4 are journaling filesystems. Starting with RHEL 7, Red Hat changed the default filesystem to XFS, a highly scalable journaling filesystem initially developed by Silicon Graphics in 1993.

The size of current filesystems has increased the importance of journaling because such filesystems are more resilient to failure. So in general, the non-journaling filesystems described in Table 7-2 are legacy filesystems. Of course, filesystems such as ISO 9660 and swap are still in common use.

| TABLE 7-2 | Some Standard Filesystems |

Filesystem Type	Description
ext	The first Linux filesystem, used only on early versions of the operating system.
ext2 (Second Extended)	The foundation for ext3, the default filesystem for RHEL 5. The ext3 filesystem is essentially ext2 with journaling.
swap	The Linux filesystem associated with dedicated swap partitions. You probably created at least one swap partition when you installed RHEL.
msdos and vfat	Filesystems that allow you to read MS-DOS-formatted filesystems. msdos lets you read pre–Windows 95 partitions or regular Windows partitions within the limits of short filenames. vfat lets you read Windows 9x/NT/2000/XP/Vista/7 partitions formatted to the FAT16 or FAT32 filesystem.
iso9660	The standard filesystem for CD-ROMs. It is also known as the High Sierra File System, or HSFS, on other Unix systems.
proc and sys	Two Linux virtual filesystems. *Virtual* means that the filesystem doesn't occupy real disk space. Instead, files are created as needed. Used to provide information on kernel configuration and device status.
devpts	The Linux implementation of the Open Group's Unix98 PTY support.
tmpfs	A filesystem stored in memory. Used on RHEL 9 for the /run partition.

TABLE 7-3   Some Journaling Filesystems

Filesystem Type	Description
ext3	The default filesystem for RHEL 5.
ext4	The default filesystem for RHEL 6.
XFS	Developed by Silicon Graphics as a journaling filesystem, supports very large files and features such as B-tree indexing and dynamic allocation inodes. It's the default filesystem for RHEL 7, 8, and 9.
JFS	IBM's journaled filesystem, commonly used on IBM enterprise servers.
Btrfs	The B-tree filesystem, developed to offer a set of features comparable with Oracle ZFS. It offers some advanced features such as snapshots, storage pools, and compression.
NTFS	The current Microsoft Windows filesystem.

Journaling Filesystems

Journaling filesystems have two main advantages. First, a filesystem check is very fast. Second, if a crash occurs, a journaling filesystem has a log (also known as a journal) that can be used to restore the metadata for the files on the relevant partition.

For RHEL 9, the default filesystem is XFS, a highly scalable, journal-based filesystem. This isn't the only journaling filesystem option available, however. Table 7-3 lists a few of the options commonly used for RHEL. From this list, Red Hat officially supports only ext3, ext4, and XFS. At the time of writing, Btrfs is no longer supported by Red Hat.

The Red Hat move to XFS is a testament to its use as a server operating system. For example, volumes formatted to XFS can theoretically be as large as 8 exabytes (EB). That's a serious increase over the maximum size of an ext3 volume: 16 terabytes (TB).

XFS supports a large number of concurrent operations, guarantees space for files, guarantees faster checks, and more. As XFS has been a part of the Linux kernel since 2004, it is proven technology.

Filesystem Format Commands

Several commands can help you create a Linux filesystem. They're all based on the **mkfs** command, which works as a front end to filesystem-specific commands such as **mkfs.ext3**, **mkfs.ext4**, and **mkfs.xfs**.

If you want to reformat an existing partition or logical volume, take the following precautions:

- Back up any existing data on the partition.
- Unmount the partition.

There are two ways to format a volume. (As noted earlier in this chapter, *volume* is a generic name that can describe a partition or a logical volume.) For example, if you've just created a partition on /dev/sdb5, you can format it to the XFS filesystem by using one of the following commands:

```
# mkfs -t xfs /dev/sdb5
# mkfs.xfs /dev/sdb5
```

You can format partitions, logical volumes, and RAID arrays to other filesystems. Some of the options available in RHEL 9 include the following:

- **mkfs.ext2** formats a volume to the ext2 filesystem.
- **mkfs.ext3** formats a volume to the RHEL 5 default ext3 filesystem.
- **mkfs.ext4** formats a volume to the RHEL 6 default ext4 filesystem.
- **mkfs.fat** (or **mkfs.vfat**, **mkfs.msdos**, **mkdosfs**) formats a partition to the Microsoft-compatible FAT filesystem; it does not create bootable filesystems. (All these commands are the same because they are symbolic links to mkfs.fat.)
- **mkfs.xfs** formats a volume to the RHEL 9 default XFS filesystem.
- **mkswap** sets up a Linux swap area.

These commands assume you've configured an appropriate partition in the first place; for example, before the **mkswap** command can be properly applied to a partition, the Linux swap partition ID type must be configured for that partition. If you've created a logical volume, as described later in this chapter, similar rules apply.

Swap Volumes

Although Linux can use swap files, the swap space is generally configured in properly formatted partitions or logical volumes. To see the swap space currently configured, run the **cat /proc/swaps** command.

As suggested in the previous section, swap volumes are formatted with the **mkswap** command. But that's not enough. Swap volumes must also be activated with the **swapon** command. If the new swap volume is recognized, you'll see it in both the /proc/swaps file and the output to the **top** command. Second, you'll need to make sure to configure the new swap volume in the /etc/fstab file, as described later in this chapter.

Filesystem Check Commands

The **xfs_repair** command (or **fsck** for other filesystems) analyzes the specified XFS filesystem and performs repairs as required. Assume, for example, you're having problems with files in the /var directory, which happens to be mounted on /dev/sda7. If you want to run **xfs_repair**, unmount that filesystem first. In some cases, you may need to go into rescue mode before you can unmount a filesystem. To unmount, analyze, and then remount the filesystem noted in this section, run the following commands:

```
# umount /var
# xfs_repair /dev/sda7
# mount /dev/sda7 /var
```

The **fsck** command serves as a "front end," depending on the filesystem format. For example, if you're formatting an ext2, ext3, or ext4 filesystem, **fsck** by itself automatically calls the **e2fsck** command. In fact, the **fsck.ext2**, **fsck.ext3**, **fsck.ext4**, and **e2fsck** files are all different names for the same command! They have the same inode number. You can confirm this by applying the **ls -i** command to all four files, which are part of the /sbin directory.

EXERCISE 7-2

Format, Check, and Mount Different Filesystems

In this exercise, you'll work with the file format and checking commands **mkfs** and **fsck** and then review the results with the **mount** command. This exercise assumes you've completed Exercise 7-1, or at least have unmounted Linux partitions with no data.

1. Review the current status of partitions on the drive discussed in Exercise 7-1 with the **parted /dev/nvme0n2 print** command. If your first disk drive has a different device name, substitute with the correct name, such as /dev/sdb or /dev/vdb.

2. Format the partition created by the first drive with the **mkfs.ext2 /dev/nvme0n2p1** command (similarly, if your drive has a different name such as /dev/sdb, the first partition is /dev/sdb1). Review the current status of the volume with the **dumpe2fs -h /dev/nvme0n2p1 | grep features** command. What features do you see in the output? Save the output temporarily. One way to do so is to open a new command-line console. Check the system with the **fsck.ext2 /dev/nvme0n2p1** command.

3. Mount the newly formatted partition with the **mount /dev/nvme0n2p1 /mnt** command. Review the output with the **mount** command by itself. If the mount and format worked, you'll see the following output:

```
/dev/nvme0n2p1 on /mnt type ext2 (rw,relatime,seclabel)
```

4. Unmount the formatted partition with the **umount /mnt** command.

5. Run the **mkfs.ext4 /dev/nvme0n2p1** command. You will get a warning that a filesystem is already present on /dev/nvme0n2p1. Type **y** to format the partition and rerun the **dumpe2fs** command from the previous step. What's the difference between the output now and the output when the partition was formatted to the ext2 filesystem?

6. Repeat Steps 3 and 4. What's the difference in the output to the **mount** command?

7. Now on the other partition created in Exercise 7-1, apply the **mkfs.xfs /dev/nvme0n2p2** command. Run the **xfs_info /dev/nvme0n2p2** command. What information is displayed? Execute **man xfs_info** for a description of this command.

8. Mount the newly formatted partition on the **/mnt** directory and then run the **mount** command by itself. Can you confirm the filesystem type of the /dev/nvme0n2p2 partition from the output of the **mount** command?

Basic Linux Filesystems and Directories

"Everything in Linux is a file." Partitions are associated with *filesystem device nodes* such as /dev/sda1. Hardware components are associated with node files such as /dev/cdrom. Detected devices are documented as files in the /sys directory. The Filesystem Hierarchy Standard (FHS) is the official way to organize files in Unix and Linux directories. As with the other sections, this introduction provides only the most basic overview of the FHS. More information is available from the official FHS home page at http://refspecs .linuxfoundation.org/fhs.shtml.

on the
ʘ o b

In Linux, the word *filesystem* has different meanings. It can refer to the FHS or to a filesystem format such as ext3. A filesystem mount point such as /var represents the directory on which a filesystem can be mounted.

Separate Linux Filesystems

Several major directories are associated with all modern Unix/Linux operating systems. Files, drivers, kernels, logs, programs, utilities, and more are organized in these directories. The way these components are organized on storage media is known as a filesystem. The FHS makes it easier for Linux distributions to adhere to a common directory structure.

Every filesystem starts with the top-level root directory, also known by its symbol, the single forward slash (/). All the other directories shown in Table 7-4 are subdirectories of the root directory. Unless they are mounted separately, you can also find their files on the same partition as the root directory. You may not see some of the directories shown in the table if associated packages have not been installed. Not all directories shown are officially part of the FHS. More importantly, not all listed directories can or should be mounted separately.

TABLE 7-4   Basic Filesystem Hierarchy Standard Directories

Directory	Description
/	The root directory, the top-level directory in the FHS. All other directories are subdirectories of root, which is always mounted on some volume.
/bin	Essential command-line utilities. Should not be mounted separately; otherwise, it could be difficult to get to these utilities when using a rescue disk. On RHEL 9, it is a symbolic link to /usr/bin.
/boot	Linux startup files, including the Linux kernel. The default, 1GB, is usually sufficient for a typical modular kernel and additional kernels that you might install during the RHCE or RHCSA exam.
/dev	Hardware and software device drivers for everything from floppy drives to terminals. Do not mount this directory on a separate volume.
/etc	Most basic configuration files. Do not mount this directory on a separate volume.
/home	Home directories for almost every user.
/lib	Program libraries for the kernel and various command-line utilities. Do not mount this directory on a separate volume. On RHEL 9, this is a symbolic link to /usr/lib.
/lib64	Same as /lib, but includes 64-bit libraries. On RHEL 9, this is a symbolic link to /usr/lib64.
/media	The mount point for removable media, including DVDs and USB disk drives.
/misc	The standard mount point for local directories mounted via the automounter.
/mnt	A mount point for temporarily mounted filesystems.
/net	The standard mount point for network directories mounted via the automounter.
/opt	Common location for third-party application files.
/proc	A virtual filesystem listing information for currently running kernel-related processes, including device assignments such as IRQ ports, I/O addresses, and DMA channels, as well as kernel-configuration settings such as IP forwarding. As a virtual filesystem, Linux automatically configures it as a separate filesystem in RAM.
/root	The home directory of the root user. Do not mount this directory on a separate volume.
/run	A tmpfs filesystem for files that should not persist after a reboot. On RHEL 9, this filesystem replaces /var/run, which is a symbolic link to /run.

| TABLE 7-4 | Basic Filesystem Hierarchy Standard Directories *(continued)* |

Directory	Description
/sbin	System administration commands. Don't mount this directory separately. On RHEL 9, this is a symbolic link to /usr/sbin.
/smb	The standard mount point for remote shared Microsoft network directories mounted via the automounter.
/srv	Commonly used by various network servers on non–Red Hat distributions.
/sys	Similar to the /proc filesystem. Used to expose information about devices, drivers, and some kernel features.
/tmp	Temporary files. By default, RHEL deletes all files in this directory periodically.
/usr	Programs and read-only data. Includes many system administration commands, utilities, and libraries.
/var	Variable data, including log files and printer spools.

The directory on which a filesystem is mounted is known as a *mount point*. While the root directory (/) is the top-level directory in the FHS, the root user's home directory (/root) is just a subdirectory.

Directories That Can Be Mounted Separately

If space is available, several directories listed in Table 7-4 are excellent candidates to be mounted separately. As discussed in Chapter 1, it's typical to mount directories such as /, /boot, /home, /opt, /tmp, and /var on separate volumes. Sometimes, it makes sense to mount lower-level subdirectories on separate volumes, such as /var/ftp for an FTP server or /var/www for a web server.

But first, several directories should always be maintained as part of the top-level root directory filesystem. These directories include /dev, /etc, and /bin. Files within these directories are essential to the smooth operation of Linux as an operating system. Although the same argument can be made for the /boot directory, it is a special case. The storage of the Linux kernel, initial RAM disk, and bootloader files in this directory can help protect the core of the operating system when there are other problems.

Files in the /proc and /sys directories are filled only during the boot process and disappear when a system is shut down, and as such they are stored in a special in-memory virtual filesystem.

Some directories listed in Table 7-4 are designed for use only as mount points. In other words, they should normally be empty. If you store files on those directories, they won't be accessible if, say, a network share is mounted on them. Typical network mount points include the /media, /mnt, /net, and /smb directories.

CERTIFICATION OBJECTIVE 7.04

Logical Volume Manager (LVM)

Logical Volume Manager (also known as LVM) creates an abstraction layer between physical devices, such as disks and partitions, and volumes that are formatted with a filesystem.

LVM can simplify disk management. As an example, assume that the /home filesystem is configured on its own logical volume. If extra space is available on the volume group associated with /home, you can easily resize the filesystem. If no space is available, you can make more room by adding a new physical disk and allocate its storage capacity to the volume group. On LVM, volume groups are like storage pools, and they aggregate together the capacity of multiple storage devices. Logical volumes reside on volume groups and can span multiple physical disks.

Definitions in LVM

To work with LVM, you need to understand how partitions configured for that purpose are used. First, with the **fdisk**, **gdisk**, and **parted** utilities, you need to create partitions configured to the LVM partition type. You can also use an entire disk device.

Once those partitions or disk devices are available, they need to be set up as physical volumes (PVs). That process initializes a disk or partition for use by LVM. Then, you create volume groups (VGs) from one or more physical volumes. Volume groups organize the physical storage in a collection of manageable disk chunks known as physical extents (PEs). With the right commands, you can then organize those PEs into logical volumes (LVs). Logical volumes are made of logical extents (LEs), which map to the underlining PEs. You can then format and mount the LVs. For those who are new to LVM, it may be important to break out each definition:

- **Physical volume (PV)**   A PV is a partition or a disk drive initialized to be used by LVM.
- **Physical extent (PE)**   A PE is a small uniform segment of disk space. PVs are split into PEs.
- **Volume group (VG)**   A VG is a storage pool, made of one or more PVs.
- **Logical extent (LE)**   Every PE is associated with an LE, and these PEs can be combined into a logical volume.
- **Logical volume (LV)**   An LV is a part of a VG and is made of LEs. An LV can be formatted with a filesystem and then mounted on the directory of your choice.

You'll see this process broken down in the following sections. In essence, to create an LV system, you need to create a new PV using a command such as **pvcreate**, assign the space from one or more PVs to a VG with a command such as **vgcreate**, and allocate the space from some part of available VGs to an LV with a command such as **lvcreate**.

To add space to an existing logical volume, you need to add free space from an existing VG with a command such as **lvextend**. If you don't have any spare space on the VG, you'll need to add to it with unassigned PV space with a command such as **vgextend**. If all of your PVs are taken, you may need to create a new PV from an unassigned partition or hard drive with the **pvcreate** command.

Create a Physical Volume

The first step is to start with a physical partition or a hard disk drive. Based on the discussion earlier in this chapter, you should be able to set up partitions to match the Linux LVM identifier. Then, to set up a new PV on a properly configured partition, such as /dev/sda1, apply the **pvcreate** command to that partition:

```
# pvcreate /dev/sda1
```

If there is more than one partition to be configured as a PV, the associated device files can all be listed in the same command:

```
# pvcreate /dev/sda1 /dev/sda2 /dev/sdb1 /dev/sdb2
```

Create a Volume Group

From one or more PVs, you can create a volume group. In the following command, substitute the name of your choice for *volumegroup*:

```
# vgcreate volumegroup /dev/sda1 /dev/sda2
```

You can include additional PVs in any VG. Assuming there are existing PVs based on /dev/sdb1 and /dev/sdb2 partitions, you can add to the *volumegroup* VG with the following command:

```
# vgextend volumegroup /dev/sdb1 /dev/sdb2
```

However, a new VG isn't enough since you can't format or mount a filesystem on it. So you need to create an LV for this purpose.

Create a Logical Volume

The following command creates an LV. You can add as many chunks of disk space, in PEs, as you need.

```
# lvcreate -l number_of_PEs volumegroup -n logicalvolume
```

This creates a device named /dev/*volumegroup/logicalvolume*. You can format this device as if it were a regular disk partition and then mount that new logical volume on a directory.

But this isn't useful if you don't know how much space is associated with each PE. You can use the **vgdisplay** command to display the size of the PEs, or specify the size with the **-s** option of the **vgcreate** command when you initialize the VG. Alternatively, you can use the -**L** switch to set a size in MiB, GiB, or another unit of measure. For example, the following command creates an LV named flex of 200MiB:

```
# lvcreate -L 200M volumegroup -n flex
```

But that's not the last step, as described next.

Make Use of a Logical Volume

You may not get full credit unless the logical volume gets formatted and mounted when the system is rebooted. This process is described later in this chapter in the discussion of the /etc/fstab configuration file.

More LVM Commands

A wide variety of LVM commands related to PVs, LVs, and VGs are available. Generally, they are **pv***, **lv***, and **vg*** in the /usr/sbin directory. Physical volume commands include those listed in Table 7-5.

TABLE 7-5 Physical Volume Management Commands

Physical Volume Command	Description
pvchange	Changes attributes of a PV. For example, the **pvchange -x n /dev/sda10** command disables the allocation of PEs from the /dev/sda10 partition.
pvck	Checks the consistency of a PV's metadata.
pvcreate	Initializes a disk or partition as a PV; the partition should be flagged with the LVM file type.
pvdisplay	Displays currently configured PVs.
pvmove	Moves PEs in a VG from the specified PV to free locations on other PVs; prerequisite to disabling a PV. One example: **pvmove /dev/sda10**.
pvremove	Removes a given PV from a list of recognized volumes; for example, **pvremove /dev/sda10**.
pvresize	Changes the amount of a partition allocated to a PV. If you've expanded partition /dev/sda10, **pvresize /dev/sda10** takes advantage of the additional space. Alternatively, **pvresize --setphysicalvolumesize 100M /dev/sda10** reduces the number of PVs taken from that partition to the noted space.
pvs	Lists configured PVs and the associated VGs, if so assigned.
pvscan	Scans disks for PVs.

TABLE 7-6   Volume Group Commands

Volume Group Command	Description
vgcfgbackup **vgcfgrestore**	Used to back up and restore the metadata associated with LVM; by default, the backup files are in the /etc/lvm directory.
vgchange	Similar to **pvchange**, allows you to change the configuration settings of a VG. For example, **vgchange -a y** enables all local VGs.
vgck	Checks the consistency of VG metadata.
vgconvert	Supports conversions from LVM1 systems to LVM2; for example, **vgconvert -M2** **VolGroup00** converts VolGroup00 to the LVM2 metadata format.
vgcreate	Creates a VG from one or more configured PVs; for example, **vgcreate vgroup00 /dev/sda10 /dev/sda11** creates vgroup00 from PVs as defined on /dev/sda10 and /dev/sda11.
vgdisplay	Displays characteristics of currently configured VGs.
vgexport **vgimport**	Used to export and import unused VGs from those available; the **vgexport -a** command exports all inactive VGs.
vgextend	If you've created a new PV, **vgextend vgroup00 /dev/sda11** adds the space from /dev/sda11 to vgroup00.
vgmerge	If you have an unused VG vgroup01, you can merge it into vgroup00 with the following command: **vgmerge vgroup00 vgroup01**.
vgmknodes	Run this command if you have a problem with VG device files.
vgreduce	The **vgreduce vgroup00 /dev/sda11** command removes the /dev/sda11 PV from vgroup00, assuming /dev/sda11 is unused.
vgremove	The **vgremove vgroup00** command removes vgroup00, assuming it has no LVs assigned to it.
vgrename	Allows the renaming of LVs.
vgs	Displays basic information on configured VGs.
vgscan	Scans all devices for VGs.
vgsplit	Splits a VG.

As you assign PVs to VGs, you may need commands to control and configure the VGs. Table 7-6 includes an overview of most related volume group commands.

As you assign PVs to VGs and then subdivide VGs into LVs, you may need commands to control and configure the LVs. Table 7-7 includes an overview of related LVM commands.

Try the **vgscan** command. You can verify configured VGs with the **vgdisplay** command. For example, Figure 7-7 illustrates the configuration of VG rhel.

TABLE 7-7 Logical Volume Commands

Logical Volume Command	Description
lvchange	Similar to **pvchange**, changes the attributes of an LV; for example, the **lvchange -a n vgroup00/lvol00** command disables the use of the LV labeled lvol00.
lvconvert	Converts an LV between different types, such as linear, mirror, or snapshot.
lvcreate	Creates a new LV in an existing VG; for example, **lvcreate -l 200 volume01 -n lvol01** creates lvol01 using 200 extents in the VG named volume01.
lvdisplay	Displays currently configured LVs.
lvextend	Adds space to an LV; for example, the **lvextend -L 4G /dev/volume01/lvol01** command extends lvol01 to 4GiB, assuming space is available.
lvreduce	Reduces the size of an LV; if there's data in the reduced area, it is lost.
lvremove	Removes an active LV; for example, the **lvremove volume01/lvol01** command removes the LV lvol01 from VG volume01.
lvrename	Renames an LV.
lvresize	Resizes an LV; can be done by **-L** for size. For example, **lvresize -L +4GB volume01/lvol01** adds 4GiB to the size of lvol01.
lvs	Lists all configured LVs.
lvscan	Scans for all LVs.

Although a number of **lvm*** commands are installed, just four of them are active: **lvm**, **lvmconfig**, **lvmdiskscan**, and **lvmdump**. Other **lvm*** commands are obsolete. The **lvm** command moves to an lvm> prompt. It's rather interesting, as the **help** command at that prompt provides a nearly full list of available LVM commands.

FIGURE 7-7

Configuration of a volume group

```
[root@server1 ~]# vgdisplay
  --- Volume group ---
  VG Name               rhel
  System ID
  Format                lvm2
  Metadata Areas        1
  Metadata Sequence No  3
  VG Access             read/write
  VG Status             resizable
  MAX LV                0
  Cur LV                2
  Open LV               2
  Max PV                0
  Cur PV                1
  Act PV                1
  VG Size               16.00 GiB
  PE Size               4.00 MiB
  Total PE              4097
  Alloc PE / Size       4096 / 16.00 GiB
  Free  PE / Size       1 / 4.00 MiB
  VG UUID               iFwuic-tmUb-mes5-SPgb-nolA-Q3cV-OaLkTM

[root@server1 ~]# 
```

The **lvmconfig** command can modify the default settings in the related configuration file, /etc/lvm/lvm.conf. The **lvmdiskscan** command scans all available drives for LVM-configured physical volumes. Finally, the **lvmdump** command sets up a configuration report with diagnostic information.

Remove a Logical Volume

The removal of an existing LV is straightforward, with the **lvremove** command. This assumes that any directories previously mounted on LVs have been unmounted. At that point, the basic steps are simple:

1. Save any data in directories that are mounted on the LV.
2. Unmount the filesystem associated with the LV. As an example, you can use a command similar to the following:

   ```
   # umount /dev/vg_01/lv_01
   ```

3. Apply the **lvremove** command to the LV with a command such as this:

   ```
   # lvremove /dev/vg_01/lv_01
   ```

4. You should now have the LEs from this LV free for use in other LVs.

Resize Logical Volumes

If you need to increase the size of an existing LV, you can add the space from a newly created PV to it. All it takes is appropriate use of the **vgextend** and **lvextend** commands. For example, to add the PEs to the VG associated with a /home directory mounted on an LV, take the following basic steps:

1. Back up any data existing on the /home directory. (This is a standard precaution that isn't necessary if everything goes right. You might even skip this step on the Red Hat exams. But do you really want to risk user data in practice?)
2. Extend the VG to include new partitions configured to the appropriate type. For example, to add /dev/sdd1 to the vg_00 VG, run the following command:

   ```
   # vgextend vg_00 /dev/sdd1
   ```

3. Make sure the new partitions are included in the VG with the following command:

   ```
   # vgdisplay vg_00
   ```

4. Now you can extend the space given to the current LV. For example, to extend the LV to 2000MiB, run the following command:

   ```
   # lvextend -L 2000M /dev/vg_00/lv_00
   ```

5. The **lvextend** command can increase the space allocated to an LV in KiB, MiB, GiB, or even TiB. For example, you could specify a 2GiB LV with the following command:

```
# lvextend -L 2G /dev/vg_00/lv_00
```

6. If you prefer to specify the extra space to be added rather than the total space, you can use the syntax in the following example, which adds 1GiB to the logical volume:

```
# lvextend -L +1G /dev/vg_00/lv_00
```

7. Resize the formatted volume with the **xfs_growfs** command (or with **resize2fs**, if it is an ext2/ext3/ext4 filesystem). If you're using the entire extended LV, the command is simple:

```
# xfs_growfs /dev/vg_00/lv_00
```

8. Alternatively, you can reformat the LV, using commands described earlier, so the filesystem can take full advantage of the new space—and then restore data from the backup. (If you've already successfully resized an LV, *don't* reformat it. It isn't necessary and would destroy existing data!)

```
# mkfs.xfs -f /dev/vg_00/lv_00
```

9. In either case, you'd finish the process by checking the new filesystem size with the **df** command:

```
# df -h
```

CERTIFICATION OBJECTIVE 7.05

Filesystem Management

Before you can access the files in a filesystem, that filesystem must be mounted on a mount point. Linux normally automates this process using the /etc/fstab configuration file. When Linux goes through the boot process, directories specified in /etc/fstab are mounted on configured volumes, with the help of the **mount** command. Of course, you can run that command with any or all appropriate options, so that's an excellent place to start this section.

The remainder of this section focuses on options for /etc/fstab. While it starts with the default using the baseline configuration for a standard virtual machine, it includes options to customize that file for local, remote, and removable filesystems.

The /etc/fstab File

To look at the contents of the /etc/fstab file, run the **cat /etc/fstab** command. As shown in the example in Figure 7-8, different filesystems are configured on each line.

FIGURE 7-8   Sample /etc/fstab

```
[root@server1 ~]# cat /etc/fstab

#
# /etc/fstab
# Created by anaconda on Fri May 12 16:44:14 2023
#
# Accessible filesystems, by reference, are maintained under '/dev/disk/'.
# See man pages fstab(5), findfs(8), mount(8) and/or blkid(8) for more info.
#
# After editing this file, run 'systemctl daemon-reload' to update systemd
# units generated from this file.
#
/dev/mapper/rhel-root     /                       xfs     defaults      0 0
UUID=cd91e619-7226-4713-ad08-4427b6f43788 /boot             xfs       defaults      0 0
/dev/mapper/rhel-home     /home     xfs     defaults      0 0
UUID=4d603dae-6cb6-4348-b085-d1370c8d40ac none              swap      defaults      0 0
[root@server1 ~]# █
```

In RHEL 9 the default is to use universally unique IDs (UUIDs) to mount non-LVM filesystems. As you'll see in the next section, UUIDs can represent a partition, a logical volume, or an entire disk drive. In all cases, volumes should be formatted to the filesystem noted on each line and are mounted on the directory listed in the second column. The advantage of UUIDs and logical volume devices is that they are unique, whereas device names such as /dev/sdb2 may change after a reboot, depending on the order in which the disks are initialized.

But to some extent, UUIDs are beside the point. As shown in Figure 7-8, six fields are associated with each filesystem, described from left to right in Table 7-8. Each field is separated by one or more spaces. You can verify how partitions are actually mounted in the /etc/mtab file, as shown in Figure 7-9. Note the differences, especially the use of the device file in place of UUIDs, and the presence of virtual filesystems such as tmpfs and sysfs, which are discussed later in this chapter.

FIGURE 7-9   Sample /etc/mtab

```
[root@server1 ~]# cat /etc/mtab
proc /proc proc rw,nosuid,nodev,noexec,relatime 0 0
sysfs /sys sysfs rw,seclabel,nosuid,nodev,noexec,relatime 0 0
devtmpfs /dev devtmpfs rw,seclabel,nosuid,size=4096k,nr_inodes=1048576,mode=755,inode64 0 0
securityfs /sys/kernel/security securityfs rw,nosuid,nodev,noexec,relatime 0 0
tmpfs /dev/shm tmpfs rw,seclabel,nosuid,nodev,inode64 0 0
devpts /dev/pts devpts rw,seclabel,nosuid,noexec,relatime,gid=5,mode=620,ptmxmode=000 0 0
tmpfs /run tmpfs rw,seclabel,nosuid,nodev,size=357112k,nr_inodes=819200,mode=755,inode64 0 0
cgroup2 /sys/fs/cgroup cgroup2 rw,seclabel,nosuid,nodev,noexec,relatime,nsdelegate,memory_recursiveprot 0 0
pstore /sys/fs/pstore pstore rw,seclabel,nosuid,nodev,noexec,relatime 0 0
none /sys/fs/bpf bpf rw,nosuid,nodev,noexec,relatime,mode=700 0 0
/dev/mapper/rhel-root / xfs rw,seclabel,relatime,attr2,inode64,logbufs=8,logbsize=32k,noquota 0 0
selinuxfs /sys/fs/selinux selinuxfs rw,nosuid,noexec,relatime 0 0
systemd-1 /proc/sys/fs/binfmt_misc autofs rw,relatime,fd=31,pgrp=1,timeout=0,minproto=5,maxproto=5,direct,pipe_ino=18247 0 0
hugetlbfs /dev/hugepages hugetlbfs rw,seclabel,relatime,pagesize=2M 0 0
mqueue /dev/mqueue mqueue rw,seclabel,nosuid,nodev,noexec,relatime 0 0
debugfs /sys/kernel/debug debugfs rw,seclabel,nosuid,nodev,noexec,relatime 0 0
tracefs /sys/kernel/tracing tracefs rw,seclabel,nosuid,nodev,noexec,relatime 0 0
configfs /sys/kernel/config configfs rw,nosuid,nodev,noexec,relatime 0 0
fusectl /sys/fs/fuse/connections fusectl rw,nosuid,nodev,noexec,relatime 0 0
vmware-vmblock /run/vmblock-fuse fuse.vmware-vmblock rw,relatime,user_id=0,group_id=0,default_permissions,allow_other 0 0
/dev/mapper/rhel-home /home xfs rw,seclabel,relatime,attr2,inode64,logbufs=8,logbsize=32k,noquota 0 0
/dev/nvme0n1p1 /boot xfs rw,seclabel,relatime,attr2,inode64,logbufs=8,logbsize=32k,noquota 0 0
tmpfs /run/user/1000 tmpfs rw,seclabel,nosuid,nodev,relatime,size=178556k,nr_inodes=44639,mode=700,uid=1000,gid=1000,inode64 0 0
gvfsd-fuse /run/user/1000/gvfs fuse.gvfsd-fuse rw,nosuid,nodev,relatime,user_id=1000,group_id=1000 0 0
/dev/sr0 /run/media/alex/RHEL-9-1-0-BaseOS-x86_64 iso9660 ro,nosuid,nodev,relatime,nojoliet,check=s,map=n,blocksize=2048,uid=1000,
gid=1000,dmode=500,fmode=400 0 0
[root@server1 ~]# █
```

TABLE 7-8 Description of /etc/fstab by Column, Left to Right

Field Name	Example	Description
Device	/dev/mapper/rhel-root	Lists the device to be mounted; you may substitute the UUID or the device path.
Mount Point	/	Notes the directory where the filesystem will be mounted.
Filesystem Format	xfs	Describes the filesystem type. Valid filesystem types are xfs, ext2, ext3, ext4, msdos, vfat, iso9660, nfs, smb, swap, and many others.
Mount Options	defaults	Covered in the following section.
Dump Value	0	Either 0 or 1. If you use the **dump** command to back up filesystems, this field controls which filesystems need to be dumped.
Filesystem Check Order	0	Determines the order in which filesystems are checked by the **fsck** command during the boot process. For XFS filesystems, this should be set to 0. On ext* filesystems, the root (/) volume should be set to 1, and other local filesystems should be set to 2. Removable filesystems such as those associated with CD/DVD drives should be set to 0, which means that they are not checked during the Linux boot process.

When adding a new partition, you could just add the device file associated with the partition or logical volume to the first column.

Universally Unique Identifiers in /etc/fstab

In /etc/fstab, note the presence of UUIDs. Every formatted volume has a UUID, a unique 128-bit number. Each UUID represents either a partition, a logical volume, or a RAID array.

To identify the UUID for available volumes, run the **blkid** command with the name of the device as an argument. The output will give the UUID of the device. As an example, to retrieve the UUID of the root LV in the rhel VG, run the following command:

```
# blkid /dev/rhel/root
/dev/rhel/root: UUID="d1d81a61-ee4c-4573-96be-9b08bc6b1373" ↵
TYPE="xfs"
```

Alternatively, you could use the **xfs_admin** and **dumpe2fs** commands for the XFS and ext2/ext3/ext4 filesystems, respectively; for example, the following command identifies the UUID associated with the noted LV:

```
# xfs_admin -u /dev/rhel/root
```

As UUIDs are not limited to LVs, you should be able to get equivalent information for a partition from a command such as the following:

```
# xfs_admin -u /dev/sda1
```

Of course, the same is true if you have a configured and formatted ext volume, with a command such as the following:

```
# dumpe2fs /dev/mapper/rhel-test | grep UUID
```

The mount Command

The **mount** command can be used to attach local and network partitions to specified directories. Mount points are not fixed; you can mount a CD drive or even a shared network directory to any empty directory if appropriate ownership and permissions are set. Closely related is the **umount** (not unmount) command, which unmounts selected volumes from associated directories.

First, try the **mount** command by itself. It'll display all currently mounted filesystems, along with important mount options. For example, the following output suggests that the /dev/mapper/rhel-root volume is mounted on the top-level root directory in read-write mode and formatted to the xfs filesystem:

```
/dev/mapper/rhel-root on / type xfs ↵
(rw,relatime,seclabel,attr2,inode64,logbufs=8,logbsize=32k,noquota)
```

As suggested earlier, the **mount** command is closely related to the /etc/fstab file. If you've unmounted a directory and have made changes to the /etc/fstab file, the easiest way to mount all filesystems currently configured in the /etc/fstab file is with the following command:

```
# mount -a
```

However, if a filesystem is already mounted, this command doesn't change its status, no matter what has been done to the /etc/fstab file. But if the system is subsequently rebooted, the options configured in /etc/fstab are used automatically.

If you're not sure about a possible change to the /etc/fstab file, it's possible to test it out with the **mount** command. For example, the following command remounts the volume associated with the /boot directory in read-only mode:

```
# mount -o remount,ro /boot
```

You can confirm the result by rerunning the **mount** command. The following output should reflect the result on the /boot directory:

```
/dev/sda1 on /boot type xfs ↵
(ro,relatime,seclabel,attr2,inode64,logbufs=8,logbsize=32k,noquota)
```

If you've read this book from the beginning, you've already seen the **mount** command at work, and even the ISO files associated with downloaded CD/DVD images. To review, the following command mounts the noted RHEL 9 ISO file on the /mnt directory:

```
# mount -o loop rhel-baseos-9.1-x86_64-dvd.iso /mnt
```

More Filesystem Mount Options

Many **mount** command options are appropriate for the /etc/fstab file. One option most commonly seen in that file is **defaults**. Although that is the appropriate mount option for most /etc/fstab filesystems, there are other options, such as those listed in Table 7-9. If you want to use multiple options, separate them by commas. Don't use spaces between options. The list in Table 7-9 is not comprehensive. You can find out more from the mount man page, available with the **man mount** command.

TABLE 7-9   Options for the mount Command and /etc/fstab

Mount Option	Description
async	Causes all I/O to be done asynchronously on this filesystem.
atime	Updates the inode access time every time the file is accessed.
auto	Permits the filesystem to be mounted with the **mount -a** command.
defaults	Uses default mount options **rw**, **suid**, **dev**, **exec**, **auto**, **nouser**, and **async**.
dev	Permits access to character devices such as terminals or consoles and block devices such as drives.
exec	Allows binaries (compiled programs) to be run on this filesystem.
noatime	Does not update the inode access time every time the file is accessed.
noauto	Requires explicit mounting. This is a common option for CD drives and removable media.
nodev	Prevents the device files on this filesystem from being read or interpreted.
noexec	Prevents binaries (compiled programs) from being run on this filesystem.
nosuid	Disallows **setuid** and **setgid** permissions on this filesystem.
nouser	Allows only root users to mount the specified filesystem.
remount	Remounts a currently mounted filesystem.
ro	Mounts the filesystem as read-only.
rw	Mounts the filesystem as read/write.
suid	Allows **setuid** and **setgid** permissions on programs on this filesystem.
sync	Causes all I/O to be done synchronously on this filesystem.
user	Allows non-root users to mount this filesystem. By default, this also sets the **noexec**, **nosuid**, and **nodev** options.

Virtual Filesystems

This section describes some of the virtual filesystems used by RHEL 9 and listed in /etc/ mtab. Here are the most common:

- **tmpfs**   This filesystem is stored in RAM. Data is erased after a system reboot.
- **devpts**   This filesystem relates to pseudo-terminal devices.
- **sysfs**   This filesystem provides dynamic information about system devices. Explore the associated /sys directory. You'll find a wide variety of information related to the devices and drivers attached to the local system.
- **proc**   This filesystem is especially useful because it provides dynamically configurable options for changing the behavior of the kernel.
- **cgroup2**   This filesystem is associated with the control group feature of the Linux kernel, which allows you to set limits on system resource usage for a process or a group of processes.

Add Your Own Filesystems to /etc/fstab

If you need to set up a special directory, it sometimes makes sense to set it up on a separate volume. While it's nice to follow the standard format of the /etc/fstab file, it is an extra effort. On the RHCSA exam, read carefully the instructions to determine if a new directory needs to be a mount point of a partition.

So, in most cases, it's sufficient to set up a new volume in /etc/fstab with the associated device file, such as a /dev/sda6 partition, a UUID, or an LVM device such as /dev/mapper/ NewVol-NewLV or /dev/NewVol/NewLV. Make sure the device file reflects the new volume you've created, the intended mount directory, and the filesystem format you've applied (such as xfs).

Removable Media and /etc/fstab

In general, removable media should not be mounted automatically during the boot process. Although that's possible in the /etc/fstab configuration file with an option such as **noauto**, in general, setting up removable media in /etc/fstab is not standard in RHEL.

To read removable media such as smartcards and CD/DVDs, RHEL partially automates the mounting of such media in the GNOME Desktop Environment. Although the details of this process are not part of the RHCSA exam objectives, the process is based on configuration files in the /usr/lib/udev/rules.d directory. If RHEL detects your hardware, click Activities | Files; in the menu that appears, select the entry for the removable media.

If that doesn't work for some reason, you can use the **mount** command directly. For example, the following command mounts a CD/DVD in a drive:

```
# mount -t iso9660 /dev/sr0 /mnt
```

The **-t** switch specifies the type of filesystem (iso9660). The device file /dev/sr0 represents the first CD/DVD drive; /mnt is the directory through which you can access the files from the CD/DVD after mounting. But /dev/sr0? How is anyone supposed to remember that?

Fortunately, Linux addresses this in a couple of ways. First, it sets up links from more sensibly named files such as /dev/cdrom, which you can confirm with the **ls -l /dev/cdrom** command. Second, it provides the **blkid** command. Try it. If removable media (other than a CD/DVD) is connected, you'll see it in the output to the command, including the associated device file.

Just remember that it is important to unmount removable media such as USB keys before removing them. Otherwise, the data you thought was written to the disk might still be in the unwritten RAM cache. In that case, you would lose that data.

Given these examples of how removable media can be mounted, you should have a better idea of how such media can be configured in the /etc/fstab configuration file. The standard **defaults** option is inappropriate in most cases because it mounts a system in read-write mode (even for read-only DVDs), attempts to mount automatically during the boot process, and limits access to the root administrative user. But that can be changed with the right options. For example, to configure a CD drive that can be mounted by regular users, you could add the following line to /etc/fstab:

```
/dev/sr0 /cdrom auto ro,noauto,users 0 0
```

This line sets up a mount in read-only mode, does not try to mount it automatically during the boot process, and supports access by regular users.

As desired, similar options are possible for removable media such as USB keys, but that can be more problematic with multiple USB keys; for example, one may be detected as /dev/sdc once, and then later detected as /dev/sdd, if there's a second USB key installed. However, if properly configured, each USB key should have a unique UUID. There's another option: rather than using static mounts for removable devices, you can rely on the automounter, as we will illustrate later in this chapter.

Network Filesystems

The /etc/fstab file can be used to automate mounts from network filesystems. The two major sharing services of interest are NFS and Samba. This section provides only a brief overview as to how such filesystems can be configured in the /etc/fstab file; to get some practice with the configurations described in this section, see the labs at the end of the chapter.

In general, network shares are subjected to more reliability issues than direct-attached storage. The settings in the /etc/fstab file should account for that. So if there's a problem in the network connection or perhaps a problem such as a power failure on the remote NFS server, you can specify how you want the client to behave.

A connection to a shared NFS directory is based on its hostname or IP address, along with the full path to the directory on the server. So to connect to a remote NFS server on system *server1* that shares the /pub directory, you could mount that share with the following command (assuming the /share directory exists):

```
# mount -t nfs server1.example.com:/pub /share
```

Some common mount options are shown in the following /etc/fstab entry:

```
server1:/pub   /share   nfs rsize=65536,wsize=65536,hard 0 0
```

The **rsize** and **wsize** variables determine the maximum size (in bytes) of the data to be read and written in each request. Normally, these should not be required, because the client and server should be able to negotiate the largest values that they both support. The **hard** directive specifies that the client will retry failed NFS requests indefinitely, blocking client requests potentially until the NFS server becomes available. Conversely, the **soft** option will cause the client to fail after a predefined number of retransmissions, but at the cost of risking the integrity of the data. If the connection is to an NFS version 4 server, substitute **nfs4** for **nfs** in the third column.

You can configure some NFS client and server settings in /etc/nfs.conf. An excerpt of this file is shown in Figure 7-10. For example, to enable only NFSv4 and disable v2 and v3, set the following configuration parameters in /etc/nfs.conf:

```
tcp=y
vers2=n
vers3=n
vers4=y
vers4.0=y
vers4.1=y
vers4.2=y
```

FIGURE 7-10

Sample /etc/nfs
.conf

```
[nfsd]
# debug=0
# threads=8
# host=
# port=0
# grace-time=90
# lease-time=90
# udp=n
# tcp=y
# vers3=y
# vers4=y
# vers4.0=y
# vers4.1=y
# vers4.2=y
```

CERTIFICATION OBJECTIVE 7.06

The Automounter

With network mounts and portable media, problems may come up if connections are lost or media is removed. During the server configuration process, you could be mounting filesystems from a number of remote systems. You may also want temporary access to removable media such as USB keys. The automount daemon, also known as the automounter or **autofs**, can help. It can automatically mount a specific filesystem as needed. It can unmount a filesystem automatically after a fixed period of time.

Mounting via the Automounter

Once a partition is mounted manually with the **mount** command or via /etc/fstab, it stays mounted until you unmount it or shut down the system. The permanence of the mount can cause problems. For example, if you've mounted a USB key and then physically removed the key, Linux may not have had a chance to write the file to the disk. Data would be lost. The same issue applies to Secure Digital (SD) cards or other hot-swappable removable drives.

Another issue: mounted NFS filesystems may cause problems if the remote host fails or the connection is lost. Systems may slow down or even hang as the local system looks for the mounted directory.

This is where the automounter can help. It relies on the **autofs** daemon to mount configured directories as needed on a temporary basis. In RHEL, the relevant configuration files are auto.master, auto.misc, auto.net, and auto.smb, all in the /etc directory. If you use the automounter, keep the /misc and /net directories free. Red Hat configures automounts on these directories by default, and they won't work if local files or directories are stored there. The following subsections will cover each of these files.

on the job

You won't even see the /misc and/or /net directories unless you properly configured /etc/auto.master and the autofs **daemon is running.**

/etc/auto.master

The standard /etc/auto.master file includes a series of directives, with four uncommented lines by default. The first refers to the /etc/auto.misc file as the configuration file for the /misc directory. The **/net -hosts** directive allows you to specify the host to automount a network directory, as specified in /etc/auto.net.

```
/misc /etc/auto.misc
/net -hosts
+dir:/etc/auto.master.d
+auto.master
```

In any case, these directives point to configuration files for each service. Shared directories from each service are automatically mounted on demand on the given directory (/misc and /net).

You can set up the automounter on other directories. One popular option is to set up the automounter on the /home directory. In this way, you can configure user home directories on remote servers mounted on demand.

```
# /home /etc/auto.home
```

This works only if a /home directory doesn't already exist on the local system. As the RHCSA exam requires the configuration of a number of regular users, your systems should include a /home directory for regular users. In that case, you could substitute a different directory, leading to a line such as the following:

```
/shared /etc/auto.home
```

Just remember, for any system accessed over a network, you'll need to be sure that the firewall allows traffic associated with the given service.

/etc/auto.misc

Red Hat conveniently provides standard automount directives in comments in the /etc/auto .misc file. It's helpful to analyze this file in detail. We use the default RHEL version of this file. The first four lines are comments, which we skip. The first directive is

```
cd      -fstype=iso9660,ro,nosuid,nodev    :/dev/cdrom
```

In RHEL, this directive is active by default, assuming you've activated the **autofs** service. In other words, if you have a CD in the /dev/cdrom drive, you can access its files through the automounter with the **ls /misc/cd** command, even as a regular user. The automounter accesses it using the ISO 9660 filesystem. It's mounted read-only (**ro**), set owner user ID permissions are not allowed (**nosuid**), and device files on this filesystem are not used (**nodev**).

A number of other directives are commented out, ready for use. Of course, you would have to delete the comment character (#) before using any of these configuration lines, and you'd have to adjust names and device files accordingly; for example, /dev/hda1 is no longer used as a device name on the latest Linux systems.

As suggested by one of the comments, "The following entries are samples to pique your imagination." The first of these commented lines allows you to set up a /misc/linux mount point from a shared NFS directory, /pub/linux, from the ftp.example.org host:

```
#linux    -ro,soft          ftp.example.org:/pub/linux
```

The next line assumes that a filesystem is stored on the /dev/hda1 partition. With this directive, you can automount the filesystem in /misc/boot.

```
#boot     -fstype=ext2      :/dev/hda1
```

The following three lines apply to a floppy disk drive. Don't laugh; virtual floppies are fairly easy to create and configure on most virtual machine systems. The first directive, set to an "auto" filesystem type, searches through /etc/filesystems to try to match what's on your floppy. The next two directives assume that the floppy is formatted to the ext2 filesystem.

```
#floppy        -fstype=auto     :/dev/fd0
#floppy        -fstype=ext2     :/dev/fd0
#e2floppy      -fstype=ext2     :/dev/fd0
```

The next line points to the first partition on the third SCSI drive. The **jaz** at the beginning suggests this is suitable for an old Iomega-type Jaz drive.

```
#jaz         -fstype=ext2        :/dev/sdc1
```

Finally, the last command is based on an older system where the automounter is applied to a legacy PATA drive. Of course, the /dev/hdd device file is no longer used, so substitute accordingly. But **removable** at the beginning suggests this is also suitable for removable hard drives. Of course, you'd likely have to change the filesystem format to something like XFS. As suggested earlier in this chapter, the **blkid** command can help identify available device files from removable systems such as USB keys and portable drives.

```
#removable    -fstype=ext2       :/dev/hdd
```

In general, you'll need to modify these lines for available hardware.

/etc/auto.net

With the /etc/auto.net configuration script, you can review and read shared NFS directories. It works with the hostnames or IP addresses of NFS servers. By default, executable permissions are enabled on this file.

Assuming the automounter is active and can connect to an NFS server with an IP address of 172.16.0.100, you can review shared NFS directories on that system with the following command:

```
# /etc/auto.net 172.16.0.100
/srv/ftp 172.16.0.100:/srv/ftp
```

This output indicates that the /srv/ftp directory on the 172.16.0.100 system is shared via NFS. Based on the directives in /etc/auto.master, you could access this share (assuming appropriate firewall and SELinux settings) with the following command:

```
# ls /net/172.16.0.100/srv/ftp
```

/etc/auto.smb

One of the problems associated with the configuration of a shared Samba or CIFS directory is that it works, at least in its standard configuration, only with public directories. In other words, if you activate the /etc/auto.smb file, it'll only work with directories shared without a username or a password.

If you accept these unsecure conditions, it's possible to set up the /etc/auto.smb file in the same way as the /etc/auto.net file. First, you'd have to add it to the /etc/auto.master file in a similar fashion, with the following directive:

```
/smb   /etc/auto.smb
```

You'd then need to specifically restart the automounter service with the following command:

```
# systemctl restart autofs
```

You'd then be able to review shared directories with the following command; substitute a hostname or IP address if desired. Of course, this won't work unless the Samba server is activated on the noted server1.example.com system and the firewall is configured to allow access through associated TCP/IP ports.

```
# /etc/auto.smb server1.example.com
```

Activate the Automounter

Once appropriate files have been configured, you can start, restart, or reload the automounter. As it is governed by the **autofs** daemon, you can stop, start, restart, or reload that service with one of the following commands:

```
# systemctl stop autofs
# systemctl start autofs
# systemctl restart autofs
# systemctl reload autofs
```

With the default command in the /etc/auto.misc file, you should now be able to mount a CD on the /misc/cd directory automatically, just by accessing the configured directory. Once you have a CD in the drive, the following command should work:

```
# ls /misc/cd
```

EXERCISE 7-3

Configure the Automounter

In this exercise, you'll test the automounter. You'll need a DVD ISO image, such as the RHEL 9 DVD. First, however, you need to make sure that the **autofs** daemon is in operation, modify the appropriate configuration files, and then restart **autofs**. You can then test the automounter in this lab.

1. Check that the autofs RPM package is installed on server1.example.com. If not, run

```
# dnf install autofs
```

2. From the command-line interface, run the following command to make sure the **autofs** daemon is running:

```
# systemctl start autofs
```

3. Review the /etc/auto.master configuration file in a text editor. The defaults are sufficient to activate the configuration options in /etc/auto.misc and /etc/auto.net.

4. Check the /etc/auto.misc configuration file in a text editor. Make sure it includes the following line (which should already be there by default). Save and exit from /etc/auto.misc.

```
cd    -fstype=iso9660,ro,nosuid,nodev    :/dev/cdrom
```

5. Reload the **autofs** daemon. Since it's already running, all you need to do is make sure it rereads associated configuration files.

```
# systemctl reload autofs
```

6. The automounter service is now active. Insert a CD or DVD into an appropriate drive and run the following command. If successful, it should display the contents of the CD or DVD:

```
# ls /misc/cd
```

7. Run the **ls /misc** command immediately. You should see the CD directory in the output.

8. Wait at least five minutes and then repeat the previous command. What do you see?

SCENARIO & SOLUTION

You need to configure several new partitions for a standard Linux partition, for swap space, and for a logical volume.	Use the **fdisk**, **gdisk**, or **parted** utility to create partitions, and then modify their partition types with the **t** or **set** command.
You want to set up a mount during the boot process based on the UUID.	Identify the UUID of the volume with the **blkid** command, and use that UUID in the /etc/fstab file.
You need to format a volume to the XFS filesystem type.	Format the target volume with the command **mkfs.xfs**.
You need to format a volume to the ext2, ext3, or ext4 filesystem type.	Format the target volume with a command such as **mkfs.ext2**, **mkfs.ext3**, or **mkfs.ext4**.
You want to set up a logical volume.	Use the **pvcreate** command to create PVs; use the **vgcreate** command to combine PVs in VGs; use the **lvcreate** command to create an LV; format that LV for use.
You want to add new filesystems without destroying others.	Use the free space available on existing or newly installed hard drives.
You want to expand the space available to an LV formatted with the XFS filesystem.	Use the **lvextend** command to increase the space available to an LV, and then use the **xfs_growfs** command to expand the formatted filesystem accordingly.
You need to configure automated mounts to a shared network filesystem.	Configure the filesystem either in /etc/fstab or through the automounter.

CERTIFICATION SUMMARY

As a Linux administrator, you should know how to create and manage new filesystem volumes. To create a new filesystem, you need to know how to create, manage, and format partitions as well as how to set up those partitions for logical volumes.

RHEL 9 also supports the configuration of logical volumes. The process may seem a bit intricate, as it requires the configuration of a partition as a physical volume. One or more PVs can then be configured as a volume group. Logical volumes can then be configured from desired portions of a VG. Associated commands are **pv***, **vg***, and **lv***; those and others can be accessed from the lvm> prompt.

Linux supports the format of partitions and logical volumes to a wide variety of filesystems. Although the default is XFS, Linux supports several regular and journaling filesystems types, including filesystems available on Microsoft and other operating systems.

Once configured, partitions and logical volumes, whether encrypted or not, can be added to the /etc/fstab file. That configuration is read during the boot process and can also be used by the **mount** command. If desired, removable filesystems and shared network directories can also be configured in /etc/fstab.

The /etc/fstab file is not the only option to set up mounts. You can automate this process for regular users with the automounter. Properly configured, it allows users to access shared network directories, removable media, and more through paths defined in /etc/auto.master.

TWO-MINUTE DRILL

Here are some of the key points from the certification objectives in Chapter 7.

Storage Management and Partitions

- ❑ **fdisk**, **gdisk**, and **parted** can be used to configure partitions for filesystems and logical volumes.
- ❑ Disks can use the traditional MBR-style partitioning scheme, which supports primary, extended, and logical partitions, or the GPT scheme, which supports up to 128 partitions.

Filesystem Formats

- ❑ Linux tools can be used to configure and format volumes to a number of different filesystems.
- ❑ Examples of standard filesystems include MS-DOS and ext2.
- ❑ Journaling filesystems, which include logs that can restore metadata, are more resilient; the default RHEL 9 filesystem is XFS.
- ❑ RHEL 9 supports a variety of **mkfs.*** filesystem format-check commands and **fsck.*** filesystem-check commands.

Basic Linux Filesystems and Directories

- ❑ Linux files and filesystems are organized into directories based on the FHS.
- ❑ Some Linux directories are well suited to configuration on separate filesystems.

Logical Volume Manager (LVM)

- ❑ LVM is based on physical volumes, logical volumes, and volume groups.
- ❑ You can create and add LVM systems with a wide variety of commands, starting with **pv***, **lv***, and **vg***.

❑ The space from new partitions configured as PVs can be allocated to existing volume groups with the **vgextend** command; they can be added to LVs with the **lvcreate** and **lvextend** commands.

❑ Extra space on a partition can be used to extend an existing XFS filesystem with the **xfs_growfs** command.

Filesystem Management

❑ Standard filesystems are mounted as defined in /etc/fstab.

❑ Filesystem volumes are usually identified by their UUIDs; for a list, run the **blkid** command.

❑ The **mount** command can either use the settings in /etc/fstab or mount filesystem volumes directly.

❑ It's also possible to configure mounts of shared filesystems from NFS and Samba servers in /etc/fstab.

The Automounter

❑ With the automounter, you can configure automatic mounts of removable media and shared network drives.

❑ Key automounter configuration files are auto.master and auto.misc, in the /etc directory.

SELF TEST

The following questions will help measure your understanding of the material presented in this chapter. As no multiple-choice questions appear on the Red Hat exams, no multiple-choice questions appear in this book. These questions exclusively test your understanding of the chapter. Getting results, not memorizing trivia, is what counts on the Red Hat exams. There may be more than one correct answer to many of these questions.

Storage Management and Partitions

1. What **fdisk** command option lists configured partitions from all attached hard drives?

2. After a swap partition has been created, what command activates it?

Filesystem Formats

3. What is the primary advantage of a journaling filesystem such as XFS?

4. What command formats /dev/sdb3 to the default Red Hat filesystem format?

Basic Linux Filesystems and Directories

5. What filesystem is mounted on a directory separate from the top-level root directory in the default RHEL 9 installation?

6. Name two directories just below / that are not suitable for mounting separately from the volume with the top-level root directory.

Logical Volume Manager (LVM)

7. Once you've created a new partition and set it to the Logical Volume Manager type, what command adds it as a PV?

8. Once you've added more space to an LV, what command would expand the underlining XFS filesystem to fill the new space?

Filesystem Management

9. To change the mount options for a local filesystem, what file would you edit?

10. What would you add to the /etc/fstab file to set up access to the ext4 filesystem /dev/sda6, mounted on the /usr directory as read-only with other default options? Assume you can't find the UUID of /dev/sda6. Also assume a dump value of 1 and a filesystem check order of 2.

The Automounter

11. If you've started the **autofs** daemon and want to read the list of shared NFS directories from the server1.example.com computer, what automounter-related command would you use?

12. Name the configuration files associated with the default installation of the automounter on RHEL 9.

LAB QUESTIONS

Red Hat presents its exams electronically. For that reason, the labs in this chapter are available from the companion website that accompanies the book. In case you haven't yet set up RHEL 9 on a system, refer to Chapter 1 for installation instructions. The answers for each lab follow the Self Test answers.

SELF TEST ANSWERS

Storage Management and Partitions

1. The **fdisk** command option that lists configured partitions from all attached hard drives is **fdisk -l**.

2. After creating a swap partition, you can use the **mkswap** *devicename* and **swapon** *devicename* commands to initialize and activate the volume; just substitute the device file associated with the volume (such as /dev/sda1 or /dev/VolGroup00/LogVol03) for *devicename*.

Filesystem Formats

3. The primary advantage of a journaling filesystem such as XFS is faster data recovery.

4. The command that formats /dev/sdb3 to the default Red Hat filesystem format is **mkfs.xfs /dev/sdb3**. The **mkfs -t xfs /dev/sdb3** command is also an acceptable answer.

Basic Linux Filesystems and Directories

5. The /boot filesystem is mounted separately from /.

6. There are many correct answers to this question; some of the directories not suitable for mounting separately from / include /bin, /dev, and /etc. (In contrast, several directories are essentially shown as placeholders for mounting, including /media and /mnt.)

Logical Volume Manager (LVM)

7. Once you've created a new partition and set it to the Logical Volume Manager file type, the command that adds it as a PV is **pvcreate**. For example, if the new partition is /dev/sdb2, the command is **pvcreate /dev/sdb2**.

8. Once you've added more space to an LV, the command that would expand the underlining XFS filesystem to fill the new space is **xfs_growfs**.

Filesystem Management

9. To change the mount options for a local filesystem, edit /etc/fstab.

10. Since the UUID is unknown, you'll need to use the device file for the volume (in this case, /dev/sda6). Thus, the line to be added to /etc/fstab is

```
/dev/sda6 /usr    ext4    defaults,ro      1 2
```

The Automounter

11. If you've started the **autofs** daemon and want to read the list of shared NFS directories from the first.example.com computer, the automounter-related command you'd use to list those directories is **/etc/auto.net server1.example.com**.

12. The configuration files associated with the default installation of the automounter include auto .master and auto.misc, all in the /etc directory.

LAB ANSWERS

Lab 1

This lab assumes that the new drive is available as /dev/sdb. Substitute accordingly if the device has a different name.

1. Run **parted /dev/sdb**. Create the new partition with the following command:

```
(parted) mkpart
Partition type?  primary/extended? primary
File system type?  [ext2]? xfs
Start? 1MiB
End? 1025MiB
```

Note that the filesystem starts at 1MiB. What happens if you enter 0MiB?

2. Type **print** to show the partition table on the drive. Exit from **parted** by typing **q**.

3. Format the new filesystem:

```
# mkfs.xfs /dev/sdb1
```

4. Create the directory mount point:

```
# mkdir /test1
```

5. Find the UUID of the device:

```
# blkid /dev/sdb1
```

6. Add the following line to /etc/fstab (substitute the UUID with the one that you obtained from the **blkid** command):

```
UUID="629e809f-2e6d-474c-bc2d-a96121cd1e21" /test1 xfs defaults 0 0
```

7. Run **mount -a** to mount the filesystem. Confirm that the filesystem is mounted with the **df** command.

8. To test that the configuration persists after a reboot, create some files in the /test1 directory. Reboot the system and list the content of /test1. Do you see the files that you have created?

9. The second part of the lab is similar, but requires you to use **fdisk** rather than **parted**. Run **fdisk /dev/sdb**. Create a new (**n**) primary (**p**) partition whose number is 2. Accept the default for the first sector and enter **+1G** for the last sector. Tag the partition (**t**) with code **82**. Show the partition table (**p**), save the changes (**w**), and exit (**q**).

10. Format and activate the new swap partition:

```
# mkswap /dev/sdb2
# swapon /dev/sdb2
```

11. Find the UUID of the device:

```
# blkid /dev/sdb2
```

12. You should be able to confirm the configuration of a new swap partition in the output to the **cat /proc/swaps** command. You should also be able to verify the result in the **Swap** line associated with the **top** command, as well as in the output of the **free -h** command.

13. Add the following line to /etc/fstab (substitute the UUID with the one that you obtained from the **blkid** command):

```
UUID="4578ae12-857f-3a2c-cc76-184ecd23654a" swap defaults 0 0
```

14. Remember, when taking the exam, all changes should survive a reboot. For the purpose of this lab, reboot the system to confirm this. However, reboots take time; if you have multiple tasks during an exam, you may want to wait until completing as much as possible before rebooting a system.

Lab 2

This lab assumes that you have spare space on the /dev/sdb drive to create the new partition and physical volume. Even if you've configured the exact spare partitions described in this lab and followed exact instructions, it's quite possible that your LV won't be exactly 900MiB. Some of that variance comes from the differences between units of measure that rely on base 2 or base 10 numbers. Don't panic; that variance is normal. The same proviso applies to Lab 3 as well.

1. Create the new partition for the PV. Run **fdisk /dev/sdb**. Create a new (**n**) primary (**p**) partition. Accept the default for the first sector and enter **+1G** for the last sector. Tag the partition (**t**) with code **8e**. Show the partition table (**p**), save the changes (**w**), and exit (**q**).

2. Create the physical volume:

```
# pvcreate /dev/sdb3
```

3. Create the volume group:

```
# vgcreate volgroup1 /dev/sdb3
```

4. Create and format the logical volume:

```
# lvcreate -L 900M -n logvol1 volgroup1
# mkfs.xfs /dev/volgroup1/logvol1
```

5. To verify the UUID of the newly formatted volume, run the following command:

   ```
   # blkid /dev/volgroup1/logvol1
   ```

6. Add the following line to /etc/fstab (substitute the UUID with the one that you obtained from the **blkid** command):

   ```
   UUID="4813caa3-56ae-cc12-5647-58aac35b71be" /test2 xfs defaults 0 0
   ```

7. Create the /test2 directory:

   ```
   # mkdir /test2
   ```

8. If the /etc/fstab file is properly configured, you should be able to run the **mount -a** command. Then the **df** command should show the logical volume mounted on the /test2 directory.

9. As with Lab 1, all changes should survive a reboot. At some point, you'll want to reboot the local system to check for success or failure of this and other labs.

Lab 3

Based on the information from Lab 2, you should already know what the size of the current LV is. The associated **df** command should confirm the result; the **df -m** command, with its output in MB, could help.

The key commands in this lab are **lvextend** and **xfs_growfs**. While there are a number of excellent command options available, all you really need with either command is the device file for the LV:

```
# lvextend -L +50M /dev/volgroup1/logvol1
# xfs_growfs /dev/volgroup1/logvol1
```

As with Lab 2, the result can be confirmed after appropriate **mount** and **df** commands. However, to ensure that no data has been lost during the process, you could create some test files before resizing the LV and the filesystem.

Lab 4

There are several steps associated with this lab:

1. Ensure that all the partitions and volumes created in the previous labs have been unmounted, eliminated from /etc/fstab, and removed (with **{lv,vg,pv}remove**).

2. You don't need to partition the /dev/sdb and /dev/sdc drives. It is sufficient to initialize the entire drives as PVs, using the **pvcreate /dev/sdb** and **pvcreate /dev/sdc** commands.

3. Run the **vgcreate -s 2M vg01 /dev/sdb /dev/sdc** command to create the VG.

4. Create the LV with the **lvcreate -l 800 -n lv01 vg01** command.

5. Format the filesystem with the **mkfs.ext4 /dev/vg01/lv01** command.

6. Add the correct entry to /etc/fstab.

7. Create the mount point (**mkdir /test4**).

If the /etc/fstab file is properly configured, you should be able to run the **mount -a** command. Then you should see /dev/mapper/vg01-lv01 mounted on the /test4 directory.

Lab 5

The configuration of the automounter on a shared NFS directory is easier than it looks. Before you begin, make sure the shared NFS directory is available from the remote computer with the **showmount -e *remote_ipaddr*** command, where *remote_ipaddr* is the IP address of the remote NFS server. If that doesn't work, you may have skipped a step described in the lab.

As for the automounter configuration, there are two approaches. You could modify the following commented sample NFS configuration directive. Of course, you'd have to at least change ftp.example .org to the name or IP address of the NFS server and /pub/linux to /tmp (or whatever is the name of the directory being shared).

```
linux   -ro,soft,intr   ftp.example.org:/pub/linux
```

Alternatively, you could just directly take advantage of the **/etc/auto.net** script. For example, if the remote NFS server is on IP address 172.16.0.100, run the following command:

```
# /etc/auto.net 172.16.0.100
```

You should see the /tmp directory shared in the output. If so, you'll be able to access it more directly with the following command:

```
# ls /net/172.16.0.100/tmp
```

If you really want to learn how to use the automounter, try modifying the aforementioned directive in the /etc/auto.misc configuration file. Assuming the automounter is already running, you can make sure the automounter rereads the applicable configuration files with the **systemctl reload autofs** command.

If you use the same first directive in the aforementioned line, you'll be able to use the automounter to access the same directory with the **ls /misc/linux** command.

Chapter 8

Linux Security

Linux security has been based on a concept known as discretionary access control (DAC). In the DAC model, access to "objects," such as file and directories, is discretionary because it is controlled by the owner of the objects. Hence, the standard permissions and ownership associated with files and directories is an implementation of DAC.

Then, the U.S. National Security Agency (NSA) developed SELinux, which is an implementation of a different kind of security architecture, known as mandatory access control (MAC). MAC differs significantly from DAC. Red Hat expects you to work with SELinux enabled during exams. In this chapter, you will examine how to set enforcing and permissive modes, change file contexts, use boolean settings, and diagnose SELinux policy violations.

Also in the realm of security, the firewall is a crucial component. In this chapter, you'll examine **firewalld**, which provides support for different trust zones. You will learn how to allow or block services through **firewalld** using the **firewall-config** graphical utility and the **firewall-cmd** command-line tool.

A service that is installed on most Linux systems is SSH. As it is a very common service for logging in to a machine, it is also a crucial service for security. So this chapter also describes how you can improve security by using key-based authentication for SSH.

If you're starting with the default installation created during the installation process, you may need to install additional packages during this chapter. For example, if the GUI-based firewall configuration tool is missing, you'll need to install it with the following command:

```
# dnf install firewall-config
```

For more information on the package installation process, see Chapter 4.

INSIDE THE EXAM

Basic Firewall Control

firewalld is a feature-rich, zone-based stateful firewall that you can use to block or accept traffic to remote network services. The related RHCSA objectives are

- Configure firewall settings using firewall-cmd/firewalld
- Restrict network access using firewall-cmd/firewall

The Secure Shell Server

As suggested in the introduction, the SSH service is given special focus in this chapter because, as a common service for logging in to a machine, securing it is crucial. The related RHCSA objective is

- Configure key-based authentication for SSH

With key-based authentication, you'll be able to log in to remote systems by using private/public key pairs. Password transmission over the network would no longer be required. The 1024 or more bits associated with such authentication keys are a lot harder to guess than a standard password.

Security-Enhanced Linux

There's no way around it. On the Red Hat exams, you're expected to work with SELinux. It's not clear whether you can even pass the Red Hat exams unless you configure at least some services with SELinux in mind. To help exam candidates understand what's needed, Red Hat has broken down SELinux-related objectives. The first objective is fundamental to SELinux, as it relates to the three modes available for SELinux on a system (enforcing/permissive/disabled):

- Set enforcing and permissive modes for SELinux

The next objective requires that you understand the SELinux contexts defined for different files and processes. Although the associated commands are straightforward, the available contexts are as broad as the number of services available on Linux:

- List and identify SELinux file and process contexts

As you experiment with different SELinux contexts, you'll likely make mistakes. You may not remember the default contexts associated with important directories. But with the right commands, you don't have to remember everything; as suggested by the following objective, it's relatively easy to restore the default:

- Restore default file contexts

SELinux uses contexts not just for files and processes but also for network ports. By editing port labels, you can allow a service to run on a nonstandard port, or you can restrict the ports that a service is able to listen to. The related exam objective is

- Manage SELinux port labels

The next objective may seem complex at first glance, but it isn't, because the boolean settings associated with SELinux have descriptive names. In essence, this means that to run a certain service under SELinux, all you need to do is turn on one or more boolean settings (rather than having to modify the SELinux policy rules directly).

- Use boolean settings to modify system SELinux settings

Once SELinux is operational, you should monitor the system for policy violations. A violation may be the result of a misconfiguration or an unauthorized intrusion attempt. Hence, to get the most out of SELinux, you should know how to audit for policy violations and be able to address common problems. The related RHCSA objective is

- Diagnose and address routine SELinux policy violations

Basic Firewall Control

Traditionally, firewalls were configured only between LANs and outside networks such as the Internet. But as security threats increase, there's an increasing need for firewalls on every system. RHEL 9 includes a firewall in every default configuration.

The Linux kernel comes with a powerful framework, the Netfilter system, which enables other kernel modules to offer functionalities such as packet filtering, network address translation (NAT), and load balancing. In previous RHEL releases, the **iptables** command was the main tool used to interact with the Netfilter system to provide packet filtering and NAT.

Today, the functionality of Netfilter has been extended by Nftables, a new packet classification system. Before you send a message over an IP network, the message is broken down into smaller units called *packets*. Additional information, including the type of data, the source address, and destination address, is added to each packet. The packets are reassembled when they reach the destination computer. An Nftables rule examines these fields in each packet to determine whether to allow the packet to pass.

In RHEL 9, the old **iptables** tool is now deprecated in favor of **firewalld**. You can interact with **firewalld** using the graphical utility **firewall-config** or the command-line client **firewall-cmd**. While **iptables** relied on the Netfilter system within the Linux kernel to filter packets, **firewalld** uses the more advanced feature provided by Nftables. In addition, whereas **iptables** was based on the concept of "chain of filter rules" to block or forward traffic, **firewalld** is "zone based," as you will see in the following sections.

For the RHCSA exam, you need to understand how to configure a firewall to either block or allow network communication through one or more ports using **firewall-cmd**. We will also explain how to use the **firewall-config** GUI tool and the Cockpit web console to achieve the same result.

Standard Ports

Linux communicates over a network, primarily using the TCP/IP protocol suite. Different services use certain ports and protocols by default, as defined in the /etc/services file. It may be useful to know some of these ports by heart, such as those described in Table 8-1. Be aware, some of these ports may communicate using the Transmission Control Protocol (TCP), the User Datagram Protocol (UDP), or even the Stream Control Transmission Protocol (SCTP). For example, as noted in the following excerpts from the /etc/services file, the FTP service has been assigned the TCP and UDP ports listed here:

```
ftp-data        20/tcp
ftp-data        20/udp
ftp             21/tcp
ftp             21/udp
```

However, you'll see shortly that the Red Hat firewall configuration tools open only TCP communications for FTP services. This is because the default policy of the Internet Assigned Number Authority (IANA) is to register port numbers for both TCP and UDP, even if a service only supports the TCP protocol.

	Port	Description
	20, 21	File Transfer Protocol (FTP)
	22	Secure Shell (SSH)
	23	Telnet
	25	Simple Mail Transfer Protocol (SMTP); for example, Postfix, sendmail
	53	Domain Name Service (DNS) servers
	80	Hypertext Transfer Protocol (HTTP)
	88	Kerberos
	110	Post Office Protocol, version 3 (POP3)
	139	Network Basic Input/Output System (NetBIOS) session service
	143	Internet Mail Access Protocol (IMAP)
	443	HTTP, secure (HTTPS)

TABLE 8-1

Common TCP/IP Ports

The firewalld Service

You can automate the process of configuring a firewall. For that purpose, in RHEL 9 **firewalld** comes with both a console and a GUI configuration tool. Although the look and feel of the two applications differs, you can use both tools to configure access to trusted services. Before starting the **firewalld** configuration tool, check that **firewalld** is running and automatically starts during the boot process:

```
# systemctl status firewalld
# systemctl is-enabled firewalld
```

One of the features of **firewalld** is *zone-based* firewalling. In a zone-based firewall, networks and interfaces are grouped into zones, with each zone configured with a different level of trust. The zones defined in **firewalld** are listed in Table 8-2, along with their default behavior for outgoing and incoming connections.

on the Job A zone is made up of a group of source network addresses and interfaces, plus the rules to process the packets that match those source addresses and network interfaces.

on the Job On some systems, you may see a zone named "libvirt." This is not one of the default zones defined in firewalld, but it is created by libvirt to manage interfaces such as virbr0, which is used to allow communication between virtual guests and the host.

TABLE 8-2 Zones in firewalld

Zone	Outgoing Connections	Incoming Connections
drop	Allowed	Dropped
block	Allowed	Rejected with an icmp-host-prohibited message
public	Allowed	Dynamic Host Configuration Protocol version 6 (DHCPv6) client and SSH allowed
external	Allowed and masqueraded to the IP address of the outgoing network interface	SSH allowed
dmz	Allowed	SSH allowed
work	Allowed	DHCPv6 client, Internet Print Protocol (IPP), and SSH allowed
home	Allowed	DHCPv6 client, multicast DNS, IPP, Samba client, and SSH allowed
internal	Allowed	Same as the home zone
trusted	Allowed	Allowed

The GUI firewall-config Tool

You can start the graphical **firewalld** configuration tool from a GUI-based command line with the **firewall-config** command. The result is shown in Figure 8-1.

As shown in the figure, the main window includes different menus and tabs. In the top-left area, you can find which interface is linked to which zone. Next to it, there is a drop-down Configuration menu, where you can set the firewall to Runtime or Permanent mode. If it's set to Runtime, the changes applied by **firewall-config** take effect immediately but will not survive a server reboot. Alternatively, select Permanent mode to make your changes survive a server reboot. At any time, you can click Options | Reload Firewalld to make a new firewall configuration immediately effective.

w a t c h If firewall-config **is not installed, run the** dnf install firewall-config **command.**

You can only modify definitions of zones and services in Permanent mode.

FIGURE 8-1   The graphical firewall-config tool

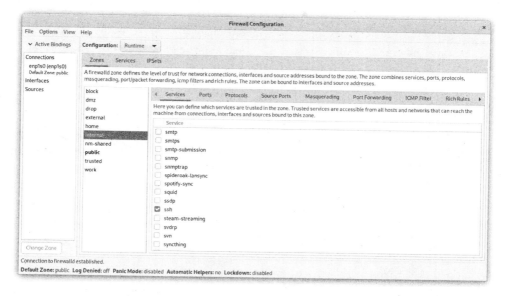

The Zones tab includes all the zones previously listed in Table 8-2. When an incoming packet hits the firewall, its source address is checked for a match with the network addresses that belong to the existing zones. If no match is found, the incoming interface of the packet is checked to verify whether it belongs to a zone. Once a correspondence is found, the packet is processed according to the rules of the zone it has been matched to.

In the main **firewall-config** window, the public zone is displayed in a bold font to indicate that this zone is the *default zone.* The default zone has a special meaning: any new network interface added to the system is automatically assigned to the default zone. In addition, the rules of the default zone are processed for all incoming packets that do not match any of the other zones. You can set a different zone to be the default by clicking Options | Change Default Zone.

To allow or deny incoming traffic through the firewall, select a zone and add or remove a checkmark in the zone's Services tab for the service you want to grant or block. As an alternative, you can also specify a protocol and port from the Ports tab.

In **firewalld**, a service is defined as a group of one of more protocols and ports. A service can also include a Netfilter helper module to support filtering for those applications that dynamically open multiple connections.

A variety of network services are already defined in the Services window. The most common are described in Table 8-3.

If you switch the **firewall-config** tool into Permanent mode, you can add new zones and services or edit existing ones. To manage services, click the Services tab, select a service, and click the corresponding icon at the bottom of the pane to remove, add, or edit the service. If desired, you can also configure custom ports for an existing service by selecting

TABLE 8-3　Common TCP/IP Ports

Service	Description
amanda-client	The client of the Advanced Maryland Automatic Network Disk Archiver (AMANDA) uses UDP and TCP port 10080.
bacula	An open-source network backup server, which uses TCP ports 9101, 9102, and 9103.
bacula-client	The client for the Bacula server uses TCP port 9102.
dhcp	DHCP is associated with UDP port 67.
dhcpv6-client	The DHCP client on IPv6 is associated with UDP port 546.
dns	The DNS service is associated with port 53, using both TCP and UDP protocols.
ftp	The FTP service is associated with TCP port 21; a Netfilter helper module tracks dynamic connections established for FTP data transfers.
http	The well-known web server uses TCP port 80.
https	Communications to a secure web server over Secure Sockets Layer (SSL) uses TCP port 443.
imaps	IMAP over SSL normally uses TCP port 993.
ipp	The standard network print server client uses TCP and UDP ports 631, based on IPP.
ipp-client	The standard networking print client uses UDP port 631, based on IPP.
ipsec	IPsec uses UDP port 500 for the Internet Security Association and Key Management Protocol (ISAKMP), along with the ESP and AH transport-level protocols.
nfs	NFS version 4 uses TCP port 2049.
openvpn	The open-source Virtual Private Network system, which uses UDP port 1194.
pop3s	POP3 over SSL normally uses TCP port 995.
radius	The Remote Authentication Dial-In User Service (RADIUS) protocol uses UDP ports 1812 and 1813.
samba	The Linux protocol for communication on Microsoft networks uses TCP ports 139 and 445.
samba-client	The Linux protocol for client communication on Microsoft networks uses UDP port 138.
smtp	The SMTP server, such as sendmail or Postfix, uses TCP port 25.
ssh	The SSH server uses TCP port 22.
tftp	Communications with the Trivial File Transfer Protocol (TFTP) server requires UDP port 69.

FIGURE 8-2   Adding custom ports to a service in the firewall-config tool

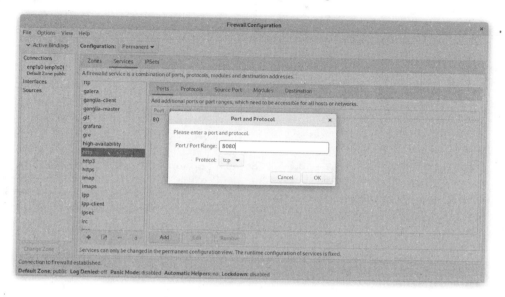

the service's port in the right pane and then clicking the Add or Edit button to open the Port and Protocol dialog box, as shown in Figure 8-2.

The Console firewall-cmd Configuration Tool

The **firewall-cmd** configuration tool has the same features and services as the corresponding GUI tool. In fact, both the graphical **firewall-config** tool and the CLI **firewall-cmd** tool are just client front ends that communicate to **firewalld**.

As with the GUI tool, **firewall-cmd** can display all the available zones and switch to a different default zone. The following example changes the default zone from the public zone to the internal zone:

```
# firewall-cmd --get-default-zone
public
# firewall-cmd --set-default-zone=internal
success
# firewall-cmd --get-default-zone
internal
#
```

The option **--list-all** is particularly useful. It lists all the configured interfaces and services allowed through a zone, as illustrated next:

```
# firewall-cmd --list-all
internal (default, active)
  target: default
```

```
      icmp-block-inversion: no
      interfaces: eth0
      sources:
      services: dhcpv6-client mdns samba-client ssh
      ports:
      protocols:
      masquerade: no
      forward-ports:
      source-ports:
      icmp-blocks:
      rich rules:
  #
```

As with many of the **firewall-cmd** command options, the default zone is assumed if no zone is specified with the **--zone** command switch. You can add and remove ports and services from a zone with the **--add-port**, **--add-service**, **--remove-port**, and **--remove-service** switches, respectively. The next example enables the http service for traffic hitting the dmz zone:

```
  # firewall-cmd --zone=dmz --add-service=http
  success
  #
```

ⓦ a t c h   You want firewall changes that survive after a reboot. To do so with the firewall-cmd **command, use the** --permanent **switch.**

By default, all configuration changes made by **firewall-cmd** do not survive a server reboot. To make a change that survives a reboot, add the **--permanent** switch to **firewall-cmd**. Then, run **firewall-cmd --reload** to implement the change immediately.

EXERCISE 8-1

Adjust Firewall Settings

In this exercise, you'll adjust firewalls from the command-line interface and review the results with the **nmap** and **telnet** commands. Although it does not matter how you address a problem on a Red Hat exam, in this exercise you'll see what happens when adding a new service via the **firewall-cmd** tool. Of course, it's possible to use the graphical **firewall-config** tool to perform the same tasks. This assumes a system with the default **firewalld** configuration described in this chapter.

Note that the Telnet application protocol is unencrypted and therefore is not considered secure. Nevertheless, this example uses the Telnet service to illustrate how to modify firewall settings. In the real world, use SSH rather than Telnet.

1. Check if the **nmap** command is present. If not, run

   ```
   # dnf install nmap
   ```

2. Review current active services on the local system with the **nmap localhost** command. Note the IP address of the local system with the **ip addr** command. If the local system is server1.example.com, that IP address should be 172.16.0.100.

3. Make sure **firewalld** is currently operational with the **systemctl status firewalld** command.

4. Go to a different system. You can do so from a different virtual machine, or you can access it remotely with the **ssh** command. If the tester1.example.com system is running, you can log in to that system with the **ssh 172.16.0.50** command.

5. Use the **nmap** command from tester1 to review what is seen through the firewall; for the noted server1.example.com system, the right command would be **nmap 172.16.0.100**. If the IP address found from Step 2 is different, substitute accordingly.

6. Return to the original system. Run the following commands to install and start the Telnet service:

   ```
   # dnf install telnet-server
   # systemctl start telnet.socket
   ```

7. Run the following command to show the current settings for the default zone:

   ```
   # firewall-cmd --list-all
   ```

8. Allow telnet traffic through the default zone, and include the **--permanent** switch to make the change persistent:

   ```
   # firewall-cmd --permanent --add-service=telnet
   ```

9. Apply the previous change to the run-time configuration of the firewall:

   ```
   # firewall-cmd --reload
   ```

10. Navigate back to the tester1.example.com system as was done in Step 4.

11. Repeat Step 5. What do you see? You should find the Telnet service in the output of the **nmap** command, indicating that the firewall is now permitting connections for this application.

12. Finally, revert the changes:

    ```
    firewall-cmd --permanent --remove-service=telnet
    firewall-cmd --reload
    ```

Firewall Configuration with the Cockpit Web Console

So far, we have seen two methods to modify the firewall configuration: the CLI utility **firewall-cmd** and the GUI tool **firewall-config**. In this exercise, we will explore how to achieve the same configuration of Exercise 8-1, but with the Red Hat Cockpit web console.

You should not be surprised that Red Hat Enterprise Linux offers many ways to achieve the same result. During the RHCSA exam, it is the result that matters, not which tool you use to achieve a configuration. Therefore, you should familiarize yourself with all the methods available to complete a task, and choose the one that most suits you.

1. Install the cockpit RPM package if it is not present:

   ```
   # rpm -q cockpit || dnf install cockpit
   ```

2. Permit the Cockpit service through the firewall:

   ```
   # firewall-cmd --add-service=cockpit --permanent
   # firewall-cmd --reload
   ```

3. Start the Cockpit service:

   ```
   # systemctl enable --now cockpit.socket
   ```

4. Open Firefox and point to the URL https://localhost:9090. Accept the server's certificate and log in with the root account credentials.

5. Click the Networking option in the navigation menu on the left. Then click the Edit Rules And Zones link, as shown next:

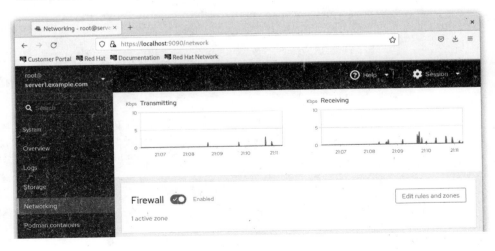

6. Click Add Services to add a service to the zone indicated:

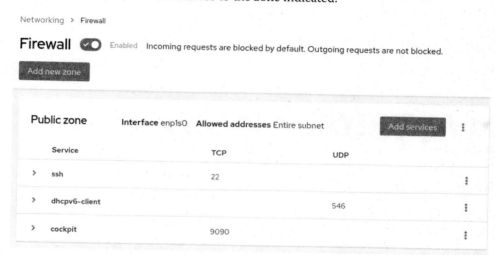

Networking > Firewall

Firewall 🔵 Enabled   Incoming requests are blocked by default. Outgoing requests are not blocked.

Add new zone

Public zone	Interface enp1s0	Allowed addresses Entire subnet		Add services	⋮
Service		**TCP**	**UDP**		
> ssh		22			⋮
> dhcpv6-client			546		⋮
> cockpit		9090			⋮

7. Select the Telnet service from the list and click Add Services:

Add services to public zone   ✕

◉ Services   ○ Custom ports

Filter services [   ]

☐ synergy
   TCP: 24800

☐ syslog
   UDP: 514

☐ syslog-tls
   TCP: 6514   **UDP:** 6514

☑ telnet
   TCP: 23

☐ tentacle
   TCP: 41121

☐ tftp
   UDP: 69

Add services   Cancel

8. The Telnet service was added to both the permanent and runtime configurations. To confirm, run

```
# firewall-cmd --list-all
# firewall-cmd --list-all --permanent
```

Securing SSH with Key-Based Authentication

Chapter 3 addressed SSH client programs, including **ssh**, **scp**, and **sftp**. The focus of this section is on securing SSH access with key-based authentication.

As SSH is an important tool for administering systems remotely, it's important to understand the basics of how it encrypts communication between a client and the SSH server. Then you'll see how to create a public/private key pair so connections won't even put user passwords at risk. But first, it may be helpful to review some basic information about SSH configuration commands and files.

SSH Configuration Commands

There are a few SSH-oriented utilities you need to know about:

- **sshd**   The daemon service; this must be running to receive inbound Secure Shell client requests.
- **ssh-agent**   A program to hold private keys used for Digital Signature Algorithm (DSA), Elliptic Curve DSA (ECDSA), and Rivest, Shamir, Adleman (RSA) authentication. The idea is that the **ssh-agent** command is started in the beginning of an X session or a login session, and other programs are started as clients to the **ssh-agent** program.
- **ssh-add**   Adds private key identities to the authentication agent, **ssh-agent**.
- **ssh**   A secure way to log in to a remote machine, similar to Telnet but with encrypted communications. The basic use of this command was discussed in Chapter 3. To make this work with key-based authentication, you need a private key on the client and a public key on the server. Take the public key file, such as id_rsa.pub, created later in this section, copy it to the server, and place it in the home directory of an authorized user in the ~/.ssh/authorized_keys file.
- **ssh-keygen**   A utility that creates private/public key pairs for SSH authentication. The **ssh-keygen -t** *keytype* command creates a key pair based on the DSA, ECDSA, or RSA protocol.
- **ssh-copy-id**   A script that copies a public key to a target remote system.

SSH Client Configuration Files

Systems configured with SSH include configuration files in two different directories. For the local system, basic SSH configuration files are stored in the /etc/ssh directory. But just as important are the configuration files in each user's home directory in the ~/.ssh/ subdirectory. Those files configure how the given user is allowed to connect to remote systems.

When DSA, ECDSA, and RSA keys are included, the user ~/.ssh/ subdirectory includes the following files:

- **authorized_keys**   Includes a list of public keys from remote users. Users with public encryption keys in this file can connect to remote systems. The system users and names are listed at the end of each public key copied to this file.
- **id_dsa**   Includes the local private key based on the DSA algorithm.
- **id_dsa.pub**   Includes the local public key for the user based on the DSA algorithm.
- **id_ecdsa**   Includes the local private key based on the ECDSA algorithm.
- **id_ecdsa.pub**   Includes the local public key for the user based on the ECDSA algorithm.
- **id_rsa**   Includes the local private key based on the RSA algorithm.
- **id_rsa.pub**   Includes the local public key for the user based on the RSA algorithm.
- **known_hosts**   Contains the public host keys from remote systems. The first time a user logs in to a system, the user is prompted to accept the public key of the remote server. On RHEL 9, the ECDSA protocol is used by default to encrypt traffic. The corresponding public key on the remote server is stored on the /etc/ssh/ssh_host_ecdsa_key.pub file and is added by the client to its local ~/.ssh/known_hosts file.

Basic Encrypted Communication

Basic encryption in computer networking normally requires a private key and a public key. The principle is the same as GNU Privacy Guard (GPG) communications, discussed in Chapter 4. A private key is stored by the owner, and a public key is sent to a third party. When the key pair is properly configured, a user can encrypt a message using their private key, while a third party can decrypt a message with the corresponding public key. This also works in reverse: a third party can encrypt a message using the public key of the receiver, while the receiver can decrypt the message with their private key. In the SSH protocol, the server shares its public key for authentication, and a symmetric session key is mutually established through a key exchange algorithm. This key is used to secure the communication channel.

Encryption keys are based on random numbers. The numbers are so large (typically 2048 bits for RSA keys or more) that the chance someone will break into the server system, at least with a PC, is practically impossible. Private and public encryption keys are based on a matched set of these random numbers.

Private Keys

The private key must be secure. Key-based authentication relies on a private key that is accessible only to the user owner of that key in the ~/.ssh subdirectory of that user's home directory. To authenticate a user, the server sends to the client a "challenge," which is a request to perform an encryption operation that requires the knowledge of the private key. Once the server receives a response to its challenge from the client, it will be able to decrypt the message and prove that the user's identity is genuine.

Public Keys

The public key is just that, publicly available. Public keys are designed to be copied to appropriate users' ~/.ssh/ subdirectories in a file named authorized_keys.

The example shown in Figure 8-3 lists the directories and files associated with SSH usage.

Most of the common issues with SSH key-based authentication are related to file permissions. As shown in Figure 8-3, the permissions for private keys are set to 600 (rw-------) and for public keys are set to 644 (rw-r--r--). In addition, the permissions of the ~/.ssh directory should be 700 (rwx------).

A key is like a password used to encrypt communications data. But it's not a standard password by any means. Imagine trying to remember the 1024-bit number expressed in hexadecimal format shown here:

```
3081 8902 8181 00D4 596E 01DE A012 3CAD 51B7
7835 05A4 DEFC C70B 4382 A733 5D62 A51B B9D6
29EA 860B EC2B 7AB8 2E96 3A4C 71A2 D087 11D0
E149 4DD5 1E20 8382 FA58 C7DA D9B0 3865 FF6E
88C7 B672 51F5 5094 3B35 D8AA BC68 BBEB BFE3
9063 AE75 8B57 09F9 DCF8 FFA4 E32C A17F 82E9
7A4C 0E10 E62D 8A97 0845 007B 169A 0676 E7CF
5713
```

FIGURE 8-3

Keys in a user's .ssh/ subdirectory

```
[michael@server1 ~]$ ls -l .ssh/
total 20
-rw-------. 1 michael michael 1822 Jan  7 21:43 authorized_keys
-rw-------. 1 michael michael  227 Sep 12 20:29 id_ecdsa
-rw-r--r--. 1 michael michael  186 Sep 12 20:29 id_ecdsa.pub
-rw-------. 1 michael michael 1679 Nov  7 18:24 id_rsa
-rw-r--r--. 1 michael michael  406 Nov  7 18:24 id_rsa.pub
-rw-r--r--. 1 michael michael  346 Jan  7 21:44 known_hosts
[michael@server1 ~]$
```

The private key is similar, *but you must keep it private*, or this whole system fails. Keeping it private means no one should have access to the key other than its owner. If your PC is public, secure your private key with a passphrase (password). The procedure to set up a passphrase is described next. Don't forget the passphrase, or you'll have to create a new key pair and again copy your public key to all the target systems.

Set Up a Private/Public Pair for Key-Based Authentication

The **ssh-keygen** command is used to set up a public/private key pair. Although it creates an RSA key by default, it also can be used to create a DSA key or ECDSA key. For example, some users may need DSA keys to comply with certain U.S. government standards. An example of the command sequence is shown in Figure 8-4.

As shown in the figure, the command prompts for an optional passphrase to protect the private key. When the identical passphrase is confirmed, the private key is saved in the id_ rsa file, and the corresponding public key is stored in the id_rsa.pub file. Both files for user michael are stored in the /home/michael/.ssh directory.

If desired, you can set up RSA keys with a larger number of bits. In our testing, we were able to set up key pairs with up to 8192 bits fairly quickly, even on a virtual machine system with just one virtual CPU. The command that starts the process is

```
$ ssh-keygen -b 8192
```

Alternatively, if a DSA key is needed, the following command can help. Only 1024-bit DSA keys are allowed. The process after this command is the same as shown in Figure 8-4.

```
$ ssh-keygen -t dsa
```

FIGURE 8-4   Command to generate an SSH key pair

```
[michael@server1 ~]$ ssh-keygen
Generating public/private rsa key pair.
Enter file in which to save the key (/home/michael/.ssh/id_rsa):
Created directory '/home/michael/.ssh'.
Enter passphrase (empty for no passphrase):
Enter same passphrase again:
Your identification has been saved in /home/michael/.ssh/id_rsa.
Your public key has been saved in /home/michael/.ssh/id_rsa.pub.
The key fingerprint is:
3f:63:1e:4e:0e:82:f1:e9:2c:c3:2b:b8:d7:7e:57:06 michael@server1.example.net
The key's randomart image is:
+--[ RSA 2048]----+
|                 |
|                 |
|                 |
|        E        |
|     .  S.       |
|      + . .o     |
|   . o. + .oB    |
|  . o =o...B +   |
|  .o oo=o.  +    |
+-----------------+
[michael@server1 ~]$ █
```

The next step is to transmit the public key to a remote system. It might be one of the servers you administer. If you're willing to transmit that public key over the network (once per connection), the following command can work:

```
$ ssh-copy-id -i .ssh/id_rsa.pub michael@tester1.example.com
```

Strictly speaking, the **ssh-copy-id** command without the **-i** option defaults to transmitting the most recently created public key. The preceding command automatically appends the noted local RSA key to the end of the *remote* ~/.ssh/authorized_keys file. In this case, that file can be found in the /home/michael directory. Of course, you may choose to substitute the IP address for the hostname.

on the job

Sometimes, after copying a key to a remote system, you may get an "agent admitted failure to sign using the key" error followed by a password prompt when you try to log in. To fix this problem, log out of the console or the GUI and log back in. In most cases, the ssh command will prompt for the passphrase.

You should then be able to immediately connect to that remote system. In the preceding case, the appropriate command is either one of the following:

```
$ ssh -l michael tester1.example.com
$ ssh michael@tester1.example.com
```

When run on a console, the **ssh** command uses the following prompt for the passphrase:

```
Enter passphrase for key '/home/michael/.ssh/id_rsa'
```

When run in a GUI-based command line, it prompts with a window similar to that shown in Figure 8-5.

FIGURE 8-5

Prompt for a passphrase

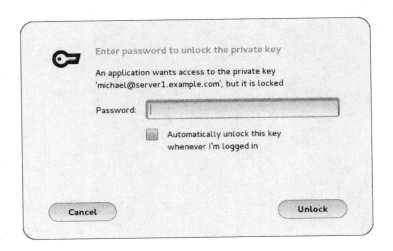

CERTIFICATION OBJECTIVE 8.03

A Security-Enhanced Linux Primer

Security-Enhanced Linux (SELinux) was developed by the U.S. National Security Agency to provide a level of mandatory access control for Linux. It goes beyond the discretionary access control associated with file permissions. In essence, SELinux enforces security rules within the kernel of the operating system. It limits the damage if there is a security breach. For example, if the system account associated with an FTP service is compromised, SELinux makes it more difficult to use that account to compromise other services.

Basic Features of SELinux

The SELinux security model is based on subjects, objects, and actions. A *subject* is a process, such as a running command or an application such as the Apache web server in operation. An *object* is a file, a device, a socket, or in general any resource that can be accessed by a subject. An *action* is what may be done by the subject to the object.

SELinux assigns different contexts to objects. A *context* is just a label, which is used by the SELinux security policy to determine whether a subject's action on an object is allowed or not. For example, the Apache web server process can take objects such as web page files and display them for the clients of the world to see. That action is normally allowed in the RHEL 9 implementation of SELinux, as long as the object files have appropriate SELinux contexts.

The contexts associated with SELinux are fine-grained. In other words, if a "black hat" hacker breaks in and takes over your web server, SELinux contexts prevent that intruder from using that breach to break into other services.

To see the context of a particular file, run the **ls -Z** command. As an example, review what this command does in Figure 8-6, as it displays security contexts in the / directory.

As noted at the beginning of this chapter, six objectives relate to SELinux on the RHCSA exam. You'll explore how to meet these objectives in the following sections.

SELinux Status

As suggested in the RHCSA objectives, you need to know how to "set enforcing and permissive modes for SELinux." There are three available modes for SELinux: *enforcing*, *permissive*, and *disabled*. The enforcing and disabled modes are self-explanatory. SELinux in permissive mode means that any SELinux rules that are violated are logged, but the violation does not stop any action.

FIGURE 8-6 SELinux security contexts of different files

```
[root@server1 ~]# ls -lZ /
total 28
dr-xr-xr-x.   2 root root system_u:object_r:mnt_t:s0          6 Aug  9  2021 afs
lrwxrwxrwx.   1 root root system_u:object_r:bin_t:s0          7 Aug  9  2021 bin -> usr/bin
dr-xr-xr-x.   5 root root system_u:object_r:boot_t:s0      4096 Jan 25 15:36 boot
drwxr-xr-x.  21 root root system_u:object_r:device_t:s0    3400 Apr 30 18:59 dev
drwxr-xr-x. 135 root root system_u:object_r:etc_t:s0       8192 Apr 30 18:22 etc
drwxr-xr-x.  10 root root system_u:object_r:home_root_t:s0  124 Jan 27 05:18 home
lrwxrwxrwx.   1 root root system_u:object_r:lib_t:s0          7 Aug  9  2021 lib -> usr/lib
lrwxrwxrwx.   1 root root system_u:object_r:lib_t:s0          9 Aug  9  2021 lib64 -> usr/lib64
drwxr-xr-x.   2 root root system_u:object_r:mnt_t:s0          6 Aug  9  2021 media
drwxr-xr-x.   2 root root system_u:object_r:mnt_t:s0          6 Aug  9  2021 mnt
drwxr-xr-x.   2 root root system_u:object_r:usr_t:s0          6 Aug  9  2021 opt
dr-xr-xr-x. 303 root root system_u:object_r:proc_t:s0         0 Apr 30 18:59 proc
dr-xr-x---.   8 root root system_u:object_r:admin_home_t:s0 4096 May  1 04:36 root
drwxr-xr-x.  45 root root system_u:object_r:var_run_t:s0   1220 May  1 04:31 run
lrwxrwxrwx.   1 root root system_u:object_r:bin_t:s0          8 Aug  9  2021 sbin -> usr/sbin
drwxr-xr-x.   2 root root system_u:object_r:var_t:s0          6 Aug  9  2021 srv
dr-xr-xr-x.  13 root root system_u:object_r:sysfs_t:s0        0 Apr 30 18:59 sys
drwxrwxrwt.  26 root root system_u:object_r:tmp_t:s0       4096 May  1 04:37 tmp
drwxr-xr-x.  12 root root system_u:object_r:usr_t:s0        144 Jan 25 15:15 usr
drwxr-xr-x.  20 root root system_u:object_r:var_t:s0       4096 Jan 25 15:36 var
[root@server1 ~]#
```

If you want to change the default SELinux mode, change the **SELINUX** directive in the /etc/selinux/config file, as illustrated in Table 8-4. The next time you reboot, the changes are applied to the system.

If SELinux is configured in enforcing mode, it protects systems in one of two ways: in *targeted* mode or in *mls* mode. The default is the targeted policy, which allows you to customize what is protected by SELinux in a fine-grained manner. In contrast, MLS goes a step further, using the Bell–LaPadula model developed for the U.S. Department of Defense. That model supports layers of security between levels c0 and c3. Although the c3 level is listed as "Top Secret," the range of available levels goes all the way up to c1023. Such fine-grained levels of secrecy have yet to be fully developed. If you want to explore MLS, install the selinux-policy-mls RPM.

TABLE 8-4   Standard Directives in /etc/selinux/config

Directive	Description
SELINUX	Basic SELinux status; may be set to enforcing, permissive, or disabled.
SELINUXTYPE	Specifies the level of protection; set to **targeted** by default, where protection is limited to selected "targeted" services. The alternative is **mls**, which is associated with Multi-Level Security (MLS).

on the job

If you just want to experiment with SELinux, configure it in permissive mode. It'll log any violations without stopping anything. It's easy to set up with the SELinux Administration tool, or you can set SELINUX=permissive **in /etc/selinux/config. If the** auditd **service is running, violations are logged in the audit.log file in the /var/log/audit directory. Just remember, Red Hat likely wants candidates to configure SELinux in enforcing mode during the exams.**

SELinux Configuration at the Command Line

SELinux is today a mature piece of software, and it has become much more useful with the releases of RHEL 7 and RHEL 8. Nevertheless, given the complexity associated with SELinux, it may be more efficient for system engineers who are not very familiar with it to use the SELinux Administration tool to configure SELinux settings.

The following sections show how you can configure and manage SELinux from the command-line interface. However, because it's easier to demonstrate the full capabilities of SELinux using GUI tools, a detailed discussion of such capabilities will follow later in this chapter.

Configure Basic SELinux Settings

There are some essential commands that can be used to review and configure basic SELinux settings. To see the current status of SELinux, run the **getenforce** command; it returns one of three self-explanatory options: enforcing, permissive, or disabled. The **sestatus** command provides more information, with output similar to the following:

```
SELinux status:                 enabled
SELinuxfs mount:                /sys/fs/selinux
SELinux root directory:         /etc/selinux
Loaded policy name:             targeted
Current mode:                   enforcing
Mode from config file:          enforcing
Policy MLS status:              enabled
Policy deny_unknown status:     allowed
Memory protection checking:     actual (secure)
Max kernel policy version:      33
```

You can change the current SELinux status with the **setenforce** command; the options are straightforward:

```
# setenforce enforcing
# setenforce permissive
```

This changes the /sys/fs/selinux/enforce boolean. For booleans, you could substitute 1 and 0, respectively, for enforcing and permissive. To make this change permanent, you'll have to modify the **SELINUX** variable in the /etc/selinux/config file. However, changes to detailed SELinux booleans require different commands.

Alternatively, if SELinux is disabled for some reason, the output would be

```
SELinux status:      disabled
```

	If SELinux is disabled, it may	the process is less time-consuming than it
	take a few minutes to reboot a system after	was for the previous RHEL releases.
	setting SELinux in enforcing mode. However,	

In that case, the **setenforce** command does not work. Instead, you have to set
SELINUX=enforcing in the /etc/selinux/config file. And that requires a system reboot
to "relabel" all files, where SELinux labels are applied to each file on the local system.

Configure Regular Users for SELinux

To review the status of current SELinux users, run the **semanage login -l** command. Based
on the default installation of RHEL 9, it leads to the following output:

```
Login Name          SELinux User        MLS/MCS Range       Service
__default__         unconfined_u        s0-s0:c0.c1023      *
root                unconfined_u        s0-s0:c0.c1023      *
```

In other words, regular "default" users have the same SELinux user context of the
root administrative user. To confirm, run the **id -Z** command as a regular user. Without
changes, it leads to the following output, which suggests that the user is not confined by
any SELinux settings:

```
unconfined_u:unconfined_r:unconfined_t:s0-s0:c0.c1023
```

The preceding string defines what is called a *label* in SELinux jargon. A label is made up
of several context strings, separated by a column: a user context (which ends with **_u**), a role
context (which ends with **_r**), a type context (which ends with **_t**), a sensitivity context, and a
category set. The rules of the targeted policy, which is the default SELinux policy in RHEL 9,
are mostly associated with the type (**_t**) context.

Although it may not be an exam requirement, regular users can be confined by SELinux.
When user accounts are compromised, and they will be compromised, you want any damage
that might be caused limited by SELinux rules. The following example specifies a confinement
rule that adds (**-a**) regular user michael, specifying (**-s**) the user_u context for confinement:

```
# semanage login -a -s user_u michael
```

TABLE 8-5	Options for SELinux User Roles

User Context	Features
guest_u	No GUI, no networking, no access to the **su** or **sudo** command, no file execution in /home or /tmp
xguest_u	GUI, networking only via the Firefox web browser, no file execution in /home or /tmp
user_u	GUI and networking available
staff_u	GUI, networking, and the **sudo** command available
sysadm_u	GUI, networking, and the **sudo** and **su** commands available
unconfined_u	Full system access

The user_u role does not have the ability to run the **su** and **sudo** commands, described in Chapter 6. If desired, you can reverse the process with the **semanage login -d michael** command. The available user contexts listed in the latest Red Hat documentation are shown in Table 8-5.

When a user role is changed, it doesn't take effect until the next login. For example, if we were to change the role for user michael to user_u in a GUI-based command line, the change would not take effect until we logged out and logged back in to the GUI. If you were to try this on your system, you would no longer be able to start any administrative configuration tools, and you would not have access to the **sudo** and **su** commands.

On some networks, you may want to change the role of future users to user_u. If you don't want regular users tinkering with administrative tools, you could make that change for future default users with the following command:

```
# semanage login -m -S targeted -s "user_u" -r s0 __default__
```

This command modifies (**-m**) the targeted policy store (**-S**), with SELinux user (**-s**) user_u, with the MLS s0 range (**-r**) for the default user. Here, "__default__" includes two underscore characters on each side of the word. As long as user_u is in effect for the default SELinux user, regular users won't have access to use administrative tools or commands such as **su** and **sudo**. The following command reverses the process:

```
# semanage login -m -S targeted -s "unconfined_u" \
-r s0-s0:c0.c1023 __default__
```

on the
🛈 o b

The MLS policy adds complexity to SELinux. The targeted default policy with appropriate booleans and file contexts normally provides more than adequate security.

The full MLS range is required (s0-s0:c0.c1023) because the unconfined_u user is not normally limited by MLS restrictions.

Manage SELinux Boolean Settings

Most SELinux settings are boolean—in other words, they're activated and deactivated by setting them to 1 or 0, respectively. Once set, the booleans can be retrieved from the /sys/fs/selinux/booleans directory. One simple example is **selinuxuser_ping**, which is normally set to 1, which allows users to run the **ping** and **traceroute** commands. Many of these SELinux settings are associated with specific services.

These settings can be read with the **getsebool** command and modified with the **setsebool** command. For example, the following output from the **getsebool user_exec_content** command confirms that SELinux allows users to execute scripts either in their home directories or from the /tmp directory:

```
# getsebool user_exec_content
user_exec_content --> on
```

This boolean can be disabled either temporarily or in a way that survives a reboot. One method for doing so is with the **setsebool** command. For example, the following command disables the noted boolean until the system is rebooted:

```
# setsebool user_exec_content off
```

You can choose to substitute **0** for **off** in the command. As this is a boolean setting, the effect is the same: the flag is switched off. However, the **-P** switch is required to make the change to the boolean setting survive a system reboot. Be aware that the changes don't take effect until the next time the affected user actually logs in to the associated system.

A full list of available booleans is available in the output to the **getsebool -a** command.

For more information on each boolean, run the **semanage boolean -l** command. The output includes descriptions of all available booleans, and it can be searched with the help of the **grep** command.

List and Identify SELinux File Contexts

If you've enabled SELinux, the **ls -Z** command lists current SELinux file contexts, as shown earlier in Figure 8-6. As an example, take the relevant output for the anaconda-ks.cfg file from the /root directory:

```
# ls -Z /root/anaconda-ks.cfg
system_u:object_r:admin_home_t:s0 anaconda-ks.cfg
```

The output specifies four elements of SELinux security: the user, role, type, and MLS level for the noted file. Generally, the SELinux user associated with a file is system_u or unconfined_u, and this generally does not affect access. In most cases, files are associated with object_r, an object role for the file. It's certainly possible that future versions of the SELinux targeted policy will include more fine-grained options for the user and role.

The key file context is the type, in this case, admin_home_t. If you configure a service such as FTP and HTTP, the files served by the FTP or HTTP service must have appropriate SELinux contexts. You can change the type of files and directories with the **chcon** command.

For example, to configure a nonstandard directory for an FTP server, make sure the context matches the default FTP directory. Consider the following command:

```
# ls -Zdl /var/ftp
drwxr-xr-x. root root system_u:object_r:public_content_t:s0 /var/ftp
```

The contexts are the system user (system_u) and object role (object_r) for type sharing with the public (public_content_t). If you create another directory for FTP service, you'll need to assign the same security contexts to that directory. For example, if you create an /ftp directory as the root user and run the **ls -Zd /ftp** command, you'll see the contexts associated with the /ftp directory as shown:

```
drwxr-xr-x. root  root  unconfined_u:object_r:default_t:s0   /ftp
```

To change the context, use the **chcon** command. If there are subdirectories, you'll want to make sure changes are made recursively with the **-R** switch. In this case, to change the user and type contexts to match /var/ftp, run the following command:

```
# chcon -R -u system_u -t public_content_t /ftp
```

If you want to support uploads to your FTP server, you'll have to assign a different type context, specifically public_content_rw_t. That corresponds to the following command:

```
# chcon -R -u system_u -t public_content_rw_t /ftp
```

You can also use a different variation on the **chcon** command. The following command uses user, role, and context from the /var/ftp directory and applies the changes recursively:

```
# chcon -R --reference /var/ftp /ftp
```

But wait, what happens if a filesystem gets relabeled? The changes made with **chcon** won't survive a filesystem relabeling because all file contexts will be reset to the default values defined in the SELinux policy. Hence, we need a way to modify the rules that define the default file context for each file. This subject will be covered in the next section.

on the job

Using restorecon **is the preferred way to change file contexts because it sets the contexts to the values configured in the SELinux policy. The** chcon **command can modify file contexts to any value passed as an argument, but the change may not survive a filesystem relabeling if a context differs from the default value defined in the SELinux policy. Hence, to avoid mistakes, you should modify contexts in the SELinux policy with** semanage fcontext **and use** restorecon **to change file contexts.**

Restore SELinux File Contexts

Default contexts are configured in /etc/selinux/targeted/contexts/files/file_contexts. If you make a mistake and want to restore the original SELinux settings for a file, the **restorecon** command restores those settings based on the file_contexts configuration file. However, the defaults in a directory may vary. For example, the following command (with the -**F** switch forcing a change to all contexts rather than just the type context) leads to a different set of contexts for the /ftp directory:

```
# restorecon -F /ftp
# ls -Zdl /ftp
drwxr-xr-x.  root   root   system_u:object_r:default_t:s0   ftp
```

You may notice that the user context is different from when the /ftp directory was created. That's due to the first line in the aforementioned file_contexts file, which applies the noted contexts:

```
/.*       system_u:object_r:default_t:s0
```

You may also list all default file contexts rules in file_contexts with the **semanage fcontext -l** command. See Figure 8-7 for an excerpt of the output.

As you can see, SELinux context definitions use regular expressions, such as the following:

```
(/.*)?
```

The preceding regular expression matches the / character, followed by an arbitrary number of characters (the .*). The **?** character means that the entire regular expression within parentheses can be matched zero or one time. Hence, the overall result is to match a / followed by an arbitrary number of characters, or nothing. This regular expression is widely used to match a directory and all the files in it.

As an example, a regular expression that matches the /ftp directory and all files in it is given by the following:

```
/ftp(/.*)?
```

FIGURE 8-7   SELinux context definitions

```
/var/ftp(/.*)?                        all files     system_u:object_r:public_content_t:s0
/var/ftp/bin(/.*)?                    all files     system_u:object_r:bin_t:s0
/var/ftp/etc(/.*)?                    all files     system_u:object_r:etc_t:s0
/var/ftp/lib(/.*)?                    all files     system_u:object_r:lib_t:s0
/var/ftp/lib/ld[^/]*\.so(\.[^/]*)*    regular file  system_u:object_r:ld_so_t:s0
/var/games(/.*)?                      all files     system_u:object_r:games_data_t:s0
/var/imap(/.*)?                       all files     system_u:object_r:cyrus_var_lib_t:s0
/var/kerberos/krb5kdc(/.*)?           all files     system_u:object_r:krb5kdc_conf_t:s0
/var/kerberos/krb5kdc/from_master.*   all files     system_u:object_r:krb5kdc_lock_t:s0
/var/kerberos/krb5kdc/kadm5\.keytab   regular file  system_u:object_r:krb5_keytab_t:s0
/var/kerberos/krb5kdc/principal.*     all files     system_u:object_r:krb5kdc_principal_t:s0
/var/kerberos/krb5kdc/principal.*\.ok all files     system_u:object_r:krb5kdc_lock_t:s0
```

Using this regular expression, you can define an SELinux policy rule that assigns to the /ftp directory and all files in it a default type context. You can do so with the **semanage fcontext -a** command. For example, the following command assigns a default type context of public_content_t to the /ftp directory and all the files in it:

```
# semanage fcontext -a -t public_content_t '/ftp(/.*)?'
```

Once you have defined a new default policy context for a filesystem path, you can run the **restorecon** command to set the contexts to the corresponding default policy values. The following command restores the context recursively (**-R**) to the public_content_t value defined previously:

```
# restorecon -RF /ftp
# ls -Zdl /ftp
drwxr-xr-x.  root  root  system_u:object_r:public_content_t:s0  /ftp
```

EXERCISE 8-3

Configure a New Directory with Appropriate SELinux Contexts

In this exercise, you'll set up a new directory, /ftp, with SELinux contexts that match the standard directory for FTP servers. This exercise demonstrates how to do this with the **chcon** command and shows the effect of using the **restorecon** and **semanage** commands.

1. Create the /ftp directory. Use the **ls -Zd /ftp** command to identify the SELinux contexts on that directory. Contrast that with the contexts on the /var/ftp directory.

2. Change the contexts on the /ftp directory to match those on the /var/ftp directory. The most efficient method is with the following command:

   ```
   # chcon -R --reference /var/ftp /ftp
   ```

   While the **-R** switch is not required, we include it to help you get used to the idea of changing contexts recursively.

3. Run the **ls -Zd /ftp** command to review the changed contexts on that directory. It should now match the contexts on the /var/ftp directory.

4. Run the following command to see what happens when SELinux is relabeled:

   ```
   # restorecon -Rv /ftp
   ```

   What did this command do to the contexts of the /ftp directory?

5. To make changes to the /ftp directory permanent, you need help from the **semanage** command, with the **fcontext** argument. As there is no analog to the **chcon --reference** command switch, the following command specifies the user role and file type, based on the default settings for the /var/ftp directory:

   ```
   # semanage fcontext -a -s system_u -t public_content_t "/ftp(/.*)?"
   ```

6. Review the results. First, the **semanage** command does not change the current SELinux contexts of the /ftp directory. Next, review the contents of file_contexts .local in the /etc/selinux/targeted/contexts/files directory. It should reflect the **semanage** command just executed.

7. Rerun the **restorecon** command from Step 4. Does it change the SELinux contexts of the /ftp directory now?

SELinux Port Labeling

The SELinux policy controls every action that a process can execute on a certain object, such as a file, a device, or a network socket. Opening a TCP socket and listening to a network port is one of those actions you can control and restrict via the SELinux policy.

If one of the services covered in the previous section is configured to listen to a nonstandard port, by default the SELinux targeted policy will deny this action. In fact, SELinux uses labels to control access not only to files or devices but also to network ports.

You can list all SELinux port labels by running the **semanage** command:

```
# semanage port -l
```

Filtering for a certain string can help in identifying which ports a service is allowed to listen to. As shown in the following example, the SSH service is restricted to listening to port 22:

```
# semanage port -l | grep ^ssh
ssh_port_t               tcp          22
```

Similarly, the http_port_t label regulates the ports that Apache can listen to, whereas http_cache_port_t identifies the ports allowed by web proxies:

```
# semanage port -l | grep ^http
http_cache_port_t        tcp          8080, 8118, 8123, 10001-10010
http_cache_port_t        udp          3130
http_port_t              tcp          80, 81, 443, 488, 8008, 8009, ↵
8443, 9000
```

If you need to change a label to allow a service to listen to a nonstandard port, use the **semanage** command. In the following example, the SELinux policy is modified to allow Apache to listen to port 444:

```
# semanage port -a -t http_port_t -p tcp 444
```

Identify SELinux Process Contexts

As you will see in Chapter 9, the **ps** command lists currently running processes. In an SELinux system, there are contexts for each running process. To see those contexts for all processes currently in operation, run the **ps -eZ** command, which lists every (**-e**) process

FIGURE 8-8   SELinux security contexts of different processes

```
system_u:system_r:systemd_logind_t:s0 785 ?        00:00:00 systemd-logind
system_u:system_r:devicekit_disk_t:s0 786 ?        00:00:00 udisksd
system_u:system_r:devicekit_power_t:s0 787 ?       00:00:00 upowerd
system_u:system_r:avahi_t:s0          793 ?        00:00:00 avahi-daemon
system_u:system_r:alsa_t:s0           808 ?        00:00:00 alsactl
system_u:system_r:chronyd_t:s0        818 ?        00:00:00 chronyd
system_u:system_r:modemmanager_t:s0 823 ?          00:00:00 ModemManager
system_u:system_r:firewalld_t:s0      824 ?        00:00:00 firewalld
system_u:system_r:NetworkManager_t:s0 890 ?        00:00:00 NetworkManager
system_u:system_r:cupsd_t:s0-s0:c0.c1023 897 ?     00:00:00 cupsd
system_u:system_r:sshd_t:s0-s0:c0.c1023 899 ?      00:00:00 sshd
system_u:system_r:rhsmcertd_t:s0      900 ?        00:00:00 rhsmcertd
system_u:system_r:rhcd_t:s0           993 ?        00:00:01 rhcd
system_u:system_r:crond_t:s0-s0:c0.c1023 996 ?     00:00:00 atd
system_u:system_r:crond_t:s0-s0:c0.c1023 997 ?     00:00:00 crond
system_u:system_r:xdm_t:s0-s0:c0.c1023 998 ?       00:00:00 gdm
system_u:system_r:rpm_t:s0           1080 ?        00:00:00 rhc-package-man
system_u:system_r:rhcd_t:s0          1081 ?        00:00:19 rhc-worker-play
system_u:system_r:rpm_t:s0           1135 ?        00:00:07 packagekitd
system_u:system_r:NetworkManager_t:s0 1136 ?       00:00:00 wpa_supplicant
system_u:system_r:realmd_t:s0        1345 ?        00:00:00 realmd
system_u:system_r:colord_t:s0        1371 ?        00:00:00 colord
system_u:system_r:vdagent_t:s0       1394 ?        00:00:02 spice-vdagentd
```

SELinux context (-**Z**). Figure 8-8 includes a varied excerpt from the output of that command on our system.

Although the user and role don't change often, the process type varies widely, frequently matching the purpose of the running process. For example, from the figure you can see how the Avahi daemon (avahi-daemon) is matched by the avahi_t SELinux type. You should be able to identify how at least some of the other SELinux types match the associated service.

In other words, although there is a large variety of SELinux types, they're consistent with the name of the running process.

Diagnose and Address SELinux Policy Violations

If SELinux is running in enforcing mode and a problem arises, and you're sure there are no problems with the target service or application, don't disable SELinux! Red Hat has made it easier to manage and troubleshoot. According to Red Hat, the top two causes of SELinux-related problems are contexts and boolean settings.

SELinux Audits

Problems with SELinux should be documented in the associated log file, audit.log, in the /var/log/audit directory. The file may be confusing, especially the first time you read it. A number of tools are available to help decipher this log.

First, the audit search (**ausearch**) command can help filter for specific types of problems. For example, the following command lists all SELinux events associated with the use of the **sudo** command:

```
# ausearch -m avc -c sudo
```

Such events are known as Access Vector Cache (**-m avc**) messages; the **-c** allows you to specify the name commonly used in the log, such as httpd or su. If you've experimented with the user_u SELinux user described earlier in this chapter, there should be several related messages available from the audit.log file.

Even for most administrators, the output is still a lot of gobbledygook. However, it should include identifying information such as the audited user ID (shown as auid), which can help you identify the offending user. Perhaps the user needs such access, or perhaps that user's account has been compromised. In any case, the alert may cause you to pay more attention to that account.

In contrast, the **sealert -a /var/log/audit/audit.log** command may provide more clarity.

SELinux Boolean Issues

After deactivating the user_exec_content boolean described earlier, we created a simple script named script1 for a user governed by the user_u label. After making that script executable, we tried running it with the **/home/examprep/script1** command. Even though that user had ownership of the file, with executable permissions set, that attempt led to the following message:

```
-bash: /home/examprep/script1: Permission denied
```

That led to the log excerpt from /var/log/messages shown in Figure 8-9. Note that the message explicitly cites the command required to address the problem. As an administrator, you need to decide whether such users should be given the ability to execute their own scripts. If so, then the noted command would address the problem.

FIGURE 8-9   An SELinux alert and a solution

```
May  1 05:41:15 localhost setroubleshoot[7783]: SELinux is preventing /usr/bin/bash from exec
ute access on the file script1. For complete SELinux messages run: sealert -l 25bad1ab-edb9-4
6e4-905f-465baec7f2a1
May  1 05:41:15 localhost setroubleshoot[7783]: SELinux is preventing /usr/bin/bash from exec
ute access on the file script1.#012#012***** Plugin catchall_boolean (89.3 confidence) sugge
sts  ******************#012#012If you want to allow user to exec content#012Then you must te
ll SELinux about this by enabling the 'user_exec_content' boolean.#012#012Do#012setsebool -P
user_exec_content 1#012#012*****  Plugin catchall (11.6 confidence) suggests   **************
*************#012#012If you believe that bash should be allowed execute access on the script1
file by default.#012Then you should report this as a bug.#012You can generate a local policy
module to allow this access.#012Do#012allow this access for now by executing:#012# ausearch -
c 'bash' --raw | audit2allow -M my-bash#012# semodule -X 300 -i my-bash.pp#012
```

The GUI SELinux Administration Tool

If you've taken the time to learn SELinux from the command line, this section should be just a review. For many users, the easiest way to change SELinux settings is with the SELinux Administration tool, which you can start with the **system-config-selinux** command. If the command is not available, install the tool by running

```
# dnf install policycoreutils-gui
```

As shown in Figure 8-10, the tool shows a basic view of the status of SELinux on the local system, reflecting some of the information shown in the output to the **sestatus** command.

As you can see, there are options labeled System Default Enforcing Mode and Current Enforcing Mode, which you can set to Enforcing, Permissive, or Disabled. Generally, you don't need to activate the Relabel On Next Reboot option unless you've changed the default policy type.

Three of the categories shown in the left pane of the SELinux Administration tool window are described in the following sections. The other categories are out of scope of the RHCSA exam.

FIGURE 8-10   SELinux status in the Administration tool

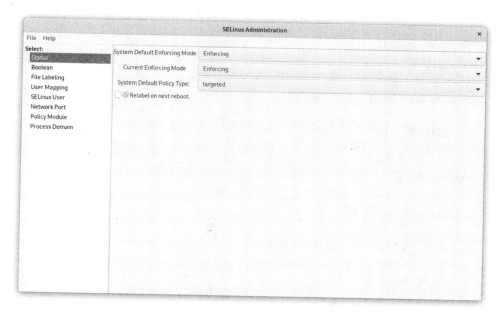

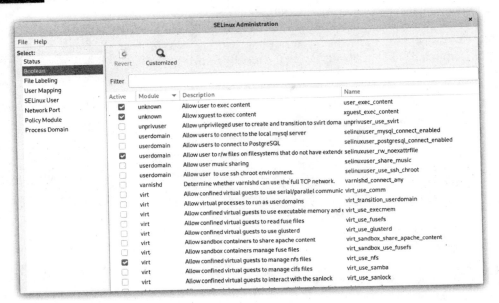

FIGURE 8-11 Booleans in the SELinux Administration tool

SELinux Boolean Settings

In the SELinux Administration tool, click Boolean in the left panel, as shown in Figure 8-11. Scroll through available modules. As you can see, an SELinux policy can be modified in a number of different categories, some related to administrative functions, others to specific services. A select number of these options are shown in Figure 8-11. Any changes you make are reflected in boolean variables in the /sys/fs/selinux/booleans directory. Module categories of interest for the RHCSA exam include cron, mount, virt, and that catch-all category: unknown. A list of selected booleans is included in Table 8-6. The booleans appear in the order shown in the SELinux Administration tool.

File Labeling

Clicking File Labeling in the left panel of the SELinux Administration tool enables you to change the default labels associated with files, some of which are described earlier in this chapter (and in other chapters discussing SELinux contexts). Some of the options are shown in Figure 8-12. Any changes to this screen are written to the file_contexts.local file in the /etc/selinux/targeted/contexts/files directory.

TABLE 8-6   Selected SELinux Boolean Options

Boolean	Description
fcron_crond	Supports fcron rules for job scheduling
cron_can_relabel	Allows cron jobs to change the SELinux file context labels
mount_anyfile	Permits the use of the **mount** command on any directory or file
daemons_use_tty	Lets service daemons use terminals as needed
daemons_dump_core	Supports writing of core files to the top-level root directory
virt_use_nfs	Supports the use of NFS filesystems for virtual machines
virt_use_comm	Supports a connection for virtual machines to serial and parallel ports
virt_use_usb	Supports the use of USB devices for virtual machines
virt_use_samba	Supports the use of CIFS (Common Internet File System) filesystems for virtual machines
user_exec_content	Gives user_u users the right to execute scripts

FIGURE 8-12   File types in the SELinux Administration tool

Network Port

The Network Port section of the SELinux Administration tool associates standard ports with services.

SCENARIO & SOLUTION	
The SSH service is not accessible on a server.	Assuming the SSH service is running (an RHCSA requirement), make sure the firewall supports SSH access with the **firewall-cmd --list-all** command; revise as needed with the **firewall-config** tool.
Enforcing mode is not set for SELinux.	Set enforcing mode with the **setenforce enforcing** command. Check the default boot settings in /etc/selinux/config.
Need to restore SELinux default file contexts on a directory.	Apply the **restorecon -F** command to the target directory. Use the **-R** switch to change the contexts recursively for all files and subdirectories.
Unexpected failure when SELinux is set in enforcing mode.	Use the **sealert -a /var/log/audit/audit.log** command to find more information about the failure; sometimes a suggested solution is included.
Need to change SELinux options.	Apply the **setsebool -P** command to the appropriate boolean setting.

CERTIFICATION SUMMARY

This chapter focused on the basics of RHCSA-level security. On any Linux system, security starts with the ownership and permissions associated with a file. Firewalls can prevent communication on all but the desired ports. Standard ports for most services are defined in the /etc/services file. However, some services may not use all of the protocols defined in that file. The default RHEL 9 firewall supports access only to a local SSH server.

The **ssh-keygen** command creates passphrase-protected key pairs, which can be used to authenticate to an SSH server without transmitting a user's password over the network.

SELinux provides another layer of protection using mandatory access control. With a variety of available objects and file types, SELinux controls can help ensure that a breach in one service doesn't lead to trouble with other services.

TWO-MINUTE DRILL

Here are some of the key points from the certification objectives in Chapter 8.

Basic Firewall Control

❑ **firewalld** is based on the Netfilter kernel system and on Nftables.

❑ You can find some of the common ports and protocols in /etc/services.

❑ The default RHEL 9 firewall supports remote access to the local SSH server.

❑ The RHEL 9 firewall can be configured with the GUI **firewall-config** tool or the CLI **firewall-cmd** tool.

Securing SSH with Key-Based Authentication

❑ SSH key authentication commands include **ssh-keygen** and **ssh-copy-id**.

❑ User home directories include their own .ssh subdirectory of configuration files, with private and public SSH keys.

❑ Private/public key pairs can be configured with passphrases using the **ssh-keygen** command.

❑ Public keys can be transmitted to users' home directories on remote systems with the **ssh-copy-id** command.

A Security-Enhanced Linux Primer

❑ SELinux may be configured in enforcing, permissive, or disabled mode, with targeted or MLS policies, with the help of the **setenforce** command. Default boot settings are stored in the /etc/selinux/config file.

❑ SELinux labels contain different contexts, such as user, roles, types, and MLS levels.

❑ SELinux booleans can be managed with the **setsebool** command; permanent changes require the -**P** switch.

❑ SELinux contexts can be changed with the **chcon** command and restored to defaults with the **restorecon** command.

❑ The **sealert** command can be used to interpret problems documented in the audit.log file in the /var/log/audit directory.

SELF TEST

The following questions will help you measure your understanding of the material presented in this chapter. As no multiple-choice questions appear on the Red Hat exams, no multiple-choice questions appear in this book. These questions exclusively test your understanding of the chapter. Getting results, not memorizing trivia, is what counts on the Red Hat exams. There may be more than one right answer to many of these questions.

Basic Firewall Control

1. What TCP/IP port number is associated with the HTTPS service?
2. What is the full **firewall-cmd** command to permanently allow incoming HTTPS traffic for the default **firewalld** zone?
3. How do you reload firewall rules without restarting the **firewalld** service?

Securing SSH with Key-Based Authentication

4. What command configures a private/public key pair using DSA?
5. What subdirectory of a user home directory contains the authorized_keys file?

A Security-Enhanced Linux Primer

6. What command configures SELinux in enforcing mode?
7. What command lists all boolean settings for SELinux?
8. What command adds TCP port 4443 to the http_port_t label?
9. How do you restore default SELinux security contexts to a file?

LAB QUESTIONS

Red Hat presents its exams electronically. For that reason, the labs in this chapter are available from the companion website that accompanies the book. In case you haven't yet set up RHEL 9 on a system, refer to Chapter 1 for installation instructions. The answers for the labs follow the Self Test answers.

SELF TEST ANSWERS

Basic Firewall Control

1. The TCP/IP port number associated with the HTTPS service is 443.

2. The **firewall-cmd** command that permanently allows incoming HTTPS traffic for the default **firewalld** zone is

```
# firewall-cmd --permanent --add-service=https
```

3. Use **firewall-cmd --reload** to reload the firewall rules without restarting the service.

Securing SSH with Key-Based Authentication

4. The command that configures a private/public key pair using DSA is

```
ssh-keygen -t dsa
```

5. Every user with public keys stored in the authorized_keys file can find that file in the .ssh/ subdirectory of the user's home directory.

A Security-Enhanced Linux Primer

6. The command that configures SELinux in enforcing mode is

```
# setenforce enforcing
```

7. The command that lists all boolean settings for SELinux is

```
# semanage boolean -l
```

8. The command that adds TCP port 4443 to the http_port_t label is

```
# semanage port -a -t http_port_t -p tcp 4443
```

9. Run **restorecon -v /path/to/file** to restore the default SELinux security context for the specified file.

LAB ANSWERS

Lab 1

This lab is designed to raise awareness of the time and effort required to disable and re-enable SELinux in enforcing mode. If you switch between disabled and permissive mode, the time and effort required should be about the same. If you have to reconfigure SELinux in enforcing mode, you may lose precious time during a Red Hat exam because nothing else can be done while the system is being rebooted and relabeled.

Lab 2

In this lab you learn how to configure a firewall for a web server.

1. On server1.example.com, confirm that SELinux is running in enforcing mode with the following command:

    ```
    # systemctl status firewalld
    ```

2. Install the httpd RPM package:

    ```
    # dnf install -y httpd
    ```

3. Start and enable the httpd service to start at boot:

    ```
    # systemctl start --now httpd
    ```

    On server1.example.com, open Firefox and point the browser to the URL http://localhost. You should see the default web page. Try opening the same page from tester1.example.com, using the IP address of the web server (i.e., http://172.16.0.100). What output do you get?

4. Check the current firewall zone and set the zone to dmz:

    ```
    # firewall-cmd --get-default-zone
    # firewall-cmd --set-default-zone dmz
    ```

5. Add the http service to the current default zone:

    ```
    # firewall-cmd --permanent --add-service=http
    # firewall-cmd --reload
    ```

6. From tester1.example.com, point the Firefox browser to http://172.16.0.100 (substitute accordingly if the IP address of your server1.example.com machine differs). You should see the default test page of the web server.

7. Remember that during Red Hat exams, all changes must survive a system reboot. Reboot your system and check if you can still access the web server's test page. If not, you may have forgotten to enable Apache to start at boot or to make your firewall changes permanent.

Lab 3

In this lab you run the web server on TCP port 81 rather than on port 80. To do so, you will have to update the http service on the firewall to allow port 81 in addition to the default port 80.

1. Open the /etc/httpd/conf/httpd.conf file and change the **Listen 80** directive to **Listen 81**.

2. Restart the httpd service:

```
# systemctl restart httpd
```

3. The test web page should be visible from the local server1 machine after you point the browser to http://localhost:81.

4. From another system such as tester1, you should not be able to load the page.

5. From the GNOME terminal, run **firewall-config** on server1. Select Permanent from the Configuration drop-down menu. Then, select the Services tab, scroll until you find the http service, click Add, and enter **81** for the port number in the window. Choose Options | Reload Firewalld to reload the configuration. If you performed all the changes correctly, you should be able to load the test web page from tester1.

6. Next, reboot server1:

```
# reboot
```

Lab 4

This lab is similar to Lab 3, but because you'll be running the web server on a nonstandard port, you will need to configure SELinux to label the new port.

1. Open the /etc/httpd/conf/httpd.conf file and change the **Listen** directive to **Listen 82**.

2. Restart the httpd service:

```
# systemctl restart httpd
```

After restarting the web service, you should see an error. The error message suggests to run the **journalctl -xeu httpd.service** command. If you do so and check the logs, you will find that the server cannot bind to TCP port 82. A similar error should also appear in /var/log/messages, but in this case you should also notice that the error is caused by SELinux. This is because TCP port 82 is not included in the list of ports for the http_port_t type:

```
# semanage port -l | grep http_port_t
```

To fix this, run the following command:

```
# semanage port -a -t http_port_t -p tcp 82
```

Then, start the httpd service. This time, you should not see any errors:

```
# systemctl start httpd
```

3. From the GNOME terminal, run **firewall-config** on server1. Select Permanent from the Configuration drop-down menu. Then, select the Services tab, scroll until you find the http service, click Add, and enter **82** for the port number in the window. Choose Options | Reload Firewalld to reload the configuration.

4. If you performed all the changes correctly, you should be able to load the test web page from tester1.

Lab 5

This lab assumes that you have completed the configuration of the Apache web server that you have set up from the previous labs.

1. Open the /etc/httpd/conf/httpd.conf file and change the **Listen** directive to **Listen 80**.

2. Restart the httpd service:

```
# systemctl restart httpd
```

3. Create the new web page as suggested in the lab instructions:

```
# echo "Hello world!" > /var/www/html/index.html
```

4. If successful, you should see the new test web page from a browser running on tester1.example.com and pointing to the URL http://172.16.0.100 (substitute for the IP address of server1, if different).

5. Create the directory /html:

```
# mkdir /html
```

6. You should have modified the **DocumentRoot** directive and added a new stanza to the /etc/httpd/conf/httpd.conf file, which should look as shown next:

```
DocumentRoot "/html"
<Directory "/html">
  Require all granted
  Options Indexes
</Directory>
```

7. Create the new web page as suggested in the lab instructions:

```
# echo "A new test page" > /html/index.html
```

8. Restart the httpd service:

```
# systemctl restart httpd
```

9. You should not be able to display the new test page from a browser. If you look in /var/log/messages, you should find an error from SELinux stating that SELinux is preventing /usr/sbin/httpd from getattr access on the file /html/index.html. This is because the file does not have the right SELinux contexts. You can set the correct context by copying that of /var/www/html as a reference:

```
# chcon -R --reference /var/www/html /html
```

This will fix the issue, but the change will not survive a relabeling of the filesystem. To make the change persistent, check the file context on the /var/www/html directory (**ls -dZ /var/www/html**), and define a new file context rule to apply the same context to /html, as shown next:

```
# semanage fcontext -a -t httpd_sys_content_t '/html(/.*)'
```

Lab 6

1. On tester1.example.com, create the user bob:

```
# useradd bob
# echo changeme | passwd --stdin bob
```

2. On tester1, generate a new SSH key pair for user bob:

```
# su - bob
$ ssh-keygen
```

3. On server1.example.com, create the user alice:

```
# useradd alice
# echo changeme | passwd --stdin alice
```

4. On tester1 as user bob, copy the public SSH key to user alice's home directory on server1 (substitute the IP address with that of your instance of server1, if different):

```
$ ssh-copy-id alice@172.16.0.100
```

5. Finally, bob on tester1 should be able to SSH to alice@172.16.0.100 without being prompted for a password (substitute the IP address with that of your instance of server1, if different).

Chapter 9

System Administration Tasks

T his chapter covers functional system administration tasks not already covered in other chapters. The chapter starts with a discussion of process management and continues with system tuning. It then covers the creation and management of archive files.

In addition, this chapter helps you automate repetitive system administration tasks. Some of these tasks happen when you want to have a "life," others when you'd rather be asleep. In this chapter, you'll learn how to schedule both one-time and periodic execution of jobs. This is made possible with the **cron** and **at** daemons. In this case, "at" is not a preposition, but a service that monitors a system for one-time scheduled jobs. In a similar fashion, cron is a service that monitors a system for regularly scheduled jobs.

Bash scripting is also highlighted as an indispensable tool for automation, enabling you to create complex workflows and automate multi-step tasks efficiently.

When you're troubleshooting, system logging often provides the clues you need to solve a lot of problems. The focus in this chapter is local logging.

INSIDE THE EXAM

Resource Management and System Tuning

Administrators work on Linux systems in a number of ways. In this chapter, you'll learn various methods for meeting the following RHCSA objectives. The first of these objectives involves identifying resource-intensive processes and taking corrective actions, such as adjusting process scheduling or setting a system tuning profile:

- Identify CPU/memory-intensive processes and kill processes

These other objectives are more closely related to system administration:

- Adjust process scheduling
- Manage tuning profiles

Archives and Compression

Commands such as **tar** and **gzip** are often used for system backups. Therefore, they are essential tools for a system administrator. The corresponding RCHSA objective is

- Archive, compress, unpack, and uncompress files using **tar**, **star**, **gzip**, and **bzip2**

Running Tasks on a Schedule: cron and at

By default, every RHEL 9 system comes with preconfigured jobs that run on a schedule to perform essential maintenance tasks. System administrators can manage those jobs and configure new ones using the **at** and **cron** commands, as listed in the following exam objective:

- Schedule tasks using **at** and **cron**

Bash Scripts

The automation of system administration tasks is perhaps the most important skill for a system administrator. That means that you should be able to create shell scripts. And because the default shell of RHEL 9 is the Bourne-again shell (or bash), that means that you need to know how to write scripts using bash. There are four RHCSA objectives related to this skill:

■ Conditionally execute code (use of: **if**, **test**, [], etc.)

■ Use Looping constructs (**for**, etc.) to process file, command line input

■ Process script inputs ($1, $2, etc.)

■ Processing output of shell commands within a script

Local Log Files

Finally, you will look at where to find information logged by the systemd journal and rsyslog. The related RHCSA objectives are

■ Locate and interpret system log files and journals

■ Preserve system journals

CERTIFICATION OBJECTIVE 9.01

Resource Management and System Tuning

Several system administration commands in the RHCSA objectives are not covered in previous chapters. They're associated with process management and system tuning. Process management commands allow you to see what processes are running, to check the resources they're using, and to kill or restart those processes. System tuning profiles apply special configuration settings to optimize a system's performance for a specific usage, such as a desktop or a database server.

System Resource Management Commands

Linux includes a variety of commands that can help you identify those processes that are running on a system. The most basic of those commands is **ps**, which provides a snapshot of currently running processes. Those processes can be ranked with the **top** command, which can display running Linux tasks in order of their resource usage. With **top**, you can identify those processes that are using the most CPU and RAM memory. Commands that can adjust process priority include **nice** and **renice**. Sometimes it's not enough to adjust process priority, at which point it may be appropriate to send a signal to a process with commands such as **kill** and **killall**. If you need to monitor system usage, the **sar** and **iostat** commands can also be helpful.

The objectives related to system resource management are to "identify CPU/memory-intensive processes and kill processes" and to "adjust process scheduling."

Process Management with the ps Command

It's important to know what's running on a Linux computer. To help with that task, the **ps** command has a number of useful switches. When you're trying to diagnose a problem, one common practice is to start with the complete list of running processes and then look for a specific program. For example, if the Firefox web browser were unresponsive and using most of CPU cycles, you'd want to kill any associated processes. The **ps aux | grep [f]irefox** command could then help you identify the process(es) that you need to kill. Note the square brackets around "f": these prevent the **grep** command itself from appearing in the results when searching for the **firefox** process. It's a technique used to exclude the **grep** process from the output.

The pgrep **command is also useful because it combines the features of** ps **and** grep. **In this case, the** pgrep -a firefox **command is functionally equivalent to** ps aux | grep firefox.

The **ps** command by itself is usually not enough. All it does is identify those processes running in the current terminal. This command typically returns just the process associated with the current shell and the **ps** command process itself.

To identify those processes associated with a username, the **ps -u** *username* command can help. Sometimes there are specific users who may be problematic for various reasons. So if you're suspicious of user mjang, the following command can help you review every process currently associated with that user:

```
$ ps -u mjang
```

As an administrator, you may choose to focus on a specific account for various reasons, such as activity revealed by the **top** command, described in the next section. Alternatively, you may want to audit all currently running processes with a command such as the following:

```
$ ps aux
```

The **ps aux** command gives a more complete database of currently running processes, in order of their PIDs. The **a** option lists all running processes, the **u** option displays the output

FIGURE 9-1   Output from the ps aux command

```
[root@server1 ~]# ps aux
USER        PID %CPU %MEM    VSZ    RSS TTY      STAT START    TIME COMMAND
root          1  0.3  0.4 106532 16124 ?        Ss   16:26    0:00 /usr/lib/systemd/systemd rhgb
root          2  0.0  0.0      0     0 ?        S    16:26    0:00 [kthreadd]
root          3  0.0  0.0      0     0 ?        I<   16:26    0:00 [rcu_gp]
root          4  0.0  0.0      0     0 ?        I<   16:26    0:00 [rcu_par_gp]
root          5  0.0  0.0      0     0 ?        I<   16:26    0:00 [slub_flushwq]
root          6  0.0  0.0      0     0 ?        I<   16:26    0:00 [netns]
root          7  0.0  0.0      0     0 ?        I    16:26    0:00 [kworker/0:0-cgroup_destroy]
root          8  0.0  0.0      0     0 ?        I<   16:26    0:00 [kworker/0:0H-events_highpri]
root          9  0.0  0.0      0     0 ?        I    16:26    0:00 [kworker/u4:0-events_unbound]
root         10  0.0  0.0      0     0 ?        I<   16:26    0:00 [mm_percpu_wq]
root         11  0.2  0.0      0     0 ?        I    16:26    0:00 [kworker/u4:1-events_unbound]
root         12  0.0  0.0      0     0 ?        I    16:26    0:00 [rcu_tasks_kthre]
root         13  0.0  0.0      0     0 ?        I    16:26    0:00 [rcu_tasks_rude_]
root         14  0.0  0.0      0     0 ?        I    16:26    0:00 [rcu_tasks_trace]
root         15  0.0  0.0      0     0 ?        S    16:26    0:00 [ksoftirqd/0]
root         16  0.0  0.0      0     0 ?        I    16:26    0:00 [rcu_preempt]
root         17  0.0  0.0      0     0 ?        S    16:26    0:00 [migration/0]
root         18  0.0  0.0      0     0 ?        I    16:26    0:00 [kworker/0:1-events]
root         19  0.0  0.0      0     0 ?        S    16:26    0:00 [cpuhp/0]
root         20  0.0  0.0      0     0 ?        S    16:26    0:00 [cpuhp/1]
root         21  0.0  0.0      0     0 ?        S    16:26    0:00 [migration/1]
root         22  0.0  0.0      0     0 ?        S    16:26    0:00 [ksoftirqd/1]
root         23  0.0  0.0      0     0 ?        I    16:26    0:00 [kworker/1:0-cgroup_destroy]
root         24  0.0  0.0      0     0 ?        I<   16:26    0:00 [kworker/1:0H-events_highpri]
root         26  0.0  0.0      0     0 ?        S    16:26    0:00 [kdevtmpfs]
```

in a user-oriented format, and the **x** option lifts the standard limitation that listed processes must be associated with a terminal or console. One example is shown in Figure 9-1. While the output can include hundreds of processes and more, the output can be redirected for further analysis with commands such as **grep**. The output columns shown in Figure 9-1 are described in Table 9-1.

Incidentally, you may note that the **ps aux** command does not include the familiar dash in front of the **aux** switches. In this case, the command works with and without the dash (although slightly differently). Valid command options with the dash are also known as UNIX or POSIX style; in contrast, options without the dash are known as BSD style. The following alternative includes current environment variables for each process:

```
$ ps eux
```

Processes can be organized in a tree format. Specifically, the first process, with a PID of 1, is systemd. That process is the base of the tree, which may be shown with the **pstree** command. In a few cases, it's not possible to use a standard **kill** command to kill a process. In such cases, look for the "parent" of the process in the tree. You can identify the parent of a process, known as the PPID, with the following command:

```
$ ps axl
```

The **l** switch displays the output in long format and is not compatible with the **u** switch. You can view the PID and PPIDs of all running processes as shown in Figure 9-2.

TABLE 9-1	Columns of Output from ps aux
Column Title	**Description**
USER	The username associated with the process.
PID	Process identifier.
%CPU	CPU usage, as a percentage of time spent running during the entire lifetime of the process.
%MEM	Current RAM usage.
VSZ	Virtual memory size of the process in KiB.
RSS	Resident Set Size in KiB (the physical memory in use by the process, not including swap space).
TTY	Associated terminal console.
STAT	Process state.
START	Start time of the process. If you just see a date, the process started more than 24 hours ago.
TIME	Cumulative CPU time used.
COMMAND	Command associated with the process, including all its arguments.

FIGURE 9-2 Output from the ps axl command

```
[root@server1 ~]# ps axl
F   UID   PID  PPID PRI  NI    VSZ   RSS WCHAN  STAT TTY        TIME COMMAND
4     0     1     0  20    0 106532 16092 ep_pol Ss   ?          0:00 /usr/lib/systemd/system
1     0     2     0  20    0      0     0 kthrea S    ?          0:00 [kthreadd]
1     0     3     2   0  -20      0     0 rescue I<   ?          0:00 [rcu_gp]
1     0     4     2   0  -20      0     0 rescue I<   ?          0:00 [rcu_par_gp]
1     0     5     2   0  -20      0     0 rescue I<   ?          0:00 [slub_flushwq]
1     0     6     2   0  -20      0     0 rescue I<   ?          0:00 [netns]
1     0     8     2   0  -20      0     0 worker I<   ?          0:00 [kworker/0:0H-events_hi
1     0    10     2   0  -20      0     0 rescue I<   ?          0:00 [mm_percpu_wq]
1     0    12     2  20    0      0     0 rcu_ta I    ?          0:00 [rcu_tasks_kthre]
1     0    13     2  20    0      0     0 rcu_ta I    ?          0:00 [rcu_tasks_rude_]
1     0    14     2  20    0      0     0 rcu_ta I    ?          0:00 [rcu_tasks_trace]
1     0    15     2  20    0      0     0 smpboo S    ?          0:00 [ksoftirqd/0]
1     0    16     2  20    0      0     0 rcu_gp I    ?          0:00 [rcu_preempt]
1     0    17     2 -100   -      0     0 smpboo S    ?          0:00 [migration/0]
1     0    19     2  20    0      0     0 smpboo S    ?          0:00 [cpuhp/0]
1     0    20     2  20    0      0     0 smpboo S    ?          0:00 [cpuhp/1]
1     0    21     2 -100   -      0     0 smpboo S    ?          0:00 [migration/1]
1     0    22     2  20    0      0     0 smpboo S    ?          0:00 [ksoftirqd/1]
1     0    23     2  20    0      0     0 worker I    ?          0:00 [kworker/1:0-cgroup_des
1     0    24     2   0  -20      0     0 worker I<   ?          0:00 [kworker/1:0H-events_hi
5     0    26     2  20    0      0     0 devtmp S    ?          0:00 [kdevtmpfs]
1     0    27     2   0  -20      0     0 rescue I<   ?          0:00 [inet_frag_wq]
1     0    28     2  20    0      0     0 kaudit S    ?          0:00 [kauditd]
1     0    29     2  20    0      0     0 watchd S    ?          0:00 [khungtaskd]
1     0    30     2  20    0      0     0 oom_re S    ?          0:00 [oom_reaper]
```

With the **-Z** switch (that's an uppercase Z), the **ps** command can also identify the SELinux contexts associated with a process. For example, the **ps -efZ** command includes the SELinux contexts of each process at the start of the output. If you've read Chapter 8, the contexts should already seem familiar. For example, consider the context of the vsFTP server process in the following excerpt:

```
system_u:system_r:ftpd_t:s0-s0:c0.c1023 2059 ? Ss 0:00 ↵
/usr/sbin/vsftpd /etc/vsftpd/vsftpd.conf
```

Contrast that with the context of the **vsftpd** executable. The actual vsFTP process runs under the system_r role, while the executable has role object_r:

```
-rwxr-xr-x. root root system_u:object_r:ftpd_exec_t:s0 ↵
/usr/sbin/vsftpd
```

As you can see, context types are also different. The **vsftpd** process runs with context type ftpd_t, while, the **vsftpd** executable has context type ftpd_exec_t. The role of different daemons and their corresponding executable files should match and contrast in a similar fashion.

View Loads with the top Task Browser

The **top** command sorts active processes first by their CPU load and RAM memory usage. Take a look at Figure 9-3. It provides an overview of the current system status, starting with the current uptime, number of connected users, active and sleeping tasks, CPU load, and more. The output is, in effect, a task browser.

FIGURE 9-3   Output from the top command

```
top - 16:41:37 up 14 min,  1 user,  load average: 0.09, 0.06, 0.06
Tasks: 246 total,   2 running, 244 sleeping,   0 stopped,   0 zombie
%Cpu(s): 14.1 us,   1.3 sy,   0.0 ni,  83.6 id,   0.3 wa,   0.3 hi,   0.2 si,   0.2 st
MiB Mem :   3662.2 total,    325.3 free,   2105.7 used,   1517.4 buff/cache
MiB Swap:   2048.0 total,   1960.3 free,     87.7 used.   1556.5 avail Mem

  PID USER      PR  NI    VIRT    RES    SHR S  %CPU  %MEM     TIME+ COMMAND
 6747 root      20   0  544180  83100  32604 R  14.7   2.2   0:00.66 dnf
 2002 alex      20   0 4081832 363460 138800 S  10.0   9.7   0:25.92 gnome-shell
 6342 alex      20   0 3412064 409184 154892 S   3.7  10.9   0:07.20 firefox
 6594 alex      20   0 2669732 127320 101388 S   1.0   3.4   0:00.42 Privileged Cont
 2696 alex      20   0  847492  55028  40712 S   0.7   1.5   0:03.64 gnome-terminal-
    1 root      20   0  173392  16936   9788 S   0.0   0.5   0:00.77 systemd
    2 root      20   0       0      0      0 S   0.0   0.0   0:00.00 kthreadd
    3 root       0 -20       0      0      0 I   0.0   0.0   0:00.00 rcu_gp
    4 root       0 -20       0      0      0 I   0.0   0.0   0:00.00 rcu_par_gp
    5 root       0 -20       0      0      0 I   0.0   0.0   0:00.00 slub_flushwq
    6 root       0 -20       0      0      0 I   0.0   0.0   0:00.00 netns
    8 root       0 -20       0      0      0 I   0.0   0.0   0:00.00 kworker/0:0H-events_hig+
   10 root       0 -20       0      0      0 I   0.0   0.0   0:00.00 mm_percpu_wq
   12 root      20   0       0      0      0 I   0.0   0.0   0:00.00 rcu_tasks_kthre
   13 root      20   0       0      0      0 I   0.0   0.0   0:00.00 rcu_tasks_rude_
   14 root      20   0       0      0      0 I   0.0   0.0   0:00.00 rcu_tasks_trace
   15 root      20   0       0      0      0 S   0.0   0.0   0:00.01 ksoftirqd/0
   16 root      20   0       0      0      0 I   0.0   0.0   0:00.07 rcu_preempt
   17 root      rt   0       0      0      0 S   0.0   0.0   0:00.00 migration/0
   19 root      20   0       0      0      0 S   0.0   0.0   0:00.00 cpuhp/0
```

| TABLE 9-2 | Additional Columns of Output from top |

Column Title	Description
PR	The priority of the task. For more information, see the **nice** and **renice** commands.
NI	The nice value of the task, an adjustment to the priority.
VIRT	The virtual memory in KiB used by the task.
RES	Resident Set Size, the physical memory in use by the process, not including swap space, in KiB (similar to RSS in the output to the **ps aux** command).
SHR	Shared memory in KiB available to a task.
S	Process status (same as STAT in the output to the **ps aux** command).
%CPU	CPU usage, as a percentage of time spent running since the last **top** screen update.

The default sort field is CPU usage. In other words, the process that's taking the most CPU resources is listed first. You can change the sort field with the help of the left and right directional (<, >) keys. Most of the columns are the same as shown in Figure 9-2, as detailed in Table 9-1. The additional columns are described in Table 9-2.

One problem with the **top** and **ps** commands is that they display the status of processes on a system as a snapshot in time. That may not be enough. Processes may load a system for just a blip of time, or even periodic blips in time. One way to find more information about the overall load on a system is with two commands from the sysstat package: **sar** and **iostat**. That system activity information is logged courtesy of the **sa1** and **sa2** commands, which will be described shortly.

System Activity Reports with the sar Command

The **sar** command is provided by the sysstat RPM package. After installing the sysstat package, start the sysstat service and enable the service to start at boot:

```
# dnf install sysstat
# systemctl start sysstat.service
# systemctl enable sysstat.service
```

Note that the last command enables not only the sysstat service but also two dependent units, sysstat-collect.timer and sysstat-summary.timer.

In essence, **sar** can be used to provide a system activity report. For example, Figure 9-4 shows the output of the **sar** command. As you can see, the output shows various CPU measures at different points in time. The default settings measure CPU load at 10-minute intervals. This system has two logical CPUs, which are measured individually and as a whole.

FIGURE 9-4   Output from the sar command

```
[root@server1 ~]# sar
Linux 5.14.0-284.11.1.el9_2.x86_64 (server1.example.local)    07/01/2023    _x86_64_    (2 CPU)

04:43:02 PM  LINUX RESTART    (2 CPU)

04:50:03 PM  CPU    %user    %nice    %system    %iowait    %steal    %idle
05:00:23 PM  all     0.53     0.00      0.27       0.02       0.01     99.17
05:10:28 PM  all     0.90     0.01      0.35       0.05       0.01     98.69
05:20:03 PM  all     1.00     0.00      0.42       0.01       0.01     98.56
05:30:23 PM  all     1.43     0.00      0.36       0.03       0.01     98.17
05:40:28 PM  all     1.29     0.00      0.40       0.02       0.01     98.29
05:50:03 PM  all     0.22     0.04      0.17       0.01       0.00     99.57
Average:     all     0.90     0.01      0.33       0.02       0.01     98.74
[root@server1 ~]#
```

The high %idle numbers shown in the figure are a good sign that the CPU is not being overloaded; however, the figure shows the load for less than an hour.

The 10-minute intervals associated with the **sar** command output are driven by the sysstat-collect.timer systemd unit, in the /usr/lib/systemd/system directory. The output from those reports is collected in log files in the /var/log/sa directory. The filenames are associated with the numeric day of the month; for example, system activity report status for the 15th of the month can be found in the sa15 file in the noted directory. However, such reports are normally stored at least for the last 28 days, based on the following default in the /etc/sysconfig/sysstat file:

```
HISTORY=28
```

Variations on sar with sa1 and sa2

The **sa1** and **sa2** commands are often used to collect system activity report data. In the system-collect.service system unit, the **sa1** command is used to gather system activity data every 10 minutes. In the system-summary.service unit, the **sa2** command writes a daily report in the /var/log/sa directory.

CPU and Storage Device Statistics with iostat

In contrast to **sar**, the **iostat** command reports more general input/output statistics for the system, not only for the CPU but also for connected storage devices, such as local drives and mounted shared NFS directories. The example shown in Figure 9-5 displays information for the CPU and the storage devices since system startup on server1.example.com.

Both the **sar** and **iostat** commands can capture statistics at regular intervals. As an example, the following command shows CPU and storage device statistics every five seconds and stops after a minute (12 reports):

```
# iostat 5 12
```

FIGURE 9-5 CPU and storage device statistics

```
[root@server1 ~]# iostat
Linux 5.14.0-284.11.1.el9_2.x86_64 (server1.example.local)       07/04/2023      _x86_64_
(2 CPU)

avg-cpu:  %user    %nice %system %iowait  %steal   %idle
           4.80     0.05    1.01    0.22    0.02   93.90

Device            tps    kB_read/s    kB_wrtn/s    kB_dscd/s    kB_read    kB_wrtn    kB_dscd
dm-0            37.69      1674.40       249.54         0.00    2392336     356533          0
dm-1            18.92         1.79        75.26         0.00       2556     107532          0
sr0              0.08         2.94         0.00         0.00       4202          0          0
vda             37.92      1683.38       326.27         0.00    2405165     466159          0

[root@server1 ~]# █
```

nice and renice

The **nice** and **renice** commands can be used to manage the priority of different processes. Whereas the **nice** command is used to start a process with a different priority, the **renice** command is used to change the priority of a currently running process.

Process priorities in Linux specify numbers that seem counterintuitive. The range of available nice numbers can vary from −20 to 19. The default nice number of a process is inherited from the parent and is usually 0. A process given a priority of 19 will have to wait until the system is almost completely free before taking any resources. In contrast, a process given a priority of −20 takes precedence over all other processes. In practice, this is true for almost all processes because "real-time" tasks take precedence over the lowest nice value of −20. But this is outside of the scope of the RHCSA exam, so ignore the existence of real-time processes for now, and for the sake of this discussion assume that all normal processes can be assigned a nice value from −20 to 19.

The **nice** command prefaces other commands. For example, if you have an intensive script to be run at night, you might choose to start it with a command like the following:

```
# nice -n 19 ./intensivescript
```

Note that only the root user can assign nice priorities less than 0. The preceding command starts the noted script with the lowest possible priority.

Sometimes a program is just taking up too many resources. If you don't want to kill a process, you can lower its priority with the **renice** command. Normally, the easiest way to identify a process that's taking up too many resources is with the **top** command. Identify the PID that's taking up too many resources. That PID number is in the left-hand column of the output.

If the PID of your target process is 1234, the following command would change the nice number of that process to 10, which gives that process a lower priority than the default of 0:

```
# renice -n 10 1234
```

If you want to decrease the nice level of a process, you must run **renice** as root. Even though the output of the command refers to the "priority," it really is just listing the old and new "nice" numbers for the process:

```
1234: old priority 0, new priority, 10
```

The new nice number is shown in the output to the **top** command, under the NI column.

Process-Killing Commands

Sometimes, it's not enough to reprioritize a process. Some processes can just overwhelm a system. In most cases, you can stop such difficult processes with the **kill** and **killall** commands. In many cases, you can kill a process directly from the **top** task browser.

If there's a situation where a process is taking up a lot of memory or CPU, it's probably slowing down everything else running on that system. As shown in Figure 9-6, Firefox has loaded the CPU of the noted system pretty heavily. If it were unresponsive, we'd press **k** from the **top** task browser.

As shown in Figure 9-6, the **k** command reveals the PID To Signal/Kill: prompt, where we enter the PID of the Firefox process or accept the default of 4537, which appears to be Firefox. It applies the default signal (SIGTERM) to the process with that PID number.

Of course, you could apply the **kill** command directly to a PID number. For example, the following command is equivalent to the steps just described in the **top** task browser:

```
# kill 4537
```

FIGURE 9-6   The top task browser with heavy Firefox load

```
top - 13:57:44 up 10 min,  3 users,  load average: 0.29, 0.32, 0.25
Tasks: 257 total,   1 running, 256 sleeping,   0 stopped,   0 zombie
%Cpu(s):  9.6 us,  1.6 sy,  0.0 ni, 88.7 id,  0.0 wa,  0.0 hi,  0.0 si,  0.0 st
KiB Mem:  16153912 total,  3167324 used, 12986588 free,    1212 buffers
KiB Swap: 16383316 total,        0 used, 16383316 free.  915604 cached Mem
PID to signal/kill [default pid = 4537]
  PID USER      PR  NI    VIRT    RES    SHR S  %CPU %MEM     TIME+ COMMAND
 4537 alex      20   0 2357456 613972  57400 S  85.5  3.8   0:27.09 firefox
 3375 alex       9 -11 1147288  24136  17980 S   4.3  0.1   0:06.18 pulseaudio
 2867 root      20   0  213992  24264  12312 S   1.3  0.2   0:18.29 Xorg
 3443 alex      20   0 1800404 110844  34464 S   1.3  0.7   0:27.82 gnome-shell
 3762 alex      20   0  622768  21156  12856 S   0.7  0.1   0:00.82 gnome-term+
 2846 qemu      20   0 5688400 691360   7468 S   0.3  4.3   0:41.09 qemu-kvm
 3471 alex      20   0  461276   5672   3468 S   0.3  0.0   0:00.39 ibus-daemon
    1 root      20   0  134836   6900   3776 S   0.0  0.0   0:01.31 systemd
    2 root      20   0       0      0      0 S   0.0  0.0   0:00.00 kthreadd
    3 root      20   0       0      0      0 S   0.0  0.0   0:00.00 ksoftirqd/0
    5 root       0 -20       0      0      0 S   0.0  0.0   0:00.00 kworker/0:+
    7 root      rt   0       0      0      0 S   0.0  0.0   0:00.04 migration/0
    8 root      20   0       0      0      0 S   0.0  0.0   0:00.00 rcu_bh
    9 root      20   0       0      0      0 S   0.0  0.0   0:00.00 rcuob/0
   10 root      20   0       0      0      0 S   0.0  0.0   0:00.00 rcuob/1
   11 root      20   0       0      0      0 S   0.0  0.0   0:00.00 rcuob/2
   12 root      20   0       0      0      0 S   0.0  0.0   0:00.00 rcuob/3
```

| TABLE 9-3 | A List of Common POSIX Signals |

Signal Name	Signal Number	Description
SIGHUP	1	Configuration reload.
SIGQUIT	3	Similar to SIGINT, but produces a core dump when it terminates the process.
SIGINT	2	Keyboard interrupt (CTRL-C). Causes program termination, but it can be caught or ignored.
SIGKILL	9	Terminates a program immediately. The process cannot catch, block, or ignore this signal.
SIGTERM	15	This is the default signal sent by the **kill** command. It asks a process to terminate nicely. If ignored, the process continues to run.
SIGCONT	18	Resumes a suspended process.
SIGSTOP	19	Temporarily suspends the execution of a process.

The **kill** command can be run by the owner of a process from his account. Thus, user alex could run the **kill 4537** command from his regular account because he has administrative privileges over processes associated with his username.

Despite its name, the **kill** command can send a wide variety of signals to different processes. For a full list, run the **kill -l** command or type **man 7 signal**. Table 9-3 lists some of the most common signals.

Before the advent of systemd and scripts in the /etc/init.d directory, the **kill -1** command was used to send a configuration reload signal to service daemons. For example, if the PID number of the main process associated with the Apache web server is 2059, the following command is functionally equivalent to the **systemctl reload httpd** command:

```
# kill -1 2059
```

Without the -**1** switch (and that's a dash number 1), the **kill** command, under normal circumstances, would terminate the given process. In this case, it would terminate the Apache web server. But sometimes, processes get stuck. In some such cases, the **kill** command does not work by itself. The process continues running. In that case, you can try two things.

First, you could try the **kill -15** command, which sends the SIGTERM signal, attempting to kill the process cleanly. If the process will not exit cleanly, **kill -9** can be used to stop a process "uncleanly" by sending a SIGKILL signal. If it is successful, other related processes may still remain in operation.

Sometimes, a number of processes are running under the same name. For example, the Apache web server starts several processes that run simultaneously. It's at best inefficient to kill just one process; the following command would kill all currently running server processes, assuming no other issues:

```
# killall httpd
```

System Tuning Profiles

The Linux kernel has hundreds of settings that can be tuned to improve a system's performance. Some of those parameters are configurable via the **sysctl** command and the /etc/sysctl.conf file, others from the /sys filesystem, or by adding special boot options to the Linux kernel.

Covering all the possible tunable settings would require a book on its own. Luckily, RHEL 9 comes with **tuned**, a daemon that simplifies the daunting and complex process to optimize a system for best performance.

The tuned service should be installed and enabled by default on every RHEL 9 system. If the package is not present, run

```
# dnf -y install tuned
```

You can enable and start the service with the following commands:

```
# systemctl enable tuned
# systemctl start tuned
```

Listing tuned Profiles

The configuration of **tuned** is based on predefined profiles. Of course, you can add and define your own profiles, but this is out of the scope of the RHCSA exam.

To interact and configure the tuned service, use the **tuned-adm** command. For example, **tuned-adm list** shows a list of all available profiles; the output is shown in Figure 9-7.

As you can see, ten different profiles are available. The output also shows that the currently active profile on the system is virtual-guest. You could obtain the same information by running

```
# tuned-adm active
Current active profile: virtual-guest
```

FIGURE 9-7   tuned profiles

```
[root@server1 ~]# tuned-adm list
Available profiles:
- accelerator-performance    - Throughput performance based tuning with disabled higher latency STOP states
- aws                        - Optimize for aws ec2 instances
- balanced                   - General non-specialized tuned profile
- desktop                    - Optimize for the desktop use-case
- hpc-compute                - Optimize for HPC compute workloads
- intel-sst                  - Configure for Intel Speed Select Base Frequency
- latency-performance        - Optimize for deterministic performance at the cost of increased power consumption
- network-latency            - Optimize for deterministic performance at the cost of increased power consumption,
  focused on low latency network performance
- network-throughput        - Optimize for streaming network throughput, generally only necessary on older CPUs
  or 40G+ networks
- optimize-serial-console   - Optimize for serial console use.
- powersave                  - Optimize for low power consumption
- throughput-performance     - Broadly applicable tuning that provides excellent performance across a variety of
  common server workloads
- virtual-guest              - Optimize for running inside a virtual guest
- virtual-host               - Optimize for running KVM guests
Current active profile: virtual-guest
[root@server1 ~]# ▮
```

TABLE 9-4	Default tuned Profiles

Profile	Description
powersave	A profile to maximize power savings, at the cost of affecting performance. For example, CPU frequencies may be scaled down to save power.
balanced	A profile that provides a balanced compromise between performance and power savings.
hpc-compute	A profile optimized for high-performance computing (HPC) workloads.
throughput-performance	A profile designed to tune the system for maximum throughput. Power-saving optimizations are disabled.
accelerator-performance	A profile similar to throughput-performance that locks the CPU to low C states. Recommended when using GPU devices.
latency-performance	A profile similar to throughput-performance, but aimed at optimizing latency rather than throughput.
network-latency	A profile derived from latency-performance to optimize the system for the lowest network latency.
network-throughput	A profile derived from throughput performance to tune the network stack to work with 40 Gbps and 100 Gbps adapters.
desktop	A profile derived from the balanced profile and optimized for desktops.
virtual-guest	A profile derived from throughput-performance to optimize a system that runs as a virtual machine.
virtual-host	A profile derived from throughput-performance to optimize a system that runs as a hypervisor, such as KVM.
aws	A profile optimized for Amazon AWS EC2 instances.
intel-sst	A profile optimized for Intel Speed Select technology configurations.

Table 9-4 describes the purpose of each profile. Note that the list of profiles in your system might be slightly different, because Red Hat continuously reviews and introduces new profiles across new versions of RHEL.

Switching tuned Profiles

Switching to a different profile is achieved by the **tuned-adm profile** command. For example, to change to the throughput-performance profile, run

```
# tuned-adm profile throughput-performance
```

The new tuning optimizations are applied immediately, and the changes are persistent after a system reboot. To confirm the current profile, run

```
# tuned-adm active
Current active profile: throughput-performance
```

After installation, the **tuned** daemon determines the best profile for your system and selects that one as the default. If you have switched to another profile and don't remember which one was the default profile that **tuned** selected, you can run

```
# tuned-adm with recommend
virtual-guest
```

CERTIFICATION OBJECTIVE 9.02

Archives and Compression

Linux includes a variety of commands to archive groups of files. Some archives can be reprocessed into packages such as RPMs. Other archives are just used as backups. In either case, archives can be a terrific convenience, especially when compressed. This section explores the archive and compression commands specifically cited in the RHCSA objectives. These "essential tools" include the **gzip**, **bzip2**, **tar**, and **star** commands.

gzip and bzip2

The **gzip** and **bzip2** commands are functionally similar as they compress and decompress files, just using different algorithms. The **gzip** command uses the DEFLATE algorithm, whereas the **bzip2** command uses the Burrows-Wheeler block sorting algorithm. While they both work well, the **bzip2** command has a better compression ratio. For example, either of the two following commands could be used to compress a big document file named big.doc:

```
# gzip big.doc
# bzip2 big.doc
```

This adds a .gz or a .bz2 suffix to the file, compressed to the associated algorithms. With the **-d** switch, you can use the same commands to reverse the process:

```
# gzip -d big.doc.gz
# bzip2 -d big.doc.bz2
```

As an alternative, the **gunzip** and **bunzip2** commands can be used for the same purpose.

tar

The **tar** command was originally developed for archiving data to tape drives. However, it's commonly used today for collecting a series of files, especially from a directory, in a single archive file. For example, the following command backs up the information from the /home directory in the home.tar.gz file:

```
# tar czvf home.tar.gz /home
```

Like the **ps** command, this is one of the few commands that does not require a dash in front of the switch. This particular command creates (**c**) an archive, compresses (**z**) it, in verbose (**v**) mode, with the filename (**f**) that follows. Alternatively, you can extract (**x**) from that file with the following command:

```
# tar xzvf home.tar.gz
```

The compression specified (**z**) is associated with the **gzip** command; if you wanted to use **bzip2** compression, substitute the **j** switch. The **tar** command can store and extract access control list settings or SELinux attributes with the --**selinux** option.

If you have a tar archive created without the --**selinux** option, you can compensate. You can use commands such as **restorecon**, as described in Chapter 8, to restore the SELinux contexts of an archive.

star

The **star** command gained some popularity because it was the first to introduce support for archiving files in an SELinux system. As the **star** command is not normally installed, you'll need to install it; one method is with the following command:

```
# dnf install star
```

Unfortunately, the **star** command doesn't quite work in the same fashion as **tar**. If you ever have to use the **star** command, do practice the command. For example, the following command would create an archive, with all SELinux contexts, from the current /home directory:

```
# star -xattr -H=exustar -c -f=home.star /home/
```

The -**xattr** switch saves the extended attributes associated with SELinux. The -**H=exustar** switch records the archive using the exustar format, which allows you to store ACLs if the -**acl** option is specified. The -**c** creates a new archive file. The -**f** specifies the name of the archive file.

Once the archive is created, it can be unpacked with the following command, which extracts the archive:

```
# star -x -f=home.star
```

If desired, the archive can be compressed with the aforementioned **gzip** or **bzip2** command, or from **star** with the -**z** or -**bz** command-line option. The **star -x** command can detect and restore files from archives configured with various compression schemes.

For example, based on a **gzip**-compressed archive, the **star** command unpacks that archive, as noted by the following log information message:

```
star: WARNING: Archive is 'gzip' compressed, trying to use the -z option.
```

CERTIFICATION OBJECTIVE 9.03

Running Tasks on a Schedule: cron and at

The cron system is essentially a smart alarm clock. When the alarm sounds, Linux runs the commands of your choice automatically. You can set the alarm clock to run at all sorts of regular time intervals. Many cron jobs are scheduled to run during the middle of the night, when user activity is lower. Of course, that timing can be adjusted. Alternatively, the **at** system allows users to run the commands of their choice, once, at a specified time in the future.

RHEL 9 installs the **cron** daemon by default and incorporates the anacron system in cron. The **cron** daemon starts jobs on a regular schedule. The anacron system helps the **cron** daemon work on systems that are powered off, such as desktops or laptops. This ensures that important jobs are always run, even if a system was powered off for a period of time.

e x a m

ⓦ a t c h **Because** cron **always checks for configuration changes, you do not have to restart cron every time a change has been made.**

The cron system is configured to check the /var/spool/cron directory for jobs by user. In addition, it incorporates jobs defined in the /etc/anacrontab file, based on the 0anacron script in the /etc/cron.hourly directory. It also checks for scheduled jobs for the computer described in the /etc/crontab file and in the /etc/cron.d directory.

The System crontab and Components

The /etc/crontab file is set up in a specific format. Each line can be blank, a comment (which begins with #), a variable, or a configuration line. Naturally, blank lines and comments are ignored. In some Linux distributions, that file includes a schedule of jobs. In RHEL 9, the default crontab file just includes the format for other related configuration files.

Users run regular commands. Anyone who runs a new process, whether it be you or a daemon, inherits an "environment" that is made of various environment variables. To see the environment variables for the current user, run the **env** command. If that user is your account, some of the standard variables in RHEL include **HOME**, which should match your home directory, **SHELL**, which should match the default shell, and **LOGNAME** as the username.

Other variables can be set in the /etc/crontab and other cron files (in /etc/cron.d, /etc/cron.daily, and so on):

```
Variable=Value
```

Some variables are already set for you. For example, **MAIL** is /var/spool/mail/michael if your username is michael, **LANG** is en_US.UTF-8, and **PATH** is where the shell looks for commands. You can set these variables to different values in various cron configuration files. For example, the default /etc/crontab file includes the following variables:

```
SHELL=/bin/bash
PATH=/sbin:/bin:/usr/sbin:/usr/bin
MAILTO=root
```

Note that the **PATH** variable in a cron configuration file may be different from the **PATH** variable associated with a shell. In fact, the two variables are independent. Therefore, you'll want to specify the exact path of every command in each cron configuration file if it isn't in the crontab **PATH**.

on the
job

The MAILTO **variable can help you administer several Linux systems. The** cron **daemon sends by e-mail any output that a job sends to** stdout **or** stderr**. Just add a line such as MAILTO=me@example.net to route all the output of cron jobs to that e-mail address.**

The format of a line in /etc/crontab is now detailed in comments, as shown in Figure 9-8. Each of these columns is explained in more detail in Table 9-5.

If you see an asterisk in any column, the **cron** daemon runs that command for all possible values of that column. For example, an * in the minute field means that the command is run every minute during the specified hour(s). Consider the example shown here:

```
1   5   3   4   *   ls
```

FIGURE 9-8   The format of a crontab

```
SHELL=/bin/bash
PATH=/sbin:/bin:/usr/sbin:/usr/bin
MAILTO=root

# For details see man 4 crontabs

# Example of job definition:
# .---------------- minute (0 - 59)
# |  .------------- hour (0 - 23)
# |  |  .---------- day of month (1 - 31)
# |  |  |  .------- month (1 - 12) OR jan,feb,mar,apr ...
# |  |  |  |  .---- day of week (0 - 6) (Sunday=0 or 7) OR sun,mon,tue,wed,thu,fri,sat
# |  |  |  |  |
# *  *  *  *  * user-name  command to be executed
```

TABLE 9-5	Columns in a cron Configuration File
Field	**Value**
minute	An integer in the range 0–59 to specify the minute of the hour.
hour	Based on a 24-hour clock; for example, 23 = 11 P.M.
day of month	An integer in the range 1–31 to specify the day of the month.
month	1–12, or Jan, Feb, Mar, and so on (case does not matter).
day of week	0–7 (where 0 and 7 are both Sunday), or Sun, Mon, Tue, and so on (case does not matter).
command	The command to be executed; in a system cron job file, this is preceded by the username to run the command **as**.

This line runs the **ls** command every April 3 at 5:01 A.M. The asterisk in the day of week column simply means that it does not matter what day of the week it is; **crontab** still runs the **ls** command at the specified time.

The entries associated with the **cron** daemon are flexible. For example, a 7–10 entry in the hour field would run the specified command at 7:00 A.M., 8:00 A.M., 9:00 A.M., and 10:00 A.M. A list of entries in the minute field, such as 0,5,10,15,20,25,30,35,40,45,50,55, would run the specified command every five minutes. But that's a lot of numbers. The entry */5 in the minute field would lead to the same result. The **cron** daemon also recognizes abbreviations for months and the day of the week.

The actual command is the sixth field. You can set up new lines with a percent (%) symbol. All the text after the first percent sign is sent to the command as standard input. This is useful for formatting standard input. The following is an example of a cron file:

```
# crontab -l
# Sample crontab file
#
# Force /bin/bash to be my shell for all of my scripts.
SHELL=/bin/bash
# Run 15 minutes past Midnight every Saturday
15 0 * * Sat   $HOME/scripts/scary.script
# Do routine cleanup on the first of every Month at 4:30 AM
30 4 1 * *     /usr/scripts/removecores >> /tmp/core.tmp 2>>&1
# Mail a message at 10:45 AM every Friday
45 10 * * Fri  mail -s "Project Update" employees@example.com
%Can I have a status
update on your project?%%Your Boss.%
# Every other hour check for alert messages
0 */2 * * * /usr/scripts/check.alerts
```

Hourly cron Jobs

Now it's time for some sample cron files. The files and scripts discussed are limited to those seen on the server1.example.com system. A number of different packages add their own cron jobs. Certain jobs associated with the **cron** daemon are run every hour, based on the 0hourly script in the /etc/cron.d directory. This file includes the same variables as the /etc/crontab file just described. For hourly jobs, it includes one line:

```
01 * * * * root run-parts /etc/cron.hourly
```

Given the information provided in the preceding section, you should be able to read this line. The **run-parts** command loads each script in the directory that follows; the scripts in that directory are executed as the root user. Of course, the first five columns specify the time; the scripts are run at one minute past the hour, every hour, every day, every month, on each day of the week.

The script of interest in the /etc/cron.hourly directory is 0anacron, which reviews the contents of the /var/spool/anacron/cron.daily file to see if the **anacron** command has been run in the current day. If not, and if the system is not running on battery (for example, on a laptop disconnected from main power), the **/usr/sbin/anacron -s** command is executed, which runs scripts defined in the /etc/anacrontab configuration file.

Regular anacron Jobs

The 0anacron script in the /etc/cron.hourly directory described earlier executes the **anacron** command after a system has been powered up. That command executes three scripts defined in the /etc/anacrontab file. This includes three environment variables that should seem familiar:

```
SHELL=/bin/sh
PATH=/sbin:/bin:/usr/sbin:/usr/bin
MAILTO=root
```

The **SHELL** directive may appear a bit different, but the **ls -l /bin/sh** command should confirm a symbolic link to the **/bin/bash** command, which starts the default bash shell. The following directive means that scripts are run at a random time of up to 45 minutes after the scheduled time:

```
RANDOM_DELAY=45
```

With the following directive, anacron jobs are run only between the hours of 3 A.M. and 10:59 P.M.

```
START_HOURS_RANGE=3-22
```

While the format of /etc/anacrontab is similar to the format listed in a script for a regular cron job, there are differences. The order of data in each line is specified by the following comment:

```
#period in days    delay in minutes    job-identifier    command
```

The period in days is 1, 7, or @monthly, because the number of days in a month varies. The delay in minutes is associated with the **RANDOM_DELAY** directive. Since the /etc/anacrontab file is executed through the /etc/cron.d/0hourly script, the clock starts one minute after the hour, after the system has been started. The delay in minutes comes before the **RANDOM_DELAY** directive.

In other words, based on the following line, the scripts in the /etc/cron.daily directory may be run anywhere from 5 to 50 minutes after the **anacron** command is run, or 6 to 51 minutes after the hour:

```
1  5  cron.daily      nice run-parts /etc/cron.daily
```

For more examples, review some of the scripts in the /etc/cron.daily directory. A key script you may want to investigate is **logrotate**, which is used to archive or remove old log files.

Setting Up cron for Users

Each user can use the **crontab** command to create and manage cron jobs for their own accounts. Four switches are associated with the **crontab** command:

- ▓ **-u** *user* Allows the root user to edit the crontab of another specific user.
- ▓ **-l** Lists the current entries in the crontab file.
- ▓ **-r** Removes cron entries.
- ▓ **-e** Edits an existing **crontab** entry. By default, **crontab** uses vi, unless a different editor is specified via the **EDITOR** environment variable.

To set up cron entries on your own account, start with the **crontab -e** command. Normally, it opens a file in the vi editor, where you can add appropriate variables and commands, similar to what you've seen in other cron job files.

Once the cron job is saved, you can confirm the change with either the **crontab -l** command or, as the root user, by reading the contents of a file in the /var/spool/cron directory associated with a username. All current cron jobs for a user can be removed with the **crontab -r** command.

Create a cron Job

In this exercise, you will modify your crontab to read a text file at 1:05 P.M. every Monday in the month of January. To do this, use the following steps:

1. Log in as a regular user.
2. Create a ~/bin directory. Add a file called taxrem.sh, which reads a text file from your home directory. A command such as the following in the taxrem.sh file should suffice:

```
#!/bin/bash
cat /home/michael/reminder.txt
```

Make sure to add appropriate lines to the reminder.txt file in your home directory, such as "Don't forget to do your taxes!" Make sure the taxrem file is executable with the **chmod +x ~/bin/taxrem.sh** command.

3. Open the crontab for your account with the **crontab -e** command.
4. Add an appropriate command to the crontab. Based on the conditions described, it would read as follows:

```
5 13 * 1 1 /home/michael/bin/taxrem.sh
```

5. Don't forget directives such as **MAILTO=user@example.com** at the start of the crontab.
6. Save and exit. Run **crontab -l** and confirm the existence of the user cron file in the /var/spool/cron directory. That file should have the same name as the user.

Running a Job with the at System

Like **cron**, the **at** daemon supports job processing. However, you can set an **at** job to be run once. Jobs in the cron system must be set to run on a regular basis. The **at** daemon works in a way similar to the print process; jobs are spooled in the /var/spool/at directory and run at the specified time.

You can use the **at** daemon to run the command or script of your choice. For the purpose of this section, assume that user michael has created a script named 797.sh in his home directory to process some airplane sales database.

From the command line, you can run the **at** *time* command to start a job to be run at a specified time. Here, *time* can be now; in a specified number of minutes, hours, or days; or at the time of your choice. Several examples are illustrated in Table 9-6.

	Time Period	Example	Start Time for Jobs
TABLE 9-6	Minutes	**at now + 10 minutes**	In 10 minutes
	Hours	**at now + 2 hours**	In 2 hours
Examples of the at Command	Days	**at now + 1 day**	In 24 hours
	Weeks	**at now + 1 week**	In 7 days
	n/a	**at teatime**	At 4:00 P.M.
	n/a	**at 3:00 12/21/22**	On December 21, 2022, at 3:00 A.M.

You can use one of the sample commands shown in Table 9-6 to open an **at** job. It opens a different command-line interface, where you can specify the command of your choice. For this example, assume you're about to leave work and want to start the job in an hour. From the conditions specified, run the following commands:

```
$ at now + 1 hour
at> /home/michael/797.sh
at> Ctrl-D
```

The CTRL-D command exits the **at** shell and returns to the original command-line interface. As an alternative, you can use input redirection, as follows:

```
$ at now + 1 hour < /home/michael/797.sh
```

The **atq** command, as shown next, checks the status of the current **at** jobs. All jobs that are pending are listed in the output to the **atq** command.

```
$ atq
1       Wed Jun 21 03:00:00 2023 a michael
```

If there's a problem with the job, you can remove it with the **atrm** command. For example, you can remove the noted job, labeled job 1, with the following command:

```
$ atrm 1
```

Secure cron and at

You may not want everyone to be able to run a job in the middle of the night. You may also want to restrict this privilege for security reasons.

Users can be configured in /etc/cron.allow and /etc/cron.deny files. If neither of these files exists, **cron** usage is restricted to the root administrative user. If the /etc/cron.allow file exists, only users named in that file are allowed to use **cron**. If there is no /etc/cron.allow file, only users named in /etc/cron.deny can't use **cron**.

These files are formatted as one line per user; if you include the following entries in /etc/cron.deny, and the /etc/cron.allow file does not exist, users elizabeth and nancy aren't allowed to set up their own cron scripts:

```
elizabeth
nancy
```

However, if the /etc/cron.allow file does exist with the same list of users, it takes precedence. In that case, both users elizabeth and nancy are allowed to set up their own cron scripts. The range of possibilities is summarized in Table 9-7.

User security for the **at** system is almost identical. The corresponding security configuration files are /etc/at.allow and /etc/at.deny. The range of possibilities is summarized in Table 9-8.

If you're paranoid about security, it may be appropriate to include only desired users in the /etc/cron.allow and /etc/at.allow files. Otherwise, a security breach in a service account may allow a "black hat" hacker to run a **cron** or **at** script from the associated account.

TABLE 9-7   Security Effects of cron.allow and cron.deny

	/etc/cron.deny exists	/etc/cron.deny does not exist
/etc/cron.allow exists	Only users listed in /etc/cron.allow can run **crontab -e**; contents of /etc/cron.deny are ignored.	Only users listed in /etc/cron.allow can run **crontab -e**.
/etc/cron.allow does not exist	All users listed in /etc/cron.deny cannot use **crontab -e**.	Only the root user can run **crontab -e**.

TABLE 9-8   Security Effects of at.allow and at.deny

	/etc/at.deny exists	/etc/at.deny does not exist
/etc/at.allow exists	Only users listed in /etc/at.allow can run the **at** command; contents of /etc/at.deny are ignored.	Only users listed in /etc/at.allow can run the **at** command.
/etc/at.allow does not exist	All users listed in /etc/at.deny cannot run the **at** command.	Only the root user can run the **at** command.

CERTIFICATION OBJECTIVE 9.04

Bash Scripts

As discussed earlier in this chapter, RHEL 9 includes some system maintenance scripts, scheduled by the **cron** daemon. Those scripts are located in various files in the /etc/cron.* directories. We will analyze some of those scripts to introduce the basics of the bash shell, and cover some of the loop and condition structures. You'll then have the skills you need to create simple shell scripts. Bash, an acronym for Bourne-again shell, is a Unix shell and command language developed by Brian Fox for the GNU Project as a free replacement for the original Bourne shell (sh) distributed with Unix. It provides a command-line interface for controlling and interacting with your RHEL operating system, and also allows you to create scripts to automate a complex series of commands.

A "Hello, World" Script

A key part of any bash script is the *shebang*. The shebang is the string **#!/bin/bash**, which is a special kind of comment that tells the operating system which interpreter should be used to execute the script. It must be the first line of your script. To write a simple "Hello, World" bash script, create a file (such as my_script.sh) with your favorite editor, and copy the following content:

```
#!/bin/bash
echo "Hello, World"
```

In the script, **#!/bin/bash** indicates that the script should be run using the bash shell, while **echo "Hello, World"** prints the string "Hello, World!" to the terminal.

On RHEL 9, the **/bin/sh** path is symbolically linked to **/bin/bash**. This means that using **/bin/sh** or **/bin/bash** will lead to the same result, and they can be used interchangeably.

on the job

Some Unix systems and Linux distributions (not RHEL) link the /bin/sh **command to a shell other than bash. Unless** #!/bin/bash **is specified in the script, it may not be transferable to other distributions.**

To run the script, you first need to make it executable. You can do this with the **chmod** command:

```
$ chmod +x my_script.sh
```

Then, you can execute the script like so:

```
$ ./my_script.sh
```

If you try to run a script that is not executable, you would get the following error:

```
# ./my_script.sh
-bash: ./my_script.sh: Permission denied
```

Hence, if you get an error such as the preceding one, add the execute permission to the script file:

```
# chmod +x /usr/local/bin/myscript
```

Every bash script or command returns an exit value when it finishes running. This is a numerical value that represents whether the script completed successfully or encountered an error. By convention, an exit value of 0 indicates success, while any other value indicates an error. You can set the exit value of a script with the **exit** command. For example, **exit 0** indicates success, while **exit 1** indicates an error. If no **exit** command is provided, the exit value of the script will be the exit value of the last command in the script.

Bash Variables

You can use variables in bash to store data. Although it's sometimes common to write variable names in uppercase letters in bash, keep in mind that you cannot start a variable name with a number.

The following example illustrates how you can assign a variable from the command line:

```
# today=4
```

Take care when assigning a variable to not add spaces around the equal (=) character. To display the value of a variable, use the **echo** command and add a dollar sign in front of the variable:

```
# echo $today
4
```

You can also add braces around the variable name to avoid ambiguous expressions. For example, without braces, the following command would retrieve the value of the variable **$todayth** rather than the value of **$today**:

```
# echo "Today is the ${today}th of June"
Today is the 4th of June
```

You can use variables as part of arithmetic expressions. In bash, arithmetic expressions are enclosed in the **$((*expression*))** syntax. Here's an example:

```
# tomorrow=$(($today + 1))
# echo "Tomorrow is the ${tomorrow}th of June"
Tomorrow is the 5th of June
```

But there's more. Variables can also store the output of a command. There are two ways to do so: using the **$(*command*)** syntax and with backticks, `` `*command*` ``. Here's an example of each:

```
# day=$(date +%d)
# month=`date +%b`
# echo "The current date is $month, $day"
The current date is Jun, 29
```

The Scope of Variables

In the previous example, we have seen that the variables that we declare in bash can be passed as arguments to other commands. But are those variables available to other scripts? For example, create a script with the following lines:

```
#/bin/bash
echo $myvar
```

Save the content to a file (for example, testvar), make it executable, assign a value to myvar, and then run the script:

```
# chmod +x testvar
# myvar=hello
# ./testvar
```

The script's output is empty, so the value of myvar was not available to the script. To use shell variables with any command, you need to export those variables as *environment variables*, as shown next:

```
# export myvar=hello
```

Then, if you run the script again, you will find that the value of the myvar variable is now passed to the script:

```
# ./testvar
hello
```

Environment variables are usually declared in either the ~/.bashrc file or ~/.bash_profile file on a user's home directory, or in the corresponding global files, /etc/basrhc or /etc/profile. An example is the LANG environment variable, which tells programs which language and local setting to use.

Environment variables are useful to define variables that should be globally available to all programs. However, they are not very practical if you want to pass to a program parameters that change often. For that purpose, you can use command arguments, or positional parameters.

Parameter	Description
$?	Exist value of the last command
$$	PID of the current shell
$0	Name of the program currently in execution
$1 to $9	Command-line arguments passed to a script
$#	Number of command-line arguments

Parameters in Bash

In bash, a *parameter* is something that can store a value. Hence, a variable is a parameter. It is in fact a type of parameter denoted by a name. However, there are also two other types of parameters:

- **Special parameters**   These parameters are represented by special characters, each with a specific meaning. For example, the special parameter $? stores the exit code of the last command executed.

- **Positional parameters**   A series of parameters, $0 to $9, that store the command-line arguments.

Some of the most common special and positional parameters are listed in Table 9-9. We will cover positional parameters in more detail later in the chapter.

Parameters Expansion

A parameter's value can be manipulated using some string substitution techniques known as *parameter expansion*. To illustrate these concepts, define a variable as shown next:

```
# ch9=/home/mike/studyguide/ch9/ch9.gz
```

The first parameter expansion construct is **${*parameter:-word*}**. This gives the value of **${*parameter*}** if the parameter is defined; otherwise, **word** is substituted:

```
# echo ${ch9:-todo}
/home/mike/studyguide/ch9/ch9.gz
# echo ${ch10:-todo}
todo
```

Another useful parameter expansion construct is **${*parameter/pattern/string*}**. This replaces the longest match of **pattern** with **string**. As an example, suppose that you want to change the .gz extension to .tar.gz for the filename stored in the variable ch9:

```
# echo ${ch9/gz/tar.gz}
/home/mike/studyguide/ch9/ch9.tar.gz
# mv ${ch9} ${ch9/gz/tar.gz}
```

TABLE 9-10	Parameter Expansion

Parameter Expansion Sequence	Description
${*parameter:-word*}	Gives the value of ${*parameter*} if the parameter is defined; otherwise, *word* is substituted
${*parameter/pattern/string*}	Replaces the longest match of *pattern* with *string*
${*parameter#word*}	Removes the shortest occurrence of *word*, starting the search from the beginning of the value of *parameter*
${*parameter##word*}	Removes the longest occurrence of *word*, starting the search from the beginning of the value of *parameter*
${*parameter%word*}	Removes the shortest occurrence of *word*, starting the search from the end of the value of *parameter*
${*parameter%%word*}	Removes the longest occurrence of *word*, starting the search from the end of the value of *parameter*

You can remove a matching suffix pattern with the parameter expansion sequences **${*parameter#word*}** and **${*parameter##word*}**. These remove, respectively, the shortest or longest occurrence of **word**, starting the search from the beginning of the value of **parameter**. An example is shown next:

```
# echo ${ch9#*/}
home/mike/studyguide/ch9/ch9.gz
# echo ${ch9##*/}
ch9.gz
```

Similarly, the parameter expansion sequences **${*parameter%word*}** and **${*parameter%%word*}** remove the shortest or longest occurrence of **word**, but starting the search from the end of the value of **parameter**. This is exemplified here:

```
# echo ${ch9%/ch9*}
/home/mike/studyguide/ch9
# echo ${ch9%%/ch9*}
/home/mike/studyguide
```

A summary of the parameter expansion sequences is shown in Table 9-10.

Bash Control Structures

Scripts are filled with various command constructs. Some groups of commands are executed only if a condition is met. Others are organized in a loop, which continues to run as long as a condition is satisfied. These command constructs are also known as *conditional and control structures*. Common commands include **for**, **if**, and **test**. The end of a loop may be labeled with a keyword such as **done** or **fi**. Some commands only exist in the context of others, which will be described in the subsections that follow.

Test Operators and Conditional Constructs

The **if** operator is primarily used to check if a condition is met, such as if a file exists. For example, the following command checks if the /etc/sysconfig/network file exists and is a regular file:

```
if [ ! -f /etc/sysconfig/network ]; then
```

The exclamation mark (!) is the "not" operator and negates the result of the test. The **-f** checks to see if the filename that follows is a currently existing regular file. Test operators are very common in bash shell scripts. Some of these operators are listed in Table 9-11.

INSIDE THE EXAM

man test is an excellent documentation resource to find all test operators in **bash**.

TABLE 9-11 Test Operators for Bash Scripts

Operator	Description
STRING1 = *STRING2*	True if the two strings are equal
STRING1 != *STRING2*	True if the two strings are not equal
INTEGER1 **-eq** *INTEGER2*	True if the two integers are equal
INTEGER1 **-ne** *INTEGER2*	True if the two integers are not equal
INTEGER1 **-ge** *INTEGER2*	True if *INTEGER1* is greater than or equal to *INTEGER2*
INTEGER1 **-gt** *INTEGER2*	True if *INTEGER1* is greater than *INTEGER2*
INTEGER1 **-le** *INTEGER2*	True if *INTEGER1* is less than or equal to *INTEGER2*
INTEGER1 **-lt** *INTEGER2*	True if *INTEGER1* is less than *INTEGER2*
-d *FILE*	True if *FILE* is a directory
-e *FILE*	True if *FILE* exists
-f *FILE*	True if *FILE* exists and is a regular file
-r *FILE*	True if *FILE* exists and is granted read permissions
-w *FILE*	True if *FILE* exists and is granted write permissions
-x *FILE*	True if *FILE* exists and is granted execute permissions

The **if** operator normally is associated with a **then** operator, and possibly an **else** operator, and the command is ended by an **fi** instruction. For example, consider the following hypothetical block:

```
if [ -e /etc/fstab ];
then
      cp /etc/fstab /etc/fstab.bak
else
      echo "Don't reboot, /etc/fstab is missing!"
fi
```

In this code, if the /etc/fstab file exists (courtesy of the **-e**), the command associated with the **then** operator is run. If that file is missing, the noted message is displayed.

An Example: The 0anacron Script

We summarized the intent of the 0anacron script earlier in this chapter, but we'll analyze it in detail here. You can find the script in the /etc/cron.hourly directory. A copy of the script is shown in Figure 9-9.

The script starts with a shebang line, which tells Linux that this is a bash script. Then, there is the following **if** block:

```
if test -r /var/spool/anacron/cron.daily; then
      day=`cat /var/spool/anacron/cron.daily`
fi
```

FIGURE 9-9   The 0anacron script

```
#!/usr/bin/sh
# Check whether 0anacron was run today already
if test -r /var/spool/anacron/cron.daily; then
    day=`cat /var/spool/anacron/cron.daily`
fi
if [ `date +%Y%m%d` = "$day" ]; then
    exit 0
fi

# Do not run jobs when on battery power
online=1
for psupply in /sys/class/power_supply/* ; do
    if [ `cat "$psupply/type" 2>/dev/null`x = Mainsx ] && [ -f "$psupply/online" ]; then
        if [ `cat "$psupply/online" 2>/dev/null`x = 1x ]; then
            online=1
            break
        else
            online=0
        fi
    fi
done
if [ $online = 0 ]; then
    exit 0
fi
/usr/sbin/anacron -s
```

The **test** operator is sometimes used as a conditional within the **if**. For example, the line

```
if test -r /var/spool/anacron/cron.daily;
```

is functionally equivalent to

```
if [ -r /var/spool/anacron/cron.daily ];
```

This **if** block verifies whether the file /var/spool/anacron/cron.daily exists and is readable. If the test is successful, the content of the cron.daily file is saved into the **day** variable. In fact, the cron.daily file contains the last date (in YYYYMMDD format) that **anacron** was run.

The next lines contain another **if** block:

```
if [ `date +%Y%m%d` = "$day" ]; then
    exit 0
fi
```

This code compares two strings: the current date, as returned by the **date** command in YYYYMMDD format (note the backticks to substitute the output of the **date** command as the first operand in the test comparison), and the content of the **day** variable. As a good practice, the name of the **day** variable is enclosed in double quotes to prevent any special characters within the quoted string, apart from the dollar sign, to be interpreted by bash.

If the two dates are equal, the script exits immediately with a value of 0, indicating no errors. In other words, if **anacron** was already run today, the content of the /var/spool/anacron/cron.daily file would include today's date. In this case, the script won't run a second time and will exit with a value of 0.

The next section of code contains a **for** loop, which is explained in the next section. For now, it is sufficient to say that each of the following blocks of code will be executed for every power supply file in the directory /sys/class/power_supply:

```
if [ `cat "$psupply/type" 2>/dev/null`x = Mainsx ] && [ -f ↵
"$psupply/online" ]; then
    if [ `cat "$psupply/online" 2>/dev/null`x = 1x ]; then
        online=1
        break
    else
        online=0
    fi
fi
```

The purpose of the code in the **for** loop is to check whether the system runs on battery power or not. If the system is running on battery, the script does not run the **anacron** command, because this is I/O intensive and may drain too much power from the battery.

The first **if** conditional checks whether the type of the current power supply is Mains and the "online" file exists for the power supply. The **2>/dev/null** part is to suppress error messages by redirecting them to null.

Then, the second **if** conditional checks whether the current power supply is online (if the content of the "online" file is 1). If the condition is satisfied, that is, if the current power supply is online, then the **online** variable is set to 1 and the **for** loop is terminated (**break**) immediately; otherwise, it is set to 0.

Note the test expression:

```
if [ `cat "$psupply/online" 2>/dev/null`x = 1x ]; then
```

This gets the content of the file $psupply/online, suppressing any errors, appends the value "x" to it, and then compares this value with the string "1x". Why append the "x" string? This is an old shell scripting trick to prevent errors if the content of the file is empty. To do so, "x" is appended to make the output a valid string.

Next, the script checks the value of the **online** variable. If it is 0 (that is, the system is not on AC power), the script terminates immediately with an exit value of 0. Otherwise, the script runs the **anacron** command:

```
/usr/bin/anacron -s
```

In turn, **anacron** will read a list of jobs from /etc/anacrontab and execute them in sequential (**-s**) order.

Control Structures: The for Loop

The **for** loop executes a block of commands for all the items specified in a list. It's fairly simple and has different forms. In the following example, the command in the **for** loop is executed three times, for each value of the variable **n** in the list 1, 2, 3:

```
for n in 1 2 3; do
     echo "I love Linux #$n"
done
```

The output of the previous snippet of code is

```
I love Linux #1
I love Linux #2
I love Linux #3
```

A more complex example is shown next. The **for** loop is executed for all the users in the system, as returned by the **getent passwd** command:

```
for username in $(getent passwd | cut -f 1 -d ":"); do
    usergroups=$(groups $username | cut -f 2 -d ":")
    echo "User $username is a member of the following groups: $usergroups"
done
```

In the first line, the **getent passwd** command returns all the users in the system. This may include users defined locally in /etc/passwd, as well as users defined in a central directory service such as LDAP. The output of the command is truncated to the first column (**-f 1**), defined by a separator character (**-d ":"**). This gives a list of usernames that the **for** loop can cycle through and assign to the **username** variable at each iteration.

Then, the previous code snippet executes the **groups** command, with each username as an argument. This command returns the groups that a user is part of, in the following format:

```
user : group1 group2 ...
```

The **cut -f 1 -d ":"** command extracts all the output after the column separator, and the result is saved in the **usergroups** variable. Finally, the result is displayed by the **echo** command.

Positional Parameters

You can use positional parameters to pass information to a script, in the same fashion that you would do with arguments in normal commands. In a bash script, the first command argument is saved in the special variable **$1**, the second in **$2**, and so forth. The total number of arguments is saved in the **$#** special variable. As an example, consider the following script:

```
#!/bin/bash
echo "The number of arguments is $#"
if [ $# -ge 1 ]; then
    echo "The first argument is $1"
fi
```

Save the code in a file named args.sh and make it executable with the **chmod +x args.sh** command. Then, run the program as shown:

```
# ./args.sh orange
```

You should see the following output:

```
The number of arguments is 1
The first argument is orange
```

In Exercise 9-2, you will have a chance to put these lessons into practice.

EXERCISE 9-2

Create a Script

In this exercise, you'll create a script named get-shell.sh. The script takes a username as the first argument and displays the default shell of the indicated user, using the following format:

```
# ./get-shell.sh mike
mike's default shell is /bin/bash
```

If no argument is provided, the script must display the default shell of the current user. If more than one argument is given, the script must print the following error message and exit with a value of 1:

```
Error: too many arguments
```

If the user given as an argument does not exist, the script must display the following error message and exit with a value of 2:

```
Error: cannot retrieve information for user <user>
```

1. Create a file named get-shell.sh and assign execute permissions to that file:

   ```
   $ touch get-shell.sh
   $ chmod +x get-shell.sh
   ```

2. Open the file with your favorite editor. Start the script with the following line:

   ```
   #!/bin/sh
   ```

3. Add the following lines that check if the number of arguments ($#) is greater than one. If so, print an error message and exit with a value of 1:

   ```
   if [ $# -gt 1 ]; then
       echo "Error: too many arguments"
       exit 1
   fi
   ```

4. Add the lines that follow. If no arguments have been passed, the script saves the name of the current user (**$USER**) in the **username** variable. Otherwise, the **username** variable takes the value of the first argument (**$1**). To express this logic, use the **if-then-else** construct:

   ```
   if [ $# -eq 0 ]; then
       username=$USER
   else
       username=$1
   fi
   ```

5. Retrieve the user's information. You can query the user database with the **getent passwd** command. This command returns user information from the local /etc/passwd file and from any configured directory systems:

   ```
   userinfo=$(getent passwd $username)
   ```

6. Check the exit value of the previous command. Any nonzero exit value means that an error has occurred. If so, exit the program immediately with an exit status of 2:

```
if [ $? -ne 0 ]; then
    echo "Error: cannot retrieve information for user $username"
    exit 2
fi
```

7. Extract the user's shell from the **userinfo** variable. This is the seventh field (**-f 7**) of /etc/passwd, where each field is separated by a column character (**-d ":"**):

```
usershell=$(echo $userinfo | cut -f 7 -d ":")
```

8. Print the result. As a good practice, exit with a value of 0 to indicate that no errors have occurred:

```
echo "$username's shell is $usershell"
exit 0
```

9. Save your changes. Execute the script with different arguments to test every possible condition:

```
$ ./get-shell.sh alex
alex's shell is /bin/bash
$ ./get-shell.sh mike
mike's shell is /bin/bash
$ ./get-shell.sh daemon
daemon's shell is /sbin/nologin
$ ./get-shell.sh mikes
Error: cannot retrieve information for user mikes
$ ./get-shell.sh alex mike
Error: too many arguments
```

CERTIFICATION OBJECTIVE 9.05

Local Log Files

An important part of maintaining a secure system is monitoring those activities that take place on the system. If you know what usually happens, such as understanding when users log in to a system, you can use log files to spot unusual activity. Red Hat Enterprise Linux comes with system-monitoring utilities that can help identify the culprit if there is a problem.

RHEL 9 comes with two logging systems: a traditional logging service, rsyslog, and an enhanced logging daemon known as **systemd-journald**. We briefly discussed systemd logging in Chapter 5. Thanks to its architecture, systemd can intercept and save all boot and syslog messages, along with the output that services send to standard error and to standard output. This is much more than what a traditional syslog server can do. By default, systemd journal logs are stored temporarily (in a RAM tmpfs filesystem) in the /run/log/journal directory.

The rsyslog daemon includes the functionality of the kernel and system logging services used through RHEL 9. You can use the log files thus generated to track activities on a system. The way rsyslog logs output to files is based on the configuration defined in the /etc/rsyslog.conf file and on the files in the /etc/rsyslog.d directory.

In many cases, services such as SELinux, Apache, and Samba have their own log files, defined within their own configuration files. Details are addressed in the chapters associated with those services.

System Log Configuration File

You can configure what is logged through the /etc/rsyslog.conf configuration file. As shown in Figure 9-10, it includes a set of rules for different facilities: **authpriv**, **cron**, **kern**, **mail**, **news**, **user**, and **uucp**.

Each facility is also associated with several different levels of logging, known as the priority. In ascending order, log priorities are **debug**, **info**, **notice**, **warn**, **err**, **crit**, **alert**, **emerg**. There's also a generic **none** priority that logs no messages of the specific facility; for example, an **authpriv.none** directive would omit all authentication messages.

For each facility and priority, log information is sent to a specific log file. For example, consider the following line from /etc/syslog.conf:

```
*.info;mail.none;authpriv.none;cron.none   /var/log/messages
```

FIGURE 9-10

The rsyslog.conf configuration file

```
#### RULES ####

# Log all kernel messages to the console.
# Logging much else clutters up the screen.
#kern.*                                             /dev/console

# Log anything (except mail) of level info or higher.
# Don't log private authentication messages!
*.info;mail.none;authpriv.none;cron.none           /var/log/messages

# The authpriv file has restricted access.
authpriv.*                                         /var/log/secure

# Log all the mail messages in one place.
mail.*                                            -/var/log/maillog

# Log cron stuff
cron.*                                             /var/log/cron

# Everybody gets emergency messages
*.emerg                                            :omusrmsg:*

# Save news errors of level crit and higher in a special file.
uucp,news.crit                                     /var/log/spooler

# Save boot messages also to boot.log
local7.*                                           /var/log/boot.log
```

This line sends log information from all of the given facilities to the /var/log/messages file. This includes all facility messages of **info** level and higher, except for log messages related to the **mail**, **authpriv** (authentication), and **cron** facilities.

You can use the asterisk as a wildcard in /etc/syslog.conf. For example, a line that starts with ***.*** tells **rsyslogd** to log everything. A line that starts with **authpriv.*** means you want to log all messages from the **authpriv** facility.

By default, **rsyslogd** logs all messages of a given priority or higher. In other words, a **cron.err** line will include all log messages from the **cron** daemon at the **err**, **crit**, **alert**, and **emerg** levels.

Most messages from **rsyslogd** are written to files in the /var/log directory. You should scan these logs on a regular basis and look for patterns that could indicate a security breach. It's also possible to set up cron jobs to look for such patterns.

Log File Management

Logs can easily become very large and difficult to read. By default, the **logrotate** utility creates a new log file on a weekly basis, using the directives in the /etc/logrotate.conf file, which also pulls in directives from files in the /etc/logrotate.d directory. As shown in Figure 9-11, the directives in the file are straightforward and well explained by the comments.

Specifically, the default settings rotate log files on a weekly basis, storing the past four weeks of logs. New log files are created during the rotation, and older files have the date of rotation as a suffix.

FIGURE 9-11

Log rotation
configured in
/etc/logrotate.conf

```
# see "man logrotate" for details

# global options do not affect preceding include directives

# rotate log files weekly
weekly

# keep 4 weeks worth of backlogs
rotate 4

# create new (empty) log files after rotating old ones
create

# use date as a suffix of the rotated file
dateext

# uncomment this if you want your log files compressed
#compress

# packages drop log rotation information into this directory
include /etc/logrotate.d

# system-specific logs may be also be configured here.
```

A Variety of Log Files

Various log files and their functionality are described in Table 9-12. These files are created based on the previously described configuration of the /etc/rsyslog.conf file and of service configuration files in the /etc/rsyslog.d directory. Some of the log files (such as those in /var/log/httpd) are created directly by applications. All files shown are in the /var/log directory. If you haven't installed, activated, or used the noted service, the associated log file may not appear. In contrast, you may see log files not shown here based on additional installed services.

TABLE 9-12   Standard Red Hat Log Files

Log Files	Description
anaconda/*	Includes at least five log files: anaconda.log for general installation messages; packaging.log for package installation; program.log for calls to external programs; storage.log for storage device configuration and partitioning; ifcfg.log for network adapter initialization; and sometimes, syslog for kernel messages and X.log for the first start of the GUI server.
audit/	Includes the audit.log file, which collects messages from the kernel audit subsystem.
boot.log	Includes messages displayed at boot.
btmp	Lists failed login attempts; readable with the **utmpdump btmp** command.
cron	Collects information from scripts run by the **cron** daemon.
chrony/	Directory of log files associated with the chrony NTP service.
cups/	Directory of printer access, page, and error logs.
dnf*.log	Logs associated with the **dnf** package manager and the installation and removal of software packages.
gdm/	Directory of messages associated with starting via the GNOME Display Manager; includes login failures.
httpd/	Directory of log files associated with the Apache web server.
journal/	Directory to store systemd journal log entries persistently.
lastlog	Lists login records; readable with the **lastlog** command.
maillog	Collects log messages related to e-mail servers.
messages	Includes kernel logs and messages from other services, as defined in /etc/rsyslog.conf.
rhsm/	Directory with logs from the Red Hat Subscription Manager plugin.
sa/	Directory with system activity reports.
samba/	Directory of access and service logs for the Samba server.
secure	Authentication and access messages.
spooler	Log file associated with printers and printing log messages.
sssd/	Directory of messages associated with the System Security Services daemon.
wtmp	List of logins, in binary format; can be read with the **utmpdump** command.

Service-Specific Logs

As suggested earlier, a number of services control their own log files. The log files for the vsFTP server, for example, are configured in the vsftpd.conf file in the /etc/vsftpd directory. As noted from that file, the following directive enables the logging of both uploads and downloads in the /var/log/xferlog file:

```
xferlog_enable=YES
```

The logging of other services may be more complex. For example, separate log files are configured for access and errors in the Apache web server in the /var/log/httpd directory.

EXERCISE 9-3

Learn the Log Files

In this exercise, you'll inspect the log files on a local system to try to identify different problems.

1. Restart the Linux computer. Log in from SSH as the root user. Use the wrong password once.

2. Log in properly with the correct password as the root user.

3. In a console, navigate to the /var/log directory and open the file named "secure." Navigate to the "Failed password" message closest to the end of the file. Review what happened. Close the file.

4. Review other logs in the /var/log directory. Use Table 9-12 for guidance. Look for messages associated with hardware. What log files are they in? Does that make sense?

5. Most, but not all, log files are text files. Try reading the lastlog file in the /var/log directory as a text file. What happens? Try the **lastlog** command. Are you now reading the contents of the /var/log/lastlog file? Can you confirm this from the associated man page?

View systemd Journal Log Entries

Aside from initializing the system and managing services, systemd also implements a powerful logging system. In Chapter 5 we briefly introduced **journalctl** and explained how to enable persistent logging. In this section, we will review some of the basic functionalities of the **journalctl** command and show how to perform advanced searches.

By default, logs are stored in a ring buffer using a binary format inside the directory /run/log/journal, and they do not persist a system reboot. If you prefer to write journal log files persistently on disk, edit the /etc/systemd/journald.conf file and look for the Storage configuration option:

```
#Storage=auto
```

This parameter can be set to **volatile**, **persistent**, or **auto**. If set to **volatile**, journal logs are temporarily stored in /run/log/journal. Conversely, **persistent** stores the journal logs in /var/log/journal (and creates this directory if it does not exist). The **auto** setting uses persistent storage if /var/log/journal exists, and otherwise fails back to volatile mode. If you modify the Storage parameter, you'll have to restart the **systemd-journald** service.

Hence, to enable persistent storage, uncomment the Storage entry and set its value to **persistent**:

```
Storage=persistent
```

Then, restart the **systemd-journald** service with the following command:

```
# systemctl restart systemd-journald
```

One of the main advantages of the systemd journal over rsyslog is that it can store not just kernel and syslog messages but also any other output that services send to their standard output or standard error. You don't need to know where a daemon sends its logs because everything is captured by systemd and logged into the journal. The journal is indexed so that it can be easily searched using different options.

By default, the **journalctl** command shows all the messages in the journal in a paged format chronologically. It displays messages of **warning** severity in yellow, and it shows err, crit alert and **emerg**, **alert**, **crit** and **err** lines in red. A useful command switch is **-f**, which works in a similar way to the **tail -f** command by displaying the last 10 log entries and continuously printing any new log entries as they are appended to the journal.

You can filter the output of **journalctl** in several ways. You can use the **-p** switch to display messages whose priority is the same or higher than the one specified. As an example, the following command shows only entries of priority **err** or above:

```
# journalctl -p err
```

The command switches **--since** and **--until** can restrict the output to a specified time range. The next examples should be self-explanatory:

```
# journalctl --since yesterday
# journalctl --until "2023-05-28 11:59:59"
# journalctl --since 04:00 --until 10:59
```

FIGURE 9-12   A journal entry with metadata

```
Sun 2020-03-08 22:01:03.074289 GMT [s=6b28fd9c29aa4618ba499fc63109198e;i=31c97;b
=7afe9ed7d1c04a00ad954c9cb7cbff99;m=220188bce86;t=5115ade9c68dd;x=825a08f554ea90
65]
    _TRANSPORT=syslog
    PRIORITY=3
    SYSLOG_FACILITY=3
    SYSLOG_IDENTIFIER=nslcd
    SYSLOG_PID=11103
    _PID=11103
    _UID=65
    _GID=55
    _COMM=nslcd
    _EXE=/usr/sbin/nslcd
    _CMDLINE=/usr/sbin/nslcd
    _CAP_EFFECTIVE=0
    _SYSTEMD_CGROUP=/system.slice/nslcd.service
    _SYSTEMD_UNIT=nslcd.service
    _SYSTEMD_SLICE=system.slice
    _SELINUX_CONTEXT=system_u:system_r:nslcd_t:s0
    _BOOT_ID=7afe9ed7d1c04a00ad954c9cb7cbff99
    _MACHINE_ID=b37be8dd26f97ac4ba4a6152f5e92b44
    _HOSTNAME=server1.example.com
    MESSAGE=[7721c9] <group/member="alex"> no available LDAP server found: Serve
r is unavailable: Transport endpoint is not connected
    _SOURCE_REALTIME_TIMESTAMP=1426456863074289
```

You can also filter the output by looking at the most recent journal entries via the **-n** option. For example, you can run the next command to show the last 20 lines in the journal:

```
# journalctl -n 20
```

But there's more. Each entry in the systemd journal has a set of metadata that you can display with the **-o verbose** switch. Figure 9-12 shows how a journal entry looks when enabling verbose output.

The **journalctl** command can filter the output using any of the fields listed in Figure 9-12. For example, the following command shows all log entries associated with user ID 1000:

```
# journalctl _UID=1000
```

Similarly, the next example displays all journal entries related to the **nslcd** daemon:

```
# journalctl _COMM=nslcd
```

You can also specify multiple conditions on the same line. As you get more practice with the **journalctl** command, you will find that the systemd journal is very robust and flexible, and can be queried using a myriad of different options.

SCENARIO & SOLUTION

A system must be optimized to run KVM.	Run **tuned-adm profile virtual-host**.
A script in a crontab file is not executed.	Check /var/log/cron and /var/log/messages. Ensure that the script has executable permissions.
Regular users can't access the **crontab** command or the at> prompt.	Review the cron.allow and cron.deny files in the /etc directory to ensure that users can run the **crontab** command. Similarly, to grant users permission to schedule **at** jobs, review the at.allow and at.deny files.
Log files don't include sufficient information.	Revise /etc/rsyslog.conf. Focus on the desired facility, such as **authpriv**, **mail**, or **cron**, and revise the priority to include more detailed information. Look for log entries in the systemd journal.

CERTIFICATION SUMMARY

RHEL 9 includes a variety of system administration commands that can help you monitor and manage the resources used on a system. These commands include **ps**, **top**, **kill**, **nice**, and **renice**. In addition, you can optimize the system for a specific workload by applying a **tuned** performance profile.

File archives are a common way to back up or distribute filesystem contents in a single file. Special command options are required to back up files with specialized attributes such as those based on ACLs and SELinux.

The **cron** and **at** daemons can help you manage what jobs are run on a system on a schedule. With related configuration files, access to these daemons can be limited to certain users. While cron configuration files follow a specific format documented in /etc/crontab, those configuration directives have been integrated with the anacron system that supports job management on systems that are powered off on a regular basis.

Linux administrators need to configure scripts on a regular basis. Normally, bash scripts start with the **#!/bin/bash** line, which sets up the interpreter. Scripts can run Linux commands, along with conditional and control structures such as **for**, **if**, and **test**.

RHEL 9 includes two logging systems—the systemd journal and the rsyslog daemon—that are configured primarily for local logging. Log entries are normally collected by systemd in the /run/log/journal directory (or /var/log/journal if the systemd service is configured to write logs persistently on disk), whereas rsyslog stores log files permanently in the /var/log directory. The rsyslog daemon also supports the creation of a logging server that can collect log file information from a variety of systems.

TWO-MINUTE DRILL

Here are some of the key points from the certification objectives in Chapter 9.

Resource Management and System Tuning

- ❑ The **ps** command can identify currently running processes.
- ❑ The **top** command starts a task browser that can identify processes utilizing excessive resources on the system.
- ❑ The **sar** and related commands provide system activity reports.
- ❑ The **iostat** command can provide CPU and storage device statistics.
- ❑ The **nice** and **renice** commands can be used to reprioritize processes.
- ❑ The **kill** and **killall** commands can be used to send signals to currently running processes.
- ❑ You can list performance profiles and apply one to a system with the **tuned-adm** command.

Archives and Compression

- ❑ Archives can be created, extracted, and compressed with the **gzip**, **bzip2**, **tar**, and **star** commands.

Running Tasks on a Schedule: cron and at

- ❑ The cron system allows users to schedule jobs so they run at given intervals.
- ❑ The at system allows users to configure jobs to run once at a scheduled time.
- ❑ The **crontab** command is used to work with cron files. Use **crontab -e** to edit, **crontab -l** to list, and **crontab -r** to delete cron files.
- ❑ The /etc/cron.allow and /etc/cron.deny files are used to control access to the cron job scheduler; the /etc/at.allow and /etc/at.deny files are used to control access to the **at** job scheduler in a similar fashion.

Bash Scripts

- ❑ Standard administrative scripts can provide a model for custom scripts to automate system maintenance tasks.
- ❑ Bash scripts start with the **#!/bin/sh** or **#!/bin/bash** shebang line.

❏ Variables can store data and are available to other scripts or commands if exported as environment variables.

❏ Parameters include $?, which returns the exit value of the last command, and $1 to $9, which are the command-line arguments passed to a script.

❏ Simple loop and control structures are executed with commands such as **for**, **if**, and **test**.

Local Log Files

❏ RHEL includes the rsyslog daemon, which monitors a system for kernel messages as well as other process activity, as configured in /etc/rsyslog.conf.

❏ You can use log files generated in the /var/log directory to track activities on a system.

❏ Other log files may be created and configured through service configuration files.

❏ Log files may be rotated on a regular basis, as configured in the /etc/logrotate.conf file.

❏ The systemd journal logs all boot, kernel, and service messages in a ring buffer inside the /run/log/journal directory. Alternatively, it can store logs persistently in /var/log/journal.

❏ The **journalctl** command is used to display and filter journal entries.

SELF TEST

The following questions will help measure your understanding of the material presented in this chapter. As no multiple-choice questions appear on the Red Hat exams, no multiple-choice questions appear in this book. These questions exclusively test your understanding of the chapter. It is okay if you have another way of performing a task. Getting results, not memorizing trivia, is what counts on the Red Hat exams.

Resource Management and System Tuning

1. What command identifies all running processes in the current terminal console?

2. What is the highest priority number you can set for a process with the **nice** command?

3. How can you list all **tuned** profiles?

Archives and Compression

4. What **tar** command option can be used to archive the files of an existing directory while saving its SELinux contexts?

5. You want to create an archive of the /etc directory. What command do you need to run to create a compressed bzip2 archive of that directory? Assume that archive is named /tmp/etc.tar.bz2.

Running Tasks on a Schedule: cron and at

6. You want to schedule a maintenance job, maintenance.pl, to run from your home directory on the first of every month at 4:00 A.M. You've run the **crontab -e** command to open your personal crontab file. Assume you've added appropriate **PATH** and **SHELL** directives. What directive would you add to run the specified job at the specified time?

7. Suppose you see the following entry in the output to the **crontab -l** command:

   ```
   42 4 1 * * root run-parts /etc/cron.monthly
   ```

   When is the next time Linux will run the jobs in the /etc/cron.monthly directory?

8. What file is used to configure log file rotation?

Bash Scripts

9. What exit code is associated with success in a script?

10. If the HOME variable contains the value /*path*/*user*, where *user* is the username stored in the USER variable and *path* is an arbitrary path, how do you use parameter expansion to refer to the /*path* value?

11. Write a bash **test** command to check if a file exists and is executable.

12. Write a bash **for** statement to cycle through all the users in a system.

Local Log Files

13. What entry in the /etc/rsyslog.conf file would notify logged-in users whenever there is a critical problem with the kernel?

14. There are several files in the /var/log directory related to what happened during the installation process. What is the first word shared by the name of these log files?

15. What command displays all systemd journal entries with a priority equal to alert or higher?

16. How you can show the systemd journal entries related to the **httpd** daemon logged since the 16th of March 2023?

LAB QUESTIONS

Red Hat presents its exams electronically. For that reason, the labs in this chapter are available from the companion website that accompanies the book. In case you haven't yet set up RHEL 9 on a system, refer to Chapter 1 for installation instructions. The answers for each lab follow the Self Test answers.

SELF TEST ANSWERS

Resource Management and System Tuning

1. This is a bit of a trick question because the **ps** command by itself identifies any currently running processes in the current terminal.

2. The highest priority number that can be used with the **nice** command is –20. Remember, priority numbers for processes are counterintuitive: lower values mean higher priorities, and higher values mean lower priorities.

3. The **tuned-adm list** command lists all **tuned** profiles.

Archives and Compression

4. The **tar** command option that preserves SELinux contexts in an archive is --**selinux**.

5. The command that creates a compressed bzip2 archive of the /etc directory is

   ```
   # tar cvfj /tmp/etc.tar.bz2 /etc
   ```

Running Tasks on a Schedule: cron and at

6. The directive that runs the maintenance.pl script from a home directory at the noted time is

   ```
   0 4 1 * * ~/maintenance.pl
   ```

7. Based on the noted entry in /etc/crontab, the next time Linux will run the jobs in the /etc/cron .monthly directory is on the first of the upcoming month, at 4:42 A.M.

8. The configuration file associated with the rotation of log files over time is /etc/logrotate.conf. Additional service-specific configuration files can be created in the /etc/logrotate.d directory.

Bash Scripts

9. The exit code associated with success in a script is 0.

10. If the HOME variable contains the value */path/user*, where *user* is the username stored in the USER variable and *path* is an arbitrary path, you can refer to the */path* value as **${HOME%%/${USER}}** or **${HOME%/${USER}}**.

11. A bash **test** command to check if a file exists and is executable can be written as follows:

```
test -x /path/to/file
```

12. A **for** statement to cycle through all the usernames in a system can be written as follows:

```
for username in $(getent passwd | cut -f 1 -d ":")
```

Local Log Files

13. There's a commented entry in the /etc/rsyslog.conf file that meets the requirements of the question. Just activate it and change the priority to **crit** to notify you (and everyone) whenever a serious problem with the kernel logs occurs:

```
kern.crit        /dev/console
```

Of course, that means there are other acceptable ways to meet the requirements of the question.

14. The log files in /var/log that are most relevant to the installation process start with **anaconda**.

15. The command that displays all systemd journal entries with a priority equal to alert or higher is **journalctl -p alert**.

16. To show all systemd journal entries related to the **httpd** daemon and logged since the 16th of March 2023, run the command **journalctl _COMM=httpd --since 2023-03-16**.

LAB ANSWERS

Lab 1

Install tuned and enable the service with the following commands:

```
# dnf -y install tuned
# systemctl start tuned
```

Note that running **systemctl enable tuned** is not necessary, because when the package is installed, it already enables the service to start at boot (confirm this with **systemctl is-enable tuned**).

Next, find the active profile and switch to the balanced profile:

```
# tuned-adm active
virtual-guest
# tuned-adm profile balanced
```

After rebooting the system, **tuned-adm active** will show that the current active profile is "balanced." Finally, switch back to the default profile. If you forgot which one it was, type **tuned-adm recommend**.

Lab 2

One way to modify the login messages as noted is with the following steps (there is at least one other method, related to the /etc/cron.d directory):

1. Log in as the root user.

2. Run the **crontab -e** command.

3. Add the appropriate environment variables, at least the following:

   ```
   SHELL=/bin/bash
   ```

4. Add the following commands to the file to overwrite /etc/motd at the appropriate times:

   ```
   0 7  * * * /bin/echo 'Coffee time!' > /etc/motd
   0 13 * * * /bin/echo 'Want some ice cream?' > /etc/motd
   0 18 * * * /bin/echo "Shouldn't you be doing something else?" > /etc/motd
   ```

5. Save the file. As long as the **cron** daemon is active (which it is by default), the next user who logs in to the console after one of the specified times should see the message upon a successful login. If you want to test the result immediately, the **date** command can help. For example, the command

   ```
   # date 06120659
   ```

   sets a date of June 12, at 6:59 A.M., just before the **cron** daemon should execute the first command in the list. (Of course, you'll want to substitute today's date and wait one minute before logging in to this system from another console.)

Lab 3

To set up an **at** job to start five minutes from now, start with the **at** command. It'll take you to an at> prompt.

Currently installed RPMs are shown in the output to the **rpm -qa** command. Since there is no **PATH** defined at the at> prompt, you should include the full path. So, one way to create a list of currently installed RPMs in the /root/rpms.txt file in a one-time job starting five minutes from now is with the following commands:

```
# at now + 5 min
at> /bin/rpm -qa > /root/rpms.txt
at> Ctrl-D
#
```

Within five minutes, you should see an rpms.txt file in the home directory of the root user, /root. If five minutes is too long to wait (as it might be during the RHCSA exam), proceed to Lab 4 and come back to this problem afterward. Don't forget to set up the other **at** job to be run in 24 hours.

Lab 4

One way to set up the cron job specified in the lab requirements is detailed here:

1. Log in as the root user.

2. The lab requirements don't allow you to use the **crontab -e** command to edit the root crontab file. Hence, create a system crontab in the /etc/cron.d directory, using the following command:

    ```
    # cat > /etc/cron.d/etc-backup << EOF
    ```

3. Type the following line to set up the cron job:

    ```
    5 2 * * 6 root /usr/bin/tar --selinux -czf /tmp/etc-backup-\$(/bin/date ↵
    +\%m\%d).tar.gz /etc > /dev/null
    ```

4. Don't forget to escape the % characters in the crontab entry; otherwise, they will be interpreted as newlines.

5. Type the EOF sequence:

    ```
    EOF
    ```

6. To test the job, modify the crontab entry so that it runs a few minutes from now. Then, change the directory to /tmp and extract the generated archive using the following command:

    ```
    # tar --selinux -xzf etc-backup-$(date +%m%d).tar.gz
    ```

7. Confirm that SELinux contexts have been preserved by running the following command:

    ```
    # ls -lRZ /tmp/etc
    ```

Lab 5

Success in this lab should be straightforward. The simplest way to set up the script is to start with the fundamental requirements and then add the other functionalities. For example, the following script saves the current date in MMDDHHSS format in the **$TODAY** variable. Then, it runs the **tar** command to back up the directory passed as the first argument into the backup-MMDDHHSS.tar file within the directory given as the second argument.

```
#!/bin/bash
TODAY=$(date +%m%d%H%S)
tar cf "$2/backup-$TODAY.tar" "$1"
```

The next step is to add the other non-core functionalities. You will need a test to check whether the number of arguments is not equal to two:

```
if [ $# -ne 2 ]; then
    echo "Usage: backup.sh <source> <destination>"
    exit 1
fi
```

You will also need to add another test to confirm that the arguments passed to the script are regular directories:

```
if [ ! -d "$1" ]; then
    echo "Error: directory $1 does not exist"
    exit 2
fi
```

In addition, another test is required to check if the second argument is a directory. If the test fails, the script must create the directory:

```
if [ ! -d "$2" ]; then
    mkdir -p "$2"
fi
```

Note that if the second argument is a file but not a directory, the script will return an error. However, this is not an error condition that the exercise asks you to take into consideration.

If you put together all the blocks of code, you will have a working script. Test the script with different arguments to verify that all the exception conditions are recognized and successfully processed.

Lab 6

There are no secret solutions in this lab; the intent is to get you to review the contents of key log files to understand what should be there.

When you review the anaconda.* files in /var/log and compare them to other files, you may gain some insight on how to diagnose installation problems. The failed login should be readily apparent in the /var/log/secure file. You may be able to get hints in the output to the **utmpdump btmp** command.

When you review the /var/log/cron file, you'll see when standard cron jobs were run. Most of the file should be filled (by default) by the standard hourly job, **run-parts /etc/cron.hourly**, from the /etc/cron.d/0hourly configuration file. If you've rebooted, you may see the anacron service, and you should be able to search for the job of the same name.

While **dmesg** includes the version of the currently booted kernel, it may be the same kernel as the one associated with /var/log/anaconda/syslog if you haven't upgraded kernels. At the end of /var/log/dmesg, you can find the filesystems mounted to the XFS format, as well as currently mounted swap partitions. For example, the following lists the partitions from a KVM-based virtual drive:

```
XFS (vda1): Mounting Filesystem
Adding 1023996k swap on /dev/mapper/rhel-swap.
Priority:-1 extents:1 across:1023996k
XFS (vda1): Ending clean mount
SELinux: initialized (dev vda1, type xfs), uses xattr
```

As you've hopefully discovered, the /var/log/maillog file does not include any information on mail clients, only servers.

Chapter 10

An Introduction to Containers

The world of IT is in a constant state of evolution, with new technologies emerging and reshaping how we approach tasks and solve problems. One such transformative technology is the use of containers, a fundamental component in today's DevOps architectures and cloud deployments. This evolution is evident in the RHCSA exam for RHEL 9, the latest exam objectives for which introduce the ability to manage containers as a significant new area of knowledge and competency.

Functionally, containers bear a resemblance to virtual machines (VMs) insofar as they both provide isolated environments with their own network interfaces, filesystems, and resource controls. However, the fundamental difference lies in the fact that containers do not maintain their own operating system. This results in containers being significantly lightweight and faster to start. Furthermore, they can accommodate more applications on a given host than traditional VMs, making them an efficient and resource-friendly option.

This chapter starts with a broad overview by discussing general concepts about containers and drawing comparisons to VMs to highlight their unique benefits. After establishing that fundamental understanding, the chapter guides you through deploying your first containers. You'll then explore the workings of container images and registries and how they contribute to the overall container ecosystem.

Next, you'll learn about container management, exploring commands in more detail and how to run containers as a service, an important skill for container deployments. The final section of the chapter delves into the crucial aspect of attaching persistent storage to a container, ensuring data longevity and resilience. This knowledge will provide you with an understanding of how to integrate containers into broader IT systems effectively, an essential skill in modern DevOps and cloud deployments. Let's embark on this journey to master the art of containers!

INSIDE THE EXAM

Fundamentals of Container Technology

This initial section, while not directly linked to specific exam objectives, establishes the vital groundwork for understanding the pivotal concept of containers. Here, we delve into the reasons behind the rise of containers as potent tools in streamlining the development lifecycle, minimizing operational costs, and mitigating complexities. By drawing analogies and differences between containers and VMs, this section offers a comprehensive introduction to container technology.

Getting Started with Containers

Exam objectives emphasize both foundational and advanced aspects of Podman, an open-source tool for developing, managing, and

running containers on Red Hat Enterprise Linux. Launching the first container introduces essential Podman commands, laying the groundwork for more detailed exploration in subsequent topics.

The relevant RHCSA exam objectives addressed here include

- Perform basic container management such as running, starting, stopping, and listing running containers
- Run a service inside a container

Building and Using Container Images

Retrieving container images from remote registries and building container images are essential skills in the world of containers.

The RHCSA exam objectives covered in this section are

- Find and retrieve container images from a remote registry
- Inspect container images
- Build a container from a Containerfile

Managing Containers

The RHCSA exam objectives also focus on advanced Podman commands, extending beyond a thorough review of those previously introduced. The configuration of containers to start automatically as a system service is a critical aspect of automated deployments, which is also covered in the exam.

Due to their ephemeral nature, containers lose their content once they are removed. Hence, configuring persistent storage is crucial when running containerized services, especially for databases. This section provides an understanding of how to achieve this.

The associated RHCSA exam objectives are

- Perform container management using commands such as **podman** and **skopeo**
- Configure a container to start automatically as a systemd service
- Attach persistent storage to a container

CERTIFICATION OBJECTIVE 10.01

Fundamentals of Container Technology

This section provides a comprehensive overview of why containers have become indispensable tools for streamlining the development lifecycle, reducing operational costs, and simplifying complex IT environments. Using comparisons and contrasts with VMs, the section clarifies the unique advantages and functionalities of containers.

The Rise of Container Technologies

In the world of software development and IT operations, there's always been a tricky balance to maintain: developers are always eager to release new features or improvements quickly, while IT operations teams need to make sure that the systems they manage stay stable and reliable. This balancing act between quick changes and stable operations led to the creation of a method called *DevOps*.

DevOps is a way of working that brings together developers and operations teams. It's all about making the process of creating and releasing software faster and more efficient, without causing problems in the systems where the software runs. However, even with the best DevOps practices, there can be challenges. Some of these include making sure the software behaves the same way in different systems, getting teams with different goals to work well together, and figuring out how to safely release new software features quickly.

Containers can help solve some of these DevOps challenges. With containers, developers can pack up an application and everything it needs to run (like software libraries) into one neat package. This means the application can run the same way in different places, whether it's on a developer's personal computer or on a large computer system in a data center.

You can think of containers as little boxes that keep applications safe and separate from each other, similar to virtual machines. But, unlike VMs, which need a separate operating system to run, containers share the operating system of the machine they're running on, which means they use fewer resources and can start up and shut down quickly.

Another reason why containers are essential is their role in the microservice architecture, which is a way of designing software applications. In the microservice architecture, an application is broken down into smaller, independent pieces, each performing a specific task. These small pieces, or *microservices*, can be developed, updated, and scaled independently, which makes the whole application more flexible and easier to manage. Containers provide the perfect environment for microservices because a container can be used to package and run each microservice independently, no matter where a microservice is deployed.

So, a container is like a little bubble that holds one or more software processes. These processes are kept separate from everything else on the system. Containers offer some of the same benefits as VMs, like security and isolation, but they need less hardware power and are quicker to start and stop. This makes them a great tool for modern software development, where speed and flexibility are key.

Here are some key benefits of containers:

- **Agility**   Containers enable rapid application deployment and scaling. They can be created, replicated, or deleted in seconds.
- **Portability**   Applications packed in containers can run consistently across various platforms and environments, reducing the "it works only on my machine" problem.
- **Efficiency**   Containers share the host system kernel, making them much lighter than VMs. This enables more applications to be run on the same hardware, increasing efficiency.
- **Isolation**   Each container operates independently from others, reducing the risk of system-wide failures.
- **Version control and component reuse**   Containers support versioning, and you can share or reuse container images across different teams, which improves the overall development process.
- **Security**   Each container is isolated from others and the host system, providing an additional layer of security.

As we delve deeper into the intricacies of containers in the following sections, these benefits will become increasingly evident.

Virtualization and Containers

Virtualization technology allows us to create services that act like their physical counterparts but aren't actually tied to any specific physical device. Both virtual machines and containers are forms of virtualization, but they differ significantly in their structure and function.

Virtual machines offer a type of virtualization called *hardware virtualization*, as illustrated in Figure 10-1. This form of virtualization abstracts physical host resources, such as CPU, memory, and storage, creating a VM that acts like a real computer with its own operating system.

This abstraction is managed by specialized software known as a *hypervisor* or *virtual machine monitor*. This software runs directly on the server's hardware, and it's tasked with managing the resources for each VM. Hypervisors come in two types, as introduced in Chapter 1: type-1 hypervisors run directly on the system hardware (bare-metal), while type-2 hypervisors run on a host operating system.

Each VM operates with its own instance of an operating system, which could be Linux, Windows, or others. Within each VM, libraries and the application itself are installed and run as if they were on a standalone computer system.

In contrast, containers are a more lightweight form of virtualization. As also shown in Figure 10-1, containers don't run their own operating system. Instead, they share the host's operating system kernel. They're essentially isolated processes running on the host, but they're set up in such a way that they run as if they're operating in their own separate environments.

FIGURE 10-1

Virtual machines versus containers

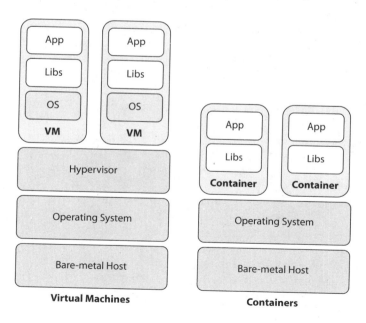

This isolation is achieved through specific technologies in the Linux kernel, such as namespaces and cgroups (discussed in the next section), which give containers the illusion of running in separate environments similar to VMs, but without the overhead of a full operating system.

When comparing VMs and containers, there are pros and cons to both approaches. VMs are fully isolated and can run different operating systems, but they also have more overhead, requiring more resources and time to start. Containers, on the other hand, are lightweight, start quickly, and are highly portable, but they share the same kernel and are slightly less isolated than VMs.

In conclusion, the decision between using VMs and using containers depends on what you need. If you need to run many different operating systems or need full isolation, then VMs are your best bet. But, if you're looking for something that's fast, efficient, and easy to move around, then containers are the way to go. They're lighter, start up quicker, and can be moved around easily while still giving you enough isolation for most use cases. This makes them a popular choice for running applications, especially in cloud computing and DevOps work. While VMs still have their uses, containers are becoming the go-to option for deploying applications quickly and efficiently.

Understanding Container Architecture

The architecture of containers is a fascinating blend of several key Linux features, specifically designed to provide process and resource isolation. These features—namespaces, control groups, and SELinux—work in harmony to create the container environment that many developers and organizations have come to rely on today.

Namespaces, at their core, are a Linux kernel feature that govern the visibility of various system resources. Imagine a process group that can only "see" certain aspects of the system, such as process IDs (PIDs), filesystems, and network interfaces. By segregating these resources between different sets of processes, namespaces create a unique "illusion" for each set, making them believe they are operating in their own isolated environment. This is a fundamental underpinning of how containers isolate processes and filesystems from each other.

While namespaces are focused on resource visibility, *control croups (cgroups)* come into play to control the actual usage of system resources. If namespaces are about "seeing," cgroups are about "using." They impose limits and manage the allocation of CPU, memory, network bandwidth, and disk I/O among various process groups. This is crucial in a container environment as it ensures that each container gets its fair share of resources, and a single greedy container cannot bring the entire system to a standstill.

SELinux adds another layer to this architecture, contributing a robust security mechanism. Known for its implementation of mandatory access controls (MAC), SELinux allows fine-grained permission control over every process and file in the system. In a container context, this is highly advantageous as it restricts what each container can do and helps limit the "blast radius" in case of a container breakout.

Moving away from the underlying Linux features, let's look at what makes a container possible in practical terms: the *container image*. An image is like a blueprint for a container; it packages the software application, its dependencies, and some configuration details into a single object. When this image is executed on a container run time (like Podman or Docker), it "comes to life" as a running container. Having such an image is essential because it guarantees the same environment can be replicated anywhere, be it a developer's laptop or a production server.

But how are these images standardized and made portable? This is where the Open Container Initiative (OCI) comes in. It's an open-source project aimed at setting common standards for container platforms. OCI primarily focuses on defining specifications for container images and run times, promoting interoperability and preventing vendor lock-in, making it easier for developers to build and deploy containers across different environments.

Lastly, just like how codebases need repositories, container images need a storage place too, known as a *container registry*. A registry is an online repository where container images can be stored, retrieved, and shared, facilitating the distribution of applications packaged as containers. Examples include Docker Hub, Google Container Registry, and Quay.io.

In a nutshell, the container architecture is a combination of these robust Linux features, standardized container images, and the efficient use of container registries, all working together to deliver the power of containerized applications.

Docker and Podman

Docker is often credited for popularizing container technology, even though the idea of containers had been around in the Linux world for years before Docker's inception. Docker, which was first released in 2013 by a company called dotCloud, was designed to simplify and accelerate the process of developing, shipping, and running applications. Docker uses containers to package and isolate applications with their entire run-time environment, making them portable across different systems. Docker's ease of use and efficient workflow quickly gained it popularity and a thriving user community.

However, Docker's architecture wasn't without its flaws. A crucial design feature of Docker is its reliance on a central daemon. This daemon runs with root privileges, presenting a potential security risk. Additionally, the Docker daemon handles all interactions with the Docker API, creating a potential single point of failure and complexity in distributed systems.

In response to these challenges, Red Hat developed Podman. Introduced around 2018, Podman addresses some of Docker's security and design issues by providing a daemonless, rootless container engine. In other words, Podman doesn't require a constantly running, high-privileged background process to manage containers. Instead, Podman launches containers and containerized services as child processes, enhancing security and reducing the attack surface.

Moreover, Podman's rootless feature allows nonprivileged users to manage containers, further reducing the security risks. Additionally, Podman offers better integration with system-level features, such as systemd for service management, cgroups for resource limiting, and SELinux for security, aligning more closely with traditional Unix philosophy.

Despite these differences, Podman was designed to be command-compatible with Docker, meaning most Docker commands work identically in Podman, which has made it easier for users to transition from Docker to Podman. With the industry's growing focus on security and efficiency, Podman presents a viable and secure alternative to Docker, while maintaining Docker's ease of use and flexibility.

CERTIFICATION OBJECTIVE 10.02

Getting Started with Containers

In this section, we'll guide you through launching your first container using Podman, an open-source tool for developing, managing, and running containers on Red Hat Enterprise Linux. This initial section introduces several basic Podman commands, each of which will be explored more thoroughly in subsequent sections.

Installing Container Tools

Getting started with containers on RHEL 9 begins with installing the container-tools meta-package. A *meta-package* does not contain any tools itself but serves as a convenient method to install a group of related packages. Use the **dnf** command to install the container-tools meta-package:

```
# dnf install container-tools
```

One of the key packages included in container-tools is Podman, the daemonless container engine responsible for developing, managing, and running OCI containers and container images. If Podman is not already present on your system, installing the container-tools meta-package will ensure it's added.

The container-tools meta-package also triggers the installation of a script named **docker**. This script acts as a wrapper around **podman**, allowing you to utilize the **docker** command just like you would with Docker, while it's actually Podman that is managing your containers behind the scenes.

Another significant utility that accompanies the container-tools meta-package is Skopeo. Skopeo is a command-line utility designed for various operations on container images and repositories, with no requirement to pull the image or create a container. This includes inspecting images directly on Docker registries and copying, deleting, or signing images. Skopeo works harmoniously with both OCI images and the original Docker Image format.

The container-tools meta-package would not be complete without Buildah, a specialized command-line tool that can build OCI container images. Buildah offers a flexible approach to creating, building, updating, and managing container images without a need for a full container run time or daemon. Podman uses Buildah behind the scenes to build container images.

Running Your First Container

Now that all the prerequisite tools have been installed, it's time to illustrate how to launch a container. In this demonstration, we'll run a container that hosts the Apache 2.4 web server:

```
$ podman run -d --name webserver -p 8080:8080 \
  registry.access.redhat.com/ubi9/httpd-24
```

After executing the command, you should see output similar to the output displayed in Figure 10-2. If all is working as expected, pointing your browser to http://localhost:8080 should display the web server's test page, as shown in Figure 10-3.

FIGURE 10-2   Create and run a container

```
[mike@server1 ~]$ podman run -d --name webserver -p 8080:8080 registry.access.redhat.com/ubi9/httpd-24
Trying to pull registry.access.redhat.com/ubi9/httpd-24:latest...
Getting image source signatures
Checking if image destination supports signatures
Copying blob 3e6d48d29678 done
Copying blob 7b3dd25bf011 done
Copying blob 0b29986fa3e6 done
Copying config 934be1fb27 done
Writing manifest to image destination
Storing signatures
a8b485b869f4f39eb31fa6e45498dcc1da1bf86b249e29b794f44a02e54950fd
[mike@server1 ~]$
```

FIGURE 10-3   The Apache web server's test page

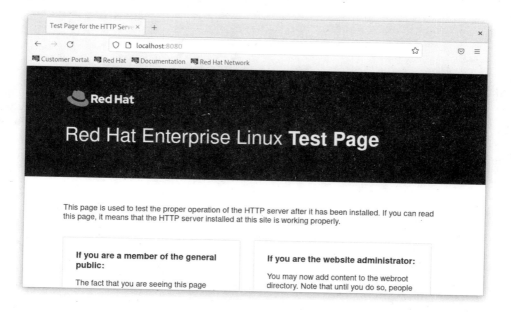

The previously mentioned command carries out multiple tasks. Initially, it checks for the presence of the httpd-24 image in the local environment. If the image is unavailable locally, Podman retrieves that image from the Red Hat registry, an operation equivalent to the following command:

```
$ podman pull registry.access.redhat.com/ubi9/httpd-24
```

Following the image retrieval, the **podman run** command initiates a new container from the httpd-24 image, with the name "webserver." The **-d** flag specifies detached mode, ensuring the container runs in the background, thereby not occupying your current terminal or shell session.

When it comes to services within the container that need to be accessible over a certain port, you can utilize the **-p** argument to expose a specific port. By using **-p 8080:8080**, you are instructing Podman to open port 8080 on the host machine and to route all incoming traffic on this port to port 8080 inside the container.

Newer versions of Docker and Podman have introduced grouping specific commands based on their usage. For instance, podman container **groups all commands related to container management, and** podman container run **would be equivalent to the simpler** podman run. **Nonetheless, Podman maintains backward compatibility; hence, newer versions of commands coexist with their traditional counterparts.**

After the httpd-24 image has been downloaded and made locally available, which you can confirm via the **podman images** command, the **podman ps** command lets you view all the containers in a running state, as shown in Figure 10-4.

The output of the **podman run** command concludes with a unique ID generated by Podman for managing the container. You can, for example, halt the container using the following command:

```
$ podman stop a8b
```

where "a8b" are the first three characters of the unique ID. For convenience, Podman doesn't require the entire ID, just the first few characters. Alternatively, you can reference the container by its given name, as shown next:

```
$ podman stop webserver
```

FIGURE 10-4   View running containers

```
[mike@server1 ~]$ podman ps
CONTAINER ID  IMAGE                                          COMMAND          CREATED      STATUS
   PORTS                  NAMES
a8b485b869f4  registry.access.redhat.com/ubi9/httpd-24:latest /usr/bin/run-http...  9 minutes ago  Up 9 minutes ago
   0.0.0.0:8080->8080/tcp  webserver
[mike@server1 ~]$ ▉
```

Keep in mind that, by default, the **podman ps** command lists only running containers. To display containers that are stopped as well, use the **-a** flag:

```
$ podman ps -a
```

Once you are done with the container, it's good practice to clean up. You can remove the stopped container by using **podman rm webserver**, and you can delete its corresponding image with **podman rmi httpd-24**.

Rootless and Rootful Containers

So far, we've been operating containers as a nonprivileged user. In the language of container technology, this is often referred to as running "rootless" containers. Conversely, when containers are run by the root user, or a user with equivalent permissions, they are called "rootful" containers. Let's dive deeper into these concepts.

Rootful containers, as the name suggests, are those run by the root user or an equivalently privileged user. This setup grants these containers broad capabilities, allowing them to fully exploit the resources and functionalities of the host system. However, this potent access also poses significant potential risks. A misstep in configurations or a container vulnerability can trigger severe security breaches. The unrestricted nature of rootful containers could potentially lay open the entire host system to exploitation.

In contrast, rootless containers are the safer counterpart, run by non-root users, without any exceptional privileges. They offer a more constrained and controlled environment, limiting the container's ability to interact with the host system. This significantly curtails the potential risk of compromising the host, making it a preferred option for prioritizing security.

Running rootless containers is like playing in a sandbox. You can do whatever you want inside the sandbox without affecting the playground around it. That's why, for most cases, rootless containers are the best choice. They give you what you need while keeping your system safe.

However, there are instances where rootful containers are necessary and advantageous. For example, when there's a need to directly interact with specific system resources or when you need to listen to network ports below 1024, which are restricted for non-root users, a rootful container might be the most feasible option.

When deciding between rootless and rootful containers, it's essential to consider the specific needs of your operations and balance them against potential security implications. By doing this, you can ensure the best possible outcome, whether your focus lies in exploiting capabilities, ensuring security, or finding a balance between the two.

CERTIFICATION OBJECTIVE 10.03

Building and Using Container Images

In this section, we delve into the world of container registries and the construction of container images. Container registries are integral to the container ecosystem, functioning as storage and distribution hubs for container images. Understanding how to interact with these registries, including how to push, pull, and locate images, is a fundamental skill for any container practitioner. Simultaneously, building your own container images can provide you with precise control over the container's environment, thereby enabling the creation of customized solutions that perfectly fit your requirements.

Image Registries

An image registry is a vital component of container-based development and deployment. It serves as a storage and distribution system for container images, enabling developers to publish their creations, and others to pull and use these images as needed. The images can be scaled and versioned, facilitating effective management. Depending on the requirements, registries can be public (accessible to anyone), private (restricted to certain users or organizations), or a hybrid of both.

The **podman images** command displays all the images that have been downloaded and are currently stored on your local machine. However, these images must initially be retrieved from a registry. When you invoke the **podman info** command, it outputs various configuration details about Podman, including the registries that are currently configured, as shown in Figure 10-5. These can be customized by editing the file /etc/containers/registries.conf.

FIGURE 10-5

Partial display of the **podman info** command output

```
plugins:
  authorization: null
  log:
  - k8s-file
  - none
  - passthrough
  - journald
  network:
  - bridge
  - macvlan
  volume:
  - local
registries:
  search:
  - registry.access.redhat.com
  - registry.redhat.io
  - docker.io
```

FIGURE 10-6 Excerpt of the output of the **podman search python** command

```
[mike@server1 ~]$ podman search python
NAME                                                                 DESCRIPTION
registry.access.redhat.com/openshift3/python-33-rhel7                Python 3.3 platform for building and running...
registry.access.redhat.com/ubi8/python-27                            Platform for building and running Python 2.7...
registry.access.redhat.com/ubi8/python-36                            Platform for building and running Python 3.6...
registry.access.redhat.com/ubi8/python-38                            Platform for building and running Python 3.8...
registry.access.redhat.com/ubi8/python-39                            Platform for building and running Python 3.9...
registry.access.redhat.com/ubi9/python-39                            rhcc_registry.access.redhat.com_ubi9/python-...
registry.access.redhat.com/ubi9/python-311                           rhcc_registry.access.redhat.com_ubi9/python-...
registry.access.redhat.com/ubi8/python-311                           rhcc_registry.access.redhat.com_ubi8/python-...
registry.access.redhat.com/rhscl/python-36-rhel7                     Python 3.6 available as container is a base...
registry.access.redhat.com/rhscl/python-35-rhel7                     Python 3.5 platform for building and running...
registry.access.redhat.com/rhscl/python-27-rhel7                     Python 2.7 platform for building and running...
registry.access.redhat.com/rhscl/python-34-rhel7                     Python 3.4 platform for building and running...
registry.access.redhat.com/ubi7/python-36                            Platform for building and running Python 3.6...
registry.access.redhat.com/ubi7/python-38                            Python 3.8 platform for building and running...
registry.access.redhat.com/ubi7/python-27                            Python 2.7 platform for building and running...
registry.access.redhat.com/codeready-workspaces/stacks-python       "Red Hat CodeReady Workspaces- Python Stack...
registry.access.redhat.com/codeready-workspaces-beta/stacks-python  Red Hat CodeReady Workspaces- Python Stack c...
registry.access.redhat.com/rhel7-atomic                              Red Hat Enterprise Linux Atomic Image is a m...
registry.access.redhat.com/rhel7/rhel-atomic                         Red Hat Enterprise Linux Atomic Image is a m...
registry.access.redhat.com/rhel-atomic                               Red Hat Enterprise Linux Atomic Image is a m...
registry.access.redhat.com/rhel7-minimal                             Red Hat Enterprise Linux Minimal Image is a...
registry.access.redhat.com/rhel-minimal                              Red Hat Enterprise Linux Minimal Image is a...
registry.access.redhat.com/rhel7-rhel-minimal                        Red Hat Enterprise Linux Minimal Image is a...
registry.access.redhat.com/rhscl/s2i-base-rhel7                      Base image delivers all the essential librar...
registry.access.redhat.com/ubi8/s2i-base                             Base image with essential libraries and tool...
registry.redhat.io/openshift3/python-33-rhel7                        Python 3.3 platform for building and running...
```

Two noteworthy registries in the list are registry.access.redhat.com and registry.redhat.io. Both these registries primarily host identical container images, but there are some images that demand a subscription, which are available exclusively from registry.redhat.io.

Another commonly used public registry in the list is docker.io, colloquially known as Docker Hub. Docker Hub houses a vast library of prebuilt Docker images for a multitude of applications and services, shared by users worldwide.

The **podman search** command is a useful tool for locating images in the list of configured registries. For instance, executing **podman search python** will instruct Podman to search for images that contain the string "python" in their name or metadata in all configured registries. By default, Podman searches across all unqualified-search registries. A part of the output generated by the command is displayed in Figure 10-6.

For a deeper understanding of a specific image, the **skopeo inspect** command comes into play. For instance, the following command provides details about the httpd-24 image:

```
skopeo inspect docker://registry.access.redhat.com/ubi9/httpd-24
```

A snippet of the output from the **skopeo inspect** command is shown in Figure 10-7. This data can be vital for evaluating whether a specific image aligns with your requirements.

FIGURE 10-7   Partial output of the **skopeo inspect** command

```
    "Created": "2023-07-17T09:45:25.086016494Z",
    "DockerVersion": "",
    "Labels": {
        "architecture": "x86_64",
        "build-date": "2023-07-17T09:42:51",
        "com.redhat.component": "httpd-24-container",
        "com.redhat.license_terms": "https://www.redhat.com/en/about/red-hat-end-user-license-agreements#UBI",
        "description": "Apache httpd 2.4 available as container, is a powerful, efficient, and extensible web server
. Apache supports a variety of features, many implemented as compiled modules which extend the core functionality. T
hese can range from server-side programming language support to authentication schemes. Virtual hosting allows one A
pache installation to serve many different Web sites.",
        "distribution-scope": "public",
        "io.buildah.version": "1.29.0",
        "io.k8s.description": "Apache httpd 2.4 available as container, is a powerful, efficient, and extensible web
 server. Apache supports a variety of features, many implemented as compiled modules which extend the core functiona
lity. These can range from server-side programming language support to authentication schemes. Virtual hosting allow
s one Apache installation to serve many different Web sites.",
        "io.k8s.display-name": "Apache httpd 2.4",
        "io.openshift.expose-services": "8080:http,8443:https",
        "io.openshift.s2i.scripts-url": "image:///usr/libexec/s2i",
        "io.openshift.tags": "builder,httpd,httpd-24",
        "io.s2i.scripts-url": "image:///usr/libexec/s2i",
        "maintainer": "SoftwareCollections.org \u003csclorg@redhat.com\u003e",
        "name": "rhel9/httpd-24",
        "release": "267.1689586475",
        "summary": "Platform for running Apache httpd 2.4 or building httpd-based application",
```

Building Container Images: A Primer

In the containerized environment, flexibility and customization often necessitate the creation of custom container images. While you can manually modify an image of a running container for specific changes or testing, the utility of Containerfiles presents a more systematic and replicable approach.

INSIDE THE EXAM

Even though the RHCSA exam objectives do not require you to author a Containerfile, understanding its contents and the process of building an image from a Containerfile is imperative.

A typical Containerfile, as illustrated in Figure 10-8, always initiates with the **FROM** instruction. This specifies the base image upon which your container will be built.

on the job

If you have prior experience with Docker, you're likely familiar with Dockerfiles. Containerfiles and Dockerfiles are essentially the same. Whether you use a Dockerfile or a Containerfile, Podman can seamlessly build an image from it.

FIGURE 10-8

A Containerfile

```
FROM registry.access.redhat.com/ubi9/python-39

LABEL maintainer="McGraw-Hill Education"
LABEL description="Simple Web Server"

COPY index.html /app/index.html

EXPOSE 8000

WORKDIR /app

CMD ["python", "-m", "http.server"]
```

The **LABEL** instruction is used to add custom metadata to the image in the form of key-value pairs. This can be helpful for documenting your image or adding custom information that can be used by run-time tools.

Next, the **COPY** instruction allows you to add files or directories from the host system to the container's filesystem. This instruction is often used to include application code or configuration files.

The **RUN** instruction (not shown in Figure 10-8) is used to execute commands inside the image during the build process. This instruction is typically used to install software packages, making it a vital element of the Containerfile.

The **EXPOSE** instruction indicates the ports that the container uses. While this instruction does not actually open any ports, it serves as a form of documentation that can be useful when running containers from the image.

Setting a working directory within the container is achieved with the **WORKDIR** instruction, which behaves analogously to the **cd** command in Linux.

The **CMD** instruction allows you to specify a default command and its arguments that will be executed when you initiate the container with **podman run**.

An optional **ENTRYPOINT** instruction can also be used to set a command that always executes upon the container's startup and remains persistent even if a command is provided to **podman run**. **ENTRYPOINT** can also be overridden, but doing so requires the explicit **--entrypoint** flag.

To translate the instructions in a Containerfile into a functional container image, the **podman build** command is used. For example:

```
podman build -t python-webserver .
```

In the preceding command, the period denotes the path to the directory containing the Containerfile (the current directory, in this case). The **-t** option assigns a name (and optionally, a tag) to the newly created image, such as **python-webserver:1.0**. If a tag is omitted, Podman will automatically assign the **latest** tag to the image.

Exercise 10-1 further explicates the process of building a custom image and running a container from it. Then, Exercise 10-2 shows you how to upload the image to the Quay registry.

EXERCISE 10-1

Building and Running a Container Image

In this exercise, you'll go through the process of creating a Containerfile, building an image from it, and subsequently running a container. This practice will solidify your understanding of managing containers using Podman.

1. Create a Containerfile using the template provided in Figure 10-8. Ensure you understand the instructions within the Containerfile, as they dictate the structure and functionality of the container image.

2. In the same directory as your Containerfile, generate a file named index.html. This file will serve as the content served by your web server. Add a simple message to it like "Welcome to our simple webserver!"

3. With your Containerfile and index.html prepared, you can proceed to build the image. Run the following command to construct the image. The **-t** flag assigns the name python-webserver to your image, and the dot refers to the location of your Containerfile—the current directory:

```
# podman build -t python-webserver .
```

4. Confirm that the image has been built and is available on your local system by running **podman images**. This lists all available images, and you should see python-webserver in this list.

5. Run a container from the image you just built:

```
# podman run -d --name simple-webserver -p 8000:8000 python-webserver
```

This starts a container named simple-webserver in the background, mapping the container's TCP port 8000 to the host's port 8000, based on the python-webserver image.

6. Confirm that the container is up and running with the **podman ps -a** command. You should see simple-webserver in the list of active containers.

7. Your container runs a lightweight web server that listens on TCP port 8000. To verify that it's functioning correctly, connect to it using a web browser or run **curl http://localhost:8000** in your terminal. You should see the content you added to index.html—"Welcome to our simple webserver!"

8. Once you've confirmed that everything is working as expected, it's good practice to clean up. Stop the container:

```
# podman stop simple-webserver
```

9. Don't remove the container image yet. You will be using it for the following exercise.

EXERCISE 10-2

Uploading an Image to Quay.io

This exercise familiarizes you with Quay.io, an image repository sponsored by Red Hat that offers some advanced features. These features include server-side image building, detailed access control, and automated vulnerability scanning of images. Your goal in this exercise is to upload to Quay.io the python-webserver image you built earlier.

1. Navigate to https://quay.io and sign in using your Red Hat account credentials. If you don't have a Red Hat account, you'll need to create one.

2. Once logged in, click the account settings located in the top-right corner of the web page.

3. In the account settings, find and click Generate Encrypted Password. This will create an encrypted password for you to use with Podman. In the same window, navigate to the Podman Login tab. Here, you'll find the exact Podman command you'll need to log into Quay.io.

4. Copy the Podman login command and paste it into your terminal. The command should resemble the following:

   ```
   $ podman login -u=<yourquayuser> -p=<yourtoken> quay.io
   ```

5. Before proceeding, ensure that the simple-webserver image is available locally on your system:

   ```
   $ podman images
   ```

6. With the image available, you can now tag it for Quay.io using the following command:

   ```
   $ podman tag localhost/python-webserver:latest quay.io/↵
   <yourusername>/simple-webserver:latest
   ```

   This command renames or "tags" your python-webserver image, prepending the Quay.io repository path to it.

7. Now, you can push or upload the image to Quay.io. Execute the following command to push the image:

   ```
   $ podman push quay.io/<yourusername>/simple-webserver:latest
   ```

8. Finally, head back to the Quay.io web page and navigate to your repositories. Here, you should see the simple-webserver image listed, confirming that the image was uploaded successfully.

Managing Containers

In this section, we dive deeper into the rich set of Podman commands, expanding your understanding of how to interact with and manage containers. We will take a closer look at a variety of commands, each with its own purpose, and how they help in making the most of container technology.

Toward the end of this section, we will shift our focus to examine how to run a container as a systemd service. This feature has immense utility in real-world applications as it offers the advantage of automatic startup during system boot, thus ensuring high availability of the containerized services. Finally, we will explore how to use persistent storage with containers.

Podman Commands

In this section, you'll get to know more about Podman commands. You've already used some of these commands, and you're going to learn some new ones as well. Podman commands are like tools in a toolbox, each doing a special job. They help us create and manage containers or images, and they let us look at details about containers or images.

To make the variety of Podman commands easier to understand, we can sort them into five main groups:

- **Container management commands** These commands are like the controllers. They help us to make, start, stop, and remove containers.
- **Container inspection commands** These commands are like detectives. They help us find out what's happening with a container, what its setup is, and what it's been doing.
- **Image management commands** These commands are the organizers for our image library. They help us make, get, name, and remove images.
- **Image inspection commands** These commands are also like detectives, but for images. They help us find out all the details about an image.
- **Miscellaneous commands** This group is for the commands that don't fit into the other groups. They do all sorts of different jobs, like managing the whole system or setting up networks.

Figure 10-9 shows the commands in each category.

FIGURE 10-9

A classification
of Podman
commands

	Management Commands	Inspection Commands
Container Commands	podman create podman rm podman run podman start podman stop	podman ps podman inspect podman logs
Images Commands	podman build podman login podman pull podman push podman rmi podman tag	podman images podman inspect podman search

Next, we'll go into each group of commands and learn about the specific jobs they do.

e x a m

ⓦ a t c h   **Remember, this**
categorization is a guide to understand
Podman commands. However, during
the RHCSA exam, you have a convenient
resource at hand—the Podman manual

page. Simply type man podman **for broad**
documentation or use a command such
as man podman-run **for specific command**
details. It's an invaluable aid during
your exam.

Container Management Commands

The commands presented in Table 10-1 are pivotal for managing containers.

We have already introduced the **podman run** command, but let's dive deeper. This command is essentially a combination of **podman create** and **podman start**. Depending on the flags you use, the behavior can differ. For instance, using **-d** (detached mode) allows the container to run in the background, whereas **-it** enables interactive mode with a terminal.

Let's consider some examples. If you want to run a container in the background, you could use

```
$ podman run -d registry.access.redhat.com/ubi9/httpd-24
```

For interactive terminal sessions, you might use

```
$ podman run -it registry.access.redhat.com/ubi9 /bin/bash
```

TABLE 10-1	Container Management Commands
Command	**Description**
podman run	Starts a new container from an image. If the image isn't locally available, it pulls it from the registry first.
podman create	Creates a new container from an image, but doesn't start it. It's useful for preparing a container for later use.
podman rm	Removes an existing, stopped container. It's used for cleaning up containers that are no longer needed.
podman start	Starts an already created but not yet started container. It's used after **podman create** to initiate the container.
podman stop	Stops a running container, making it inactive but not removing it. It can be started again with **podman start**.

The latter command would start a bash shell in the container, allowing you to interact with it directly. The **podman run** command offers several other commonly used options. For instance, you can use --**name** to designate a specific name for the container. If a name is not assigned to the container with --**name**, then Podman generates a random string name. You can also utilize -**p** to establish port mappings, as demonstrated in the section "Running Your First Container." Moreover, at the end of this chapter, we will delve into a fresh option, -**v**, which enables the mounting of a volume into the container.

on the
ⓘob

ubi9 is the Red Hat Universal Base Image (UBI), a base image provided by Red Hat. It serves as a foundation for building containerized applications and is designed to be lightweight, secure, and reliable. UBI is based on Red Hat Enterprise Linux.

If we were to decompose **podman run**, we would first use **podman create** to create the container, and then **podman start** to run it. For example:

```
$ podman create --name my-container ↵
registry.access.redhat.com/ubi9/httpd-24
$ podman start my-container
```

When you issue the **podman stop** command, the container ceases to run but still exists in the system. You can easily start it up again using **podman start**. For instance:

```
$ podman stop my-container
$ podman start my-container
```

Finally, to permanently remove a container from the system, you would use **podman rm**. It's important to note that this will delete all the data associated with the container. For example:

```
$ podman rm my-container
```

TABLE 10-2	Container Inspection Commands

Command	Description
podman inspect	Shows detailed information about a container. It provides details such as the state of a container, its configuration, network settings, and more.
podman logs	Displays the log messages from a running or a stopped container. It's useful for troubleshooting or understanding the activities of a container.
podman ps	Lists the containers currently running on your system. It provides information like container ID, image, command, creation time, status, ports, and names. With additional options, you can also see stopped containers.

Container Inspection Commands

Table 10-2 introduces a range of container inspection commands, which are indispensable for understanding the inner workings of our containers.

First up is **podman inspect**, a versatile command that provides detailed information about a container. This includes but is not limited to its ID, created time, path, args, state, and much more. This command will output a JSON representation of the container's current state, giving you valuable insight into its configuration and status. You can see an excerpt of the output in Figure 10-10.

Next, the **podman ps** command shows you all the running containers. You will see details like the container ID, image, command, when it was created, status, and names. But what if

FIGURE 10-10	An excerpt of the output of the **podman inspect command**

```
[mike@server1 ~]$ podman inspect webserver
[
    {
        "Id": "a8b485b869f4f39eb31fa6e45498dcc1da1bf86b249e29b794f44a02e54950fd",
        "Created": "2023-07-27T03:49:39.597280191+01:00",
        "Path": "container-entrypoint",
        "Args": [
            "/usr/bin/run-httpd"
        ],
        "State": {
            "OciVersion": "1.0.2-dev",
            "Status": "running",
            "Running": true,
            "Paused": false,
            "Restarting": false,
            "OOMKilled": false,
            "Dead": false,
            "Pid": 51117,
            "ConmonPid": 51115,
            "ExitCode": 0,
            "Error": "",
            "StartedAt": "2023-07-27T03:49:39.674913042+01:00",
            "FinishedAt": "0001-01-01T00:00:00Z",
            "Health": {
```

FIGURE 10-11 The output of the **podman logs** command

```
[mike@server1 ~]$ podman logs webserver
=> sourcing 10-set-mpm.sh ...
=> sourcing 20-copy-config.sh ...
=> sourcing 40-ssl-certs.sh ...
---> Generating SSL key pair for httpd...
AH00558: httpd: Could not reliably determine the server's fully qualified domain name, using 10.0.2.100. Set the 'Se
rverName' directive globally to suppress this message
[Thu Jul 27 02:49:41.410528 2023] [ssl:warn] [pid 1:tid 1] AH01909: 10.0.2.100:8443:0 server certificate does NOT in
clude an ID which matches the server name
[Thu Jul 27 02:49:41.410734 2023] [:notice] [pid 1:tid 1] ModSecurity for Apache/2.9.6 (http://www.modsecurity.org/)
 configured.
[Thu Jul 27 02:49:41.410745 2023] [:notice] [pid 1:tid 1] ModSecurity: APR compiled version="1.7.0"; loaded version=
"1.7.0"
[Thu Jul 27 02:49:41.410748 2023] [:notice] [pid 1:tid 1] ModSecurity: PCRE compiled version="8.44 "; loaded version
="8.44 2020-02-12"
[Thu Jul 27 02:49:41.410754 2023] [:notice] [pid 1:tid 1] ModSecurity: LUA compiled version="Lua 5.4"
[Thu Jul 27 02:49:41.410755 2023] [:notice] [pid 1:tid 1] ModSecurity: YAJL compiled version="2.1.0"
[Thu Jul 27 02:49:41.410755 2023] [:notice] [pid 1:tid 1] ModSecurity: LIBXML compiled version="2.9.13"
[Thu Jul 27 02:49:41.410756 2023] [:notice] [pid 1:tid 1] ModSecurity: Status engine is currently disabled, enable i
t by set SecStatusEngine to On.
AH00558: httpd: Could not reliably determine the server's fully qualified domain name, using 10.0.2.100. Set the 'Se
rverName' directive globally to suppress this message
[Thu Jul 27 02:49:41.479897 2023] [ssl:warn] [pid 1:tid 1] AH01909: 10.0.2.100:8443:0 server certificate does NOT in
clude an ID which matches the server name
[Thu Jul 27 02:49:41.480184 2023] [lbmethod_heartbeat:notice] [pid 1:tid 1] AH02282: No slotmem from mod_heartmonito
r
[Thu Jul 27 02:49:41.482746 2023] [mpm_event:notice] [pid 1:tid 1] AH00489: Apache/2.4.53 (Red Hat Enterprise Linux)
 OpenSSL/3.0.7 configured -- resuming normal operations
[Thu Jul 27 02:49:41.482769 2023] [core:notice] [pid 1:tid 1] AH00094: Command line: 'httpd -D FOREGROUND'
[Thu Jul 27 02:50:41.635705 2023] [autoindex:error] [pid 55:tid 226] [client 10.0.2.100:49570] AH01276: Cannot serve
 directory /var/www/html/: No matching DirectoryIndex (index.html) found, and server-generated directory index forbi
dden by Options directive
10.0.2.100 - - [27/Jul/2023:02:50:41 +0000] "GET / HTTP/1.1" 403 5909 "-" "Mozilla/5.0 (X11; Linux x86_64; rv:102.0)
 Gecko/20100101 Firefox/102.0"
[mike@server1 ~]$ ▊
```

you want to see all containers, not just the running ones? That's when the **-a** option comes into play. Running **podman ps -a** will list both running and stopped containers, providing a comprehensive overview of all your containers.

Finally, **podman logs** is a must-have tool in your container troubleshooting toolkit. It fetches the logs of a specified container, which can be crucial when diagnosing problems. For example, see Figure 10-11.

Together, these commands form the basis of container inspection and provide a valuable insight into the container's operations. They can be instrumental when debugging issues or understanding the behavior of your containers.

Image Management Commands

Table 10-3 reviews a variety of image management commands. These commands are essential tools for creating, retrieving, renaming, and deleting container images.

First, let's review the **podman build** command, previously introduced in the section "Building Container Images: A Primer." This command is used to build a container image from a Containerfile (or a Dockerfile). For instance, if you have a Containerfile in your current directory, you can run the following command to create an image named my-image:

```
$ podman build -t my-image .
```

The **-t** option allows you to tag your image, while the period (.) denotes that the build context is the current directory.

TABLE 10-3	Image Management Commands
Command	**Description**
podman build	Creates a new container image from a Containerfile (similar to a Dockerfile). The Containerfile contains a list of instructions to define what goes on in the environment inside your container.
podman login	Authenticates with a container registry. This is particularly useful when you need to push or pull images from private registries that require authentication.
podman pull	Downloads an image from a container registry, like Quay.io or Docker Hub. This image can then be used to create new containers on your system.
podman push	Uploads a container image to a container registry. You would use this command to share your container images with others or deploy them in different environments.
podman rmi	Removes one or more images from your local system. It's useful for keeping your system clean and free from unused or outdated images.
podman tag	Assigns a tag to a container image. Tags are usually used to manage versions of an image, but you can also use them for other purposes.

The trio of commands **podman tag**, **podman push**, and **podman pull** are essential for managing images between local and remote registries. **podman tag** is used to assign a tag or another name to an existing image, providing a convenient way to reference images. For instance, the command shown next tags the image my-image with a version designation of v1.0:

```
$ podman tag my-image:latest my-image:v1.0
```

Next, the **podman push** command enables you to push an image from your local machine to a remote registry. If you've tagged your image my-image:v1.0, you can push it to a registry such as Quay.io by running

```
$ podman push quay.io/username/my-image:v1.0
```

and replacing "username" with your Quay.io username. Note that in a private registry that requires authentication, such as Quay.io, you need to log in first with the **podman login** command.

In contrast, the **podman pull** command is used to fetch an image from a remote registry to your local machine. For example, the following command would pull the latest nginx-122 image from the Red Hat registry:

```
$ podman pull registry.access.redhat.com/ubi9/nginx-122
```

Lastly, the **podman rmi** command is used for removing images from your local storage. If you're finished with an image, or if you need to clean up storage, **podman rmi my-image:v1.0** would remove the specified image. It's good practice to keep your image storage tidy, removing unneeded images to save space.

TABLE 10-4	Image Inspection Commands

Command	Description
podman images	Lists all the container images currently stored on your system. It provides information such as the repository, tag, image ID, and creation date for each image.
podman inspect	This command, also shown in Table 10-2, can be applied not only to containers but to images as well, providing comprehensive details about them.
podman search	Helps you to find container images on a registry. It's like a search engine for container images.

Image Inspection Commands

In the following discussion, outlined in Table 10-4, we'll revisit some of the image inspection commands discussed earlier in the chapter. The objective of these commands is to provide you with extensive information about the container images that are present on a system.

One of the most basic but essential commands for working with Podman is **podman images**. It gives you an overview of all the container images that are stored locally on your system. The information it displays includes the repository name, the image tag, the image ID, when it was created, and the size of the image. For instance, if you run **podman images**, you'll see a table with details of all the images you have downloaded or built on your machine, as shown in Figure 10-12.

Next is the **podman inspect** command. While this command is versatile and can be applied to both containers and images, its usage with images provides a wealth of details about a specific image. If you run **podman inspect <image-name>**, where image-name is the name (or the ID) of your image, you'll see JSON output with detailed information about the image, including its ID, configuration, and layers, among other things.

Here's where it gets interesting: the **podman inspect** command varies from the **skopeo inspect** command previously introduced in the section "Image Registries." The difference lies in the fact that **skopeo inspect** can fetch information directly from a remote registry, while **podman inspect** only inspects images already downloaded on your system. For example, the following command retrieves the metadata of the nginx image from the Red Hat registry, without downloading the image itself:

```
$ skopeo inspect docker://registry.access.redhat.com/ubi9/nginx
```

FIGURE 10-12	A list of local container images shown by **podman images**

```
[mike@server1 ~]$ podman images
REPOSITORY                                TAG      IMAGE ID       CREATED         SIZE
localhost/webserver                       latest   0b49309eb5df   13 seconds ago  996 MB
registry.access.redhat.com/ubi9/httpd-24  latest   934be1fb277c   9 days ago      377 MB
registry.access.redhat.com/ubi9/python-39 latest   a9b24b965feb   5 weeks ago     996 MB
[mike@server1 ~]$ 
```

Lastly, the **podman search** command allows you to search for images on a container registry right from your terminal. The command **podman search <search-term>** will return a list of all images whose name matches the search term, along with a brief description and star ratings if available. It's a handy tool when you're looking for a particular image or exploring available options for a specific service. For example, **podman search ubi9** would return a list of available Red Hat Universal Base Image 9 from the default registries.

Miscellaneous Commands

Finally, we delve into a group of commands that, while not fitting neatly into our previous categories, offer unique and practical utilities in managing containers. These miscellaneous commands are outlined in Table 10-5.

Let's begin with the **podman attach** and **podman exec** commands. While both are used to interact with running containers, they have significant differences. The **podman attach** command connects to a running container's main process, allowing you to interact with it as if you were directly logged in. For example, if you've started a container in detached mode using **podman run -d my-container**, you can attach to it with **podman attach my-container** (or using the container ID rather than the name).

On the other hand, **podman exec** executes a new process within an already running container. This is useful for running specific commands or scripts within a container without interrupting its main process. For instance, the following command would list the contents of the root ("/") directory in your running container:

```
$ podman exec my-container ls /
```

Just like with all Podman commands, you have the flexibility to use either the name or the ID of a container (or image) interchangeably. This means you can refer to a specific container or image by its given name or unique identifier based on your preference or needs.

Moving on to **podman cp**, this command is akin to the familiar **cp** command on Linux, allowing you to copy files or directories between the host and a container. For instance, to copy a file from your host to a running container, you'd use the command shown next:

```
$ podman cp /host/path/file.txt my-container:/container/path/
```

To do the reverse, simply flip the source and destination.

The **podman generate** command, listed in Table 10-5, will be detailed in the next section.

Lastly, we have the **podman info** and **podman version** commands. **podman info** provides a comprehensive overview of your Podman installation, including configuration details and the status of storage, registries, and more. On the other hand, **podman version** simply returns the version of Podman you have installed, with the API version and other build details. These commands are especially useful when troubleshooting or verifying your setup.

TABLE 10-5 Miscellaneous Commands

Command	Description
podman attach	Allows you to connect to a running container's standard input, output, and error streams. It's like stepping into the running container and observing or interacting with its processes directly.
podman cp	Enables you to copy files or directories between your local system and a container.
podman exec	Runs a command inside a running container. It's useful for tasks such as checking the status of services in the container or other debugging tasks.
podman generate	Creates a systemd unit file for a container, which can be used to manage the container lifecycle with the **systemctl** command.
podman info	Provides a summary of the system's Podman configuration and state. It includes details about the host, registries, containers, images, and more.
podman version	Displays the version of Podman that is currently installed on your system. It's useful for ensuring you're running the latest version or for troubleshooting compatibility issues.

Running a Container as a SystemD Service

Let's delve into the process of running a container as a systemd service, which can be incredibly useful for containers that need to persist across reboots, such as a web server or a database container.

Back in Chapter 5, you learned how to enable and manage services using the **systemctl** command. Podman extends this capability by allowing you to create systemd configuration files for your container services using the **podman generate systemd** command.

Let's imagine that we have a web server container operating, brought to life with the following command, as described in the earlier section, "Running Your First Container":

```
$ podman run -d --name webserver -p 8080:8080 ↵
registry.access.redhat.com/ubi9/httpd-24
```

Here, the **podman generate systemd** command can take this running container and use it as a blueprint to create a service configuration file. Here's an example of this:

```
$ podman generate systemd --name webserver --new
```

This command will output the systemd configuration file necessary to run the container as a service, as shown in Figure 10-13. By employing the **--files** option, instead of outputting the configuration to your console, it will create the configuration file. If the container is running as a nonprivileged user, this file would then need to be relocated to the ~/.config/systemd/user directory. If it's running as root, it should go into /etc/systemd/system.

FIGURE 10-13

A systemd unit
configuration
generated by
**podman generate
systemd**

```
[mike@server1 ~]$ podman generate systemd --name webserver --new
# container-webserver.service
# autogenerated by Podman 4.2.0
# Thu Jul 27 06:24:19 BST 2023

[Unit]
Description=Podman container-webserver.service
Documentation=man:podman-generate-systemd(1)
Wants=network-online.target
After=network-online.target
RequiresMountsFor=%t/containers

[Service]
Environment=PODMAN_SYSTEMD_UNIT=%n
Restart=on-failure
TimeoutStopSec=70
ExecStartPre=/bin/rm -f %t/%n.ctr-id
ExecStart=/usr/bin/podman run \
        --cidfile=%t/%n.ctr-id \
        --cgroups=no-conmon \
        --rm \
        --sdnotify=conmon \
        --replace \
        -d \
        --name webserver \
        -p 8080:8080 registry.access.redhat.com/ubi9/httpd-24
ExecStop=/usr/bin/podman stop --ignore --cidfile=%t/%n.ctr-id
ExecStopPost=/usr/bin/podman rm -f --ignore --cidfile=%t/%n.ctr-id
Type=notify
NotifyAccess=all

[Install]
WantedBy=default.target
[mike@server1 ~]$ █
```

INSIDE THE EXAM

If you're feeling overwhelmed by the details in this section, the **man podman-generate-** **systemd** command will serve as a handy resource during the RHCSA exam.

Observe in Figure 10-13 that the systemd service has been named container-webserver .service. By default, **podman generate systemd** prepends "container-" to the name of the container to form the systemd unit's name, unless a different prefix is specified using the **--container-prefix** option.

Once your configuration file is in place, you can start the service and check its status using

```
$ systemctl --user start container-webserver.service
$ systemctl --user status container-webserver.service
```

Let's briefly unpack what the --**user** option does here. It specifies that we are managing services for the current user, rather than system-wide services.

To ensure the service starts automatically at boot, execute the following command:

```
$ systemctl --user enable container-webserver.service
```

If you're running a systemd service as a regular user, an additional step is needed. Without this, your container could stop shortly after you exit your SSH session. To prevent this and keep your user's systemd services running, run the following command:

```
$ loginctl enable-linger
```

This step isn't necessary if the container is running as root.

To better understand and put into practice the concepts explained in this section, proceed to Exercise 10-3.

EXERCISE 10-3

Running a Container as a Service

In this exercise, you'll walk through the practical steps to run a container as a systemd service, using the webserver container you previously set up in the section "Running Your First Container."

1. Log in as a regular user. To manage systemd user services, it's important to directly log in without using the **su** or **sudo** commands to create a session.

2. Start the Apache web server by executing the following command (previously discussed in the "Running Your First Container" section):

```
$ podman run -d --name webserver -p 8080:8080 \
  registry.access.redhat.com/ubi9/httpd-24
```

If you've previously created this container and it's currently stopped, you can get it up and running again using the **podman start** command.

3. Check if the container is actively running:

```
$ podman ps
```

4. Use the **podman generate systemd** command to take your running webserver container and create a systemd service configuration file:

```
$ podman generate systemd --name webserver --new –files
```

5. Copy the configuration file to the ~/.config/systemd/user directory; if the directory doesn't already exist, create it:

```
$ mkdir -p ~/.config/systemd/user
$ cp container-webserver.service ~/.config/systemd/user/
```

6. Stop and remove the active container:

```
$ podman stop webserver
$ podman rm webserver
```

7. Reload systemd so it recognizes the new unit file:

```
$ systemctl --user daemon-reload
```

8. Start the container service and enable it to boot automatically at startup:

```
$ systemctl --user start container-webserver
$ systemctl --user enable container-webserver
```

Alternatively, the following command accomplishes both tasks at once:

```
$ systemctl --user enable --now container-webserver
```

9. To ensure systemd services for your user account start at system boot, run

```
$ loginctl enable-linger
```

10. Reboot your system:

```
$ sudo reboot
```

11. Verify that your container is running and that the web server is accessible:

```
$ podman ps
$ systemctl status container-webserver
$ curl http://localhost:8080
```

12. Finally, clean up:

```
$ systemctl --user stop container-webserver
$ rm ~/.config/systemd/user/container-webserver
$ systemctl --user daemon-reload
```

As an additional challenge, attempt this exercise as the root user. The differences here include not needing the --**user** option for **systemctl** commands and not having to run **loginctl enable-linger**. Moreover, the systemd configuration file should be relocated to /etc/systemd/system instead of the ~/.config/systemd/user directory.

Persistent Storage

Storage in containers is often described as "ephemeral," meaning that it is temporary and its contents will not be retained once the container is removed. The fundamental nature of containerized applications is such that they operate on the assumption of always starting with a clean storage slate.

Let's break down a few terms in the context of container images:

- *Ephemeral* means temporary. Any changes made to the container, such as adding files or modifying configurations, will be lost once the container is removed unless these changes are written to a persistent volume.
- *Immutable* means that a container based on that image will always start in the exact state of the image at the time of its creation.
- *Layered* means that each change to an image creates a new layer. These layers are stacked on top of each other, with each layer containing only the changes from the previous layer. This layered approach optimizes storage, simplifies updates and rollbacks, and speeds up container startup times.

While containers operate under the presumption of ephemeral and immutable storage, in some circumstances persistent storage is required. For instance, databases and other data-intensive applications require storage that persists beyond the lifespan of a single container instance. Persistent storage is also needed when multiple containers need to access the same data, or when data must be kept across updates and restarts.

Podman provides a solution for this by enabling the mounting of host directories inside a running container. The containerized application perceives these host directories as an integral part of the container storage, akin to how regular applications perceive a remote network volume as part of the host filesystem. Unlike the ephemeral storage in the container, the content of these host directories remains intact after the container is stopped, enabling them to be mounted to new containers as needed.

Let's illustrate with an example. Assume you want to connect the contents of the directory ~/app on your host to a container named my-container under the directory /app. To achieve this, you would create the container with the following command:

```
$ podman run -d --name my-container -v ~/app:/app:Z my-image:latest
```

In this command, the **-v** option enables volume mounting, essentially linking a host directory (in this case, ~/app) to a directory inside the container (/app). The **Z** at the end instructs SELinux to apply the appropriate file context (container_file_t) to the directory.

One crucial point to note is that user IDs (UIDs) and group IDs (GIDs) inside a container differ from those of the user that initiated the container. This discrepancy occurs because containers have their own user namespaces, which can lead to permission issues when trying to access or modify files in the mounted directory. Hence, you must assign the correct permissions to the directory that you mount inside a container.

To put these concepts into practice, proceed to Exercise 10-4.

EXERCISE 10-4

Attaching Persistent Storage to a Container

This hands-on exercise walks you through a practical example of attaching persistent storage to a container, extending the webserver example from the section "Running Your First Container."

1. Log in as a regular user to your Linux system.

2. Prepare the host directory that you want to mount onto your container. Create a directory called ~/html:

   ```
   $ mkdir ~/html
   ```

3. Navigate to the ~/html directory and create a file with some simple content. For instance, create an index.html file with the message "Welcome to our webserver!" by using the following **echo** command:

   ```
   $ echo "Welcome to our webserver" > ~/html/index.html
   ```

4. With your directory and file prepared, you are now ready to create and launch your container. Here, you will mount the ~/html directory from your local host to the /var/www/html directory within your container. Run the following command:

   ```
   $ podman run -d --name webserver -v ~/html:/var/www/html:Z \
     -p 8080:8080 registry.access.redhat.com/ubi9/httpd-24
   ```

5. After creating and launching the container, ensure that it is actively running:

   ```
   $ podman ps
   ```

6. Next, verify that your web page is properly displayed. Use the **curl** command to fetch the content of the web page:

   ```
   $ curl http://localhost:8080
   ```

   You should see the message "Welcome to our webserver!"

7. Experiment with changing the permissions of the ~/html directory on the host. Modify the permissions to make it accessible only by your user:

   ```
   $ chmod 700 ~/html
   ```

8. If you now try to access the web page, you will encounter a permission error. Verify this by running the following again:

   ```
   $ curl http://localhost:8080
   ```

9. To correct this, you need to adjust the permissions of the directory to make it accessible again. You can achieve this by setting the permissions back to 755:

```
$ chmod 755 ~/html
```

10. Lastly, it's time to clean up after the exercise:

```
$ podman stop webserver
$ podman rm webserver
```

CERTIFICATION SUMMARY

This chapter delved into the transformative world of containers, an innovative technological development that has become a cornerstone in modern DevOps and cloud infrastructure ecosystems.

You can envision containers as secure, isolated boxes that encapsulate applications, functioning much like virtual machines. Yet, the comparison stops there. Containers are much more lightweight than virtual machines because they don't need a separate operating system to function. They rely on and share the operating system of the host machine they're running on. This unique characteristic allows containers to use fewer resources, and, as a result, they can initiate and terminate operations rapidly.

In RHEL 9, Podman is the tool of choice for managing containers. At the core of Podman operations is the **podman run** command, which creates a new container. This command can be customized with a plethora of subcommands and options to suit various scenarios.

The genesis of a container lies in an image, akin to a blueprint that specifies its structure and contents. These images act as templates from which containers are built. They are stored in dedicated storage locations known as registries, ready to be pulled and used whenever a container needs to be created.

In addition, images can also be tailor-made using a Containerfile, a text document that contains all the commands a user could call on the command line to assemble an image. Building images from a Containerfile opens up the possibility of creating personalized containers, fine-tuned to meet specific requirements.

Podman offers a comprehensive set of commands to manage and inspect containers and images, extending its usability far beyond mere creation. Some of the common commands include **podman create** for container creation, **podman start** for starting a container, **podman inspect** for inspecting container details, and **podman search** for searching images in a remote registry. However, this is just scratching the surface, and there are many more commands to explore.

One of the prominent features of Podman is the ability to run containers as systemd services that start automatically at boot. The **podman generate systemd** command can generate a systemd service configuration file based on a running container, enabling the seamless integration of containers into a systemd-driven system.

Despite their extensive capabilities, it's important to remember that containers are ephemeral by nature. Their contents do not survive beyond their lifecycle. However, Podman provides a mechanism to persist data across container lifecycles. Host directories can be mounted inside a container using the **-v** option of the **podman run** command, enabling data to persist beyond the container's lifespan and making it accessible to subsequent containers.

TWO-MINUTE DRILL

Here are some of the key points from the certification objectives in Chapter 10.

Fundamentals of Container Technology

- ❑ DevOps practices have supported the use of containers, lightweight tools that ensure software consistency across different platforms.
- ❑ Containers are often favored over virtual machines due to their speed, efficiency, and portability.
- ❑ Container architecture utilizes key Linux features for process and resource isolation, such as namespaces, cgroups, and SELinux, along with standardized container images and container registries.
- ❑ Docker, responsible for popularizing container technology, now has major competition from Podman, a more secure and system-integrated alternative developed by Red Hat.

Getting Started with Containers

- ❑ The **container-tools** meta-package for RHEL 9 includes Podman, Skopeo, and Buildah.
- ❑ Containers can be created and started with the **podman run** command.
- ❑ Containers can be started in the background (detached) mode with the **-d** command option.
- ❑ Containers can be managed using their unique ID or their given name.
- ❑ After usage, containers can be cleaned up, with commands such as **podman rm** to remove containers and **podman rmi** to remove local images.
- ❑ Rootful containers, run by root users, have broad capabilities but also pose potential security risks, while rootless containers, run by non-root users, offer a more secure environment.

Building and Using Container Images

❏ Container images and registries provide a mechanism for storage, distribution, and versioning of container images.

❏ The **podman images** command allows you to view locally stored images.

❏ The **podman info** command provides configuration details about Podman, including currently configured registries.

❏ Notable registries include registry.access.redhat.com, registry.redhat.io, and docker.io (Docker Hub).

❏ The **podman search** command helps locate images across configured registries.

❏ For detailed information about specific images, the **skopeo inspect** command can be used.

❏ Building custom container images can be achieved through a Containerfile.

❏ The **podman build** command translates instructions from a Containerfile into a functional container image.

Managing Containers

❏ Running a container as a systemd service involves using the **podman generate systemd** command to create a systemd unit file from a running container.

❏ For nonprivileged users, systemd unit files are located in ~/.config/systemd/user, while for root they can be placed in /etc/systemd/system.

❏ In containers, storage is typically ephemeral and immutable. However, for certain applications like databases, persistent storage may be required.

❏ The -v option of the **podman run** command can mount a local directory into a mount point on a container.

SELF TEST

The following questions will help you measure your understanding of the material presented in this chapter. As there are no multiple-choice questions on the Red Hat exams, there are no multiple-choice questions in this book. These questions exclusively test your understanding of the chapter. Getting results, not memorizing trivia, is what counts on the Red Hat exams.

Fundamentals of Container Technology

1. What are the key differences between virtual machines and containers?
2. What are the key components of container architecture and how do they function?
3. How does Podman improve on Docker's design?

Getting Started with Containers

4. What is the purpose of the **container-tools** meta-package in RHEL 9 and which key packages does it include?
5. Explain the process of running a container using the Podman tool, as well as the meaning of the **-d** and **-p** flags in the command.
6. Discuss the differences between rootless and rootful containers, their advantages, and when to use each.

Building and Using Container Images

7. What command do you run to build a container image and tag the image as dbserver if the Containerfile is in the current directory?
8. How do the **CMD** and **ENTRYPOINT** instructions differ in a Containerfile?
9. What is the function of the **skopeo inspect** command?

Managing Containers

10. How can you generate the configuration to run a container as a systemd service for a running container named ftpserver? Where should the unit configuration file be placed for a rootless container?
11. How do you ensure that a rootless container that is managed by a systemd unit named container-ftpserver.service is configured to automatically start at boot?
12. What is the meaning of the terms "ephemeral," "immutable," and "layered" in the context of container images?

LAB QUESTIONS

Red Hat presents its exams electronically. For that reason, the labs in this chapter are available from the companion website that accompanies the book. In case you haven't yet set up RHEL 9 on a system, refer to Chapter 1 for installation instructions. The answers for each lab follow the Self Test answers for the fill-in-the-blank questions

SELF TEST ANSWERS

Fundamentals of Container Technology

1. Virtual machines and containers are both forms of virtualization, but they differ in their functionality and resource utilization. VMs are completely isolated and have their own operating system, making them more resource-intensive. In contrast, containers share the host's operating system kernel, making them lighter and faster to start and stop. Containers, therefore, are highly portable and offer enough isolation for most use cases, making them popular for modern software development, particularly in DevOps and cloud computing.

2. Container architecture is composed of several Linux features designed to provide process and resource isolation, along with standardized container images and efficient use of container registries. The Linux features include namespaces that control the visibility of system resources, control groups (cgroups) that manage the allocation of system resources, and SELinux, which adds a robust security mechanism. Container images serve as blueprints for containers, packaging the software application, its dependencies, and some configuration details into a single object.

3. Podman, developed by Red Hat, addresses some of Docker's security and design issues by offering a daemonless, rootless container engine. Unlike Docker, which requires a constantly running, high-privileged daemon to manage containers, Podman launches containers and containerized services as child processes, enhancing security and reducing the attack surface. Podman's rootless feature also allows nonprivileged users to manage containers, further improving security.

Getting Started with Containers

4. The **container-tools** meta-package in RHEL 9 is used as a convenient method to install a group of related packages, and it doesn't contain any tools itself. Key commands that come along with the meta-package include **podman** (a daemonless container engine), a script named **docker** (emulates Docker CLI executing Podman commands), Skopeo (a command-line utility for container images and repositories operations), and Buildah (a tool to build OCI container images).

5. Running a container using Podman involves using the **podman run** command. The **-d** flag specifies detached mode, which allows the container to run in the background and not occupy your current terminal or shell session. The -p flag exposes a specific port of the container, making it accessible. For example, -p 80:8080 instructs Podman to open port 80 on the host machine and route all incoming traffic on this port to port 8080 inside the container.

6. A rootless container is run by a nonprivileged user, whereas a rootful container is run by a privileged user. Rootless containers, run by non-root users, offer a more constrained and controlled environment, thus posing less risk to the host system. They are generally preferred for their higher security. Conversely, rootful containers, run by the root user, have broad capabilities. For example, they can bind to network ports lower than 1024.

Building and Using Container Images

7. If the Containerfile is in the current directory, the command to build a container image and tag the image as dbserver is shown next:

```
$ podman build -t dbserver .
```

8. The **CMD** instruction specifies a default command, and its arguments that will be executed when you initiate the container with the **podman run** command. However, this can be overridden by providing a command to **podman run**. On the other hand, the **ENTRYPOINT** instruction sets a command that always executes upon the container's startup and remains persistent even if a command is provided to **podman run**. **ENTRYPOINT** can also be overridden, but doing so requires the explicit **--entrypoint** flag.

9. The **skopeo inspect** command provides intricate details about a specific image. This can be vital for evaluating whether a specific image aligns with your requirements. For example, the following command provides detailed information about the httpd-24 image:

```
$ skopeo inspect docker://registry.access.redhat.com/ubi9/httpd-24
```

Managing Containers

10. You can generate the configuration to run a container named ftpserver as a systemd service by using the following command:

```
$ podman generate systemd --name ftpserver --files --new
```

The unit configuration file must be copied to the ~/.config/systemd/user directory.

11. To ensure that a rootless container that is managed by a systemd unit named container-ftpserver .service is configured to automatically start at boot, you must run the following commands:

```
$ systemctl --user enable container-ftpserver.service
$ loginctl enable-linger
```

12. "Ephemeral" in the context of container images means temporary; any changes made to the container will be lost once it's removed, unless these changes are written to a persistent volume. "Immutable" means that an image, once created, doesn't change. Any container based on that image will always start in the exact state of the image at its creation. "Layered" means each change to an image creates a new layer, with each layer containing only the changes from the previous layer. This approach optimizes storage, simplifies updates and rollbacks, and speeds up container startup times.

LAB ANSWERS

Lab 1

BusyBox represents a valuable image for executing various tools or functioning as a foundation for additional containers.

1. Search for the image through the following command:

   ```
   $ podman search busybox
   ```

2. Once you've located the image, pull it using the following command:

   ```
   $ podman pull docker.io/library/busybox
   ```

3. To verify the size of the image, which should be less than 5MB (demonstrating its lightweight nature), execute the following:

   ```
   $ podman images
   ```

4. Attempting to run a container using the busybox image in detached mode will result in the container's immediate termination:

   ```
   $ podman run -d --name busybox busybox
   ```

5. You can verify this phenomenon using the **podman ps** command. The first command shown will not show the busybox container, as it's not running, while the subsequent command, with the **-a** option, will show all containers, including the ones in a stopped state:

   ```
   $ podman ps
   $ podman ps -a
   ```

6. Proceed by deleting the current container and creating a fresh one that runs the /bin/sh shell:

   ```
   $ podman rm busybox
   $ podman run -it --name busybox busybox /bin/sh
   ```

7. Inside this shell, you can execute the **ls /bin** command to explore the commands available within the image. Remember, this command is executed within the container's environment. You can quit this interactive shell by typing **exit**.

8. Moving to the last task, initiate a container that runs a ping to www.google.com:

   ```
   podman run busybox ping -c 5 www.google.com
   ```

Lab 2

In this activity, you're asked to build a Python image that runs a simple service that returns "pong" when pinged.

1. Search for the Python 3.9 image with this command:

   ```
   $ podman search python-39
   ```

   This shows you the Red Hat UBI 9 Python 3.9 image to use.

2. Make a Containerfile that tells Podman how to create your image. Here's what you need to put in it:

   ```
   FROM registry.access.redhat.com/ubi9/python-39
   RUN pip install Flask
   EXPOSE 8000
   COPY pingpong.py /app/pingpong.py
   WORKDIR /app
   CMD ["python", "pingpong.py"]
   ```

3. You also need to create the pingpong.py file in the same directory. Make sure you copy the content provided in the lab exercise into this file.

4. Build the image:

   ```
   $ podman build -t pingpong .
   ```

5. Create a container from the image you just made with this command:

   ```
   $ podman run -d --name pingpong -p 1234:8000 pingpong
   ```

   Pay attention to the **-p 1234:8000** command option. This tells Podman to connect TCP port 1234 on your computer to port 8000 on the container.

6. Make sure the container is running with **podman ps**.

7. Test the service with this command:

   ```
   $ curl http://localhost:1234/ping
   ```

   It should respond with "pong."

8. If something goes wrong, you can check the logs with **podman logs pingpong**.

9. Do not stop or remove the container, as you'll be using it for the next lab.

Lab 3

In this lab task, you're building upon the steps you accomplished in Lab 2, but this time as a non-root user.

1. Execute the following command to generate a systemd configuration file for your container service:

   ```
   $ podman generate systemd --name pingpong --new --files
   ```

   This command results in creating a container-pingpong.service file in your current directory.

2. Move this file into the ~/.config/systemd/user directory. If this directory doesn't already exist, you'll have to create it:

   ```
   $ mkdir -p ~/.config/systemd/user
   $ cp container-pingpong.service ~/.config/systemd/user
   ```

3. Stop and remove the current pingpong container:

   ```
   $ podman stop pingpong
   $ podman rm pingpong
   ```

4. Refresh systemd and set up the service to automatically start when your system boots:

   ```
   $ systemctl --user daemon-reload
   $ systemctl --user enable container-pingpong.service
   $ loginctl enable-linger
   ```

5. To verify that everything is set up correctly, reboot your system and check if the container is running:

   ```
   $ systemctl --user status container-pingpong.service
   $ podman ps
   ```

6. Use the following commands to stop and remove the container and its image:

   ```
   $ systemctl --user stop container-pingpong.service
   $ podman rmi pingpong
   ```

To replicate this task and run the container as a root user, please be aware of a few subtleties. You should first move the existing container-pingpong.service file from the ~/.config/systemd/user directory to the /etc/systemd/system directory. It's important to ensure that the rootless container has been halted and deleted beforehand. Furthermore, verify that the pingpong image has been built by the root user.

After ensuring this, proceed with the following commands to configure the service to initiate automatically at boot:

```
$ systemctl daemon-reload
$ systemctl enable container-pingpong.service
```

Note that for a container running as root, the command **loginctl enable-linger** is not necessary.

Lab 4

This lab dives deep into the dynamics of ephemeral and persistent storage in containerized applications. Understanding the difference between these two storage types is crucial as it directly impacts the behavior and longevity of data within your containers. Ephemeral storage, as the name implies, is temporary and does not survive container re-creation, while persistent storage allows data to survive beyond the life of a single container.

1. Set up and run a container that uses the Apache 2.4 web server (as covered earlier in the chapter). Before you begin, ensure that no other containers are currently using the same port; otherwise, the command to start the container will fail. Run the following command to start the container:

```
$ podman run -d --name webserver -p 8080:8080 \
  registry.access.redhat.com/ubi9/httpd-24
```

2. With the container running, open a shell inside it using the following command:

```
$ podman exec -it webserver /bin/bash
```

3. Within this shell, create the /var/www/html/index.html file and populate it with the text "Welcome to our webserver!":

```
$ echo "Welcome to our webserver!" > /var/www/html/index.html
```

4. You can confirm that the newly created index.html page is being served by running the following command on your host:

```
$ curl http://localhost:8080
```

5. Explore the ephemeral nature of container storage by stopping and removing the container and creating and running a new one with the same command:

```
$ podman stop webserver
$ podman rm webserver
$ podman run -d --name webserver -p 8080:8080 \
  registry.access.redhat.com/ubi9/httpd-24
```

6. If you check your web page now, you'll see that the changes you made have been lost and the web page has reverted to its default state. This demonstrates the ephemeral nature of container storage:

```
$ curl http://localhost:8080
```

7. Stop and remove the container again:

```
$ podman stop webserver
$ podman rm webserver
```

8. Explore the concept of persistent storage by creating a local ~/html directory on your host machine and adding the index.html file to it:

```
$ mkdir ~/html
$ echo "Welcome to our webserver!" > ~/html/index.html
```

9. Re-create the container, but this time, mount the local ~/html directory to /var/www/html inside the container:

```
$ podman run -d --name webserver -p 8080:8080 \
 -v ~/html:/var/www/html:Z \
 registry.access.redhat.com/ubi9/httpd-24
```

10. Confirm the visibility of the web page:

```
$ curl http://localhost:8080
```

Notice that even if you stop and delete the container and re-create it using the command provided in Step 9, the index.html file, which is now a part of persistent storage, is retained. This demonstrates the persistence of the storage—your changes are preserved across container lifetimes.

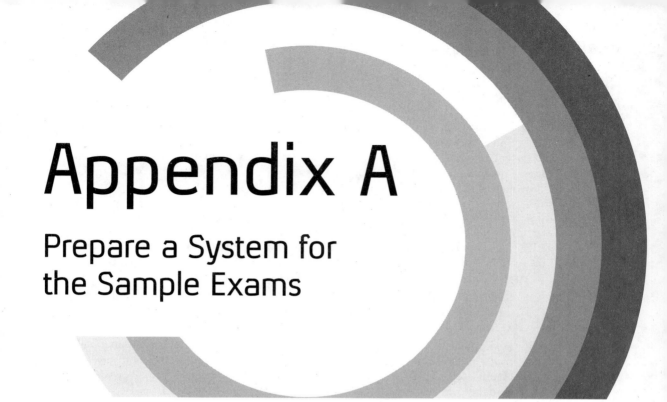

Appendix A

Prepare a System for the Sample Exams

Randy Russell, the Director of Certification at Red Hat, revealed in a blog post that Red Hat exams no longer mandate a "bare-metal installation." Put simply, you will be provided with a pre-installed system when you sit for a Red Hat exam today. This appendix guides you through the setup of a pre-installed system suitable for the two sample exams accessible on McGraw Hill's companion website. Details regarding each exam are provided on the first few pages of Appendixes B and C, respectively, followed by their solutions.

Sample Exam System Requirements

As highlighted in Chapter 1, a genuine RHEL 9 subscription is ideal for this purpose. Exercise 1-1 described how to enroll in the Red Hat Developer Program and obtain a Red Hat Developer Subscription for Individuals at no cost. Rebuild distributions, such as AlmaLinux, should function just as effectively since they are grounded on the openly available RHEL 9 source code. However, we strongly advise against using Fedora Linux for studying for Red Hat exams. Despite RHEL 9 being rooted in Fedora Linux, RHEL 9 presents a distinctive look and feel and, in certain instances, differs in functionality from the most similar Fedora release, Fedora 34.

Keeping these considerations in mind, we recommend using the server1.example.com and tester1.example.com virtual systems that you initially set up in Chapter 1. However, you will need to reinstall RHEL 9 on both systems and configure them according to the following specifications before commencing the sample RHCSA exams:

- **Network settings** For server1.example.com, assign a random IPv4 address and netmask during installation to render the system network unreachable. On tester1.example.com, leave the IPv4 default settings to use DHCP and set the hostname to tester1.example.com. These settings can be found on the Networks and Hostname configuration screen, as shown in Figures 1-6 and 1-7.

- **Root password** On server1.example.com, set a random password and forget about it (you will execute password recovery during the sample exams). On tester1.example .com, set the root password to changeme.

- **Disk space** On server1.example.com, select custom partitioning and manually configure the /boot and / partitions. Do not format the entire disk, and leave 1GB unallocated. On tester1.example.com, select automatic partitioning. For additional guidance on this topic, please consult the "Partition Creation Exercise" section in Chapter 1.

- **Software selection** In the Software Selection screen, keep the default option Server with GUI selected, as shown in Figure 1-13.

- **System subscription** After the installation is completed, on tester1.example .com, set up the system to obtain packages from the Red Hat Network using the following commands:

```
# subscription-manager register
# subscription-manager attach --auto
```

- **Web service** On tester1.example.com, install an Apache web server by executing the following command:

```
# dnf install httpd
```

In the /etc/httpd/conf/httpd.conf file, change the following line:

```
DocumentRoot "/var/www/html"
```

to the following:

```
DocumentRoot "/html"
```

Also change this line:

```
Listen 80
```

to the following:

```
Listen 8234
```

Then, add the following lines at the bottom of the file:

```
<Directory "/html">
  Require all granted
</Directory>
```

Finally, run the following commands:

```
# mkdir /html
# echo "Success!" > /html/index.html
# systemctl enable httpd
```

INSIDE THE EXAM

While the setup of an Apache web server is not an RHCSA exam requirement, you should be able to "configure firewall settings using firewall-cmd/firewalld" and "manage SELinux port labels" and "file contexts" to make a service operational.

- **NFS service** On tester1.example.com, set up the NFS. First, add the following lines to /etc/exports:

```
/exports/sam *(rw,sync,no_root_squash)
/exports/nfsshare *(rw,sync,no_root_squash)
```

Then, run the following commands:

```
# dnf install nfs-utils
# firewall-cmd --permanent --add-service=nfs
# firewall-cmd --reload
# systemctl enable nfs-server --now
# mkdir -p /exports/{sam,nfsshare}
# chwon 1234 /exports/sam
# chmod 700 /exports/sam
```

INSIDE THE EXAM

Again, setting up an NFS server isn't an RHCSA exam requirement, but you should be able to "mount and unmount network file systems using NFS."

Appendix B

Solutions to RHCSA
Sample Exam 1

The questions in the RHCSA Sample Exam 1 will help measure your understanding of the material covered in this book. As indicated in the introduction, you should be capable of completing the RHCSA exam in 3 hours. However, we have capped the time for this lab at 2.5 hours to accustom you to working under time constraints.

The RHCSA exam follows a "closed book" format. Nevertheless, you are permitted to refer to any documentation available on the Red Hat Enterprise Linux computer. Although test centers permit note-taking, these notes cannot be taken out of the examination room.

In the majority of cases, there isn't a single solution or method to resolve a problem or install a service. With the plethora of options available in Linux, it is impossible to cover every potential scenario.

For the forthcoming exercises, avoid using a production computer. Even a minor error in any of these exercises could render Linux unbootable. If you cannot recover using the steps provided in these exercises, you might need to reinstall Red Hat Enterprise Linux. Consequently, you may not be able to recover any data saved on the local system.

Red Hat conducts its exams electronically, which is why the exams in this book can be accessed from the McGraw Hill companion website. This exam, named RHCSAsampleexam1, is available in Microsoft Word format. For instructions on setting up RHEL 9 as a suitable system for a practice exam, please refer to Appendix A.

RHCSA Sample Exam 1 Discussion

In this discussion, we'll describe briefly one way to meet the requirements listed for the RHCSA Sample Exam 1.

1. To complete this task, review Exercise 5-2, "Recover the Root Password," in Chapter 5.

2. Assuming that the network interface is named eth0, that the NAT subnet address of your VMware Workstation Player setup is 192.168.0.100, and that the IP of the default gateway/DNS is 192.168.0.2, execute the following commands:

```
# nmcli con mod eth0 ipv4.addresses "192.168.0.100/24"
# nmcli con mod eth0 ipv4.gateway "192.168.0.2"
# nmcli con mod eth0 ipv4.method manual
# nmcli con mod eth0 ipv4.dns "192.168.0.2"
# nmcli con down eth0
# nmcli con up eth0
# nmcli con show eth0
# hostnamectl set-hostname server1.example.com
```

3. To complete this task, review Exercise 4-2 in Chapter 4.

4. Create a file named /etc/yum.repos.d/epel.repo and add the following content:

```
[epel]
name = epel
baseurl = http://linuxsoft.cern.ch/epel/9/Everything/x86_64/
gpgcheck = no
```

Then, run the following command to install the htop RPM:

```
# dnf install htop
```

5. Use the **parted** command to create a new partition. Assume that your hard drive is /dev/vda, the new partition is number 3, and there is some free space starting at about 19GB. Start the **parted** utility with **parted /dev/vda** and type

```
(parted) unit mib
(parted) print
(parted) mkpart primary 19000MiB 19500MiB
(parted) set 3 lvm on
(parted) quit
```

Then, run the following commands:

```
# pvcreate /dev/vda3
# vgcreate -s 8M vg01 /dev/vda3
# lvcreate -l 32 -n lv_project vg01
```

6. Format the volume and create the mount point:

```
# mkfs.xfs /dev/vg01/lv_project
# mkdir /project
```

To make sure that the volume is automatically mounted the next time the system is booted, configure it in /etc/fstab to the appropriate format, with the UUID associated with the volume, as provided by the **blkid** command:

```
# blkid /dev/vg01/lv_project
```

Then, add the following line to /etc/fstab:

```
UUID=<substitute with UUID value> /project xfs defaults 0 0
```

7. Run the following command to complete this task:

```
# find /etc -type f -name "*.conf" >/root/configfiles.txt
```

8. To complete this task, run:

```
# tar -cjf /tmp/etc.tar.bz2 /etc
```

9. The /home/engineers directory should be owned by the group engineers. As long as users donna and mike are not part of that group, and other users don't have permissions (or ACLs) on that directory, access should be limited to members of the engineers group. The directory should also have SGID permissions:

```
# useradd nancy
# echo "changeme!" | passwd --stdin nancy
# useradd randy
# echo "changeme!" | passwd --stdin randy
# useradd donna
# echo "changeme!" | passwd --stdin donna
# useradd mike
# echo "changeme!" | passwd --stdin mike
# groupadd -g 2000 engineers
# usermod -aG engineers nancy
# usermod -aG engineers randy
# mkdir /home/engineers
# chgrp engineers /home/engineers
# chmod 2770 /home/engineers
```

10. If you've modified user mike's account to make his account expire in seven days, the right expiration date should appear in the output to the **chage -l mike** command. To complete the task, run

```
# chage -E $(date -d "+7 days" +"%Y-%m-%d") mike
```

11. There are a number of ways to set up a cron job; it could be configured in the /etc/crontab file or as a cron job for the user root or mike with the **crontab -u <user> -e** command. To complete the exercise, you can add the following line to /etc/crontab:

```
50 3 2 * * root /bin/find /home/mike/tmp -type f -exec /bin/rm {} \;
```

12. One effective way to share a file between users is to create a group, add the relevant users to that group, and then change the file's group ownership to that group. Create a new group, for example, "projectgroup":

```
# groupadd projectgroup
```

Add users mike and donna to projectgroup:

```
# usermod -aG projectgroup mike
# usermod -aG projectgroup donna
```

Next, as user mike, create the file, change its group ownership, and modify the file permissions to enable read access for the group:

```
$ touch /opt/project.test
$ chown mike /opt/project.test
$ chgrp projectgroup /opt/project.test
$ chmod 640 /opt/project.test
```

13. Create a file /usr/local/bin/backup.sh with the following content and make it executable with **chmod +x /usr/local/bin/backup.sh**:

```
#!/bin/bash

# Check if an argument is provided
if [ "$#" -ne 1 ]; then
    echo "Usage: backup.sh <DIRECTORY>"
    exit 1
fi
# Check if the provided argument is a directory
if [ ! -d "$1" ]; then
    echo "Error: $1 is not a directory."
    exit 1
fi
# Create a tar.gz archive
tar -czf backup_$(date +%Y%m%d%H%M%S).tar.gz -C $1 .
```

Next, schedule the script to run automatically at 2:00 A.M. daily to create a backup of the /home directory in the /tmp filesystem. To do so, add the following line to /etc/crontab:

```
0 2 * * * root /usr/local/bin/backup.sh /home
```

14. First, create the user sam:

    ```
    # useradd -u 1234 -d /nethome/sam sam
    ```

    Then, configure NFS automounting. Install the autofs package:

    ```
    # dnf install autofs nfs-utils
    ```

    In the /etc/auto.master file, add the following line:

    ```
    /nethome /etc/auto.nethome
    ```

    Now, you need to create and configure the map file (/etc/auto.nethome) you just referenced in the auto.master file. This file will contain the following line (substitute for the IP address of tester1.example.com):

    ```
    sam -rw <ip_address_of_tester1.example.com>:/exports/sam
    ```

    After the configuration files are set up, start and enable the autofs service:

    ```
    # systemctl enable autofs --now
    ```

    Now, if you open a shell as user sam (**su – sam**), the NFS share from tester1.example.com:/sam will be automatically mounted as user sam's home directory. The **-rw** option ensures that the NFS share is mounted in read-write mode.

15. On tester1.example.com, run

    ```
    # semanage port -a -t http_port_t -p tcp 8234
    # systemctl restart httpd
    ```

    After running this command, Apache should be able to bind to port 8234. You can verify this with the following command on tester1.example.com:

    ```
    # ss -tlpn | grep 8234
    ```

16. Run the following commands on tester1.example.com to allow other hosts to connect to the web server on port 8234:

    ```
    # firewall-cmd --add-port=8234/tcp --permanent
    # firewall-cmd --reload
    ```

    Change the SELinux context of the /html directory to the type httpd_sys_content_t. This type is used for static web content that should be accessible by **httpd**:

    ```
    # semanage fcontext -a -t httpd_sys_content_t "/html(/.*)?"
    ```

    The argument "**/html(/.*)?**" is a regular expression that matches the /html directory and all its subdirectories and files. The **-a** option is used to add a record. After that, use the **restorecon** command to apply this context mapping to the running filesystem:

    ```
    # restorecon -R -v /html
    ```

Then, the following command on server1.example.com should display the "Success!" test page (substitute for the IP address of tester1):

```
# curl http://<ip_address_of_tester1>:8234
```

17. Run the following commands as user mike to start the container:

```
$ mkdir ~/html
$ podman run -d --name httpd \
 -v /home/mike/html:/var/www/html:Z \
 -p 8081:8080 \
 registry.access.redhat.com/ubi9/httpd-24
```

Execute the following command to generate a systemd configuration file for the container service:

```
$ podman generate systemd --name httpd --new --files
```

This command results in creating a container-httpd.service. Next, copy this file into the /home/mike/.config/systemd/user directory. If this directory doesn't already exist, you'll have to create it:

```
$ mkdir -p /home/mike/.config/systemd/user
$ cp container-httpd.service ~/.config/systemd/user
```

Afterwards, you'll need to stop and remove the current httpd container:

```
$ podman stop httpd
$ podman rm httpd
```

Now, it's time to refresh systemd and set up the service to automatically start when your system boots:

```
$ systemctl --user daemon-reload
$ systemctl --user enable container-httpd.service
$ loginctl enable-linger
```

To verify that everything is set up correctly, reboot your system and check if the container is running:

```
$ systemctl --user status container-httpd.service
$ podman ps
```

18. Just like with all Red Hat exams, it's essential for your modifications to endure a system reboot. Therefore, reboot the system and verify that your configurations remain fully functional.

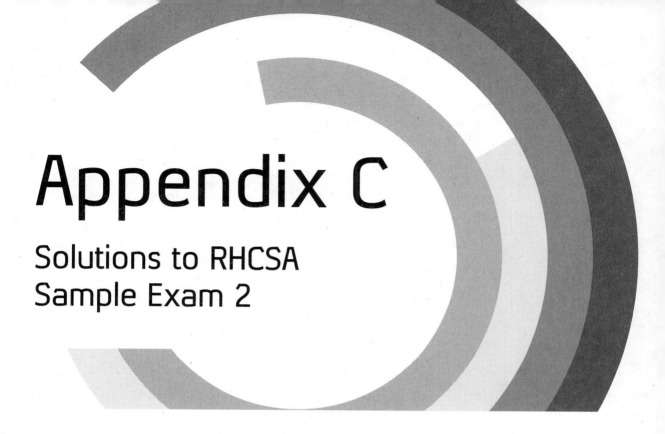

Appendix C

Solutions to RHCSA Sample Exam 2

The questions in the RHCSA Sample Exam 2 will help measure your understanding of the material covered in this book. As indicated in the introduction, you should be capable of completing the RHCSA exam in 3 hours. However, we have capped the time for this lab at 2.5 hours to accustom you to working under time constraints.

The RHCSA exam follows a "closed book" format. Nevertheless, you are permitted to refer to any documentation available on the Red Hat Enterprise Linux computer. Although test centers permit note-taking, these notes cannot be taken out of the examination room.

In the majority of cases, there isn't a single solution or method to resolve a problem or install a service. With the plethora of options available in Linux, it is impossible to cover every potential scenario.

For the forthcoming exercises, avoid using a production computer. Even a minor error in any of these exercises could render Linux unbootable. If you cannot recover using the steps provided in these exercises, you might need to reinstall Red Hat Enterprise Linux. Consequently, you may not be able to recover any data saved on the local system.

Red Hat conducts its exams electronically, which is why the exams in this book can be accessed from the McGraw Hill companion website. This exam, named RHCSAsampleexam2, is available in Microsoft Word format. For instructions on setting up RHEL 9 as a suitable system for a practice exam, please refer to Appendix A.

RHCSA Sample Exam 2 Discussion

In this discussion, we'll describe briefly one way to meet the requirements listed for the RHCSA Sample Exam 2.

1. To complete this task, review Exercise 5-2, "Recover the Root Password," in Chapter 5.

2. Assuming that the network interface is named eth0, execute the following commands:

```
# nmcli con mod eth0 ipv4.method auto
# nmcli con mod eth0 ipv4.gateway ""
# nmcli con mod eth0 ipv4.address ""
# nmcli con down eth0
# nmcli con up eth0
# hostnamectl set-hostname server1.example.com
```

3. To complete this task, review Exercise 4-2, "Subscribe a System to the Red Hat Subscription Management," in Chapter 4. Then, install the tmux RPM package with the following command:

```
# dnf install tmux
```

4. Use the **parted** command to create a new partition. Assume that your hard drive is /dev/vda, the new partition is number 3, and there is some free space starting at about 19GB. Start the **parted** utility with **parted /dev/vda** and type

```
(parted) unit mib
(parted) print
(parted) mkpart primary 19000MiB 19500MiB
(parted) quit
```

5. Run the following commands to format the filesystem and create the mount point:

```
# mkfs.xfs /dev/vda3
# mkdir /sysadmins
```

Add an entry to the /etc/fstab file. You will use the UUID (Universally Unique Identifier) of the partition for this, which you can obtain by running the **blkid** command as follows:

```
# blkid /dev/vda3
```

Then, add the following line to /etc/fstab:

```
UUID=<substitute with UUID value>   /sysadmins   xfs   defaults   0 0
```

And mount the filesystem:

```
# mount /sysadmins
```

6. Use the **parted** command to create a new partition. Assume that your hard drive is /dev/vda, and the new partition is number 4. Start the **parted** utility and type

```
mkpart primary 19500MiB 19600MiB
set 4 swap on
quit
```

7. Format the new partition as swap:

```
# mkswap /dev/vda4
```

Find the UUID of the partition:

```
# blkid /dev/vda4
```

Then, add the following line to /etc/fstab:

```
UUID=<substitute with UUID value>    none swap    defaults    0 0
```

And mount the filesystem:

```
# swapon /dev/vda4
```

8. The following command shows one method to complete this task:

```
# find /etc -type f -exec grep -l redhat {} \;↵
>/root/etc-redhat.txt
```

9. New local users should be listed in /etc/passwd and /etc/shadow. To specifically deny regular users access to a directory, you can create a dedicated group for this purpose, for example "sysadmins". You should be able to confirm that users bill and richard don't have access to the /sysadmins directory by trying to list its contents or creating a file in it.

To complete the task, run the following commands:

```
# useradd linus
# useradd richard
# useradd mark
# useradd bill
# echo "redhat123" | passwd --stdin linus
# echo "redhat123" | passwd --stdin richard
# echo "redhat123" | passwd --stdin mark
# echo "redhat123" | passwd --stdin bill
# groupadd sysadmins
# usermod -aG sysadmins linus
# usermod -aG sysadmins mark
# mkdir /sysadmins
# chgrp sysadmins /sysadmins
# chmod 770 /sysadmins
```

10. Install the autofs and nfs-utils packages:

```
# dnf install autofs nfs-utils
# systemctl enable autofs --now
```

Then, add the following line to /etc/auto.misc:

```
dvd -fstype=iso9660,ro,nosuid,nodev :/dev/cdrom
```

To confirm your change, add an ISO file to the virtual drive on the virtual machine. Then, run the **ls /misc/dvd** command, and the automounter should mount the DVD and provide file information on that drive. This should be an easy configuration, based on a slight change to the default /etc/auto.misc file. Of course, you'll need to make sure the autofs service runs after a reboot, which you can confirm with the **systemctl is-enabled autofs** command.

11. To set the system to boot into the multi-user target by default, use the following command:

```
# systemctl set-default multi-user.target
```

You can verify that the default target has been set correctly with this command:

```
# systemctl get-default
```

12. Open the file /etc/chrony.conf and locate any lines that start with server or pool. Comment those lines out by adding a # character at the beginning of each line. Then, add a new line to specify time.google.com as the server:

```
pool time.google.com iburst
```

Restart the **chronyd** daemon to apply the changes:

```
# systemctl restart chronyd
```

To verify the current NTP sources, run

```
# chronyc sources
```

13. Open the /etc/selinux/config file. Locate the line that starts with **SELINUX=**. This line specifies the SELinux mode. Change it to **SELINUX=permissive**, save the file, and reboot the system. To verify that SELinux is set in permissive mode, run the **sestatus** command.

14. Make sure the NFS client utilities are installed. You can do so with the following command:

```
# dnf install nfs-utils
```

Create the directory where the NFS share will be mounted:

```
# mkdir /mnt/nfs
```

Then, add the following line to /etc/fstab (substitute for the IP address of tester1 .example.com):

```
<ip_of_tester1>:/exports/nfsshare  /mnt/nfs  nfs  defaults  0 0
```

To mount the filesystem, run

```
# mount /mnt/nfs
```

15. As user mark on server1.example.com, generate an RSA SSH key pair with a key length of 4096 bits:

```
$ ssh-keygen -t rsa -b 4096
```

Now, create user mike on tester1.example.com:

```
# useradd mike
# echo "changeme" | passwd --stdin mike
```

Then, on server1.example.com, copy the public key to the destination server tester1 .example.com. You can do this using the **ssh-copy-id** command (substitute for the IP address of tester1.example.com):

```
$ ssh-copy-id mike@<ip_of_tester1
```

You will be prompted to enter user mike's password for tester1.example.com to allow the copy operation. Now, user mark from server1.example.com should be able to SSH into tester1.example.com as user mike using key-based authentication. When you initiate the SSH connection, you'll be prompted to enter the passphrase for the key.

16. First, make sure that the tuned RPM is installed and the service is running. If not, install the package, start the service, and enable it to start at boot:

```
# dnf install tuned
# systemctl start tuned
# systemctl enable tuned
```

Now, to activate the virtual-guest profile, use the **tuned-adm** tool:

```
# tuned-adm profile virtual-guest
```

To verify the active profile, you can use the following command:

```
# tuned-adm active
```

17. As user bill, create a Containerfile with the following content:

```
# Use the Red Hat UBI 9 image as the base
FROM registry.access.redhat.com/ubi9/ubi:latest
# Execute the "sleep 1d" command
CMD ["sleep", "1d"]
```

Use the following command to build the image:

```
$ podman build -t ubi-test .
```

18. Just like with all Red Hat exams, it's essential for your modifications to endure a system reboot. Therefore, reboot the system and verify that your configurations remain fully functional.

Appendix D
About the Online Content

This book comes with online resources, including the labs for each chapter, a copy of Appendix A, "Prepare a System for the Sample Exams," and files for the simulated sample RHCSA exams in a downloadable .zip file.

Single User License Terms and Conditions

Online access to the digital content included with this book is governed by the McGraw Hill License Agreement outlined next. By using this digital content you agree to the terms of that license.

Access   To download your online content, simply follow these easy steps.

1. Go to https://www.mhprofessional.com/redhatlinux.
2. You can also go to this URL: https://www.mhprofessional.com and type the ISBN **9781260462074** into the Search By ISBN box.
3. You will be taken to the book's page. Click the Downloads & Resources tab, where you will find a link to download the online content for this book.

Duration of License   Access to your online content through the Web site will expire one year from the date the publisher declares the book out of print.

Your purchase of this McGraw Hill product through a retail store is subject to the refund policy of that store.

The Content is a copyrighted work of McGraw Hill, and McGraw Hill reserves all rights in and to the Content. The Work is © 2024 by McGraw Hill.

Restrictions on Transfer   The user is receiving only a limited right to use the Content for the user's own internal and personal use, dependent on purchase and continued ownership of this book. The user may not reproduce, forward, modify, create derivative works based upon, transmit, distribute, disseminate, sell, publish, or sublicense the Content or in any way commingle the Content with other third-party content without McGraw Hill's consent.

Limited Warranty   The McGraw Hill Content is provided on an "as is" basis. Neither McGraw Hill nor its licensors make any guarantees or warranties of any kind, either express or implied, including, but not limited to, implied warranties of merchantability or fitness for a particular purpose or use as to any McGraw Hill Content or the information therein or any warranties as to the accuracy, completeness, correctness, or results to be obtained from, accessing or using the McGraw Hill Content, or any material referenced in such Content or any information entered into licensee's product by users or other persons and/or any material available on or that can be accessed through the licensee's product (including via any hyperlink or otherwise) or as to non-infringement of third-party rights. Any warranties of any kind, whether express or implied, are disclaimed. Any material or data obtained through use of the McGraw Hill Content is at your own discretion and risk and user understands that it will be solely responsible for any resulting damage to its computer system or loss of data.

Neither McGraw Hill nor its licensors shall be liable to any subscriber or to any user or anyone else for any inaccuracy, delay, interruption in service, error or omission, regardless of cause, or for any damage resulting therefrom.

In no event will McGraw Hill or its licensors be liable for any indirect, special or consequential damages, including but not limited to, lost time, lost money, lost profits or good will, whether in contract, tort, strict liability or otherwise, and whether or not such damages are foreseen or unforeseen with respect to any use of the McGraw Hill Content.

Downloadable Book Resources

The following sections detail the resources available with your book. You can access these items by selecting the Download & Resources tab toward the bottom of the page at the URL listed above and clicking on the Download link. All the resources are available in one convenient .zip file. Download the .zip file to proceed.

Lab Files

The lab files for each chapter are arranged in a directory within the .zip file with a folder for each chapter. The lab files are available in Microsoft Word format. The lab solutions can be found in the Self Test section of each chapter.

Appendix A: Prepare a System for the Sample Exams

Appendix A provides instructions on how to prepare your system to take the sample RHCSA exams. The PDF can be found in the Appendix A folder in the .zip file.

Sample Exams

Two sample exams are available, each simulating the RHCSA exam experience. Each sample exam is available in Microsoft Word format in the Sample Exam 1 and Sample Exam 2 folders.

Technical Support

For questions regarding downloadable book content, visit https://mhedu.force.com/CSOM/s/.

INDEX

H

I

Q

R